Penguin Books
George

D0231590

Emlyn Williams was born in North Wales in 1905 and educated at Holywell County School, in France and at Christ Church, Oxford. Today he is a famous actor and writer; in 1962 he was awarded the C.B.E.

Among his best-known plays are *A Murder Has Been Arranged*, *Night Must Fall*, *The Corn is Green* and *The Light of Heart*. His film appearances include *The Citadel*, *Major Barbara*, *Hatter's Castle*, *Ivanhoe*, *I Accuse*, *The Walking Stick*, *David Copperfield*: also *The Last Days of Dolwyn* (which he also directed, having written it for Edith Evans and Richard Burton), and an historical curiosity, the unfinished *I, Claudius*, in which he played Caligula.

In 1951 he created a theatrical revolution when he compiled and presented *Emlyn Williams as Charles Dickens*, a solo performance which has been acclaimed all over the world. He followed this with another 'one-man show', *Emlyn Williams as Dylan Thomas Growing Up*, which was to become equally popular: in 1977 and 1978, in London and New York, he presented *The Playboy of the Week-End World*, a third solo performance from the stories of Saki. In between his other commitments, he is always happy to return to these ventures.

In 1960 he fulfilled a life's ambition – to write a book. This was *George*, the first part of his autobiography, followed by *Beyond Belief*, 'A Chronicle of Murder and its Detection', and by *Emlyn*, the sequel to *George*. In 1978 the *Reader's Digest* Association published his *Doctor Crippen's Diary*; 1980–81 marked the appearance, in London and New York, of a first novel, *Headlong*.

Emlyn Williams

George

An Early Autobiography

Penguin Books

Penguin Books Ltd, Harmondsworth, Middlesex, England
Penguin Books, 625 Madison Avenue, New York, New York 10022, U.S.A.
Penguin Books Australia Ltd, Ringwood, Victoria, Australia
Penguin Books Canada Ltd, 2801 John Street, Markham, Ontario, Canada L3R 1B4
Penguin Books (N.Z.) Ltd, 182–190 Wairau Road, Auckland 10, New Zealand

First published by Hamish Hamilton 1961
Published in Penguin Books 1976
Reprinted 1982

Made and printed in Great Britain by
Hazell Watson & Viney Ltd, Aylesbury, Bucks
Set in Linotype Pilgrim

To my wife and our two sons,
Molly, Alan and Brook

Thank you J. L. Bedrock, Josephine Bott,
Richard Clowes, Desmond Gill, Mary Haynes,
D. V. Hill, Rosemary Howells, Lilla Jones,
Nellie Jones, Roy Jones, Raymond Mander,
Joe Mitchenson, Hilda Morris, Eira Parry,
E. Whitford Roberts, John Roberts,
Edward Rogers, Hannah Southward,
Dorothy Swinnerton, Edward Walsh,
Steven Watson, Gwladys Williams,
John Williams, Margaret Williams,
Nancy Williams, Rhydwen Williams

Contents

Part Three

Oxford (1923–1927)

Part One

Glanrafon, Trelogan
(1905–1916)

Chapter 1

Richard and Mary

The world was waiting. Waiting for me, to whisper my incantation, 'I am George Emlyn Williams and ...' I was lying with my head on my fist on morning grass, dry of dew and warm with the first heat of the year. All was still, even the stalks clutched in my hot fingers. I had come up into the fields to gather shaking-grass, a weed with a hundred beads tremulous to the touch, which my mother would inter in two vases where it would frugally desiccate and gather dust for ever. Spring smells and earth feelings crept into my seven-year-old body; nine-tenths innocent, one-tenth conscient, it responded. I rolled one cheek up till it closed an eye, and squinted down at the sunlit village. A dog lay asleep in the road. Mrs Jones South Africa was hanging washing, and quavering a hymn. Cassie hung on their gate and called to Ifor, 'Time to go to the well!' The bleat of a sheep. A bird called, careless, mindless. Eighteen inches from my eye, a tawny baby-frog was about to leap. It waited.

Everything waited: the hymn had ceased, the bird was dumb and suspended. 'I was born November the 26th 1905 and the world was completed at midnight on Saturday July the 10th 4004 B.C.' – our Bible stated the year at the top of Page One, the rest I felt free to add – 'and has been going ever since, through Genesis Revelation the six wives of Henry the Eighth the Guillotine and the Diamond Jubilee right until this minute 10 a.m. Sunday April the 14th 1912, when the world has stopped. The sun will not set tonight, or ever again, and I am the only one who knows.'

No sound: the spool of time has run down, the century is nipped in the bud. I shall never grow up, or old, but shall lie on the grass for ever, a mummy of a boy with nestling in the middle

of it a nameless warmth like the slow heat inside straw. This is
the eternal morning.

The frog jumped. Cassie called again, I scrambled up, brushed
my best knickerbockers, pulled the black stockings up inside
them, raced down and hopped between my water-buckets into
the wooden square which kept them well apart so as not to
splash. The sun did set, and by the time it rose next morning the
Titanic had been sunk. If the world *had* stopped, they would not
have drowned; I thought about it for days.

The century, un-nipped, has crept forward, and the knickerbockers are no more. They encased one brother till he burst out
of them, then another till they fell exhausted away from him,
turned into floor-rags and at last were decently burned. But I am
still here, not yet decently burned or a floor-rag or even exhausted, George Emlyn Williams, born 26 November 1905.

My family tree is the shortest in the wood. The Japanese
variety, healthy but stunted. It would be the neatest feature of
any landscape, for hardly a twig ventures outside Flintshire, the
smallest county in Wales, the one in the top right corner next
to Chester and Liverpool. My mother was Mary the daughter of
Job Williams, collier, and his wife Eleanor (Elin Jones), midwife,
both of Treuddyn, a tiny village in the hills above the small
market-town of Mold, around which both families had lived for
generations. From my sheaf of half a dozen birth certificates, I
learn that my mother was born in 1869, and that two days after
her first birthday my father was born fifteen miles way. Before
they met they had in common surname, county, sturdy peasant
stock and the Welsh language, for their four parents spoke no
other. The four also felt their way along the same precarious
financial line, a couple of shillings away from the precipice of
pauperdom, and none of them could read or write : whatever the
savings-book may have lacked in noughts, the birth certificates
made up in crosses.

Yma fe ddyliwn roi syniad o'r iaith Gymreig, which is the
Welsh for 'I ought here to give an idea of the Welsh language'.
I was brought up in it, but even I can see that it is peculiar,

bearing no relation to English in either vocabulary or grammar, and indeed little to any modern tongue except its first cousins, Irish, Gaelic, Breton and Cornish; in Britain, Welsh was already widely spoken in the sixth century, having been handed down from the Britons, the direct ancestors of the Welsh. To imagine the sound of it, take Italian, drain off a measure of southern languor and infuse the same quantity of northern vigour.

My mother's father, Job, born in 1831, was one of the several sons (all miners, one killed in Coedllai Colliery) of Thomas Williams, itinerant tea-seller with donkey and cart, himself married to a Jones and domiciled at 'Tŷ Capel Wesle', Wesleyan Chapel House. (Thomas the tea-seller's father had ventured a variation on the tune of Williams-Jones by marrying a Miss Ponsonby, daughter of the organist at Gresford Parish Church ten miles away.) My mother's mother Elin came of farming stock, her father was a master miller in the old lead-works. Her uncle John Jones had gone far afield as civil engineer – 'fe adeiladodd bont yn y Ffrainc' (he built a bridge in France), besides taking out a patent for a thrashing-machine – and her Aunt Mary (I heard more than once from a great-aunt) 'moved in high circles' in Newcastle-under-Lyme, Staffordshire. For me this evoked great drawing-rooms and kissing of hands, until the same aunt spoke of another sister who had 'bettered herself wonderful you see, George, and been taken as a lady's maid'. A relative of more reliable distinction, allotted twenty-three lines in the Welsh Dictionary of National Biography, was a great-uncle of my mother's named John Dafis Nercwys, Nercwys being a village two miles from Mold: '(1799–1879) A Methodist preacher noted for his fluency and wit ... His "Commentary on the Book of Proverbs" attracted great attention ... An ardent supporter of the movement to repeal the Corn Laws, he was much more broadminded than most ministers of his time.'

At Treuddyn National School Mary, with her elder brother and sister, Jabez and Sarah, learnt the rudiments of English; and rudiments they were, all her life she was to write 'I have been' as 'i of being'. Outside school the language was never heard, and the only books were *Y Beibl* and the Welsh commentaries thereon; aged ten, she acquired a tiny cardboard 'Award for Religious Knowledge'. As she was growing up, so grew the reputation of nearby Mold as the home of the first major Welsh novelist, Daniel Owen, but it is doubtful whether Treuddyn children had access to *Rhys Lewis* as it came out in serial parts. Her parents were staunch chapel-goers, living simply and cleanly in the dark corners of a four-roomed cottage in Bridge Terrace, the standard set by the thrifty mother, the only horizon the billow of hills round Moel Fammau, Flintshire's only real mountain and a suave one at that.

Their mother had a cross to bear: Job the Sabbatarian had falls from grace, usually on Saturday night. He drank. And when he was 'dan y cwrw', under the influence, he was a mettlesome customer: once, exhorted to repent and read aloud from the Old Testament which had given him and his children their names, he is reputed to have lugged a great Bible into the street and bawled passages new to his window-and-door congregation. When recovering from his bouts, the only person he would allow near him was his Mary fach, small, pink and white, with light blue eyes and curly fair hair, her gaiety already at odds with an innate timidity; to his wife's distaste, he would perch the child on his knee, swing her to and fro to the tune of 'Hob y derri dando', and gather her to a beery breast. When Jabez was nineteen, a collier, he came upon his father attacking his mother in a drunken fury, thrashed him, and walked out never to return. On thirteen-year-old Mary, this must have had a powerful effect. Jabez went to 'Lerpwl', the teeming metropolis Liverpool, with a vow to make good, toe the straight path, and never touch drink. He kept all these resolutions: he was apprenticed to a tea-blender named Jones – inevitably – settled among the Welsh colony in Bootle, where he joined the Wesleyan Chapel in Trinity Road, and was a lifelong teetotaller except for a glass of port on Christmas Day. In the chapel he was 'Goruchwyliwr y Tlodion' (Steward of the Fund for the Poor) and for many years deacon, 'Arweinydd y Gân' (hymn leader), Sunday-school teacher and a fine pray-er. All this need not make a man of integrity, but that is what he was.

A year after he had stormed out, with Sarah already in service at a girls' school outside Dolgelley, fourteen-year-old Mary's tin box was packed and her fair hair twined up under a black straw hat; she was driven in a farmer's trap down to Mold – 'paid a anghofio i newid yn Nghaer, don't forget to change at Chester' – and at Liverpool, in the shadow of the birds of prey on the Liver Building, she stepped off the ferry-boat and in the terrifying maelstrom caught sight of brother Jabez's glasses and walrus moustache. He escorted her, on her first tram, to 16 Yew Tree Road, the imposing stockbroker's house near Walton Jail where she was to be a housemaid. She did the silver, the steps, the washing, the dusting, anything. Liking her work and her mistress, she was always to speak of both with pride, while Mrs Ellsworthy took a fancy to the little monosyllabic foreign child, toiling noiselessly with no thought of time. Whoever heard of a servant so scrupulous that she would wind bits of string round her finger and stack them in a drawer, next to used paper-bags folded like doll's linen? Bobbing came naturally, but she felt peculiar saying 'ma'am', was it not what she had called her mother since she could speak, 'Mam'?

Sunday was Welsh day, when Mary went by tram to her brother in Bootle, and Treuddyn came nearer. Sunday-school in Trinity Road, back to Jabez's lodgings for high tea, back for the evening service, then back again, perhaps with the minister and a couple of chapel members for cold ham, tea and gossip, theological and thereabouts. By the end of the day the stockbroking dinner-parties ('This is sherry, Mary my dear, and that one's called port') seemed far away, and adventure further. Several years passed. Jabez acquired a Welsh wife and a house in a row with a bow window, but while other girls looked about them (maybe without seeing much) Mary lived, as she was to go on living, with eyes modestly to the ground.

In Welsh chapels at this time, after the preacher had prayed and one or two of the deacons enshrined in the 'Sêt Fawr' (the Big Seat beneath the pulpit) had renewed their weekly intimacies with Jehovah, it was not unknown for an inspired member of the congregation to come forward and give his 'profiad' (his experience) just as at bullfights in Spain, a headstrong onlooker will vault the barricade with a stick and a red rag. These boys are called espontáneos. But while the Spanish clap the intruder into jail, the Welsh ask him back for tea and seed-cake. One turned up at Trinity Road, in the summer of 1889. The hymn had died away and Mary had dutifully rearranged herself beside her brother, when she heard a Sunday squeak in the aisle. These amateurs of imprecation tended to shamble and the divine light was often obscured behind pince-nez, but this was different. A thick-set young man with a confident slightly rolling walk opened the gate-door of the deacons' den – he too could have vaulted – and settled down to pray steadily and aloud, the congregation following silent suit. This particular Wesleyan espontáneo was to be my father. And my mother's first view of him, one eye open over her muff, was kneeling with his hands clasped.

'O Arglwydd, rho lais i dy was, o Lord give to thy servant a voice ...' Twenty, she guessed, same age as me. Dark close-cropped hair, widow-peaked – in truth a crew-cut, for he was a stoker aboard the transatlantic *Lucania* – a face square-to-round, eyes shut and out of action. 'Pechaduriaid igyd, pob dyn, pob ddynes – sinners all, every man, every woman ...' A trim moustache over lips perhaps too curved for the rarefied discourse emanating between them; a resonant voice; a splendid command of Biblical Welsh, histrionic but sincere; and a touch of the 'hwyl' – the vocal trapeze on which Welsh preachers swung to dizzy heights – just enough to show he could do it, 'amen'.

Collecting brolly and pulling on gloves in the dim porch, one was introduced. Now that Stoker Williams had taken leave of the Deity and his eyes were open, they were revealed to be deep-set and blue; after his stern demeanour in the celestial witness-box, his flashing smile and chuckle were startling. What part of Wales? That settled it, brother Jabez – impressed, a pray-er himself – asked him back for refreshments. It was a warm evening, On the stroll, past the trams and the slums, Mr and Mrs Jabez flanked the minister in front while the other two brought up the rear; Mary found herself on the inside, his manners were impeccable. All in black – bowlers, ties, gloves, umbrellas – they were a small funeral. But the praying stoker's conversation was not very redolent of the end of life, or even of the Sabbath; she was surprised to hear him poking fun at the gentleman who had prayed before him. He made her laugh outright twice, but she would have felt more comfortable laughing on a weekday. She thought he was a little 'gwyneb galed', the epithet she most often applied in disapproval; it means hard of face, bold. Her instinct was infallible, but with the bold she condemned the original and the whimsical. Two slum children ran up, barefoot, poor things; he stooped and talked like a young Father Christmas and gave them a penny each, it was nice but he did not know them. He was from Ffynnongroew, no, she had never been, it must be a good fifteen miles from – had Mr Williams ever been as far as Treuddyn? No, but he had been to Trincomalee, Tripoli, and Panama, in each of which he had a wife, was Treuddyn worth a visit? She gave him a swift sideways look and quickened her elastic-sided boots. Was she married? No, a maid. Even in Welsh – 'forwyn' – that had a Shakespearean ring. A maid, outside Walton Jail.

Reverently they sauntered, past shop-windows shrouding weekday delights as unthinkable to her as wrapped-up moonlight, past murkily respectable side-streets which a high-minded councillor had dedicated to learning: Balliol Road, Exeter Road, Wadham Road. If a passer-by had informed Richard and Mary that these were named after Oxford colleges, they would have listened respectfully. The scholastic yielded abruptly to the theatrical: Viola Street, Portia Street, Juliet Street, one dingy bow-fronted heroine followed another, while lower down Othello and Macbeth jostled sulkily back to back. The cortège turned into Benedict Street. It is a temptation to report that Richard told Mary he lodged there; only to discover that she dwelt opposite in the Street of Beatrice; but she was still below stairs near Walton Jail and he considerably above, in the attic of a Seamen's Hostel, they were bound for Mr and Mrs Jabez's house.

17

An enjoyable cold supper (Paned arall, peidiwch a bod yn swil, another cup, don't be shy!') and he was invited back when the *Lucania* would next be in dock.

Richard Williams was born in Ffynnongroew – 'the clear well' – a village on the Dee estuary next to Mostyn, a station on the Chester–Holyhead line from London to Ireland. Most of the inhabitants worked at the adjacent Point of Air colliery, which gave the long straggling street, and the people, a smear of grit very different from the green of Treuddyn. Ffynnongroew was as Welsh, but tougher; the one nestled, the other wrestled, and the Clear Well had acquired a film of coal dust. My father was born, in 1870, at 1 Denbigh Row, the son of Robert Williams, collier, and Catherine, Griffith : of his father's antecedents nothing is known, but Catherine was one of the eight children of William Griffith and his wife Catherine, Williams, of Capel Curig, who early in their married life moved here from Llanrwst, thirty miles away in Denbighshire, where the Griffith family still farms and deals in horses. This William Griffith, my father's grandfather, had a sister who maried a Mr Berry; their son became the Rev. R. G. Berry, M.A., for forty years minister at Gwaelod-y-Garth, South Wales, and a well-known dramatist in Welsh who toured the United States lecturing to Welsh Americans. His half-dozen plays, all in print, are simple studies of village life with racy natural dialogue; the best-known, *Ar y Groesffordd* ('At the Cross-roads', later to win the Lord Howard de Walden Prize), treats of a minister's love for a poacher's daughter and his clash with his congregation, then a daring subject. While I was growing up, playwrights were small enough fry in Wales for the existence of this fairly distinguished relative – my grandmother's first cousin – to be unknown to me.

Not long after Richard's birth his parents left Wales, and him, to settle in Thatto Heath, near St Helens, Lancashire, which they proceeded to populate with regularity. As five of his maternal uncles and aunts followed and did the same, I see the main street of St Helens, on a Saturday night, thronged with my kin; and as one sister married a Joe Tickle, so becoming a legendary

Auntie Polly Tickle, I claim all Lancashire Tickles as my own.
In Ffynnongroew, Richard was brought up by his mother's
mother – indeed answered only to the name of Dic Griffith, a
name which for me has always had a picturesque scampish ring,
and when I first heard the adjective 'gruff' I took to it at once.
He attended Moriah Chapel and the village school, where he was
a 'rough boy'; at twelve he quarrelled with his grandmother,
climbed out in the middle of the night, walked the thirty miles
to Liverpool and signed on at the docks, there to recur as a
familiar figure till the Sunday night when the sailor was washed
up on the mercy-seat in Trinity Road.

Every time the *Lucania* docked, there were sing-songs on
Saturday evenings and out of the Benedict Street bow window,
Richard's voice would soar in a curve more suitable to Naples
than to Bootle – 'O na byddai 'n hâf o hyd', Would it were Ever
the Summer ... Presents were brought, a framed engraving of
the ship, a china ring-tree (Mary had no rings, what an odd present). He would call for her at the top of the Ellsworthy area
steps, the location of which never failed to amuse him – 'I picked
up your Mam outside the Jail!' – and then, by permission, he
would be invited down like any Victorian policeman, given tea
and presented to Mary's mistress, who was taken by the young
man's grand manner and pedantic diction: 'whether she
poisoned him or not, no doubt whatever but what Mrs May-
brick is in a desperate corner, isn't it?' 'He has fine hands,' said
Mrs Ellsworthy, 'and he uses them very nicely in describing, my
dear are you going to marry him?' Timid Mary – 'oh no ma'am!'
– went red at the thought. She did not really like him.
But Stoker Williams knew what he wanted, and travelled the
five-year courting road so patiently that his progress was only
just perceptible. He even negotiated a tricky corner in any
Welsh relationship, or French, German, Spanish: the moment
when 'vous' becomes 'tu' and 'chwi' in Welsh becomes 'ti'.
When is the suitor to change from 'Ydi chwi 'n aros, are you
staying' to 'Wyti 'n aros, art thou staying'? This negotiated, he
called Jabez 'Jab', and Mary he christened 'Poll'. Jab disapproved

and so did Poll, but it was his name for her for ever : rapscallion, warm and unsuitable. Though she knew that to the world he was Dic, she never called him anything but Richard. It was indicative of their two natures.

He took her to a Music Hall called the Rotunda, 'Daddy wouldn't Buy me a Bow-Wow', 'Oh, Mr Porter', 'Ta-ra-ra-boom' ... When they heard 'In Trinity Church I met my Doom', no doubt Richard slapped his knees with laughter and Mary tut-tutted and blushed, for they were to be married in Trinity Road Chapel. The only time they patronized the legitimate theatre was to see, from the gallery of the old Royal Court, *Romeo and Juliet*. Jab, to whom Shakespeare seemed permissible for a Wesleyan sister, can have had no idea what an inflammatory example the evening might have set to two young walkers-out, but Mary came to no harm. 'I did not understand much of what they said,' she said of it later, 'because they talked so old-fashioned.' Once or twice her betrothed put her oddly in mind of her father, whom he did not resemble. Unaccountably., as he helped her on with her jacket she would be sitting on Job's knee, hob y derri dando ... Then she realized, with a shock, that the connection was not visual, but nasal. The praying stoker smelt of beer. But she brushed aside her doubts ('Led astray by shipmates') and hoped her brother would not notice. Jabez was already frowning on the long absences afloat as well as on the financial outlook, which was simple : both parties were impecunious. Every penny would have to be watched, and it became equally clear that the watching, as well as the waiting, would be done by the wife. Richard was honest and good-hearted, but nobody could call him money-minded.

On 3 December 1894, Richard bent the knee for the second time in Trinity Road, but on this occasion Mary, lost to the area steps, knelt by his side : she Spinster, twenty-five, he Mariner, twenty-four. Jabez could not have put into words why he was loth to give her away. Her mistress parted with her even more reluctantly, giving her a clock, a tea-set, a hug and a tribute which the bride was to cherish : 'Mary my dear, I'll never find another maid like you.'

The happy pair, as often happens when the confetti has dribbled into the dustbin, found themselves in essential ways ill-suited. She was conventional to the point of defeatism, shy of strangers and painfully conscious of the immorality of spending one penny unless there was a halfpenny behind it; her idea of married life was to sit by a careful fire with the coal-hole replenished. She liked to know what the neighbours were up to, was even something of a curtain-tweaker, but had no desire to have them in her house or to enter theirs, while he, sanguine and impulsive, loved people, odd or ordinary : she called this 'soft-hearted'. When he entered a room every soul – 'and how *are* you, this long time !' – was made to feel that he or she shared a private joke with Dic. If these two could have pooled resources, he the optimist, she the realist, they would have made a rare character.

But the confetti was still fresh, and 39 Elwy Street Toxteth Park a mansion, four rooms between two people ! Dic had a fine scheme : he had heard afloat that there was money in singing-birds, and hung a dozen cages in the back room. Mary could not take to them, and when she stripped the parlour paper only to recoil from a wall swarming with life, she convinced herself that the birds had wooed the bugs. But they sang sweetly if not in harmony; after an untidy three-day honeymoon she waved her husband on to the tram, returned, a Penelope whose Ulysses was not due back till two weeks Friday, and started to settle in. Elwy was the only Welsh thing about a mean street flanked with low gravy-coloured dwellings debouching straight on to the pavement, the only sounds the grumble of a tram or the wail of a fog-horn, lowering to the spirit of an inland wife wed to the Atlantic. No dog, no cat, she had never known either. But everything found its place.

The parlour, over the years, was to move with her to other homes. Grandfather clock, corner-cupboard ensconcing the tea-set never to be used, and a mug – which had mysteriously stayed with Richard, cracked and mended, since he was seven, 'On the Coming of Age of Llewelyn Mostyn Esquire'; two horsehair chairs and sofa with castors and antimacassars; on the mantelpiece, two brass candlesticks, two solid glass spheres – leaden-heavy to hold and shot through, like gigantic marbles, with the hues of the spectrum – and an unexpected dinner-gong, a hot-headed oriental buy. On the dresser, amid the few family photographs and the ring-tree, a vaulted glass globe housing a minuscule fairyland : three glass birds, with the delicatest spun-rainbow wings, poised amid crystal flowers and a frozen crystal fountain. On the main wall, the twin symbols of genteel matrimony : the paintings of the pair, heavily gilt-framed, copied from a daguerreotype with appalling expertise, the groom handsome and severe in stiff collar and braided coat, the bride handsome and meek in fichu and Alexandra fringe bunched on the forehead. Opposite, two smaller frames, also twin-gilt, each enshrining a quantity of lumpy foliage and a Welsh waterfall liberally laced with blancmange. The immense Beibl, the minister's wedding present, squatted on the spindliest of legs next to the hymn-book; these comprised the family library. Stiff spotless lace curtains, a blind decently drawn a quarter of the way; on a small table in the window, glimpsed by the passer-by as the edge of a red petticoat is for a second vouchsafed, a timid fuchsia. The tiny penurious shine was complete.

Housekeeping passed the time and saved the pence, Sundays helped, and the Friday dawned. Richard had his jobs aboard to finish, then a bath, ashore and home by six for high tea and the Rotunda. Mary's plain cooking had done its unobtrusive best : lobscouse – 'a sailor's dish, meat stewed with vegetables and ship's biscuit' – and rice pudding flavoured with salt as only she could make it. The kettle was simmering, the little kitchen shone like a jewel that had been lived in for a year, he had called it that, a jewel. There it came, six o'clock tinkling from the wedding present. Several times she was sure she heard that springy step, spelling foolishness and fun.

By the time seven tinkled, then eight, she felt she had been in her jewel for two years. A tram clanged callously past Elwy Street in the dusk, she would never get used to them, rampaging urban animals ready to maul you. Had he just stepped off?

Through the wall a neighbour poked at a grate, she remembered again that she had no idea who lived on either side.

She lifted off coal, to be restored when the front d– there it was, rat-a-tat. But he had his key – she was in the lobby by now, another sixpence for a new key – 'paper missus', the boy was gone. In an access of bookishness Richard had made her a subscriber to *Horner's Penny Stories*, one of the humbler stations in the Northcliffe pilgrimage to the House of Lords; she looked down at the journal, her still unfamiliar wedding-ring bleary in the gaslight. Two people passed, strangers ... She sat down to read. 'Duchess or Dairymaid, a Wife's Dilemma', no, the words were too difficult and she was not in the mood. Mending? His shirts and long underwear lay immaculate in the drawer with the blue serge and the clothes-brush. If she had the sewing-machine – but at three shillings a week, put by in her secret tin box under the bed ... She peered at the lobscouse, it was spoiling. From the three tea-caddies on the mantelpiece Gladstone, Disraeli and the Queen stared coldly down at her, filled with coiled string and bootlaces. She went and for the first time sat in the parlour, thought of the bugs and shuddered. From the dresser, postcard-framed and stern, she caught her brother's eye behind his glasses.

There must have been a storm, you can have it breathless in a port and three miles out, he had told her, the water boiling like fat ... She picked up the hymn-book and turned the black fly-leaf under the lamp to catch the gleam of his writing, 'Richard and Mary Wms, 39 Elwy St.' A firm, godly hand, so unlike her own tottery pot-hooks – she lifted her head. A step.

She flew into the lobby; a measured tread, a policeman of advanced years. It stopped – peering for the number? A knock, to wake the street. Richard rolling lifeless in the Atlantic deeps ... She opened the door. No policeman. Richard was rolling, but not in the Atlantic.

Wedding bowler on the back of his head, he was smiling as benignly as if he had won a lottery. The trim little moustache was stale with beer, and the blue eyes, candid and comfortable with children, were a pair of fumed oaks. He lunged at her for a safe-in-port kiss, stubbed his boot against the step and nearly knocked her over. She caught the parcel he was carrying, and backed panting into the kitchen. She could smell drink and burnt rice pudding.

At the cross-roads of our life there should hover, on the shoulder of us all, a second self to whisper the couple of words we should speak, and to stifle the rest; and we can be one another's other self, she was later (resented, often) to be mine. But at that moment she stood, white and trembling, in need of hers: in need of a voice to say, 'Smile, get off the subject, remember the Rotunda? When the clown fell over and what the red-nosed parson said? Hang on to that, say "yea verily a pint too much ...", you will pretend to laugh too and he will fall burbling into bed. You may cry yourself to sleep, but tomorrow will be yours ...'

'Cwilydd! Shame on thee!' It was a bolt from the pulpit. She said more. It was somebody else talking, quicker than she could think, and the somebody was her own overheard mother, with behind her thousands of pathetic wives with answers-back as futile in Welsh as in English, a fine husband my brother warned me sitting like a slave dinner going to ruin let me finish if it's the last thing I say ...

He stared at her. This afternoon at the Shore Arms, his kit-bag under the counter, that bubble of light where he had run into the two sailors from Llanrwst who had known his grandfather and they had sung a Welsh hymn in harmony to hilariously bad words, and the two had told him of a funny house in Algiers and he had told them how luckily he had married ... the bubble had burst. Not a virago, you could fight that, but a kitten, whimpering righteous abuse.

They stood staring. Just as she was unrecognizable, so he had changed: his eyes glittered molten-blue with hate – where was the merry mariner, the child-lover? If she had gone upstairs, the evening might still have been retrieved. But she banged the shrivelled meal on the table. He looked from it to her, and walked out into vast Liverpool. 39 Elwy St, home of Richard and Mary Wms.

She stood a long time. A draught, he had not shut the front door. No curtains twitching, thank goodness... She looked down at his loose parcel and drew out a shawl, too garish to wear, and a printed card, 'From a Sailor Boy to a Bowery Gal, N.Y.' She blew out the lamp and went upstairs, the step of an older woman. When she did sleep, the birds in the back room taunted her awake. He was back in the morning with his kit-bag, but they did not speak till evening. The die was cast.

But the Welsh language had no word for divorce, and if the procedure had been explained to her, she would have taken it as personally as the details of a cannibal feast. Though there was never to be question of another woman, she had two rivals, and a powerful and perfidious pair they turned out to be: the slut Beer, and her mad-eyed sister Whisky. It was to be a tough fight, but gradually the enemy succumbed and the marriage won long before the end, which came with death forty-nine years later. Once, when for the first time in the memory of her family she was to collapse ill into bed, he was to look down (just home from work) at the knife and fork laid for his dinner, then round the empty kitchen – empty with three sons standing in it – and burst into tears. They loved each other.

Chapter 2

The Tavern and the Convent

The matrimonial boat was patiently baled out by the wife, and settled to choppy seas. The drink problem was allied to the financial one; Richard may not have been money-minded, but he cherished one fixed idea about wages which was to exasperate Mary till the day he retired: he would never disclose the amount of his weekly pay-packet, not under duress or caress, not by wheedle or needle. Every week a certain sum was handed over, the rest a private matter. She, harvesting pennies as she hoarded string, would close her eyes and see him breezing along a quay waving to strangers, with unnumbered coins clinking one after the other out of a hole in his pocket and into a tavern-till. He craved company, and company meant drinking. 'If only he would bring it home,' she would sigh, as if it were a wild animal to be tamed – but neither their class nor their period favoured combining the crackle of home-fires with the pop of corks.

. The Sunday visits to Jabez continued, though Richard did not again venture his bended knee into the Big Seat. There were agreeable evenings, and when his chuckle had a sober ring Mary was as happy, in her deprecating way, as the rest. After the bad days she would swallow her pride, take the tram to Benedict Street and pour it all out to Jabez; plainly the evil genie of father Job's bottle was by no means laid. Jabez's wife died in 1898; late in the following August Mary's sister arrived and took over the back room (from the birds?); Mary, five years wed, was expecting her first child. Sarah, now a strong-willed married woman with a straight tongue, was the only woman who withstood Dic's spell: he knew from her first quizzical look that his arrows of merriment would swoop to earth. She treated him as a delinquent schoolboy ('Twt lol,' she would say, 'nonsense') and in her presence he stood sullenly by, invisible cap in hand.

In the front of the great Beibl, in Richard's firm writing, 'Jabez, born September 8, 1899'. On the next line, less firm, 'Died April 22, 1900, aged 7 months'. The infant was buried with the wife of his Uncle Jabez. There survived a receipted bill : 'J. Powell Evans, with thanks, To Good Oak Coffin, Shroud, Best Brougham, Reopening of Grave, Kirkdale Cemetery, £2.8.od.' The document anticipates modern advertising with a woodcut of the Evans headquarters, a thriving three-storey Tudor mansion in the heart of Liverpool, with 'Funeral Furnishers' splashed cheerfully over the façade. Such a set-back cannot have wooed Dic from temptation, but he had decided over the years that the sea was not the life for a married man; he would settle down, in Wales. Mary's heart lightened. She had always fancied a little shop, with a bell on the door and bootlaces and liquorice and bottles with a marble inside. In Mold? ... Then, over midday dinner, the great decision. It was to be Ffynnongroew – 'fy ngwlad fy hun, Poll, my own home' – and a public-house.

She stared, appalled. The equivalent reaction nowadays would be of a wife informed that her husband plans to open their home as a house of ill-fame and that she is to help him run it. 'You see, Poll, the secret of a –' 'No,' she cried – 'no!' He stared back, carving-knife in air, as she pressed the stays to her heart. 'Yes Richard, I *know* you are the life and soul, and that is the very reason ... Richard – don't do it!' It only made him cajolingly more obstinate. 'Poll, let us go there, as the English say, "on spec" – to look round, meet old friends, see how the land lies!' So be it. They waved good-bye at the landing stage, and Jabez turned sorrowfully away.

At Chester they changed to the coast railway to Rhyl, and as the train slid under a grey sky through one begrimed near-town after another, her spirits foundered : this they did easily, and were not inclined to bob back to the surface. The scenery was not elevating; to the left the gentle Flintshire hills shrank from the sullen roofs, to the right puddled stretches merged into flat and flooded Cheshire – the Sands of Dee, where another sad Mary, Kingsley's, had called the cattle home. Gleefully Richard pointed out the bridge at Queensferry, which he had crossed when he had run away from his grandmother. With luck, thought Mary, she will still be there . . . A workman joined them, and Richard spoke first. The other's face lit up. 'Dic Griffith Tai Roc? Man, I remember you and that Tan-y-Rhiw lot walking into the Gyrn Arms and rolling out a baby barrel of beer, not more than twelve can you have been!' Richard gurgled like an old lag, Mary tweaked her veil and looked out at the estuary. At Mostyn the stranger, now an old friend, helped the meagre luggage on to the trap. The exile was home.

After the flurry of family handshakes, they settled into Glasdir, a little house above the village with a tiny orchard and a glimpse of the sea; Richard's uncle got him a surface job at Point of Air, stoking, and his Nain – his grandmother – was a pious warm-hearted old lady. And the countryside was near; once the steep Rhiw was climbed, Rhewl Fawr, a cluster of hill cottages, led on all sides to fields and lanes with a green distance of woods. On the evenings when they went strolling up there, her arm through his, Richard spruce and debonair and bowing to all and sundry, Mary observed that he put on his grand manner (when his relatives called him 'Lord Mostyn') as easily as a coat. Lapses were few, it was a not unhappy time. Then, in the Beibl, 'Sarah Blodwen, born March 22 1902'. On the next line, 'Died May 6 aged 7 weeks'. Something had gone wrong with 'the feeding', frantic journeys to the little surgery, but there it was – over a span of seven years, two healthy parents had lost two children.

The cloud dispersed, never to be mentioned again. For Richard, the novelty of stoking on dry land dispersed too. The next move was up to Rhewl Fawr, to 1 Jones Terrace, a row of houses, up steps from the road : four rooms as usual, but with the front room stacked with garden produce and by the front door, a card in Richard's copperplate: R. Wms, Greengr'c'y. And no vegetarian could wish for a finer parlour, scrubbed as clean as at 39 Elwy. Where the twin paintings had hung, two Seed Almanacs; where the glass paradise had stood on the dresser, a pyramid of carrots as neat and gleaming as hot-house grapes; where the great Beibl belonged, a vegetable marrow quite as unwieldy. It was surprising that the potatoes had dirt on them.

Richard was to function with tiny horse and cart and Mary behind the counter. It sounded idyllic, but it did not work. The front room was much too small, the window – not a bow – inadequate for display : one respectable cabbage and the light of day was blotted out. The margin of profit proved exiguous, and Richard got bored. Mornings he would set forth up the hill with the cart, waving pleasantries and spick-and-span, though the little horse, another impulsive bargain, seemed to have aged considerably since joining the firm. Late afternoon, the neighbours would watch the same cart come teetering obediently down the hill, the same amiable animalkin between the shafts and the same carrots and turnips aboard, dusty by now; but Rosinante had mislaid her Quixote. No Dic; the travelling salesman had travelled, but had neither sold nor returned. Then Mary was pregnant again, in time for the day when he came home radiant with news – to hell with the peas and the spuds, he had got a public-house, a Free House, a gold mine! He had sold the horse to Parry Gyrn Arms for five shillings, and they were to move in next March, three months after the child was born. She accepted her fate. In November inevitable Sarah arrived, good-humoured and sardonic, and Dic again became the bad penny. 'A tavern, Richard, won't the smell of the beer turn you faint?' Mary told her about her husband's truancies, and about faithful little Dobbin trotting home. Said Sarah, threading a needle, 'You should have married the horse.'

The child was born in the front bedroom, and with its first breath inhaled the healthy whiff of vegetables for sale. But an hour later the mother's sister came in from her tasks to find it choking to death : childless Sarah held it upside down, or smacked it, or did something right, and Richard, having described himself on the birth certificate as 'General Labourer', wrote in the Beibl 'George Emlyn b. Nov 26 1905'. Underneath that, when he came to record the next arrival, he was realistic enough to leave a blank line. The child was the first to be christened up the road at new Gwynfa Chapel, and gained weight; Richard saw Sarah off at Mostyn with a sigh of schoolboy relief, and prepared for the great move.

The new home was hardly a mile from the last, inland. Described outside as 'The White Lion Inn, licensed to RICHARD WILLIAMS' in brazen letters, it was always called Pen-y-Maes, Top of the Field. A large slate-roofed white-washed box perched on a hillock, not picturesque, not ugly, it dominated Glanrafon, which must be the easiest less-than-a-village in the world to describe: it contained, in a green and shallow hollow, a row of fourteen stone cottages. Across the road from them, the 'river' – trickling water three feet wide and two inches deep except when in spate, when it was six.

From Pen-y-Maes, on every hand around the village there rose a gentle swell: to the left, the swell of field up to woods, and to the right, behind the cottages, the swell of back-gardens (each with its pig-sty) up to a protective ridge. Straight ahead the road, after dipping from us into Glanrafon and crossing a lane, skirted the gamekeeper's cottage on the edge of the wooded Gyrn Castle estate, swelled up on the other side, past Parry's Farm and the pump, and disappeared between trees up to Llanasa, the hamlet whose parish we were in. Our own village lay so sheltered that it was hard to believe that the white specks scattered sometimes on the green slope of field were not enormous flowers until they soared, all marvellously together, and turned into seagulls. For out of sight were the blue-grey stretches of the estuary, with half in sky and half in sea, the white blur of ships. From the height behind Pen-y-Maes, a field away, you could see across to the Cheshire plain; and once, sitting with my father in the trap on his way down to Mostyn for beer, I asked him what that place was over the water, with all that sand? He said it was another country, where Welsh was not spoken and the public-houses were open on Sunday. I remembered the Sahara, and asked if it was Africa? He laughed and said it was, and that on a clear day you could see elephants walking in and out of Parkgate.

But from our house nothing was visible of this world of surmise, only the warm bowl of peace that was Glanrafon. It was inhabited by farm-hands, colliers at Point of Air and workers on the estate : whether John Jones South Africa was a former gold prospector or a veteran of the war, I never asked. It was a Welsh-speaking community, English being studied but rarely spoken, and then brokenly : humble, godly and isolated. The formative years I spent there were television-less, radio-less, film-less, theatre-less : they also lacked concert, gramophone, telephone, electricity, gas and tap-water. We walked up to Llanasa for the post-office and down to Ffynnongroew for everything from a bottle of medicine to a box of matches : once a week the E. B. Jones van trotted in from Prestatyn with provisions, as to a lighthouse. There were no buses, the nearest station was Mostyn (nearly three miles) and a motor-car was so rare that as it chugged along every child ran after it; it left us not only an exotic smell of exhaust, but a trail of pennies. The nearest I came to the miracle of the telephone was to put my ear to the poles growing out of the hedgerows on the Llanasa road, and in the sunlight listen to the endless thrum of a million business men ululating deals between Liverpool and Llanberis, between Birmingham and Bettws-y-Coed. They even thrummed on Sundays; could it be the sound of preachers?

Pen-y-Maes, to four-roomed Mary, was a rambling castle. Off the lobby, between back-kitchen and bar, a tiny room called 'y snug' (a word from Liverpool) where I was to spend most of my indoor life; from it stone steps led down into a musty cob-webbed cellar full of barrels. Behind the house, next to the tiny ammoniac fortress where customers paid toll to nature, a disused garden scrabbled round a dusty laurel; behind that, a great shabby unloved yard with rain-butt, hen-coops, pig-sties, abandoned cart-wheels and in the far corner, lurking discreetly behind the stable, the earth privy for the household, called 'y petty'. (If I mention bodily functions more often than I would choose, it is because living as we did they became an important nuisance; to this day, the generous gush of clear water into a lavatory-bowl gives me a satisfaction almost aesthetic.) Sloping downhill to the woods, a morose kitchen-garden. All this was

31

never to change, for Mary's house-pride had enough to fight inside; there was never a flower in Pen-y-Maes, either growing or as a frivolous transient indoors.

Even happy-go-lucky, she would have found the life wearing; how she managed, as partner in what was to turn out a nine-year bacchanal, it is hard to know. She bore two more sons, Job Percival, 1908, and Thomas, 1912; after Job's birth she employed a girl of thirteen as nurse-help, but there was never to be any other servant. On top of her domestic duties, she could never relax in a house that was indeed public : there were no licensing hours, her front door was open to the world, wherever she went she was dogged by popping corks and raucous laughter, and the very horsehair in the little parlour seemed to reek of beer. Many a night she jostled her way behind the bar to polish glasses; customers, drawn by the personality of mine host, loomed up out of nowhere – travellers deflected from main roads, poachers, bibulous farmers, bucolic local preachers fallen from grace, nomadic tramps. Richard tabled their debts in a small account book, in his meticulous hand – 'Tom Evans Fat 1/1½d, Ned Engineman 7½d' – but what larger sums were neither entered nor collected, is not known.

After nightfall the party spirit thickened, with drinks galore on the house; on the stairs, I spent many draughty minutes squatting in the dark, in my nightshirt, listening to the guffaws and the singing. Once was wafted up a mournful and yet sprightly sound which I could connect neither with earth nor heaven, and which must have been a concertina; once a voice sang jaunty Welsh songs in exquisite falsetto. Then Mam would come hurrying through to the cellar with beer jugs to be filled – 'go back, before I get the stick!' – and I would scamper to bed – 'I wanted a drink of water' – and out into ambush again in three minutes.

Sunday was her haven; Saturday night, last weary thing, the front door creaked to and was bolted till Monday dawn. Sunday morning meant two extra and balmy hours abed while a beer-weary smoke-sodden house lay blessedly shrouded in silence and rested its aching limbs. Later in the day though, the Sabbath peace would be broken by discreet thirsty knocks at the back door. Any bit of gossip was excuse for replenishment, such as when Mr Hughes the Policeman (on behalf of Miss Jones Post-Office whom both the Tai Mawr twins had courted) called at Tai Mawr with an affiliation order, found the twins seated on the doorstep staring up at him mute and identical, and turned back for home. Mary was not amused. Another Sunday, warned that the same harassed officer was on the prowl, Richard led his cronies into the open air, stood them outside the Gentlemen, and as the law stalked powerlessly past, conducted a pious choir through the Welsh hymn 'O Watch Our Shepherd Guard His Flock'. His wife did not find this funny either. She longed for evening chapel, her link with respectability and her one chance to wash a week of ale-froth out of her system.

But on rare fine Sunday evenings Richard would accompany her – best serge, false front, bowler, Albert watch-chain, walking-stick and Sunday look – on a sedate stroll over the brow of Pen-y-Maes, me between them : along the thorn hedges decked with the fluttering wool of sheep, past the munching Welsh-speaking horses. They would nod at acquaintances, Richard would have liked a chat, 'Watch the sun, Georgie, it's got a lid on it!' And if you braved the glare, there *was* a smooth lid slithering over the molten cauldron, would it set the earth afire? When we came to a stile, there were jokes about her showing 'dipyn o bais', her petticoat. 'Hush, Richard,' she would gurgle, and I was content to see them alone and at ease. Then we passed the haunted place, a roofless barn in a field, nettles waist-high. 'One dark night, Georgie, a man stumbled into that pond and drowned, and his ghost lives in that barn, crys croes tân poeth, cross my heart!' 'Dad, was he ill?' 'No,' said Richard sadly, swiping a daisy, 'drunk my boy, dead drunk.' Mary stepped round a cow-pat, and smoothed a glove.

The thirteen-year-old help, who came when I was three, was Annie Roberts, from a cottage up over the hill where she lived with her mother and sister and a mysterious man called Jacky Milwr, Jack the Soldier, a quiet well-spoken customer with an undefined shadow upon him. 'No,' Mam answered me, 'he is not her father and the house too small for a lodger,' a Welsh sentence which I realize now could be run together into one portmanteau word meaning 'lover'.

Annie was a merry fresh-cheeked girl with pigtails, black stockings and high boots. As my mother had perforce to become a scolding and overworked figure in the background – she may have caressed her children in babyhood, but not later, it was not in her nature – so Annie turned into my mother-sister. Neither I nor my brothers would have dreamt of addressing our parents as 'ti', thou – once when I did to tease my mother, she was vexed and said it was 'gwyneb galed' and lacking in respect – but Annie was 'thou'. She and I shared a bed, and I would wait for her to come upstairs and chatter to me while under her nightdress she tugged her stays round, unhooked them, dropped them, rolled them neatly on to the cane chair with a hole in it, and got in beside me. Once, as she snuggled down, she broke innocent wind; she had reproved me for the same peccadillo, the tables were turned, and we giggled. 'Paid a dweud gair wrth dy fam, don't tell thy mother!'

My first pleasures were with Annie. 'Annie, oes gennyti fferin yn dy ffedog, hast a sweet in thy apron?' She helped me to toast my bread; when I was in bed with a bad cold and scared by thoughts of disused quarry-shafts and the idiot faces forming in the wall-paper, she brought me home from a chapel-social a prodigal pile of old many-coloured paper streamers: it was to her I showed how I could spring off a stair and swing from the ledge above twice by my finger-tips, a thing I did for luck every new morning. One evening, one of the few when the cloud lifted from my mother, Annie and I sat while she sang 'Oh, Mr Porter' and 'Wass You Ever See' ('such a funny sight before') and Annie learnt them to sing to me. It was she who pointed out the Gyrn Castle flag blowing above the trees, 'to show they were there'. Her information was not always so accurate, for she warned me never to drink from a glass in the dark, because it would very likely have a frog in it. At the roadside, on the way to Rhewl Fawr, was a bank where flowered tiny wild strawberries, enough to make a dwarf's nosegay; there Annie helped me to scrape out a cave the size of a head, in which we arranged pebbles as eggs and criss-cross twigs to bar the entrance, then we left it, our secret colony. For months, whenever I passed, I would give the overgrown entrance a look of complicity. Another time we would dig up jagged old saucers and bottles, once nearly a whole jug, wash them and play shop, twirling squares of newspaper into holders for stone sweets and dirt sugar.

My tiny horizon crept outwards. In red petticoat and pinafore edged with frayed lace, and big bedraggled straw hat over a fierce fringe in my eyes, I was soon emerging alone and staggering down the hill to join in the games of the five other children : Idris and Bet (the policeman's two), Ifor and Cassie Owens, and John. We hoarded the lids of biscuit-tins, floated them flashing in the sun with a ten-strong crew aboard on to the mighty two-inch river, and watched them sweep bravely into the tunnel under the path; then the race over the top and the tense wait. Sometimes the precious vessel came bobbing impertinently out of the blackness, mostly not; sometimes, days later, freed by a whim of the current, it would swirl wondrously into view.

We would sneak to the back of a horse-and-trap and clamp on as it started off; this was forbidden – 'he'll give you the whip!' – and he did. Then we would squat along a high wall, like crows, and watch the sheep being ruthlessly sheared; Dad dabbled in beasts as he had in birds, and occasionally a denuded animal would bound up branded with 'R.W'. When I passed these sheep in the fields, I was surprised that they did not re-cognize me. There was leap-frog, hide-and-seek among the hay-stooks, somersaults; it was during the latter that I had a fleeting view of five-year-old Bet and was surprised to note that she was ungarnished. I thought the tiny pearly twin folds beautifully neat but was disconcerted, it was like seeing a closed hand with a gracious dimple where the thumb should be. I meant to ask Annie, but forgot ... We dragged a stick to make a shell-whorl for hopscotch and stored marbles in jam jars, but our toys were mostly home-made; there was a race with buttons, moistening the thumb and pressing it on the button to pick it up, but that was an end-of-tether game. Then there was the 'olwyn', an iron hoop donated from the blacksmith's sparking hell-fire; as the wheel lunged down the hill before me, the hook in my hand making a fine rasp, I would race after it, splendidly aware of myself. We would kick at a blown-up ball, veined and greasy, which I found repulsive even before I discovered that it had been extracted from the pig to whose death-screams I had listened aghast. After that I could not touch a 'swigan'.

Those nine years, not only was it rare for me to venture out of Glanrafon, I never set foot in anybody else's house : no neighbours could be more friendly, but when we called for each other we waited discreetly outside. So the excitement when Annie announced a picnic to Llannerch-y-Mor, the Side of the Sea, was so unbearable that she would do so only on the hot morning of the day. There was only one query, 'It's not the day for the ice-cream man?' For his arrival from Prestatyn was a great afternoon moment : no bell, the word was round before he was out of Ffordd Ddwr, the Lane of Water, into the clear of the cross-roads. It was the only time I begged an extra halfpenny from my mother and got it : it bought a cornet or a wafer, and the decision was hard.

Annie and her plain friend, Mary Pugh the milliner's apprentice, would make sandwiches, and we would set out after early mid-day dinner – 'paddling, but no bathing, mind' – up Ffordd Ddwr to where on a very clear day you could see the funnels of ships in the Mersey (and even, they said, the mountains of Cumberland) then down through Gwespyr and Gronant to Talacre, where we would hurry over the railway, the same line from Chester to Rhyl, for we could smell the sea. Then a knoll, and – look, at our feet, between prickly grass – sand! Over and down a hillock by the snowy lighthouse, and we were on the honey-edge of the Dee. Not a soul but us; crabs, jellyfish, castles, we took off shoes and stockings and ran and sang and splashed and tasted the horrible salt; then we paddled. The adventure was complete. Then departure for home after foreign travel, drunk with air and a million tiny waves and a trillion grains of sand. Glanrafon looked smaller.

All this was when I was not at school, which I started at the age of four: Mam wanted me out of the public-house as much as possible. The only school near enough for me to walk to alone was Talacre Convent, a mile up Ffordd Ddwr, across fields and lanes and down into a tree-shaded scoop on the way to the estuary; the other Glanrafon children must have been old enough to attend Llanasa. The first couple of days Annie took and fetched me, but I was soon off on my own, lank hair shorn off, petticoats folded away and into my navy ganssi (a version of guernsey) buttoned at one shoulder, and my new corduroys – the torture of that smell! – swinging sandwiches by the string and a tin of cold tea with 'G.W.' scratched on the lid.

The school was conducted by nuns, and at home there were Wesleyan qualms: 'If you see any graven images keep your knees stiff and don't pick up any beads lying about.' But from the first my apprehensions were soothed by the gentle blanched faces under the starched coifs, as they twittered prettily like holy birds. I had heard English spoken only in stray phrases, but was now puzzled not to recognize one word in fifty, never mind in ten. 'That is not English,' said a scoffing boy of seven, 'it is from "dros y môr", over the sea!' They were French nuns; so that after Welsh, French was the first language I heard consecutively spoken.

It was a mild benevolent school, boys and girls, two big rooms with crayons and blocks, a-b-c frames with battered beads, slates to be breathed on hotly, oleographs of Bible catastrophes – the Flood, Lot's Wife, and Moses looking like our bearded neighbour Issmael Jones angry in a nightgown. At noon we would file out, lift our tins off the stove and settle in corners; the tea tasted tinny, but it was different from home and that was good. I learnt my English letters, while not yet speaking English, by copying words printed in exquisite copperplate: 'silence is golden', 'virtue is its own reward'. Over the door stood the lady against whom I had been warned: a pale plaster figure, chinless head meekly bowed, fingers raised in blessing. She looked kind, though for the first few days I avoided catching her sightless eye; filing through, I would dive past in case I was tripped into the wicked act of genuflexion.

In the holidays I looked forward to school, but made no close friends there any more than at Glanrafon, where I played happily with the other children without thinking of them as people to talk to; I tended more and more to lead an interior life, a square silent child, gentle-mannered, left-handed, clumsy, given to sudden smiles. But I was not content with that life, something was lacking. One Sunday I realized what it was. 'Mam, what can I do?' 'Find a verse to learn.' I lugged down the great book, glumly turned a page and read 'Jabez ... died April 22, 1900.' I hurried to her, what did it mean? She was sharp with me – 'but Mam, it's in the Beibl!' If God had willed it I would now have a brother six years older, hurry up and find a verse.

An elder brother! He would be stalwart and popular, with a strong happy face, like Dad at his best, and protective like Annie, with his arm round my shoulders – the fantasy blossomed – curly brown hair, warm frank eyes to be turned to in every trouble ...

But where was he?

But for a week or two I forgot him, and school too, in the January of Woodbine Town. Christmas had been stimulating – whatever our mother's worries, Santa Claus never forgot to fill our stockings with modest surprises, plus orange and apple – but it had worn off. I had watched Cassie playing with her new doll; I would not have told even Annie that I coveted it, but I did. Not to nurse, but to talk to and be talked to by, it seemed unfair. One evening, when Annie was too busy for snakes and ladders, and all drawings had been mutilated with crayons, and the novelty had worn off the houses of cards, and off the little M-less rubber printing-set (ƆEOƆЯE WILLIⱯ S, PEN-Y- ⱯES, NEЯⱯ OSTYN), Annie brought into the snug an old thin catalogue from Lewis' Liverpool and suggested 'torri allan', cutting out the figures: men, women and children sketched in every sort of costume, description and price attached. It sounded dull enough, but I made a start.

Annie returned to find me absorbed. I had snipped out a haughty creature on her way to a ball in a fourreau of ivory chameuse just escaping the ground at ninety-nine shillings, propped her against a tea-caddy and was talking to her, and for her. Not Welsh – was she not named 'The Lady Mary Line'? – but an inane English picked up from the nuns and from the bar. 'Attention the Lady Mary look sharp now the curfew shall not ring tonight isn't it?'

From under the bar Annie retrieved a Woodbine cigarette-box, cardboard lid attached, which we placed on the table, folding the lid back on to old play-bricks; the box became the living-room – and the lid the bedroom – of a special roofless house. The front door, cut into the wall, looked like a low gate, and was;

then we made a staircase of concertina-ed cardboard, then chairs, tables, beds and windows – the frames only, folded at the base to stand unaided. Within a week, the snug table was Woodbine Town.

And an odd colony they were, making up for dead sameness of physiognomy by their unpredictable behaviour. Ladies would promenade the oil-cloth street, all using the same kangaroo hop, in filmy nightdresses of Liberty Satin (69/6); at the corner, by the flicker of the candlestick lamp-post, they would engage in halting converse with a gentleman leaning against it in a bathing costume. Names were borrowed from local gentry : 'Good evening, is the gun loaded, Colonel Batters?' 'Yes Lady Bates.' 'Right-ho, good night . . .' After this sinister exchange, Lady Bates would bound home again and retire for the night in full view of neighbours collected outside for long expressionless chats; they would watch her through the window, and indeed through the wall, prostrate on her bed in a tea-gown with kimono sleeves and a hat like a tub, both hands tucked into a muff as if overcome by wine at the moment of leaving to pay a social call.

They also proved a morbid lot, prone to standing about for hours, on the very edge of the horrific table-mountain, discussing sudden death. 'I heard,' remarked Lady Bates, now in deerstalker and cycling bloomers and anxious to tell a true story Annie had told me, 'that a nurse in Llandudno –' The door would open : Mam hastening into the cupboard, and I would wait for her to go, but more often it was Dad on his way through with great beer jugs. Even in a hurry he would stop behind me; I would pretend not to know and continue, while he gave Annie a conspiratorial wink to make fun of the performance in an appreciative way that was all his own. 'Llandudno?' interposed the Colonel, in top hat and opera cloak. 'Yes, a cliff called the Great Orme, good evening Colin' – a prim boy eavesdropping against the lamp-post in cricket-wear – 'not too near the edge my lad least said soonest mended, well Colonel there was this nurse holding this baby, well such a wind, pray Colin do not fidget, the baby was blown – *Colin!*' At a signal, Annie had waved a *Liverpool Echo* and paper-thin Colin was lying with every bone

broken on the cracked tiles thirty inches below. At this point
Dad would remember his duties and go clumping down to the
cellar. In the meantime Mrs Batters would be sitting at home
supping in a motoring veil, with opposite her a gentleman who
had arrived – and evidently been made welcome – in snug com-
binations at three guineas. The catastrophe having been reported
to her by an impulsive caller in a deep elastic belt (£3/13/6) the
absolute comfort of which was assured, 'When is he for to be
buried pray?' said Mrs Batters, 'I would be sorry to miss Colin's
funeral ...' And so it would go on till bedtime, when they were
bundled away into one chaotic living-room all unseemly-piled
one on top of the other, parasols and cricket bats and opera hats
and all.

This sport lingered past the Easter holidays. Then, as my invention wore as thin as my dramatis personae, a new lesson
started at school : the fortuitous basis of a second fantasy which
for two or three years was to be as powerful as the other.

I had called the boy Colin after a class-book entitled *Colin,
His Story*, with opposite every page a picture illustrating it –
'He leapt on his horse', ' "I've lost my puppy," sobbed Colin'.
Many leaves were loose, and Sister Marie had the ingenious idea
of detaching them all, distributing them daily and asking each
child to copy out his two pages. Colin's pranks thus presented
a chaotic pattern, and every morning I wondered what would
fall to my lot. Would he be off on the holiday he returned from
last Friday?

As I deciphered other tales, there began to lodge in my mind
the idea of a Book, by an omniscient Author who at the end of
each day wrote, straight into print with an illustration opposite,
one more page in *George, His Story*. Every night in bed after my
quick Welsh prayer – 'God bless Dad Mam Job Thomas Annie
Amen' – I would think, what was today's page? Sometimes it
would be the photographer at the convent, and us all in our
best : me in faintly candy-striped long-shorts over my stockings,
with best ganssi and a soft hat with a wide brim turned up all
around. Job, by now in my red petticoat and pinafore – new

lace – was brought by Annie, and at last our turn came to be posed on the lawn. 'Dyma'r 'deryn iti!' said the man, 'watch the bird!' 'The child would have fallen off the chair but for George standing by his side.' The illustration would show just that, the caption reading 'The nuns applauded'. I sighed contented into my pillow, and fell asleep to the rustle of the page turning ready for tomorrow. I told nobody about the Story, not even Annie.

Then there was the day I looked down into a disused quarry and saw a skeleton of a sheep; then 22 June 1911, a Coronation tea in the convent, with cakes and 'bara brith' – speckled bread – and jellies such as I had never seen, and bunting, when we each went home staggering with patriotic surfeit and clutching a bright red-white-and-blue mug with portraits of their Majesties and 'O'r Arglwyddes Mostyn, from Lady Mostyn'. A gay and greedy day. 'George, named after the new King, received a message from him which was read out to the school.' Mam placed the mug in the corner-cupboard next to my father's.

I was always hoping Gwen would provide material for the Story. Gwen – Parry's Farm – had fits; and often in Ffordd Ddwr, under the high gilly-flowered wall, I would listen fearfully, callously, for the strangled sounds I had heard about. They never came. She had one accomplishment which even then seemed a pointless one : one day Annie proudly handed me a neat ruled book which Gwen had filled with stuff copied out of a newspaper. But she had copied it backwards, you had to hold it to the looking-glass. I connected this feat in some way with epilepsy. Then there was Glyn, a lump of a boy who jumped up and down, quite high, to show the slighest pleasure; we realized he was in his teens and looked on him as a talking pet.

But neither he nor Gwen ever earned a mention; and at the end of most days it was hard to know what the Author would have put. That George was woken up by his father shouting and then stumbling, or lost his weekly penny down a rain grid? Dull. I did ponder over the morning I was offered a ride on a horse by a customer, dared not refuse, and was tossed up on to a terrifying mountain of herculean muscle which heaved under

me like the sea. 'Dwisho disgyn!' I screamed, 'I want to get off!'
'Be thou not a Mary Ann,' laughed Dad, but Mary Ann screamed
more and was lifted down. It was a cart-horse from Issmael
Jones's farm by the name of Lloyd George. I rejected the episode
as lacking in incident.

Then there were the days of active boredom, when I would
sit on the stile beside Pen-y-Maes, one leg bent under me ('Don't
sit on stone, Georgie') and survey the village in the morning sun.
A bee buzzed, a horse grazed, a butterfly butterflew. But none of
this warranted even a look; for a country child, I was ignorant
of nature and incurious. I was indeed fascinated by birds, not
only for the grace and mystery of their swoops across the evening heavens, but for their elusiveness: it was my wistful hope
to watch a high dive into long grass, and then to creep slowly
up, snatch, and hold the beating wings in the heat of my hand.
Then I would lovingly cast them free again. But always, as I got
as near as two feet, there would be a flurry of sward and feather,
and the bird would spring twenty feet into the air. I liked to
stare for minutes at a rabbit immobile before the race, but the
touchable world of dogs and cats held no interest; our black
bitch Nel, lying meek on the rag rug in the kitchen, was a lodger
and no more. Again, though I had recurring dreams of vast hills
of thick-packed foliage where I would roam like a monkey from
one laden branch to the next, I was rarely able to call a tree by
its name. Nothing in any of this for the Story.

Then there were the incidents which seemed unsuitable, I did
not quite know why. Such as the afternoon of hide-and-seek
when Fat Maggie and I decided to make the petty our hiding
place, and Mam opened the door, found us giggling happily, and
was so oddly upset, 'Come *out* the two of you!' Later, trotting
alone into the road in the early evening, I came abruptly upon
Dad at grips with a vicious customer, just as Annie ran up, said
'He is holding him till they get the policeman!' and must have
whisked me away. For what is bitten into my memory is the
eternally still picture of a sunlit landscape empty but for two
men sprawled in the roadway at the blazing cold heart of a fight,
one pinning down, the other spread-eagled in the dust: the only

sound the inexorable panting, the only motions the vein throbbing in the neck and the other's maddened fingers clawing at
the sun.

Also unsuitable was the hot overcast afternoon, in school,
when we sat drawing our own pointing left hand. Suddenly tall
Mother Jeanne stalked through, immensely stern and carrying a
cane, and in her wake shambled one of the few older scholars, a
hulking boy with a reddened face. His offence must have been
serious; Mother Jeanne was God, His-Her wrath glowered in the
thundery air, the wretch was damned. She opened the heavy
arched door of the porch and turned to him. They were both
breathing fast. It was the first look I had ever seen between a
man and a woman, even though the one was disguised as a
schoolboy and the other as a nun : she flashing with authority, he
smouldering with rebellion. I knew that she was saying to him,
in unspoken French, 'Savage, you see me as a woman but I will
teach you a lesson,' and that he was saying to her, in unspoken
Welsh, 'You pious bitch, you will cry before I do'. A moment of
suspension; in the other room, Sister Marie, 'God is love, repeat.'
For a second, it looked as if he might snatch the cane from her,
then he strode insolently past. The door crashed behind them,
the crack of doom. Silence. I felt hot and frightened. The boy
next to me whispered, 'She's taking his trousers down,' and
sniggered. Past my drooping hand being drawn as a paw, I saw
the two of them in that ascetic porch – she, the avenging angel,
pulling his braces round and over his arms, he flailing at her
swirl of black – and I held back from the brink of something bad.
Then Sister Thérèse said quickly, 'Let me see your drawings,
please,' and the picture shattered. Three minutes later Mother
Jeanne crossed, followed by the culprit : she a benevolent casti-
gator, he a sulky child. Had I imagined something I knew nothing of? Or had I known something I thought I was imagining?
It did not somehow fit into *George, His Story*.

Then there was the morning when bored with arithmetic, I
saw a beetle slowly approach over the floor and disappear
directly under me. To get a view, I had to lean over the front of
my desk, my whole body resting on it, arms and knees sloppily

bent. The beetle stopped dead. Lazily waiting for an insect to move, my mouth loosely open the way children's go, I felt suddenly at ease, floating, held up not by a child's desk but by a wickedly strong grandfather. Sweetly, in the unquestioning infant marrow of my bones, I felt beneath the desk a flicker which I could not savour or even, at the back of my child's mind, suspect. The beetle scuttled, and I sat back to Fractions.

But that night it was on a horrid episode earlier that I pondered, when at the end of spelling, Mother Jeanne had entered : 'Somebody with eggs to show you.' In lounged a self-possessed person in a sailor-suit, at least twelve years of age, bearing a glass case and saying, 'Gather round and don't push.' I realized with a thrill that he was English, for he ran one word into the next with superb nonchalance; but his eyes were cold and sandy. The eggs quite interested me, though I would sooner have come upon the box on my own, every shell miraculously intact, abandoned by highwaymen. The only wild eggs I had seen were vaguely blue, and some of these were dappled, or even streaked with yellow. He explained the birds, then, 'Any inquiries?' Our English was not up to an articulate question, but I raised an impulsive hand. 'Please, sir,' I said carefully, 'does the paint come off the eggs?'

I had never spoken up before; there was a titter, I went crimson. The ovologist stared at me, and spoke one word. 'Ass,' he said. We had several rude English words to bandy meaninglessly in the playground, and one of these he would seem to have applied to me. Arse. The hilarity was immense. I was a chubby child, and felt my face crumple. Back at home Annie laughed and said, 'Fi sy'n gwybod, a tin hardd sydd gennyti 'nghariadi, I'm the only one that has seen thy bottom, love, and it's beautiful, Georgie why didn't you ask him how long since he laid the eggs?' We both rollicked with laughter, and in bed I settled on the incident for today's page, though I tampered with the ending. 'George alone spoke up. "How long pray," asked he, "since you *laid* these eggs?" The crowd roared, George had won.'

That made a fine page, making up for the impending Sunday.

For the one blank day was the seventh; mine was a weekday story.

Nothing can ever irk again as badly as the boredoms of child-hood. More and more, the Sabbath for which my mother prayed I dreaded, particularly in the summer. I would wake with the daylight bursting the blind, and lie for an hour and a half, no Annie, racked with unrest. One Saturday evening, called in to bed – 'Georg-IE!' – from a timeless sunny orgy of rounders, I saw Annie putting on her hat. 'Annie,' I wailed, 'do they never skip Sunday and go Friday, Saturday, Monday?' 'I never heard of it,' said Annie, buttoning briskly, 'what would the poor preachers do, dressed up and straining at the leash?' 'But if you wanted Sunday crossed out, who would you write to?' 'Lloyd George. Now off with your singlet.' 'Issmael Jones's horse?' 'Now say your prayers, Georgie, and not a word to God about it.'

The Chancellor of the Exchequer was not appealed to; behind smiling Saturday, Sunday continued to rear its sepulchral head. Weekdays the village was somnolent but alive – a sudden greet-ing, a ringing laugh as a loaf would roll out of the van and send a pig squawking, the whir of the knife-grinder, a black-faced collier flashing over the cross-roads on his bicycle, the traffic through our front door of thirsty sinners – but Saturday over, for twenty-four hours Glanrafon held its breath in a black-gloved hand, coming to on Monday morning with lungs bursting and blue in the face. It was my belief that the birds knew about Sunday, for I never seemed to see or hear any; I imagined them packed feather to feather inside some seventh-day sanctuary, feet meekly in Sabbath lime, a choir godly and mute. The feel-ing in the air was that somebody had died, that nobody knew who it was and that everybody was too afflicted to ask.

I got up straight into my Sunday best – chafing boots, celluloid collar and creaking knickerbockers – so my every movement was circumscribed: no playing shop (dirt) no hop-scotch (dust), just sit. Yet the forbidden regions of bar and porch I roamed at will. The porch was lit only through the frost of the locked front door, glass blandly smooth on the outside, but inside ribbed like corduroy and wonderfully nasty to flick with my nail; in the watered light it was weirdly empty and still. The bar smelt voluptuously of stale beer, stale tobacco, stale ribaldry. The only sound was the tick of the grandfather clock; this was my chance to clamber on to a stool to scrutinize the delicate little landscapes painted on its face like coquettish birthmarks. Then its stomach would give a sudden grind and, in my startled face, begin to strike.

The old *Liverpool Weekly Post* Almanacs which my mother had tacked over stains had a Sunday lure, for each, amid its desert of dates – 7 August, Ninth Sun. after Trin., 29 March, Ch. Wesley d. – bore a rotogravure ('Her Fatal Mistake', 'The Letter Delivered'). I would then watch a dusty sunbeam point a fastidious finger at the spittoon on the floor; then I would drag the spittoon to the bar, stand tiptoe on it, plant my Sunday elbows next to the still-wet rings, heave myself up and peer over at the tin full of my father's beer-sticky change, the tobacco scales and the disused roulette wheel. On the floor, grey-clogged sawdust and Woodbine butts, squashed into the stone like flies. The room was dead and dirty, but to me it meant the free-and-easy forbidden, with ranged on the shelves the medicine bottles of the damned. Once I took the mystic whisky and held it up to the sunbeam. It gleamed, amber-wicked, what devil lurked in there, and how was he conjured out and into a man? I sniffed the debauched air like ozone.

The door creaked open: my mother, bucket in hand. 'Put that bottle *down*! ... Have you tasted it?' I ran out, or rather walked, there was nothing to run for. Dinner – it never rained just then – was shadowed by Sunday-school at Capel y Groes, a gaunt stone rectangle a mile away, on the hill before you dipped into Llanasa. Home for tea, then a listless half-hour turning weighty slabs of family album. In the middle, cheek by jowl and scowl with ghostly wedded couples staring me defiantly out, I found one aunt who for some reason was looking past me, so sweetly that I wished she were facing. She had signed herself, boldly, 'Ellen', the n obscured by the cardboard setting, but when I asked Mam which she was, she had no idea and could not recall the picture. Years later I recognized my Auntie Ellen as Ellen Terry, and with reluctance yielded her to other nephews who had more claim on her.

Then back for the evening service, with my mother; in the hymns, her meek voice hid behind the contraltos. As I stepped inside, I knew this would be the lost time, the moth-ball hour of desolate hymns and faltering 'gweddi', the prayer, a shredded patchwork of platitude. With Mam bowed beside me – perhaps wistfully remembering the praying stoker and wondering what was afoot at home – I would bend forward, close my mouth over the back of the pew in front and to the rhythm of jargon, worry that hallowed varnish till I heard a protesting crackle and felt saliva about to drool.

The sermon was the test of endurance. I trained myself not to watch the clock for five minutes on end, for if watched it never moved; then, staring at the woman's hat in front, I tried to imagine her at home before the glass, settling it and spearing it, but could not, she had sat here always. Then a bluebottle would grumble up to a tiny opened pane, slip, climb, slip, climb and – out! Looking from the bare walls to the pulpit, I knew there was nothing between me and the pit of boredom except the private thoughts into which I learnt to retire. As the long words washed over me, endlessly repeated but so empty that I never took in their meanings – 'edifeirwch' repentance, 'trugaredd' mercy, 'tragwyddoldeb' eternity – I sank into the story, what a good boy is that George Pen-y-Maes, never takes his eyes off the preacher. I was so far into it by the end, that Mam would have to shake me for the hymn and for going forward with the other children to mumble my verse. 'Yr Iesu a wylodd, Jesus wept.' Then I would emerge to out-of-doors gulping like a deep-sea diver, leap down the steps, take a quick look at Y Gop, the green volcano-like cone showing over the rim of Llanasa hill where Queen Boadicea is reputedly buried, and soberly suit my step to my mother's.

Every early summer came the Gymanfa, the Festival, when I went to chapel Monday evening as well. This might have been the hellish night of the year, but was not; changing into best after a normal day and sitting in a chapel crowded to the doors was new, *not Sunday*! And the only time I was ever wooed from my inner life was one of these Mondays. The preacher, famous for holding his audience, spoke of the carpenter's son in the gentle hill-country of Nazareth: I found myself listening. I suddenly saw it as the pastoral Flintshire around me and watched, walking past the chapel in tunic and sandals, the shy child solemn beyond his years, walking down into Llanasa and past the mansion called Golden Grove, surely the most beautiful name ever given to a house; I saw the shepherds of Bethlehem, they were the farm-boys round Glanrafon. In the crowded chapel, not a rustle: when the preacher paused, there was a silence I had not heard before. He spoke of the trial, of Pilate; here was a Story, under my nose, which I had missed ... But the sermon over, the congregation relaxed into respectable torpor and my mind clicked off again.

Before my sleep-walking eyes, trees burgeoned and spread their leaves and lost them; harvests ripened and were gathered, my brother grew unnoticed below me and I grew unnoticed above him. Then even the weekdays began to pall. I used to hear of Bands of Hope, Penny Readings and Eisteddfodau – festivals of competitive singing and reciting – but Glanrafon was so remote that I never went. The games lost their savour too, and I developed an antipathy to any communal activity, such as group singing; I had no voice anyway, and no ear. One Guy Fawkes day, we children were marching through the village, sooty-faced and singing, in comic costumes; the more my companions enjoyed our inane clowning, the more embarrassed I became. As we filed past the crowded door of Pen-y-Maes, I burst into inexplicable tears and dived through to the snug, to wash and withdraw into myself in my continued search for escape. What was to provide it?

Chapter 4

Three Friends, and
a Funeral March

Reading. The reason I remember Glanrafon as mostly summer is because in bad weather, when not at school, I was in the snug, arched over print. The process was gradual, starting with the disembowelled career of Colin, then I was to totter through stray books from the Convent shelves : *Tales for Little People*, then *What Katy Did*, but once I had tracked down the page to which the frontispiece referred – Katy high on a swing, and the branch splintering – and made sure she was badly hurt, I was done with her. *In His Steps* was set in a wicked city called Chicago, but started with a preacher preparing his sermon; *Jessica's First Prayer* I did not open. The only books in Pen-y-Maes (I did not count the Beibl and the hymns) were Old Moore's Almanac, unreadable, and under Dad's counter, a large thin tattered volume with on the cover a faded golden-curled child blowing bubbles. I knew my father was known far and wide as Dic Pen-y-Maes, but why was this boy named Pears Eng Dic? I had a confused idea that he had invented all the words inside and was exhaling them through a pipe, and anyway dismissed a tiny-printed endless list, from A to Z, as tedious; it was put firmly back.

Then Dad, on one of his annual trips to Rhyl to renew his licence – it seemed to take two days – one morning cleared his head of business cares enough to walk into a bookseller's and inscribe my name on the fly-leaf of *The Water Babies*, abridged, with drawings; I sat eagerly down to it. I enjoyed the first part, became the little chimney-sweep, hated Mr Grimes, and was carried away by the hue-and-cry after Tom and his spectacular climb down Vendale; but as soon as he sank to the pool-bed and became a winsome baby strolling finger to lip, a wisp of weed across his middle, through a half-world of luminous fish and frond – why didn't he *drown*? All stories for children had this effect; my stomach-eye was caught by the House of Sweets, but the prattling rabbits and the goblins peeping from behind toadstools I looked at with a fishy eye. Peter Pan would have left me cold – boys flying in at windows!

After *The Children's Gulliver*, though, I would spend an hour watching inch-high people swarming up ladders on to my knee-cap and picnicking deep in the folds of my knickerbockers; I heard their squeaks of laughter and their sudden petrified silence as the shadow of my hand, a great bird of prey, crossed slowly between them and the sun. Another day, this mood of benevo-lent power would give way to the opposite one, with which was mingled curiosity. I myself, the manikin, set a ladder against a giant buckled shoe, and climbed timorously on to a lower leg encased in thick wool and smelling of sheep-shearing, with above me, gleaming in the sun, the rolling uplands of leather breeches; higher up, athwart the sleeping rhythmic-heaving shirted belly, a sinewy outcrop of arm with hair on it like yellow gorse. And I thought a lot about the eagle flying the universe, swinging from its claws the helpless traveller. Crusoe, too: many a time, on a walk, I stood rooted – a footprint! And the Swiss Family's boa constrictor, swallowing animals *alive* ... But none of it could ever be obsessive enough to dislodge my real life, barren though that seemed.

Then again, I was so unfamiliar with English that the few grown-up books to fall into my hands were far beyond me. In the drawer behind the accounts, I came upon a shabby tome as long as the Beibl – which put me off to start with – called *David Copperfield*, left behind by an absent-minded customer (an Uncommercial Traveller?). I was puzzled by the name, thinking it belonged to a boy living in a field where there was a copper mine, and found the first couple of pages incomprehensible. The only sentence I understood bewildered me, and I turned to my mother, treading away at the sewing-machine, 'Mam, how

.can you have a baby without a father?' The wheel stopped dead. 'What did you say?' 'Well, it says here' – I spelt out the words laboriously – ' "My father's eyes had closed upon the light of this world six months, when mine opened on it" – how could he be born if his father wasn't there?' She must have given a swift and equivocal answer, for I immediately lost interest in David. Next day, when I decided to give him a second chance, he was nowhere to be seen. I fancy my mother was one of the few parents ever to put Dickens out of bounds.

Then Lytton's murderer, Eugene Aram, so long-winded that after thrashing through thickets of words in hopeful search of a dead body, I gave up. Then I tried *The Wide Wide World*, a genteel Victorian classic through a little girl's eyes. On the first page she went to buy 'merino', which they wrapped up for her to take home; I remembered Pears Eng Dic the bubble-boy, but he failed me by stating firmly 'merino : a sheep'. I was also discouraged by brougham, which I prononuced brew-gam; but when I read of 'furtive creatures lurking in doorways', I felt no need of help, I knew it meant creatures covered with fur. There was nobody to read to me, to clarify, highlight dramatic scenes and omit intermediate ones; before my fancy could catch fire, I required a plain story with a clear style, a high-coloured treatment to lift me out of my surroundings, and yet apparently realistic grown-up characters. The answer came.

'Annie, mae'n glawio, it's raining!' It was the holidays and I was lolling sluggishly in the snug. She brought in something she had fished up from her tin trunk, a novel which had long ago frittered away its cover. *A Welsh Singer* threatened religion, and I opened it gingerly. It would be fitting that the first work to fire my blood with love of words, and of people created by words, should have been *Hamlet, Endymion,* or back-of-a-drawer David of the copper-field; but it was *A Welsh Singer*. 'On the rocky coast of Wales, the sun flushed the pale eastern sky. A boy and a girl stood in earnest conversation; the tears ran down her face, he looked grave . . .'

I was a not unhappy child, and had no idea that through nobody's fault I was being starved of something as necessary to my nature as breath to the lungs : Romance. I was an exile from a country to which I could have given no name. It was early to be starved, I was not yet eight, but not only did I not know of the theatre, I had never heard a note of music – I discount the wheezy chapel organ – and no child or adult had ever *said* anything to me : it was with a shock of pleasure that I turned the pages of my first real book. It was like hearing a vast wind, then looking up and seeing, beyond the Glanrafon woods, a curtain of cloud sweep up and away in gigantic folds, revealing the world. For the rest of the holidays, there was not a free waking minute, free from washing or cleaning boots or seeing if there were any real eggs next to the pot one, when I was not immersed in *A Welsh Singer*. One morning I was so engrossed that when my mother put her head in and asked me to bring her the pepper, quick, I rose from my book, crossed to the cupboard, walked out of doors, and stalked down the back yard and into the petty; there I came to, gaping stupidly into distasteful depths and clutching a pepper-pot. I hurried out, red in the face, to meet Dad holding his sides. 'I've heard of other pots, Poll, but *pepper*!' 'It's that reading,' said Mam, pursing her lips, 'first his eyes will go and then his brain will turn to water.' 'But Poll, pepper in the petty!'

'Allen Raine' had done this, a lady novelist who could have been dubbed the Marie Corelli of below stairs; but she wrote with sincerity and I am glad there was nobody to disillusion me. The story would appear unlikely to enslave a child whose one need was the escape-hatch of the imagination – a tale set in Wales and dealing with 'humble folk', even quoting the Welsh language, what was the escape? Romance. The initial familarity was just enough to act as a spring-board, and I was off. I did not find the book easy to read, but it was written simply enough to encourage me to battle with the difficult parts. Anyway, after the first page, I grasped all manner of things with a bemused extra sense. The word 'enigmatic' came twice – 'her enigmatic eyes' ... 'his enigmatic tone' – and this time Eng Dic did not fail me : 'full of mystery'. A rigmarole of words had become a treasure.

Suspicious: mistrusting (pronounced suspickuss). Cynical: unbelieving (prononuced kinnical). Agitate: disturb (pronounced
aggie-tate).

The story too was simple. The shepherdess Mifanwy, fifteen,
shy and sun-browned and plain, has lost yet another sheep over
the crag. She is comforted by her foster-brother, Ieuan the shepherd, and when they return to the farm in their rags, it is he
who takes the blame, and the thrashing (my elder brother ...).
The boy has a talent for sculpture – 'the art of making statues',
I looked it up – and is adopted by a renowned artist; Italy and
fame beckon him, while barefoot Mifanwy stays to train for the
Eisteddfod: her teacher recognizes her voice as a great one. To
earn her living she joins a circus ('Be'di circus Mam, what is a
circus?') where she comes under the wing of a warm Cockney
family ('Be'di Cockney Mam?' I never got the answer to that),
the Pomfreys and their son Tom, a simple-hearted stalwart boy
of eighteen; in the caravan, after the nightly performance when
Mifanwy has floated round the ring on their horse Sultan, Tom
teaches her to write, falling in love over the pot-hooks. They
reach London (Chapter Seven, Visit to the West End) 'where the
shops, the carriages, the fine ladies took Mifanwy's breath away'
and Tom takes her to Park Lane to see a great house whence
emerges 'a young man, broad-shouldered and tall, with crisp
brown hair and an open brow'. Ieuan, my brother Jabez again ...
Mifanwy goes sadly back to the East End. But after three years
of study, during which she slowly turns into a beauty, the little
shepherdess becomes the opera star La Belle Russe; at a soirée
Ieuan is presented to her. ' "How charming she is," he thought,
"in her simplicity." '

But the scene I knew by heart was the one in 'The Opera
House', which puzzled me at first by sounding like an edifice
where operations are performed. La Belle's public is there to see
her triumph, including faithful Tom. Ieuan is in her dressing-
room to give her a pearl necklace, 'How could I leave for Wales,
before tonight?' The scene shifts to the audience; I was again
puzzled by 'The lights were lowered, and the curtain rose'. A
few lines later, Tom observes a bewildered face in one of the

wings (this quite baffled me – a great stuffed bird?) and from then on the drama drove marvellously on, many many times was I to race up and down the page, picking out the mesmeric words. 'Face blanched with horror – "if we can get out well and good, if not, God help us" – "let me implore you to be calm, the dressing-rooms are one fire ..." ' Back to La Belle – 'she coughed – that far window – yes, lighter – yes, a lurid red! – the door jammed – shaken frantically – gasping – burst into tears – "Mr Powys – Ieuan – I am ..." – slipped from his arms – door burst open – Tom – Ieuan dragged to safety – Tom raised her and rushed through the flames ...' This was probably where I took the pepper out of doors.

Then the hospital. 'There lay poor Tom, the beauty of his manly form disfigured by bandages. "Is it Mifanwy? ... You will take Sultan, will you not?" "My beloved brother ..." ' (Brother! My fantasy was doubled.) ' "Are you crying for me, Mifanwy? Shall you ... miss me ... from your life?" She looked into the fast-darkening eyes ...' Her happiness with Ieuan was assured, but for me, with the death of Tom the wonderful story was over.

I had lived through it so powerfully that the microcosm of Glanrafon, my parents, Annie even, faded into unreality. How could companionable shadows who said, in Welsh, 'Good morning, Georgie. Glyn has got a cold,' compete with beings who came out with 'Shall you ... miss me ... from your life?' I identified myself completely with hero and heroine. Like Ieuan I was Welsh, poor, handsome one day (I prayed so) and though something told me I was not cut out for sculpture, there would be something else? Like Mifanwy, did I not pass unnoticed, was I not easily hurt, might I not join a circus and go on from there? Standing on Sultan, in spangled tights – after Lloyd George the horse? no – well, I could collect the takings ... I fell deeply in love with them both, and with Tom; the picture of these two in the caravan, bent over their books, the gentle uneducated boy coaching the illiterate girl, touched me infinitely. Sundays, I stood at the cross-roads and waited for my three friends to walk down the lane arm-in-arm (no chapel for them); joyously they would recognize me, I would wave and they would be upon me, laughing and arms extended, Ieuan and his bride as radiant as the dawn, and brave Tom ... But Tom was dead, in Kensal Green. My eyes blurred with tears.

Suppose I looked up in the snug, and they were standing there, glowing like lamps in this tiny room into which apple-cheeked fustian Annie fitted like furniture? 'Annie, who wouldst thou be most surprised if they walked in?' She answered promptly, biting a thread, 'Jesus Christ.' This took me aback, and in the Welsh, Iesu Grist, it sounded more like a person we knew. 'But Annie, he would never come here.' 'He went among the publicans,' said Annie, 'so he could not be above talking to us.' 'In Welsh?' 'He talks Welsh in the Beibl, what else would he talk?' 'Annie, why is Iesu Grist born the same date every year but dies a different Good Friday every time?' Annie ignored this. 'Georgie, why dost thou not want Iesu Grist in the snug?' I hesitated: 'because he looks like a lady.' Annie stared, 'a lady?' 'Long hair,' I explained, 'and skirts.' She caught my eye; shocked at ourselves, we giggled. 'It is the way he is,' she said, 'he would cure Gwen of those fits.' 'Would he order a glass of beer?' 'He might,' said Annie, stitching, 'he turned the water to wine, he might want the beer so as to turn it to water – hush Georgie, don't tell your Mam. I don't like Mifanwy as a name ...'

No, even Annie could not understand. My friends were introduced into my prayer, God bless Dad Mam Job Thomas Mifanwy Ieuan Tom Annie. The climax of the fire I examined minutely, as an art student might put his puzzled eye to the brushstrokes of the picture which from the right distance has stirred him. Although I would not face the idea that these three were fictions, I thought subconsciously, how wonderful to write something like that ... Mam, to get me out of the snug, had insisted on my entering a competition for the Llanasa Sports, 'Best Bunch of Wild Flowers', and as I plunged aimlessly in undergrowth tugging objects up by their roots – primrose or foxglove, what did it matter? – I would repeat like a lesson, 'Are you crying for me, Mifanwy?' Sitting in Sunday-school and shut off as usual, I thought of Tom in the hospital; the organ began to play, and I heard it as if for the first time. My tears coursed down, and the startled teacher bent to ask if there was bad news. I wanted to step into the pulpit and tell them, to music, how Tom had died. All he way home, past the throbbing telegraph poles, I talked to the three of them, invisible, indivisible. I was bewitched.

George, His Story was hard to get back to, but what else? I tried *Eric, or Little by Little* but though the school interested me – ' "there's to be an awful lark in the dormitories tonight" ' – and Eric's surname was Williams, the odour of sanctity was continuous enough to make me queasy.

But you never knew what the day held in store, in the way of a page. One afternoon I wandered into the forbidden woods encircling Gyrn Castle; it was so quiet that I could hear my corduroys rub as I walked. Alone in the world with the twitter of birds and the mossy gurgle of hidden streams, I passed the time pretending I was mad, shouting gibberish interspersed with falsetto whoops. Suddenly I found myself by a water-lilied lake, the only figure in a wide landscape of leaves, each sun-silvered and unwinking, watching me. I stood as disembodied as the birds – who was I? where was I going? – when up above I saw the Castle, the corner of a balustrade : beyond, I imagined the moat and the crumbling donjon. A woman swam into view holding a cup and saucer. It was Lady Enid, a guest in the haunted wing; lovesick, in Rotten Row she had thrown herself off a galloping horse and been brought here to calm down. She gave the sky a sad look and disappeared to make aimless chatter; I was alone in the world again, turned to go, and saw, lying in a bed of bluebells ten yards from me, a dead man. In the same second that I knew he was dead, I saw that his right arm had been hacked off.

His face, rammed into the pit of his left arm, showed a week's beard; no coat, and the shirt-sleeve, outflung on the bruised flowers, lay hideously flat from shoulder to broken wrist-button. A dragon-fly darted. A bird squawked. I ran.

I tripped, I fell, I ran; I ran, I tripped, I fell. I found myself at a fence, soared over it and fell breathless on to grass, nettle-stung, briar-torn. I lay for five minutes, got up, and hurried down into

the village – Mr Hughes the Policeman, there would be a reward!
I was halfway to him when a figure emerged from the woods : a
tramp who cheerfully stretched himself, or rather half-stretched,
for he was one-armed. He seemed refreshed after his siesta, and
wandered up the hill towards Llanasa. I was glad I had seen him
before claiming the reward.

But as I was returning to Eric with a sigh, along came, for the
Story, a red-letter page : or rather black, for it was the day we
children were invited into Mr Edwards the keeper's cottage to
see Kate. She had died of something called pew-monia, aged
fourteen, and it was the summer morning of the funeral. My
mother, her instinct infallible, had been doubtful of the rightness
of this private view, but nothing could have kept me out of the
little house unrecognizable with the hooded windows.

Stiff in our Sunday best, the six of us were to be ushered in
one by one, out of the sun, by the hollow-eyed mother. Doffing
my cap at the front door, I remembered our standing just here
six months ago, gaping in at a forbiddingly empty cornucopia;
its black bowels had been emitting, in a shrill frenzied refrain,
'Daisy Daisy gibby your answer do!' As I tiptoed now into the
first house I had ever visited, the maniacal voice echoed in my
head. There was one floor, and I found myself straight in the
bedroom. In the sudden twilight I could see nothing at first,
conscious only of the overpowering smell of the strange flowers
everywhere, smothering pictures and ornaments; I identified
them later as carnations. The coffin lay deep on the bed, handles
gleaming opulently in the half-dark; it looked too large for a
pitiful room shrunk smaller still in grief. In the glassy wood I
could dimly see myself; face to the wall, as if disgraced, was the
gramophone horn, Daisy Daisy ... I stood on my toes, cap
clutched tight, eyes and mouth wide with curiosity, and looked,
for the first time, upon Death.

And Death was an exquisitely pale doll who might at any
minute creak up to a sitting position, open her eyes, and say
Mamma. But it was Kate all right, I could see the mole she had
once pointed out to us; she was wearing a nightdress, like
Annie's, but she will never get up, never ... 'Cusan i Kate fach,

said a well-meaning aunt, 'would you like to kiss her?' I shrank
back; as I had never embraced anybody, it seemed effusive to
kiss a dead neighbour. But I steeled myself to put my finger-tips
to the brow, just to say I had. I had never handled ice, and the
feel was chilling beyond imagination; the warm flower-smells
and the hot bee-buzzing village shrivelled into nothing, the world
was numbed for ever. I tried to see Annie lying there, but could
not. I was back in the sun. Cassie and Ifor and John stood apprehensive, but more alive than I had ever imagined anybody;
gleaming, glowing, alive. 'Welsoti hi,' they whispered, 'what's
she like?' 'All right,' I said, and walked home, composed but
more dazed than I knew. I had never heard the village so full of
noises. I shall never die, I thought, as I ate my lobscouse, never.

Afternoon came. The six of us were planted firmly in the procession, and toiled up the hill in the heat: a funereal pace in
truth. From Sundays I knew every inch of the road – the crenel-
lated gates of the Castle, the mushroom field, the telegraph poles;
only today I could not listen to them, or even laugh insanely.
The Dead March. It grew hotter; as my collar softened, my heart
hardened, and the opium of fancy wreathed inside my head. The
mourners dabbing their eyes in the cool of the carriage, *they*
should be doing the walking, they wouldn't perspire like this,
when you mourn the only water comes out of the eyes ... We
were passing a cart with two stupid black-faced sheep in it, like
emaciated negresses in great dirty fur coats; they stared at the
hearse. Could sheep smell a death? Except there was nothing to
smell, only a wax doll.

Squeak creak cough. Cough creak squeak. *George, His Story*,
Chapter Forty-two. 'There was a tremor in the procession as
George, pale and resolute, stepped out. "Stop!" His steady blue
eyes told all, as he called out modestly to the hearse, "Kate!" A
horrified murmur, the splinter of wood ...' Ifor whispered,
'Your stocking has come down.' I hopped twice, diving for my
garter at the same time; the Dead March again. I saw the doll
sit up in the coffin, saw her eyelids swing back, heard her say
Mamma. Then she floated glass-eyed to the dusty road, waxen
hands still crossed over her breast, her whiteness a dazzle against

the mourners. All eyes were upon George as he turned the handle in the small of her back; as she walked to the head of the procession, a whir of wheels. Passing Groes Chapel, her father seized George's hand. 'On Sunday, you will be thanked in Westminster Abbey!'

The daydream had served its purpose, and we were defiling at last into the hollow of Llanasa. I put on a bereaved face; I saw a girl nudge her friend. But I was pulled out of myself when the coffin was lowered, what a waste of gleaming wood, and I heard the distraught sobs of the mother; none of us should be there to gape at such suffering. But I could not be moved, they were putting into the ground not Kate, but a doll who would never, now, say Mamma. As the first grains of soil thundered on to the lid, the scent of flowers enveloped me again. I longed for Annie, but Annie was in Pen-y-Maes making herself useful, which we six were not.

Wandering among head-stones I lost the others, and walking home alone got back to the Story, taking a bold leap forward to the final page. To my own funeral, no less. ' "Mother" – George spoke only English – "my heart is ceasing to beat." ' (We would be in the snug.) ' "Nonsense," retorted Mrs Williams, and boxed his ears. The day dawned, the finest of the year. His friends waited, with whom he was so popular. But George lay arms crossed ...' Outside Gyrn gates, the empty mourning carriage passed me, but I was too absorbed, was I not watching my own procession going the other way? Dad and Mam holding each other up, 'Never another like him ...' The illustration? Of course, 'Never another ...' What would be the very last line? 'With George in the cold earth, Glanrafon was not the same. THE END.' As I got to the keeper's cottage, and looked at the blinds being sadly raised, there were tears in my eyes. Kate's father was in the road, about to turn wearily in at his gate. He saw the tears, and patted my shoulder. I was glad he had noticed, and been touched.

Ten minutes later, I was changed into ganssi and corduroys and in the field playing rounders as if I had not died at all. Or Kate either.

Chapter 5

Boredom, Death and Martyrdom

But days like that were rare, mostly they would promise a page and then let the Author down with a bump. One morning that autumn, sitting on my stile on my leg, I heard two men approach down the hill, then a voice, a rich and measured English, 'Mind you, there is a difference in outlook, is there not, between the Catholic Mostyns and the Church of England Mostyns?' I remembered that Sir Percy Bates of Gyrn Castle was passing through, and awaited my first glimpse of the English gentry. The voice continued, 'Mind you too, sir ...' I looked, it was not Sir Percy addressing my father, it was my shirt-sleeved father addressing Sir Percy, an amiable rubbed-out-looking man with a straggly fair moustache and gaiters. 'This is my son,' said Dad. 'Splendid,' said Sir Percy, 'looks a strong little feller, like to be a bitter on Saturday and earn a shilling?' He got into his trap and trotted off.

A bitter? In a garden, cutting the weeds into bits, elegant over a trowel? I was to meet my first English, as real as the ones Mifanwy and Ieuan knew in London! That night, after an hour with Eric, I lay awake and pre-created the following day. At the Castle gates, in the sun, four or five tall men on horseback; one vaults off with a disarming smile. 'George? Let me present myself, the Honourable Rupert, but who cares about that, and my nephew the Honourable Eric, known as Curly.' As I turn to Curly Eric, something tells me that he will be my Elder Brother: his honest eyes look into mine as if they knew me well, yet he retains a manly reserve. The drawbridge clanks down. 'Before the bitting, George, let me show you the dungeons, and Lady Bates.' Eric strides on. 'George,' whispers Rupert, taking my arm, 'the family are worried about Eric. He has taken to smoking and is everybody's enemy. Can *you* help?' Under the illustration, ' "George, the family are worried" '. I could feel his mysterious English presence across the village and the tramp-haunted woods. I shivered at that, then listened to the wind rise; my thoughts, as always in bad weather, turned to Kate, clay-cold in the wet ground, and one by one, I saw my family the same. On the edge of tears, I fell asleep.

The morning of the 'bitting' was dark and gusty, just the weather for the snug with Annie and Eric and the rain spitting ineffectively against the window. I hooked on a short weatherproof cape of my mother's, short on her, to the knees on me; I fancied myself in it and liked to squat inside so that it trailed the ground all round me, my private tent where I could hoard objects; then, rising and walking, I would feel it swing from my shoulders, fold my arms under it and stride with historical head high. By the time I reached the Castle gates, I was damp. A dozen other boys, older, from outlying farms, were sheltering under a tree; they did not speak to me, but stood making determined jokes. No horses, but two English gentlemen, lounging under their own tree and examining guns, identically inflexible in stiff breeches and leggings and both with Sir Percy's moustache. I stood lamely by, numbed hands crossed under my cape, and lending surreptitious ear to my first English conversation, as far as I can reconstruct it. Last week in the bar, I had been allowed to watch an amateur ventriloquist; these would seem to be his assiduous pupils. 'Come far?' 'Chester.' 'Poor morning.' 'Very poor.' (To me.) 'What are those fellers jabberin' about, what's the lingo?' 'Lingo, sir?' 'What are they talkin'?' 'Welsh, sir.' 'Welsh? Good God, bad as abroad.' Something told me that I was not going to run into the Honourable Eric.

We were each given a stick by a wet bad-tempered underling-turned-overseer. I discarded my cape at the lodge, and with the others stumbled after forty moustached leggings into the dripping woods, were we were detailed off to plod in front and belabour the undergrowth to scare out the birds. 'Bitter' had been the English way of saying 'beater'. The woods, known to me only in the languor of summer, had become a welter of dank jungle, thorny pitfalls, and brambles that whipped wetly round knees and clawed at cheeks; the trees dripped malice, Nature was doing the beating. Surely the weather would wash out the whole day – then the rain spitefully cleared. I thought in despair, am I to be here till sundown? Is *this* what being grown-up, outside books, is like? Suppose it had to be every day, this is what it must be like down the coal-mine ... Then the rain started again, and every branch overhead was a frail but pitiless drainpipe. The order was, fan out, keep in front, keep travelling.

I fanned out, I kept in front, I kept travelling. And as I got dirtier and more tired and half wet through, I did not scare out a sparrow. Shots rang out, there were scurries and excited bellows. I tripped, spread-eagled backwards into a showering thorn-bush, picked myself up, thought of Eric and Co waiting for me in the snug, and sank on to a decayed log so as to get wet right through. I was alone. Voices receded, animated, dedicated, then the scuttle of a terrified bird, then a distant babble; let it escape, poor proud thing, with me in its claws, like Gulliver. I heard stealthy footsteps and hid behind a tree, a peasant on the side of the pheasant.

The shouts and the shots died away and I crept back to the gate: a Mary Ann, but I did not care. A driver under the tree, a sack over his head, munching at his damp dinner. He was from Gronant and knew Dic Pen-y-Maes, who did not? I took my cape, and hooked it on with shivering fingers. I was cold, to be sure, but was shivering them on purpose. 'Well my boy?' 'I've caught cold, Mr Blythin,' I said, 'and got to give up my beating.' 'Too bad for thee.' I coughed. 'Mr Blythin, about my shilling?' He looked at me. 'Not till the end of the day, from Owen the head beater.' 'Oh.' My teeth were on the brink of chattering. 'I hope,' I said, 'I have not got a fever.' A pause, then a jingle. 'Here is thy shilling, I will claim it back, run home now.' I ran home, gave the coin to Mam – my first income, unearned – changed into dry clothes, thought what a good life was mine and settled into the snug with Eric. My sporting days were over.

Winter, spring ... and then, when least expected, with summer a thing happened too big even for a red-letter page, an event which for weeks I was to try to relive, in words. And the illustration! No, too big ...

Reconstructing, I would start with the day before, a Sunday. I had nothing to read, and between the services, was reduced to playing dominoes by myself. I debated whether to walk down and listen under the wall in case Gwen might be having a fit, but I was too lazy. I did not even mind being sent to bed before the sun had gone. I scrambled through my prayers, then trailed to the window for a last glassy look round. The heartless caw of rooks; Issmael Jones's horse clopped past in the half-light, led by Aneurin, the long-jawed farm-hand as dull as his master – why could not a mad bull come stabbing his horns into our back door? A man approached down the hill, tell-tale unsteady, on his way to us for further Sunday sanctuary – but he evidently thought better and weaved down the dark of the hill. I went to bed and reviewed the week. Mam, Monday mid-day dinner, saying to Dad as he carved the cold lamb, 'Your hand is shaking, after the day of rest,' and him turning to her with thunder in his face, pointing the knife across me, and saying – his hand *was* shaking – 'another word, and ...' Not worth remembering.

Next morning Annie was back, but without the book she had promised to borrow for me, it had been thrown away. Thrown away! I sat on my stile; the village below had not the faintest heart-beat. Tall spinsterish Jane Williams picked flowers in her garden, and went in; for five minutes, not a dog, not a cat. A bicycle glided over the cross-roads, then funny Glyn loped out of his gate, crossed to fill a bucket, and back in. He did not even jump up and down. John emerged and strolled across to the slaughter-house to store potatoes. I sighed, the long heaving sigh children expel when alone – 'oh-h-h ...' – and wandered into the house; then Mam, holding baby Thomas, called me into the parlour, where I never ventured. We were followed by Nel. Then Mam – how I recall the details – placed the baby back into his cradle and went to the dresser to sort linen, while I resigned myself to rocking; Thomas's mewing petered out into breathing. The room was in cool morning twilight. Nel lay on the rug, a fly burbled against the sealed window. Was it the same fly I had seen just a –

Many things happened at once. A sharp shout – a swift shadow across the window – a woman's shrill gasp – the smack of feet along the passage – then the door wrenched open, hitting the wall and knocking framed Auntie Sarah to the ground. It was Annie, lips bloodless, unrecognizable. 'Mae Issmael Jones wedi crogi 'hun!' He had hanged himself.

In the first stupefied moment, I heard myself say inside, quicker than any one spoken word, 'This is not happening, I am reading it.' Then, a vision stabbed by a jagged second of lightning, I saw him behind her, just out of sight, slumped for ever from the hook on the kitchen door, possessing the house. 'Ble?' I said, 'where?'

In the slaughter-house, John had found him. But I had seen John, in the sunlight, cross the road – it could have been me ... Mam clutched her breast, 'Nefoedd annwyl, dear Heaven ...' She and Annie stared at each other, two frightened animals; the only sound, crockery tinkling from the jolt of the door. Then Annie ran, Mam followed, turned – 'stay by the cradle, don't move' – and ran after Annie.

It was as if there had been a deafening explosion, every window shattered, now me alone in a silent room with a sleeping baby and a dog. My knees were locked to my stool; I felt my face white. The clock ticked. Waxwork Richard and Mary stared at me, new-frozen with horror, but Nel was blinking, and her indifference made the new morning doubly dreadful. For all was changed. Issmael Jones, a farmer with a beard whom I had beheld in the distance, a human being like any other who had been a baby like the one asleep at my feet ... A pair of boots, gently swinging ... The clock ticked.

They were breathlessly back. 'Don't talk about it!' called Mam, 'is the baby all right? No, George, put it out of your mind, I know you ...' She sat and rocked furiously, which woke Thomas, 'Terrible ...' Annie went out, lips painfully sealed; I followed her and looked down, at the hollow which five minutes ago had been a sleepy mother's-lap of a village, now a buzzing valley of death. In the road and at garden gates there were thirty people, spectres in the sun. Jumping Glyn stood rooted to a flagstone, old Mrs Davies's bedridden father was miraculously in his doorway, six or seven bicycles, three carts and even a motor had appeared out of nowhere, smelling tragedy like a forest fire. I whispered, 'Tell me . . .'

It was all she needed, the oath of silence was killing her. John had run out and straight to Mr Hughes the Policeman (shattered though I was, I remembered my tramp and felt a pang of envy) to tell him that Mr Jones was in there having a swing'. The policeman had raced across with a knife and cut him down, they tore up the door and carried him up the hill, past us, with a bed-sheet over him, they'll never never sleep under that again, he was owing money, no family thank Heaven, in his Sunday best which he never put on since not going to chapel, the last to see him was Aneurin last night, standing by the gate there (I stared at it, that turnip-headed boy, now unique) and Aneurin said, 'Mr Jones, a bit late for chapel?' and Mr Jones said, 'Better late than never' and what do you think he did then Georgie, gave a kiss to Lloyd George! A horse! 'Nos da Lloyd George,' he said, his last words on earth, and then he walked down, terrible . . .

I could not speak. I had looked out of my window, yawning – yawning! – and in the light between day and night, *he* had passed disguised as a patriarch like any other, but this one unique among millions, for was he not accursed . . . enigmatic? Instead of sighing myself to mundane sleep, I should have thrown back the bed-clothes . . . 'Come along,' said Annie, 'forget it now.'

But I could not, and that night she stayed by me till I was asleep. And asleep, I was back in my dream. Down the hill in my nightshirt, noiseless as a bird, I catch up with him as he presses on: alone under the moon, the child and the self-destroyer. I pluck him by the sleeve, 'Meddyliwch eto, Mr Jones,' I whisper, 'think twice.' 'I have thought, thrice,' and he enters into the house of death. My bare feet stand chill to the ground, as the last village candle is blown out, a night like every night, still as the tomb. How shall I tell them? Like Judgment Day, count three and then a thundering rat-tat? Or like Herod, next to each door the mysterious mark, to be gaped at in the dawn? I turn just in time to see the flicker of his match and am in past the door, the door tomorrow to be wrenched from its sockets ... He is lighting a stub of candle; the naked corpses of swine hang motionless, their great shadows swinging over us. He is Dad, Dad with a beard; he is fastening the noose, with the method of the drunken and the damned, and for the first time in the history of the world a child looks up into the face of a man about to ... I made myself count sheep, un dau tri pedwar ...

Questioning John, I was envious enough to be relieved when all he had to contribute was 'I ran in and I thought it was an extra pig, then I saw it had got trousers on and I ran out.'

One Sunday evening in January 1914, after chapel, I was in the snug, once more with nothing to read. 'Try this book,' said Mam, 'the E. B. Jones man persuaded me to take it every week, and it *is* good.' I knew her good was not mine and took up the 'book' without interest: a weekly journal named the *Sunday Companion*, One Penny, another Northcliffe offspring. Page One did not fire me, articles artfully sprinkled with advertisements: Church Worship and Family Life, Don't Wear a Truss, Our Conversation Corner for Mothers and Daughters, De Witt's Kidney Pills, The Power of Prayer, Superb Magneto Corset, Drunkards Cured, Save Your Loved Ones – had Mam seen that? – then I turned the page.

'Mam, what's a serial?' 'I don't know,' said Mam, 'something serious by the sound.' The name was blazoned across the top, in fancy printing: *'Neath Nero's Rule*, by May Wynne. 'Mam, what does "'Neath Nero" mean?' She pondered. 'Neath,' she said at last, 'is in South Wales, your father went there when he was at sea, but I never heard him talk of Nero.' My eye idled down the page. I saw the word 'Christians' twice, and sighed; 'The Christians patiently await their summons' conveyed to me chapel-goers in a police-court. I was about to put the paper away when my eye caught the pen-and-ink illustration: the Roman

Colosseum. A sweep of faces, two lone figures, a giant black cat bounding through an opened barrier. 'Between the angry panther and its prey stood the tall fair stranger.' In the top corner, a synopsis. 'Ælia and Stephen the Briton, Christians under the monster-emperor Nero, are in deadly peril, now read on.'

I obeyed greedily. 'Another roar of execration as three white-robed girls entered the blood-stained arena ...' For me the trumpets had sounded again, I was transported. I sipped my Oxo and munched my bread-and-dripping without raising my eyes: 'His mighty stature, dazzling skin, golden hair ... Nero lounged on his couch, magnificently robed and an emerald in his eye, jesting and drinking while indulging in those excesses which made the Court of Rome a byword ... "I swear by Jupiter Liberator that Cæsar will find fiendish delight in torturing those mighty limbs of yours,"' another enthralling instalment next week. Next week! Last week's copy? Burnt. I scoured the rest of this week's, but it was good thoughts (*The Flower of Forgiveness*, a Quiet Story Beautifully Told). While I waited, I re-read every paragraph of the serial, with dips into Eng Dic:.. Excesses: going beyond the proper amount. Instalment: a portion. Orgy: revel. I rhymed it with doggie.

Friday, from three p.m. on, found me stationed at the crossroads, ear cocked for the thrilling clop-clop down Ffordd Ddwr. The van would halt at the keeper's to deliver seed-cake or Peek Frean biscuits, and at the same moment the driver would throw me my Roman dispatch. I then raced up the hill and into the snug, there to settle into the first century where I belonged. The *Sunday Companion* became a Friend, for every day of the week; hidden between the columns of a pious panacea for housewives on nodding Sabbath afternoons, I found my own pagan ambrosia: barbaric pageantry, vicious splendours and (again) Romance. When the *Companion* announced at the foot of a page that 'our Great New Serial continues to attract attention throughout the Kingdom', I believed it.

As week by week I cut out the instalments and pinned them raggedly together, I became utterly absorbed: not in the almost painfully personal way in which I had been drawn to *A Welsh*

Singer, more sweepingly. The idea that the world had been fascinating in olden times had not occurred to me : as week by week I saw the title across the top of the page, the name 'Nero' became deeply exciting to the eye, bold and terrible. Marcellus and Aurelia had a noble ring, and the Siamese-twinned vowels of Cæsar and Ælia an exotic appeal; I copied out my own name, George Æmlyn. With rain pattering against the snug window and villagers scuttling to shelter, I sat in Ancient Rome, where people moved not spasmodically in bad weather, but slowly and gracefully in the sunlight of my mind.

The Christians and their catacombs became dear and desperate; 'catacomb' (not in Eng Dic) I had guessed at first to be a religious head-dress, possibly trimmed with the hair of the wild-cat. Pale and beautiful they stand in the face of death, in their snowy tunics – the heart-breaking alto of a boy's voice – ten thousand throats are silenced – the panther bounds into the arena, the flash of great claws in the sun, the jungle-smell – and as my young blood soaks into the sand, I sink unconscious on the snug table, 'Georgie, be' sy'n dy gorddi, what is churning thee?' Two thousand years ago, seven hundred and thirty thousand days, I counted them ... I walked my lanes, and my bedlam leaps and bounds gave way to the tread of the martyr. I even snapped off two branches, tied them athwart each other with grass and held them to my bosom, till a cart approached and I would beat nettles with them. Over a five-barred gate, leading up from the dungeons, 'Courage Ælia child,' I would exhort, 'one more step, remember our faith ...' The fact that I dreaded Sunday as much as ever, had nothing to do with it.

Chapter 6

Pictures, Persecution and Invasion

But it is with serials as with humanity, the flattered newcomer (Our Best Yet, Order NOW) finds itself, with time, edged towards the back page : as the breaths in life get shorter, so do the instalments. The week came when the usual illustration to which I avidly looked forward had been replaced by a photograph (a photograph!) of two missionaries leaving Tilbury in the rain; Nero's days were numbered. 'Ælia took him to her bosom, her eyes streaming, to be concluded, see Page One for details of *The Hammer of Poverty* and *free* gift of photogravure "Feathered Friends" by Sheridan Knowles.' By Jupiter Liberator, I was depressed. There started the rumour of a circus to visit Ffynnongroew, with wild beasts, but it never came; I was relieved, how could a panther turn up in a place where I went every six weeks for a hair-cut?

But life did not stand still for long. Lying in wait to tame a bird, playing hide-and-seek in a hayfield, taking home a Coronation mug, dreaming of Roman splendours : in between all the to-and-fro rhythm of the sleep-walking days, occasionally reality would smite like a smell. After Issmael Jones, the Monster of Picton.

When the new Picton Council School opened a mile away, in June 1914, I was moved to it. It had exciting whiffs of wood and plaster, with two brand-new asphalt yards, each with its stone portal stamped sternly 'Bechgyn', boys, and 'Genethod', girls. Picton was bigger, more intimidating than the convent, and there were masters; but I started under Miss Dawson from Prestatyn, English, firm and kind. On her desk lay an old atlas; I had never seen one before and was irresistibly drawn to the colours as the pages turned, England blue, France pink, Italy booting Sicily towards Gibraltar in apple-green, and several times Miss Dawson caught me staring at it. One Monday she announced for the child who in the next week would behave the best, a prize: the atlas. To me it was a rainbow to yearn for, I sat the whole week with arms folded on my slate, painfully good. My desire for sanctity got on my mind. I lay awake imagining the fame of my goodness spreading up to Llanasa and down to Ffynnon-groew – 'old beyond his years, Georgie is' – and I even tried to make six-year-old Job good too, by telling him gently, as I had been told at school, to sit with mouth closed and not open, and showing him how to use a knife and fork. He would have none of it. I found that in class (as in life) to be good and attract attention is not possible; but Miss Dawson read my eyes, the atlas was mine, and I could forget about goodness. Her name was on it, 'Winifred Dawson'. She was a person! What was she like . . .?

Two days later she would have kept her atlas. 'Tyd yma,' hissed an older boy, nine he must have been, 'sit here.' I was an obedient child, and it was arithmetic; I settled next to him at the back. Beside him sat two round-faced, fringed knicker-bockered nobodies, but there was adventure in the air. I waited for sweets to be passed; nothing, they were all looking guilelessly at the teacher. I was puzzling what they – when I saw, with the candid eyes of childhood, that behind the long desk they had undone their buttons and were sitting on nonchalant hands with three pink shells impudently on display. A display to the chill morning air, for nobody could see but me. Feeling daring, I followed suit, sat on my hands, and turned the same look of blank innocence on to Miss Dawson. The lesson ended, and with it the cherubim show. I never saw it repeated and never heard it referred to. But I would have lost my atlas.

Mischief was one thing, evil another. One warm mid-day a week later, it was arithmetic again: the squeak of chalk on the board, the room sleepily and ominously still. Seven eights fifty-six, eight eights . . . The door opened like a whirlwind, somebody

71

strode in, up to Miss Dawson, and in the tolerant sunlight that blinks at nothing, struck her across the face.

Her sudden whimper, like a dog run over, would have been enough of a shock; but coming from one who a second before had been the all-powerful adult ('Hywel Davies, mark my words, you will get the cane!') it was shattering. The attacker was, unbelievably, a woman, a termagant with a lantern-jaw and a man's cap. In the sickened silence, Miss Dawson, suddenly a white and terrified girl, uttered one English word, which I have never heard spoken since. 'Blaggard,' she gasped, rhyming it with laggard, 'blaggard!' – years later I realized that the word is written 'blackguard'. 'Dyna wers iti,' said the intruder, 'that'll teach thee, teacher!' and strode out. Miss Dawson looked at us, bewildered, burst into tears and scurried. We sat dumbfounded; I felt a wave of shame that it should be a creature of Welsh tongue and blood that had committed such an outrage, and with it a disgust, rooted in some loam of chivalry, that a woman should so demean both herself and another. Her child had apparently been detained; she was from Tai Trap, Trap's Houses, a row of slums near Rhewl, Fawr. A master hurried in and took flustered charge.

But full in the face of childhood, cruelty had defeated authority; into the Headmaster's bland smile I spelt fear, and saw him crumple into a corner, an overturned scarecrow with a slate broken over his pate. We had felt earthquake, and could never be quite so footsure again. Walking home, I peered into hedges – everywhere, darkening the sunlight, the rasp of the voice, the yelp of the victim. Annie knew the Cap by sight. 'She drinks at home,' she said, 'and she beats her husband.' This somehow made it better for poor Miss Dawson.

Next day, Saturday, after my *Companion – Dark Peril* by Marie Connor Leighton – dawdling up Ffordd Ddwr in the morning sun, I saw a dirty perambulator outside a cottage gate. 'Watch the baby,' said a slatternly girl, 'while I get the cwrw-dalan-poethion, the nettle beer.' 'Yes,' I said meekly. She had holes in her stockings, a thing never seen in our community. 'Where do you live?' I said, without knowing why I asked. 'Tai

Trap,' she said, and slopped up the path and into the cottage. 'Tai Trap,' I repeated aloud, and stared into the pram.

The child must have been two, with a slobbered face and a stale sickly smell. I had never really looked at a baby; this one opened its sore old eyes and stared at me, straight back. It was a look of such vacuity that I was startled. It licked its lips, foolishly, and then dribbled on to the disembowelled eiderdown; I thought of the slut its mother and felt my face harden. I was alone with a child. Does evil breed evil? For as I stood, still stained with the brutality of the harpy in the schoolroom, the creature gaping at me looked so stupid that I wanted to pinch its face hard so that it would snivel, I wanted to kill it. I felt hair prickle at the back of my neck, and walked away. The child was soon forgotten – I realize now that it must have been a cretin – but the other bony sexless monster was to stay with me, as formidable as Attila.

Monday, no Miss Dawson. I was sorry, and would have liked to apologize to her for Wales. I was even sorrier when I saw the tall thin-lipped man – was cruelty in my mind? – who was to be my first male teacher. With the instinct of the bird of prey, the first time his cold eye swept the room, out of thirty upturned faces Mr Hedges scented me. The eye flicked, as if to note, that's a timid shrimp, the solemn one ... After the first lesson, I went to the blackboard, wiped it clean, and was going back when I saw Mr Hedges looking at me with raised eyebrows. I stopped, then blushed, a double mistake. 'Well,' said Mr Hedges, 'what was that for?' 'Please sir,' I said, my English leaving me, 'always it was me for the board, sir, cleaning it for Miss Dawson.' 'I see,' said Mr Hedges; then he used the underhand device of the question to which a negative answer will be rude and a positive one disastrous, 'Am I right in thinking you are a Teacher's Pet?' There was a titter; my face felt twice the size. 'Am I right?' 'Yes, sir.' When the laughter had subsided 'Sit down T.P.,' said Mr Hedges. His victory was complete. Walking home, I realized that I had always enjoyed school and that I was dreading tomorrow.

Morning came, fine and buoyant, and swinging on the stair ledge I felt renewed; I thought, walking to school, he will have a different coat and feel different, or even a different head, a dog's, and he will bark and they will laugh at *him* for a change. But Mr Hedges did not bark and wore not only the same coat but the same expression. His first lesson was History, my favourite Princes in the Tower. Sarcastically they informed their keeper that they loved him, sneeringly the keeper informed them that he would rather have his own eyes burnt out than – all was changed, and this was life, for ever. Sitting with arms folded in my 'good' pose, eyes thoughtfully on my teacher, I wished he might catch a fever and die.

He would leave me severely alone except for about three public jabs spaced through the day. I would be polishing my penknife for woodwork. 'Don't we,' said Mr Hedges, and like a fox in covert, I heard the hunting note, 'need a little more elbow-grease?' 'Yes, sir,' I said, and half got up. He saw the move; I was lost, wavered down to my seat again, and the class waited. 'Weren't you,' said Mr Hedges, hideously waggish, 'going to fetch some elbow-grease?' 'Yes, sir,' I said, guessing as I spoke that it must be an idiom. He pressed on. 'And where does one buy such a thing?' I looked at the expectant Welsh faces, none of them had ever heard the word either, and I thought recklessly, here goes, hit or miss. 'Please, sir,' I said, 'you buy it from the blacksmith, for the rheumatics, only you got to remember not to rub with the same arm that got the rheumatics, because if you do you cannot reach round to rub the elbow.' A pause; then giddily, I heard laughter. My enemy's joke had back-fired.

But that was the only time. Later that day, reading nervously aloud, I pronounced 'reap and sow' to rhyme with 'bough'. 'Come,' said Mr Hedges, 'there must be a lot of pigs where you come from.' At the break 'Hwch Pen-y-Maes,' shouted a boy, 'the Sow of Pen-y-Maes!' It was taken up in chorus. The nickname was meaningless but abhorrent to me, and when two days later, from the playground, I saw a farmer approaching with two great pigs before him, I hid in the lavatories till they were past.

I became stupid and could not even deal with questions to which
I had the answer; I found myself, as in chapel, clicking off. Was
it now to be Sunday every weekday too?

Annie was away with a cold; Mam asked me why I looked
depressed, 'Wti'n sâl, art thou ill?' I told her I didn't like the
master, but not to tell Dad in case he called me a Mary Ann; he
had just returned from the annual two days in Rhyl and was in
the doldrums. I thought no more of it. Then one dinner-time, the
playground full of shrill humanity pointlessly pushing, and me
dragging a stick along the railing, hard, to make a loud useless
rat-a-tat, I saw a figure walking down the road. My father.

I could not remember ever having seen him outside Pen-y-
Maes; also my day at school was as sealed off from my evening
at home as a diver is from his ship. It was like seeing a ghost.
He looked strange too, collar, dickey, Albert, and Sunday bowler
level across a serene brow. He did not see me, a crouched non-
entity behind the railings; I watched him walk into the playground and up to 'Bechgyn', with the air of an indulgent
inspector who has arrived by surprise. In the doorway, he
beckoned to a large boy who had once or twice patronized me;
the boy ran obediently up. My father beamed a benevolent question down at him, he answered; Dad looked as if he might give
him a penny, and walked into the school. The boy called to me,
with awe and glee. 'He's looking for Mr Hedges, watch out!'

I thought of the shrew in the man's cap. By all counts, remembering my father on black days, I should have either curled up
to die or run to entreat him not to humiliate me before the
school. But I had just seen my father for the first time, and knew
from his leisurely gait, bespeaking ownership of something or
other, that I had nothing to fear. A calm settled on me too, and
I sat supine, on my haunches. Five minutes passed, the bell rang;
he issued forth, gave the pupils an avuncular smile, saw me,
pretended with superb tact not to, and walked unwavering home
to shirt-sleeve and spittoon. We filed into class : about to squeeze
through, I felt a hand on my arm. Mr Hedges, face carved into
a winter smile. 'I am told,' he said, 'that I am to leave you alone.'
'Yes, sir,' I said dully, and followed the others. He did leave me

alone and paid the penalty due for good behaviour, for I remember nothing more about him.

The *Companion* stayed faithful: *Out of Egypt*, a serial about the persecuted Israelites – 'on on, across the burning desert' – and the offer, for 4d. post free from Fleetway House, of *'Neath Nero's Rule* in paper-back book form, '120 pp. of thrilling romance'. There was even a picture of the book, pages fluttering with illustrated cover. I desired this so strongly that even Mam saw that the money had to be sent; after my ragged cuttings, the pleasure of unwrapping the little package and handling the exquisite new-bound volume was a sensual delight.

In the issue of 1 August, under the serial stood a whole family knee-high in the sea in knee-low bathing costumes, which Mam glanced at with pursed lips; underneath, 'A Holiday Reminder, Use Zam-buk Ointment'. It is doubtful if the reminder was effective that year, for a day or two later the slumber of Glanrafon, and of many another village, was broken. There was even a sleepy turning-over; I saw newspapers fluttering at garden gates like sea-gulls. Rhyfel, War. It touched us scarcely at all, I hardly ever saw khaki, and Dad was forty-four. Tiny flags with pins for poles – the Japanese with its lop-sided sun the prettiest – Belgium two sad and ugly syllables, strange anthems in class with English words: the Marseillaise springy and brave, the Russian strange and stirring, so that when I found the Russian words on a cigarette-card, I learnt them, was stood on the settle in the bar and sang them tunelessly to my father; my parrot-accent, being Welsh, was possibly not bad. I had dreams of being invisible, slipping through the lines into Berlin, in to Kaiser Bill asleep in bed, stabbing him to death, saving the world and acquiring a V.C.; but there my interest ended, and when I watched for the evening post, it was not bulletins I was after but the flash of the postman's bicycle. For he liked Annie, and unknown to Mam, I would fly in and warn her, a corduroyed Cupid, slightly jealous.

'The Germans!' called Annie one day, with some of the panic of the Issmael morning – 'look!' A knot of people stood at the cross-roads, pointing; but it was only our first glimpse of an aeroplane, grinding high over the Gyrn woods, and as it did not have Gulliver hanging from its claws I was not held for long. Even when I heard that twenty-year-old Tom Parry had been killed in France, it made little impression, I had never really seen him. The *Companion* was full of war; within two weeks *The Flag of Honour*, an absorbing special serial, had got under way, and there was an announcement of '*The Penny War Weekly* out today!!!' With the editor nimbly straddling his twin steeds Patriotism and Piety, there were hasty drawings – 'nothing rouses the simple Russian soldier to action so thoroughly as the sight of his priest bearing aloft a symbol of his church' – and on the cover, pacific family scenes were ousted by Lord Kitchener and once by Lloyd George nervously Examining An Explosive Fuse In The House Of Commons. Only the Superb Magneto Corset stayed unyieldingly the same. But at the time I noted little of this, for I was safe between the columns of *Out of Egypt*.

So when the *Liverpool Daily Post* was left lying in the snug, it was not the news from France that caught my eye but the photograph of a gentleman on the front page (dislodging the war!) which had been of peculiar interest to Dad, Mam, Annie and everybody in the bar. Over his head was splashed 'THE BRIDES IN THE BATH!' He had pulled them up one by one by the legs and drowned them for their money; the blurred photograph was plain and thick-spectacled, a chapel-goer if ever I saw one. It sounded comic and drab. 'George, if your mother caught you at *that*! Read the war news, look, nice maps!' I turned the page absently, Annie sewing and singing, 'Wass You Ever See . . .' 'New Fight for Calais' – 'Mont St Eloi Blown Up' – then a heading, 'Nuns Raped'. 'Annie, be'di Nuns Raped?' Annie pondered, needle to apple-cheek. 'Must be a part of their service. Look in your book, Georgie bach.'

Eng Dic informed me that rape meant ravish, and that ravish meant delight; I was no wiser. But I wallowed on. 'The nuns' – I saw Talacre – 'were dragged to the wash-houses, where they had been toiling among the troughs and mangles, and there the Hun soldiery submitted them to tortures.' How? I wondered. By putting them through the mangles? I glanced at the more official news, which I never saw. 'The houses were still burning –' then incredibly, my eye caught a familiar name. 'The village of Glanrafon suffered severely ...' I stared, it was Glantillon, near Neuve-Chapelle. 'Before the population could be evacuated, it is feared that more than twenty women and children were killed.' I remembered Annie's face when she had said 'The Germans!' ... then, in the lamp-lit snug, it all seemed further than Nero.

But in bed, I rambled on. 'The Huns, having occupied Chester, are advancing along the Dee and all are ordered to flee before night.' A black-bordered letter, my mother's frozen face. 'The Huns have taken Bootle, your Uncle Jab was marched into Trinity Road Chapel and shot.' Queensferry Bridge jammed with refugees, starving, despairing, then a crunch, a scream and all, all are swept away. 'Talacre is surrounded ...' The nuns are filed out to the lawn; on the spot where we were all photographed, a giant washing mangle. Drums and prayers, as Mother Jeanne is flung forward to her knees, her wimple trailing. She is lifted by the brutish hands of the boy she caned, now a Hun, who arranges the wimple between the great rollers. Spare them, spare them –

I opened my eyes, heart beating. Through the window, the flicker from the oil-lamp by the front door became the glare of distant fires. Mifanwy and Ieuan, trapped in the Opera House ... I strained for a whoop of laughter from downstairs, not a sound. Annie, in the panic of packing, thinks I am with Mam, and Mam, clutching the others, thinks I am with Annie, I alone am left ... What's that? Over the top of Pen-y-Maes, the echoing clatter of hooves. A horse rears, neighs, halts. In the corner I espy a family chest, slither out of bed and just as the jackboot creaks on the stair, leap inside and close the lid. Choked by dust, I lift it an inch; on the wall, the shadow of a helmet. A guttural swear-word, the clang of a sabre as it is plunged through the bed. A stumble – cursing – nearer ...

A guffaw from the bar, a step on the landing. 'Annie!' I shouted, strangled, 'Annie!' In two seconds she was sitting on my bed unplaiting her hair, and in another minute we were laughing about the nuns in the mangles. Prayers were repeated, for luck. 'God bless Dad Mam Job Thomas Mifanwy Ieuan Tom

Annie the Nuns but not the Huns Amen.' Another giggle, and asleep.

Gradually shadows lengthened along the grass, the shadows of impending change. Poor Nel died of old age; then one day, as I copied from the *Liverpool Echo* a hasty drawing of last week's *Lusitania*, taking pains to etch in the puppets writhing on to capsized lifeboats, I think I felt I was doing some sort of war work, Annie put her head in the snug door and said, 'You're going to live in a town miles away, twenty at the least, your mother just told me!' 'Will you come?' 'I expect so,' she said vaguely, 'not a tavern, a house, in Wrexham.'

I could prise no details, but I had them all, from *The Wide Wide World* and from Eric. For though on the map Wrexham was in Wales, I settled that it was English. The house would be large and sedate, with – glimpsed from my den at the top – gas-lamps, a red pillar-box and hansom cabs passing at a genteel trot; I would be a worldly city child attending a great wise school nearby. I might even wear a top hat, and Annie would go shopping in a hobble-skirt from Woodbine Town (the Lady Mary Line?). There would be no spittoons, no Gents and no Sundays to speak of. Dad would be in a frock-coat with his English voice permanently in place; Mam would be in her best every day, except when she put on a stiff pinafore and unexpectedly did the steps. Job would behave impeccably and sit for hours, at my command, alternately reading and practising with a knife and fork, while in my den I would be reading steadily and with furrowed brow through a pile of *Sunday Companions*, an occupation which in some way covered the expenses of the whole house with extras for needy passers-by. Mam taps at my door and kisses me on the brow, which unfurrows at once. 'Dear boy, Papa and I are thinking of going to buy a merino.' 'Of course, my dear, but I am nervous of the coachman.' 'I know, your father thinks he drinks.' The swish of a tea-gown with kimono sleeves, and Mam, humming 'The Man that Broke the Bank', settles back into the brougham pronounced brew-gam. We never went to Wrexham.

Chapter 7

Parting, and Departure

The false alarm had been a straw in the wind, for change was imminent, and the rhythm of the days I found jolted by bad things. Richard was being tugged so far into excess that even cronies shook their palsied heads, and the point came when he was forbidden the public-houses in Ffynnongroew. A publican exiled by his own kind, in Dic's own birthplace! I never saw him at meals.

Then came the moonlight night, not for the Story, when I was woken, long after the bar had closed, by loud banging. The back door was sharply bolted. Outside, a cry. I crept to the window in my nightshirt, numb with fright: not the self-aroused panic of the German nightmare, but the cold fear of the real thing, I could feel it grip at the very centre of my body, fear of violence toppling into madness. The house that had lately echoed with hollow jollity stood silent, eyes averted. I pressed my nose to the pane, and looked down on a scene that was no longer a green and pleasant land, but blanched by the moon; the loose-stone walls, the blotched whitewash of the outhouse, the stone ribbon disappearing uphill, all was drained of substance or colour, a barren crater on another planet. And in the midst, bereft in the wilderness, stood my mother: a frail ghost in the apron she never took off, hatless, friendless, homeless. I could not bear it. 'Mam,' I whispered, and pounded on the sill, not on the window, it might break and she would scold, 'Mam!' But more than a window stood between us, there was the frosted glass of reserve. 'Richard,' I heard her cry, 'Richard ...' and she put her hands to her face. I wept myself to sleep, not Mifanwy or Tom or all the Christians in Rome were any help to me now, then I heard the back door unbolted. Swiftly I crossed, squatted and listened. The door closed, and was bolted; I heard her step. She was inside, she was home. From the stairs, she spoke to him; and though, as always, it would have been wiser to say nothing, the banality of her speech comforted me. 'Don't you go to sleep over my lamp, the house is not insured, good night.' I crept back into bed, my face still wet, but feeling better.

One evening Annie barged into the snug. I looked up, startled out of the blue Mediterranean; I was copying Corsica out of the atlas. She was crimson, I had never seen her angry before. 'Be' haru ti, Annie,' I said, 'what's the matter?' 'Your father,' she said, 'he is a horrible man.'

My jaw dropped. While Mam complained about him – the one outlet which her reticence seemed to allow – and though I would speak against him to Annie, it was always Annie who said, 'Mrs Williams fach, he is a good husband when he is all right.' She had obviously defended my mother to him, to be told sharply to mind her own business. A week later, tying her bow to go out, she said, 'I am leaving.' 'I know you are,' I said, 'you are meeting Mary Pugh.' 'No, Georgie, proper leaving, to be a maid in Prestatyn, in a house called Skelton Dowell.' She knew the name would take my fancy, as indeed it did, I never forgot it. I looked at her, stupidly. 'What for?' 'Your father,' she said redly, knowing she was offending me again, 'I am going on Saturday.'

Like all bad news, even death, it was somehow fresh, as news, before turning quite bad; it had the novelty of something departing which I had always known. I was interested to watch her try on a new apron and pack her clothes, 'No, I'll leave these old boots, look at my new low shoes!' She put them on for me, her ankles beautifully trim. 'An English family you see, Georgie, two minutes from the sea and the one boy named Francis the same age as you that says good-gracious-me like a grown person and got sticks for fishing and a tricycle and a gramophone – good-gracious-me, Georgie, I shall have to sharpen my English!'

On the Saturday, I helped her lift her tin trunk, the one she had found *A Welsh Singer* at the bottom of, on to the trap. There she sat, upright and tight of nineteen-year-old waist in her unfamiliar best, though I knew those stays, cheeks rosier than ever, jocund eyes smiling into a future I could not even guess at : the new world of Skelton Dowell and handsomer postmen and golden Prestatyn beaches. She clasped her gloves and umbrella and lavender-scented handkerchief, but no farewell keepsake : we did not move in the world of presents. But with her she took one intangible gift which she had gaily fashioned for herself over the years, the love of a country child. 'Georgie, if I see Mifanwy or Ieuan I will write, don't take pepper to the petty now, ta ta . . .'

Mam and I waved her off : clip-clop down to the cross-roads, gone. But my mind was not ready for it. I read *Out of Egypt* again; 'On on, sun-blackened limbs aching, 'twixt the Pyramids . . .' Happily the domestic cloud had lifted; a commercial traveller had called with news from Uncle Jab, and as he did not drink to excess it warmed Mam's evening, and I went to bed feeling no more than the usual pre-Sunday depression. I slept. Grief stabs in the back, unawares. Sunday, with Annie never at Pen-y-Maes, was the one day when the routine need not remind me of her; yet when I opened my eyes and saw the sun shafting down past the blind on to her dusty boots, one overturned on the other, I knew my heart was broken.

The sun meant nothing to me, and I closed my eyes again; for the first time in my life I felt ill. Not like when I had had bad colds, and had to roll Peps round my tongue and swallow assafetta; this was an ache right through. I did not want to get up. 'Wti'n sâl?' said Mam sharply, the familiar 'Art thou poorly?' 'A bit,' I mumbled, 'hot and a headache,' which was to get out of chapel. She made me swallow something (paregoric?) and I dressed slowly in my old clothes, washed mechanically behind my ears and went downstairs. It was the first time I remembered not swinging on the ledge for luck.

The Sunday desolation was desolate indeed. I opened the door of the snug. In the corner stood Annie's old work-box, neatly closed. I crashed on my knees on the window-seat, almost enjoying the jolt it gave the knee-caps, and pressed my nose to the glass : a thing for rainy days, but today was sunny and I should be outside. I glanced at the dead village and walked out to the back yard, to the discarded barrels on which she and I had once arranged the board and the shards to play shop with; blindly I groped backwards, 'Look Georgie, nearly a whole saucer!' The clothes-line had never been free of something of hers, stockings or a pinafore skittish in the wind. Down in the long grass there had been the secret picnic, 'Don't tell thy mother!' The nest we had made with our bodies was gone. I walked up the hill to the cottage where she had lived all her life. I had never looked at it before, she had only, for me, shiningly existed in our house; I stared at the nondescript door, suddenly unique, and walked away.

Dinner made no impression, except that there was everyday talk and no bottomless pits of silence. An hour passed. I could not remember ever being at home at this time on a Sunday, and the strange afternoon echoed on. Thomas slept while Job, seven, squatted in the sun playing with bricks; leaving them under my supervision, our parents disappeared for their 'Sunday rest'. On the rug, I saw Nel's invisible dark shape and knew, for the first time, that she would never lie there again – was Annie dead too? I saw Kate in her coffin and she changed into Annie, the apple-cheeks drained by death; I looked round, dazed with grief, looked and listened. The house which contained four of my flesh and blood was as empty as a shell, as empty as life. I mooned into the parlour, a musty Sabbath tomb, and slumped on to the sofa, its cold chilling me through my trousers; ends of horsehair nagged at my wrist. The waxworks faced me, Richard and Mary Williams of Elwy Street, united in the eyes of God. I was not to know – or did I, deep deep down, adding to my isolation? – that over my head they were united again, and that for a fleeting hour recrimination had been stilled by the long-stifled murmur of an indissoluble love.

The wall-faces looked through me with such indifference that I raised my boots on to the horsehair, slid flat and turned to the wall. I thought, this feeling has nothing to do with any emotion I have read about and then imitated; as for the Story, it would be like slipping in an account of a raging toothache. In the wall-paper, I saw Francis in a splendid seaside snug, velvet curtains, a piano, plants in urns and a pile of buckets and spades. I saw him turn pages of the *Sunday Companion* bound in leather, and heard Annie say, in English, which I had never heard her speak, 'George Williams was his name, Francis, always his nose in a book and could not fish or play the gramophone, used to cut out dolls, quite a Mary Ann and a horrible father too, Francis will you take me to the beach on your tricycle?'

'Wti'n sâl?' Mam's voice, apprehensive. To find me lying in the parlour on holy horsehair, my face to the wall, must have been alarming. 'No, Mam,' I said, turning over, 'just sleepy, I am better now' (too late for chapel). She was fixing a comb into her hair. Then she said, 'Job has been crying, he might have cut himself on those bricks.' She turned at the door, 'Oes rhywbeth wedi digwydd, has anything happened?' I had a feeling that she knew after whom I was sorrowing, but I could say nothing. Neither could she. She went back to her work.

Next day the bustle of school; but once home I drooped again. I would write to her! I sat down to my first letter and first composition; even Mam corresponded with her sister in laborious English, we had been taught to write in it and it was the accepted mode of communication. 'White Lion Inn. Dear Annie' (dear Annie, she was in a story) 'I hope when you receive this that you are well. I hope that you are happy in Skelton Dowell. I hope that you like the life with English people like with Welsh people like us. Have you paddled yet like we did. Can Francis swim I expect he can swim. Nothing is changed please write George.' As a literary exercise it had nothing to offer, but between the ruled lines was pain, and hunger, and love.

Annie's going heralded the big change; the doctor had ordained that if Richard did not give up his way of life, there could be no answering for that life. Financially no regrets, for what should have been a fine property had turned out nothing but a great nine-year bath copiously filled and at the same time, a fraction a day, more copiously emptied. My mother could hear the gurgling which presages the end.

Before I realized it, at the beginning of the holidays of July

1915, the morning was upon us when we sat, as if waiting for a train, in an echoing house with pictures stacked against walls and unbelievable blotches on the paper. My father, dusty and harassed, threw me papers to count. I started, flicking them over, then stared: pound-notes! I had never seen more than one and I lost my place; Dad shouted at me, I started again, hastily. Ninety-eight, ninety-nine, a hundred ... Reverently I handed back the crackling treasure – where was Francis now? Little did I know that this was the inadequate total received for his lease, and that except for the squirrel-savings in the surreptitious tin box, it represented all we possessed.

We moved. When Mary saw her chattels brought unrecognizably out into the open, she was so ashamed that she hurried in and busied herself at that end until all was done. But when not fetching and carrying, I was watching. Sections of a bed would teeter drunkenly round the stair-corner, and under the impassive gaze of standers-by, be flung into a cart, dismembered and dishonoured; washing baskets piled with worn bedclothes and faded curtains were followed by objects I had never seen, dragged from my parents' bedroom to reel with a workhouse look into the merciless light of day. Then emerged the glass-faced family portraits, unflinchingly returning the stares of the peasantry only to reveal, from behind, brown paper riddled with the lounges of spiders which house-pride had annually routed. Just when the worst seemed past, out would lurch a dazed and senile sofa, groaning from old wounds new-broken and with the stuffing dribbling down its pendent haunches. With everything out and even the windows bare, the piebald house stared down at the village, like a shabby old pig, through four sightless eyes. A man on a ladder was painting out RICHARD WILLIAMS; Mam, helping the last exhausted wash-stand on to a handcart, gave his back a loving look.

We moved. The lease had gone so promptly that we were to stay with distant relatives of my father's while he did his 'looking around'. 'Stay with relatives!' Incurably inventive, I saw terraces and tea on the lawn; they lived in Rhewl Fawr, in the row of houses where I was born.

Dad's bargain with his kin must have been made, in the

smallest hours, through a haze of goodwill towards all men including Aunties Lizzie (Liz Fawr as Mam called her, Big Liz), who looked not unlike the Cap who had invaded Picton School. My heart hardened to her with a snap, and she had a grown-up daughter (the Young One), a down-at-heel slut. Mam recognized them at once as 'sothach', shoddy stuff: they were not chapel, kept a dirty house and belonged to 'the bad side of your father's family'. The first night we slept on mattresses in the large empty front bedroom, where I fell asleep, to fitful candlelight, with Belgian parentage and fleeing from the Boche hordes. I woke up a Welsh refugee in Rhewl Fawr. It was not easy to emerge from our quarters, for passage and stairs were crammed with the furniture that had been cleared out to make room for us; and the parlour, already crowded, was gradually stacked with our poor chairs and sofas and wash-stands, perched on end, like somnambulist invalids, against other people's rubbish.

Pen-y-Maes gone, my mother's spirits were good and from the first she tried her best. Though not one of the pound-notes had found its way into the tin box – and there must have been powerful wassails – Richard must have turned decorous by each evening, for there were no returns unduly late to a 'home' where the dark journey upstairs, past jutting castors and vases on their sides, would have daunted a preacher. But for the first and only time we were adrift, five in a room, and the atmosphere worsened. My mother would try to clean up some corner that had not been touched for years, Big Liz would demand if her house wasn't clean enough for homeless people, and so on till the day they were Not Speaking. I looked forward to walking past with high averted face, and thought once of shouting something but was not brave enough. The house was soon bursting with such claustrophobic hate that the families clamped to it on either side must, on still nights, have been conscious of an ominous crackling.

Groes Chapel was now too far, and on Sundays I was dispatched up the road to Gwynfa; even chapel was an escape from the furniture jungle. And I had my serials: Saturday mornings, I would burrow my way into the parlour, past haunts of fern pot and strawed crockery, past blancmange waterfall and bamboo what-not, to a nest I had made myself in a tiny arm-chair, feathered, under a wizened cushion, with old *Companions*. Between me and the window was a sideboard, but I could see to read if the sun was out. From where I sat I could glimpse my waxwork parents, he with his face to the enemy wall, she the right way round but upside down with a mad stare and a moustache under each eye. My only uninterrupted view was of a luxuriant-haired young woman, framed behind cracked glass, clinging in her nightgown, deep in thought, to a stone cross jutting out of a storm-racked ocean. Under a table I could watch my own booted feet in a mirror. In a nightmare way, I enjoyed the parlour.

I remember little of the month except one evening when it was still daylight and Job and I were going to bed. The windows had neither curtain nor blind, such birds of passage were we, and the late sun poured kindness into our unhappy room; from the road two older boys spied us in our singlets. They whooped, we ducked shamefaced, then hopped to the window, half to show off and half for company; we waved, I even gave one of my mad falsetto calls and jumped like Glyn. Three others had joined them, when Mam stormed in; Big Liz had seen, and laughed at her. 'Disgracing us in front of those women, into bed before I get the stick!' I realized how desperately she was clinging to her self-respect, harder than the woman in the parlour was holding on to her cross. After that we padded in a circle away from the window.

Then one evening my father returned quicker of step, brighter of eye; our future was in place, we were to move in a week.

A week! All was bustle and change. Next morning the five of us set out in a borrowed donkey-drawn cart with a parcel of wall-paper, a bucket of paste and a brush. Mam wore her black straw and carried Thomas in a shawl, Dad held the reins, clear-eyed and with Job on his knee, and I was huddled in the back, watching the road do its exciting familiar trick of flowing endlessly out from under me. We trotted past Gwynfa Chapel where the three of us had been christened, past the haunted barn, past the pond – 'look Georgie, they're pulling the poor drunken fellow out!' – and bowled along a country-side that was our fresh-faced father's by birth and the joy of living, while Mam clucked and stifled a smile, oh let it stay like this ... Then zestful up the hill, past Annie's (a pang, but the donkey was going fast) past Issmael Jones's farm (a look at his bedroom, but somebody waved out of it so it was hard to imagine a hanged man) then jogger-trot, jogger-trot, the White Lion Inn, licensed to JOHN MUNRO; for one second I glimpsed myself sitting watching us, arms demurely folded, on the garden wall next to the Gents with the dusty laurel behind me, then I was gone. Dad called 'Last orders!', slapped his thigh with a chuckle and down into Glanra-fon, on which he bestowed the Lord Mostyn bow and the Dic wink. Mam turned to him, laughing, her profile suddenly like Annie, let it be like this always ...

Although we could not move yet, I felt this was farewell : and on, donkey-borne, to a fresh chapter. Good-bye to the hedgerow of pebble-caves, good-bye to the wild strawberries – farewell the Gyrn woods, with Curly Eric on the terrace and the dead tramp in the bluebells, farewell the beaters, Kate's father, Nero, Mifanwy, farewell ... Up the hill, past the lonely smithy of the glowing heart, steeper, all get down to give the poor donkey a chance, up through Afon Goch, up the tiny Everest of Trelogan village, a landscape rambling and open to the winds – but look, a shop – two shops! Over the top, under a scurry of sunlit clouds, past the school – look Georgie, bechgyn, genethod – and down a toy hill to toy cross-roads. 'Dyma ni', cried Dad, pointing masterfully with borrowed whip, 'here we are!' It was a nice little cottage attached to a twin, with a lot of neglected garden and a tumbledown petty. We wheeled round past the Traveller's Rest, the neat little tavern on the corner – Mam gave it a quick glance – and we were at the gate of One Mainstone Cottages, Berthengam.

Four rooms, each with the desolate look of any empty house, never mind a cottage pock-marked with poverty, but it was ours. Dad was in his element, Dic the shirt-sleeved sailor anchoring into port. Mam doffed her hat, donned her apron, put Job in the garden to watch Thomas, and we set to work. Dad stripped the parlour walls, no bugs, and then papered them, singing the song as he did so, 'When Father Papered the Parl-ah', while I helped Mam wash the floors. In fact, the parlour would not be the parlour, for it contained the tiny oven next the grate, and would have to be kitchen and living-room. Fetching water from our rain-butt at the back, Mam exchanged pleasant words with next-door, whom she could tell at a glance were 'all right'. The sun shone, we picnicked in our house, life had a sparkling new taste, I could even think of Annie without constriction. Mid-afternoon, Dad crossed to the Traveller's Rest to meet Mr and Mrs Morgan Licensed to Sell, but took Mam with him; she cannot have been averse to sitting for half an hour enfumed in alcohol and tobacco and not responsible for any of it. Dad returned rich with tales of local eccentrics which I was too young to savour: John Price the spiritualist, who lived by the lake Llyn Helyg with hens and a white donkey, and Bob yr Hendre, a cheery recluse inhabiting an immense shed chock-a-block with the spoils of prowling (perished tyres, wheels prised off lorries, prams, sewing-machines) who, having once openly carried home an anvil up Trelogan hill, could surely have laid claim to the heavy-weight championship of the light-fingered world.

Then we bowled down again through Trelogan, up past darkling John Munro and back to the horrible house, but we were dead tired and immune. Days of this, then the move, a fine August one. I helped to lug furniture out into the back yard, with orders 'not to speak'; there had been disputes over bills. Let one foot take a false step, and the house would blow up.

The step was taken, by the Young One. We were out in the alley – I tying up sticks and the two umbrellas, Mam packing crockery, Dad straining at a table, fine and stern and glowing – when the Young One stalked out, blouse tight over her stayless dirty 'big front', as Annie and I had called the stylish busts in Woodbine Town. Her hair was coming down. She looked at my mother, turned and shouted to hers, 'Mam, our teacups, she's a thief!' Mary stood fixed, clasping her wedding teapot and lucent with honesty, while Richard slowly put down the table, wheeled, put his hand to an umbrella, drew it carefully like a sword, and looked at the Young One; his face was so terrifying that she gave a sharp yelp, picked up her skirts, and ran. Then the splendid thing happened. At her heels, as if at the bark of a starting gun, down the alley and up the road pounded an avenging angel with a furled brolly held like an Olympic torch. It was the height of the village morning, and it was marvellous to see them all drop everything and gape. The quarry, dirty hair streaming, big front galumphing, swerved down an alley and into some scurvy sanctuary. My father slowed down, veered, and returned to us with measured tread, breathing heavily but well, and stared at with respect by half Rhewl Fawr.

An hour later the van left with his family possessions, from the framed S.S. *Lucania* to the vases of shaking-grass. An hour after that the family itself departed, donkey-drawn and without a stain on its character.

Chapter 8

A Bad Time, and a Better

I felt so at ease that afternoon, as we settled into One Mainstone Cottages, that I made a family joke. Carrying waxwork Mary gingerly in through the front door, I called, 'Here comes Queen Alexandra!' Dad laughed appreciatively, Mam putting up the blind in the back kitchen tut-tutted, I blushed with grown-upness. It was a busy and creative day.

A week later my mother set me to oil my winter boots, I tied the red scarf Auntie Sarah had knitted for me, and I joined Trelogan Council School, on the crest of the hill. It was smaller than Picton; the headmaster Mr Fidler, who toiled up every day on his bike from Rhewl Fawr, was a bachelor – of science – with thick glasses, a little moustache, and knickerbockers with belted waist and foppishly low shoes: a kind two-wheeled owl. In the hall, behind glass, were four minute exquisitely uniform books with bright covers which I desired as I had desired the atlas: they were New Testaments, French, Italian, Spanish and Portuguese (this being 1915, the Bible had never been translated into German). School was easy and pleasant except for the allotments, where each child tended a square of peas and beans which, if encouraged, would apparently win the war. There was raffia work – I brought home a lop-sided pincushion I had made, it went into the parlour for ever – and flag-signalling, and nutting excursions up to the bushy hillside called 'y Glol'. My mother baked her own bread, and when she had kneaded the indecently amorphous stuff into the tin – 'don't touch it with your dirty fingers!' – I would carry the tin, under my cape if it was raining, over through Trelogan to the bakehouse; next day I would call for the new-born loaf, still warm, and on the way home stealthily peel from the side a sliver of delicious crust.

We were too far for the *Companion*; but every Monday after school I would walk the two miles down to Glanrafon, already in the nostalgic past, and call on Mrs Hughes the Policeman. I felt half shy at asking for her copy before she could have had time to finish it, and half afraid she might not let it go. The serial was *In the Realm of the Tsar*, and halfway up the first lane I would start to read, pacing rhythmically. The first couple of times I found myself in the ditch, but I learnt to keep to the middle of the road; colliers cycled round me, humouring me like a sheep. By the time I was scaling the populated hilltop I had fortunately arrived, with a sigh of surfeit, at 'Another enthralling inst. next week'.

Life at home darkened again, and I was to look back with longing on that week of plans and picnics. The sailor who had bobbed to the surface and gulped ozone, was now to sink with deadly purpose into the deeps; Father, having papered the parlour, never gave the house another look. For the first time in his life he was idle, and cooped in a remote countryside with wife, three children and no hope of a companionable stranger breezing in through an open door. He had, moreover, the best part of a hundred pounds.

When Mam had given that quick look at the Traveller's Rest, her intuition had not played her false. 'I will talk to the wife,' she said, 'even though she is a bit simple.' One afternoon when Dad was sleeping it off, she stole across, and arrived back puzzled. 'She was very nice with promising to stop him being tempted, but she is absent-minded, looking out of the window and speaking to herself.' It took another visit for it to dawn on my usually second-sighted mother that as much as any stay-at-home Traveller, Mrs Morgan needed her Rest, and to get it was inclined to quaff, deep and surreptitiously, the strong waters of Lethe.

Like a worker clocking in, every morning Richard reported at the tavern, and often remained at his post all day, missing the meal which his wife, with bitter memories, would watch disintegrate before her eyes. The savings too shrivelled and shrank; the momentum could only quicken. Sitting in that tiny topery, demoted from mine host to workless cottager – what demon of maladjustment drove him to such self-spoiling? Was there an element of guilt – he was a sensitive man – the disgust of standing by while the war news worsened? One altercation was settled by a loaf being placed squarely on the glowing coals; bread in the fire, the neighbours whispered in horror, in *war-time*! At one crisis we were all four banished and offered sanctuary next door, leaving the Welshman in solitary possession of his castle. We were back in two days and had somehow known we would be, but it was galling to glimpse neighbours peering over hedges. We did not welcome pity.

Our waste of garden was used by the school as extra allotments, Mam being paid a few shillings a month of which Dad knew nothing; and once a week twenty boys, including myself, were marched down the hill and into our gate to plant war-winning potatoes. I dreaded two contingencies, that Mam should cross to the petty in front of all the boys, or that Dad should appear. The first never happened, the second was inevitable.

After our spade war-work, one autumn afternoon, Mr Fidler marched us two by two out of our gate, with my mother tweaking her curtain as if to peer at a midget army of occupation. Satisfied that one or two were shabbier than I, she went back to her chores. We plodded past the pond, and at the Traveller's Rest had just wheeled when I heard a titter; he was in the doorway. They all turned to him, twenty pairs of cruel eyes; and I had no choice but to view him through them. I saw, holding a glass, a grand foolish-looking tramp with a two days' beard and an empty smile. I looked away and stared at the neck in front; he called something. Mr Fidler heard, halted the march – O kind owl, your kindness to me over weeks is obliterated – focused in the stillness and realized, too late, that this parent was not up to examination standard. 'Sut mae'r mab,' called Sir Tramp thickly, benevolently, 'how is't with thee, my son?'

An eternity of two seconds; the communal titter, 'forward march!' and it was over. Would I get a nickname, I wondered as I copied 'King noun, Dardanelles proper noun, torpedo noun ...' On the way home, I was still too disturbed to give more than a look to Bob yr Hendre sauntering by with a one-wheeled bicycle over his shoulder. I did not tell Mam. Next day, as if to make up, Mr Fidler took the four Testaments out of their case and sat me down with them at a desk; in wonderment, I handled them with the same gentle physical joy I had derived from my paper-backed *Nero*. I compared one with the other, or with the English. Jesus, in French, had a mark over the second letter, the Lord's Prayer in Italian looked like a bunch of flowers. I mouthed unknown words, feeling outlandish, privileged. Mr Fidler, passing, said, 'It's not as different from English as Welsh is!' I had not thought of that.

It was a bleak Christmas, and when I sniffed the frosty air, it held no promise. For my mother, the shadow of the word she dreaded most, 'workhouse', loomed over Mainstone Cottages; she must have come as near despair as she can ever have been. One night, in imitation of a band of children who had raised piping voices at front doors and then been remunerated, I made a secret sally. Money was on my mind; having learnt 'While Shepherds Watch' in class, I set off through the drizzle in my cape, an emissary of the Tsar, and crept up to the bow-windowed houses behind the school. I would sound tremulous and proud and poor, and take a shilling home. In a dark porch, I cleared my throat, was glad Mam was not near, and started. I sounded tremulous and poor, but not proud. A light flickered through the glass, I broke off and dived into the shadows. The door opened. 'Cath oedd hi,' said Mrs Lloyd General Stores, 'it must have been a cat.' The door closed. That was Christmas 1915.

But not entirely. I took Job into the woods for holly, there was 'potas' to fill us, delicious dripping with bread drowning in it, and 'ponsh maip', mashed turnips piquantly salted; and Mam made a plum-pudding. And late on Christmas Eve, in the tiny moonlit cave of our back bedroom, I was woken by sounds such as I had never heard; as I swam up into drowsy consciousness, I thought I had died and that these deep and plangent harmonies were the first intimations of immortality. Our little family shames were washed clean; the world was still, and listening. I crept to the window, and looked up the ghostly transfigured hill. On the crest, next to the school, a choir of miners were singing carols. 'While Shepherds Watch' ... I was glad I had run away. I was facing Bethlehem Hill, and again I felt that these were the same shepherds who had sung two thousand years ago, just as it was the same moon, with its same look of impassive benediction. That was Christmas too, and anyway 1916 must be going to be better.

Something had to happen; in the spring, my father enrolled as munition worker at Sandycroft, on the estuary just our side of Chester; he was to live in lodgings in Shotton. It was a cloud lifting. To be sure, under where the cloud had been there was nothing except the tin box, but for the first time in years my mother could relax and run her home. And every Sunday, Dad was to come home for the day, the train to Mostyn and then the steep mile-walk up through the woods. Which meant, as she reasoned, that even if there had been a Saturday lapse, the early start and the cold air would have cleared the head. She was right, the first Sunday he arrived crackling with health, a wage-earner delighted to see the family from whom, for the first time, he had been separated; and his pockets were full of treats, including his pay-packet, or as much of it as he thought fair to part with. In the evening, we accompanied him part of the descent to Mostyn, and our peaceful fatherless week started again. It was an ideal schedule. Richard was himself again.

Of the treats, one I loathed, the other loved. The first was black-puddings, which we ate immediately for Sunday dinner: I was not aware that these war-time delicacies were made from blood, but I did not need to know this to be revolted by the greasy grey beads of fat stuck together like the mashed eyes of myriads of mice. The second was a Sunday newspaper – in itself a daring novelty, like a picnic on a tombstone – called, boldly, the *News of the World*. My nose sniffed past the robberies and the rapes ('Annie, be'di Rape?' I still did not know). 'Artillery-men Show Photos to Schoolgirls.' Of cannons? ... Then – 'Our Great Serial, *The Exploits of Elaine*, from the sensational film'; this last meant nothing to me ('film', a light layer) and I glanced underneath at the weekly music-sheet. 'Miss Violet Loraine, Tongue-Twisting 'Triumph (Dedic. to the Boys Over There) " 'E Misses 'Is Missus's Kisses"!!!' I glanced back. 'For New Readers: Elaine is hot on the trail of the fearsome Clutching Hand and suspects the criminal Wu Fang, read on.' Once more I obeyed, and went on obeying, every Sunday.

On my trek to Glanrafon, I told Mrs Hughes I was reading another serial, but found it difficult to describe Elaine. 'Never mind, Georgie,' he said, 'you must bring her and the Chinese down to Glanrafon!' I smiled politely, but walking home (*The Shell Girl*, an uneasy amalgam of Methodism and munitions) I stopped, struck with a thought. Why not?

Though I had never seen, or even thought of, two or more persons addressing one another in public in an assumed guise – walking along, the *Companion* under my arm, I worked out a detailed plan; one or two black-faced cyclists who knew my habits must have looked wobblingly back, for I was not only walking without reading, I was talking to myself as if I had known myself for years. First, I decided, a staff of three from Trelogan (Willie Savage, a practical boy you could rely on, plus two) will slip down to Mrs Hughes earlier in the day and stow away ornaments, pull the sofa round, also arm-chairs and stools and chairs from the bedrooms – bound to be a shed in the back, a bench, that will do – all into the parlour, to face an arrangement, in the back part, of small table, chair, telephone and behind, the half-open door into the kitchen. Telephone? All I knew from General Knowledge was that it meant speaking through an instrument to people miles away and that it was vital to Elaine.

In the kitchen the characters prepare themselves: Job, eight, young but can be trained, Ifor, John: and Cassie will be Elaine, I the detective. And I will use the telephone. I enter and take it. Out of a drawer? We shall see. 'Hello ... (pause, Dad nudges Mam) ... Yes, I understand ... (The others look at one another, amazed.) ... Chinatown? Spell that, please ... In danger, I understand ...' In the flickering oil-light, the faces are intent. Outside, the dark Glanrafon road and opposite, the outhouse where once hung ... 'Please do not wipe the blood till I arrive in my motor. Well, Wu Fang?' Job has shuffled in from the kitchen in an old blouse of Mam's, his plump cheeks smeared with yellow chalk and smoking opium. 'What news from China-town –' Before he can answer, the telephone rings (a table-spoon rat-tatted against a plate) as Elaine is brought in, gagged, 'Hello, Detective speaking ...' I arrived home, felt the whole evening had happened and was content.

Two weeks later, by coincidence, one mid-week Mam sud-denly announced an outing, and an evening one at that; she must have been given three tickets and could not bear to waste them. Thomas was left in the neighbour's charge, a pony and trap were lent and after school, as the spring night darkened, we drove two miles to the strangely named village of New-market. I had never been out with her before without my father, it was like accompanying a recent but serene widow. 'What are we going to see?' I asked as we jogged along. ' 'Dani am weld drama,' said Mam, 'we are going to see a play.'

It was an amateur group from Ffynnongroew, of which I remember nothing except a real anvil which exuded real sparks when hit by what seemed to be a real blacksmith. It was in the Town Hall, no curtain, not that I expected one, no scenery to speak of, and no lighting. The play must have been an inferior imitation of my cousin Mr Berry's work, one of those homely pieces written about 'village-folk' to be acted, or rather spoken self-consciously at one another, by 'village-folk'. There was talk of righteousness, and of the drunken son of the preacher (the vice mentioned but not portrayed) and maybe a feud between two farmers; it was, moreover, in Welsh and so, to me, as dull as real life without having me in the middle of it. My pleasure came from being out with my mother at her ease.

Yes, the fact that it was in Welsh was to me a major draw-back; even if it had been a brilliant translation of *Romeo and Juliet* acted by Ieuan and Mifanwy come to poetic life, I would have resisted the sound of my own language. The harm had been done, by those stagnant chapel hours still going on, and words which should have sounded wonderful from the stage –

'gogoniant', glory, 'datguddiad', revelation – would have been mere echoes of incarceration; and the English language was becoming the symbol of escape. 'Very nice,' said Mam in the trap going back, as I nodded beside her and Job slept on her knee, 'I liked the fire coming out of the anvil. The blacksmith had a look of those Protheroes that worked with your father's cousin, I must ask on Sunday, fancy doing *this* in his spare time.' She was more interested than I was.

The match to a sluggish fuse was to come from another quarter. As spring turned to summer my father, anxious to show us off to his new cronies in Shotton, insisted that we come and stay the night at his 'place' – no, baby Thomas too, the blue of his eyes was flecked with green and he was the bonniest. Mam had her doubts, but one Saturday morning, in the sun, we took the short cut down through the woods, she and I taking turns to carry Thomas. It was my first train journey; the week-end bustle of the tiny station, the parcels, the porters, the smell of the sea and then, out of nowhere, the ruthlessly steady approach of the monster, the smoke and the whistle-shrieks and the doorbangs, it all excited and frightened me. Mam sat like a statue, a bundle on each side – I never saw her trust anything to a luggage-rack – and her eyes fixed on the communication cord as we shot past a vast black smoking crashing burning devilish city which she said was the Mostyn Ironworks. The estuary to the left, and several stops; but nothing so good happened again till Shotton, where Dad awaited us, straight from work, washed and brushed and smiling, proud of us and himself.

I clutched at my parents with my eyes – my hands were full of luggage – and thought, I must not lose sight of them, I shall be swallowed up in this eddy of faces and voices and houses and shops and footsteps, I cannot take it in I cannot ... Shotton and Connah's Quay, merging into each other with indifference on both sides, were at that time a couple of hasty townships, wood and bricks and mortar run up at the behest of commerce; but on me, that busy Saturday, they had the effect of strong drink. Not only were the bicycles going quicker and ringing sharper bells, but the people with the preoccupied faces were walking brisker, the smoke from the strange houses blew faster, and even the town-clouds, brown at the edges from smuts and sophistication, raced swifter over a man-made sky. My head swam with the multiplication of fellow-beings, with the plurality of shops (ten in a row!) and with the danger of being lost. The swarthy old woman with the limp and the hat with a feather, swaying round a corner – had she gone for ever? Had I seen her? There was a man playing a cornet, for pennies, with a cap at his crippled feet, a man dedicated to sadness – I must have had a small fever, that Saturday – he was the beggar outside the Opera House to whom Mifanwy slips a sovereign, the maimed slave in the dust of the Colosseum, he was Life, half of it the life which was undoubtedly his, squatting there, and half the life which *I* breathed, the breath of fiction ...

I emerged somewhat from this metropolitan dream when we reached 3 Clarence Street, a lodging house which, unlike Big Liz's, contained the furniture of half of one. Mrs O'Neill was pleasant, a kind Irish cousin of the same Big Liz. Richard must have hinted that Poll, while a pearl, might not prove the easiest guest for a biddy who could scramble a couple of eggs between one Guinness and the next, and Irish charm worked on Welsh steel in a new way, eating into it not with acid but with honey. 'What a *good* husband, ever speakin' of his Old Dutch and his three wee ones!' Mary smiled, and turned from the timid country cousin into the district visitor from the family seat, Richard hovering like an anxious student. After nine years as mine-hostess-of-all-work, she must have enjoyed it. Her English was nothing like as wieldy as her husband's, and she had the craft to rely on balanced monosyllables. 'No? ... Indeed? ... Fancy!' She even attempted the English for 'tewch, tewch!' – 'you don't say!' – but translated it literally by repeating 'Be quiet, be quiet,' in a hushed tone, luckily Mrs O'Neill was not listening, 'No! Fancy! Be quiet, be quiet ...' The visit was a success.

The afternoon I spent on some waste ground with the *News of the World* : tonight there would be a girl to watch Thomas and we four were to go to the 'livin' pictiars'. These I imagined to be lantern slides, and they did not take my mind off the Clutching Hand. It was already dark when we set out along the milling Saturday-night street, shopping, hurrying, dawdling, arguing, eating, courting, Liverpool-Echoing, past sign after sign, Station Arms, Maypole, Co-operative Stores, Fish and Chips, Arcade (pillars!), Glazier's Furniture Emporium (Nero!). Then, lit up in a window, arm-chairs, sofas – and a bed! I saw us sitting on them and the crowd pressed against the glass, my mother crimson with exposure, Walton's Clock and Watch Shop, Custom House Lane ... To the right, a train savaged through, a deafening billow of light and fire: the Irish Mail, Dad said, Holyhead to Chester, and then to London, and as he said it, it was proudly gone, leaving a lazy insolent question-mark of smoke. London ... We reached a crowd outside a corrugated place called the Connah's Quay Hippodrome.

It was disgorging what Dad called 'the first house', drugged and blinking, into the gaslight; I had never seen so many people before, let off a firework behind them and they could turn into the crowd pouring out of the flaming Opera House. My father called to us as he jostled into a group, 'Dyma'r cyw!' 'Cyw,' prononuced 'kew', is Welsh for chicken; I looked round puzzled, till he explained that it meant lining to get in. He looked as if he owned the place, as he waved two twopence-ha'penny stubs and two halves and we trooped down the echoing side-alley to the front: a pervasive smell of smoke, gas, sweat, dust and orange peel. 'Run,' said Dad to me, 'four in the middle, far back as you can!' I knew exactly what he meant, darted past the dawdlers and sat with my cap next to me on the wooden back bench, with just behind it the barrier to the fourpennies. He had sweets to distribute and it was delightful to sit chewing and watching the place fill: where had all *these* come from? I sat back, content to be part of the Roman populace.

There was a glowing curtain, alive with advertisements and lit from below, with on either side a draped Roman female extending a plaster arm which had once held aloft a gassy torch at some rich man's gate. A haughty young woman entered from a little door, unbuttoned a short fur cape, sat at an upright piano, twiddled her rings with the abstracted air of one who knows she is being watched, and began to play. The only time I had ever known the piano had been at school, grinding out marches or choruses : now I heard it for the first time. She darted from rag-time to ballad, from ballad to dramatic fragment, then back to rag-time : 'Swanee', 'The Last Rose of Summer', 'I Wouldn't Leave my Little Hut', all transported me. Then the lights went out and the curtain rolled up to show, bathed in unearthly coloured light, an exquisite girl in a flowing green and red dress, a tiara in her hair; she was holding a violin, motionless. Expecting a 'living picture', I looked from her to the two Roman ladies and was thoroughly confused. I whispered, 'Is she a statue?' – as I did so, the figure moved, and played the violin. It is doubtful if she played well, but I had never heard one before. The tender ebb and flow of the other-world voice stirred me to wonder. I forgot my family; I thought not only of Ieuan and Mifanwy and Tom and the Romans and the Egyptians toiling to build the Pyramids, I saw the swirling crowds outside, the crippled beggar and the tipsy gipsy. To the strains of a fiddle, I was bright-eyed and bright-bodied with love of life.

The curtain bumped down, and – of its own accord! – up again; the girl came forward and bowed, a story-heroine with unbelievably red mouth arched over pearly teeth, great blue-lidded eyes ... Down again, a deafening Saturday-night roar of talk, and just as I wondered how it could ever be countered, the curtain rolled up, to display a dull white sheet. Utter silence. At my back, a whirring noise; but before I could turn my head, the sheet was a rectangle of blinding light. A sign, 'Pathé's Animated Gazette', then the words 'A London Street', then a photograph – of a London street. Then a gasp through the four Williamses, a Welsh wind of 'Mae 'nhw'n symud, they are moving, symud symud symud ...' And they were – jerkily, perkily, in a snow-storm, but moving! Then King George the Fifth came toddling smartly at us, overcoat-less in the same snowstorm, shook hands with a Chinaman and plainly asked him, I assumed in Welsh, how he was, 'A sut mae'r teulu?' As they exchanged courtesies the lady pianist attacked a gavotte and I sank, already exhausted

by the special day, into a bath of melody and movement. Then
... *The Juggernaut*, in Four Reels.

Juggernaut? Reel? ... No snow, no jerking. The train was in
danger: the audience murmured fearfully as the two bad men
were seen, to pounding ominous music, tampering under the
great bridge over which the Juggernaut had twice circled
superbly. A great white shimmering sign 'The day dawned ...
What will it bring?' Then I was a lone onlooker, hidden in the
branches swaying in the foreground. The Train came into view,
fearing nothing; but as it glided round the curve and towards the
bridge over the waters many feet below, the music mounted
steadily in warning fury; my heart began to beat ... Then the
unbelievable happened – fifty feet in front, a cloud of dust, then
a yawning gap. The music stopped dead, and in appalled silence
I watched the train race on and slowly, inevitably (horrified
gasps) plunge to watery doom. A carriage thrashing in the
water, like a great beast – a frenzied fist breaking the glass –
people pulled through like sacks, one drowning – then a quick
rescue, an embrace, the lights up and the audience rising, to the
National Anthem, dazed and murmuring.

I was more than dazed, as if from the shock after a real accident. With the capacity to walk and answer questions – 'where
didst thou leave thy cap?' – I was, near enough, unconscious. We
had to wait for my father and his mates to return before sleeping
arrangements could be improvised, and I ended up sandwiched
between Dad and another lodger. I spent a sleepless night trapped
in a narrow valley between two black mountains of snore and
belch and hiccup and sweat; but I would not have slept anyway,
for my fever of soul was at uncontrollable pitch. I was one
moment in the train, Mam clutching two great shopping bags
with Thomas in one and Job in the other – nearer – only *I* knew
– the communication cord, we must pay five pounds or die, so
we die ... Then I would be among the day's crowds, brandishing
a ticket for the Train, I must get there to warn the guard, but
every time I tried to duck past they trampled me into the gutter;
then I would doze, till the real-life shriek of an engine would
start me off again. The day dawned. What will it bring?

It brought, like after reading, an unreal reality. I took in nothing of the journey back to Mostyn, by an unsabotaged slow train, or of the sleepy toil up through the woods. I sealed up that hectic memory, air-tight. In the meantime, I was content to feel the tempo slow down : my heart more measured, the smoke from the Trelogan chimneys back to the right meander, the passers-by and the dogs and cats with less on their minds.

Chapter 9

Set-back, and Forward

My mother's role of district visitor was not to be repeated, indeed there was to be one painful relapse. Whitsun week-end, Dad was to come home Saturday and stay the night: a fine prospect, Mam would have his dinner ready. She had. She waited, until at ten to five I came dragging my boots up the garden path, a schoolboy Cassandra: Dad had been seen walking up Trelogan, 'waving and full of fun', at three o'clock.

Mam looked at me, went to the back door, shaded her eyes against the sun, and stared at the Traveller's Rest; behind those harmless lace-curtains a fly was caught once more, waving and full of fun, in an alcoholic web. I sat in the back room and started a new chapter in *Westward Ho!*, feeling in the nape of my neck the gathering of the storm; I was glad Job was out. I saw her eyes move from the ruined war-time meat to the rest of her home. Solvency was so delicately adjusted that one bad week could make the difference between being All Right and Owing. Th sun moved inexorably across the wall-paper as if to show up her house as a pitiful little museum of spit-and-polish. The bang of the front door.

The familiar silence. I covered my ears and went on reading, knowing that the words would slowly empty of meaning. 'The thought of the Inquisition crossed their minds. "Frank! Men, to the rescue, give it the black villain!" What were those dull thuds' – the door banged again, my head shot up. She had said something, swift as an arrow; he had swayed, said nothing, and gone. I heard her suddenly call out, a voice I could not recognize, shrill, distracted, 'Rho'r arian imi, give me the money – rho'r arian imi!' Then I heard her wrench the front door indecently open and sat numbed, the old thrill of horror striking at the centre of my body. On the page swimming before me, Frank Leigh was dying, 'confused mass of negroes and English ... he lying in the boat, weak, half blind with blood', no good, I rose and walked to the back door.

The scene was caressed by a late afternoon sun which picked out the details like an old painting. My father was striding past the Rest, a Saturday-night crowd at the door and several housewives at theirs; and who could blame them, it was painful and watchable, I was watching too. Her tiny figure came into view round the corner, I could just see her head over the hedge as she stumbled after him, calling 'Richard, Richard' ... I could tell by her tone that in front of the crowd which she had spent her life avoiding, she was making a desperate effort to keep the proprieties, as if she were catching him up with a forgotten pipe. But she was given away by one damning detail : she was out in the road, every hair in place, but without a hat. I had never seen her bareheaded in public, it was like watching a stranger.

In an evening light made for lovers, he took pound-notes from his pocket, with some change, and flung them at her feet. It was very still weather, and I heard the clink of the coins. Then he strode up the hill, his back turned on all that belonged to him, bound for nowhere. She stared after him. I would have run to her, knelt for her and picked up her wages and brought her home, but I remembered the tone in which she had once said, 'Whatever you do, keep out of it.' The crowd was twenty by now, and I groped blindly back; I could not have borne to watch her kneel, in front of those pitying faces, kneel with the dignity of the utterly poor and proud and gather up the pennies. I made myself read. 'The boat seemed paved with bodies. "Dead!" shrieked Amyas. "For God's sake run – run!"' ... No don't run, after this nothing can be worth running for because nothing I shall ever read about, nor the Juggernaut plunging, nor the dead in Flanders, can be as awful as this. I clutched my head long enough to know that she must be indoors. If only she could have walked into that back room and into my ten-and-a-third-year-old arms, already ten years older than the two she had lost ... But it was not our way.

The memory was hard for her to bear; yet it was bearable. To the passer-by, it could only have been a working-class brawl, cruel and vulgar: but he was not cruel, and neither of them vulgar. And even then I knew that in spite of incompatibility and hardship and hurt, each needed the other; and that one day, when the restless blood had cooled, the wounds would heal. It was bearable. Monday morning (Whit, so a holiday) she insisted on my going with her up to the shop, I evidently supplied a feather-weight of moral courage. As we passed the Rest, Mrs Morgan was at the top of a ladder, vaguely dabbing at a window. 'Dangerous,' murmured my mother. 'Her eyes,' I said, 'are running again, there's water coming out.' 'Funny,' said Mam, 'with none going in ...'

But in the evening, brooding between bouts of cutting bread-and-margarine, me sitting with *Westward Ho!*, for the Inquisition had swerved back into focus, she said suddenly, 'If he can drink, so can I.' I could not have been more suprised if she had announced that she had joined up as a private. 'Once it is dark, I want thee to slip down to Afon Goch, *not* the Rest, for a bottle of stout, doctor's orders, keep it under the cloak and if anybody asks, it's a book.' A bottle-shaped book? I set out, disguised royalty in cannibal Trelogan, threading our way through. But nobody challenged me, and at the side-door the potman was too preoccupied to wonder about me. 'Mae Kitchener wedi boddi,' he said, 'Kitchener has been drowned.' Mam received the bombshell as if she could have warned him not to sail. 'It's the way the world is going,' she said. I watched her curiously as she poured the stout with the expertise of nine years, then drank it as if it were medicine. Funny, I thought, the first drink in our house drunk by our mother. I read, and after five minutes looked up. She had finished the glass, and sat rocking her chair in sour satisfaction. The rest of the stout was with us for days, then poured away and the Royal Messenger sent to throw the bottle down a disused pit-shaft.

It was not good, the next mornings, to watch her watch the postman pass the gate. On the eve of Dad's birthday, she gave me a penny to buy a postcard with 'To My Dear Father' entwined in forget-me-nots; I wrote carefully on the back 'Hoping you are quite well, we shall be glad to see you at home on Sunday from your loving sons, George, Job and Thomas.' The printed legend was more eloquent. 'May this Little Token, dear Father, convey, The wishes unspoken, my Fond Heart would Say.'

The feud was to be healed, at one breath, by misfortune. Friday morning, she soaping the front step, Job and I off to school, there was a click at the gate : the postman, tendering something utterly new, a telegram. I read it to her. Instead of Mrs Morgan falling off a ladder it was Dad, at work, and he was in Chester Infirmary. I looked down at her, crouched on a square of sacking with her buttoned boots showing, the scrubbing brush in her wet hand; her face was stricken. I helped her to her feet, and all was action. She sent me to get the pony-and-trap for Mostyn Station, she called over the wall to the neighbours to take Thomas, and in half an hour she was off, worried but free of the other look. She was home in the evening, exhausted, relieved : he was patched up. Obviously another hurt had been patched up too.

The summer of 1916 flowed by, in country fashion. I read *A Prince of the House of David*, a Victorian 'novel' made up of letters written by imaginary onlookers to the life of Jesus – centurions, great ladies and all sorts : conventionally reverent, but with a fresh enough outlook, as well as a whiff of my Rome, to engage me. One evening, as I returned with firewood, the idyllic stillness inspired holier thoughts in me than any indoor Sunday had ever done. Suppose I were to will every fibre of my being to being good, good, good? Unselfish thoughts, peace of mind for ever, a goodness that with one look would heal my father, not only of his leg but of any deeper sickness ... Issuing from the woods and thinking of Him with a capital H, I looked down the lane to the cross-roads; the sun was setting, every leaf serene and expectant. Far off, there approached one solitary man, haloed against the golden glow : the only sound, the note of one enchanted bird. I put down my bundle and waited, emptied of all wickedness, waited to be filled to the brim by a look as He passed, then I would know that my life was dedicated. Nearer and nearer, until – just as the glow, as if blown upon, gently faded from the sky – he turned into Bob yr Hendre, empty-handed for once (but the night was young) and ruddy from his third pint at the Rest. Like Mam with the stout, it was my first venture into the realm of religious experience, and my last.

One morning, in my class, we were told to write ten lines on 'Where We Would Like To Live'. Next day the master, a young pupil-teacher, criticized the results as usual, one by one. 'Olwen Jones, "were" without an "h" is different from "where" with an "h". Idwal Rowlands, Chester has got a capital C . . .'

Then he said, 'One effort is outstanding, perfect punctuation, one spelling mistake and a good idea of English, by George Williams.' I flushed with surprise and pleasure. He then read out my effort; I half wished he wouldn't and half enjoyed it. 'I would like to live in a town. A town is inevitably full of people, and this would mean a lot of variety on every side of oneself. Also the number of shops is exceedingly startling, a veritable treasure trove. I would like to live in a town near the raleway where the Juggernauts roar all the night. In a town there is always a new visage. In a village the faces are ever the same, and this is exceedingly monotonous.' I found myself stared at with new eyes by twenty ever-the-same village faces, and for the first time I was special not only to myself, but for a moment, to others. At mid-day, the teacher stopped me. 'You have got brains,' he said, 'you carry on.' 'Thank you, sir,' I said. I hoped he would ask me what a Juggernaut was, but he didn't. It did not particularly fire me to 'carry on', but I raced home to tell Mam. 'Your father will be glad,' she said, 'I hope it has not made anybody jealous.'

The following week Mr Fidler stopped me in the corridor with a blink and said, 'A note for your mother.' Mystified, I delivered it. In Welsh, it was to say that though I was young for it he wished to enter me, with Elfyn Roberts the greengrocer's son, for a scholarship to Ysgol Sir Treffynnon, Holywell County School. Mam sat down to scan the missive with the wariness she accorded to any written matter. 'I shall have to leave it to your father on Sunday.'

I was interested, but not excited. Holywell, which I knew vaguely by name, was a picturesque market hill-town five miles from Trelogan, on the top road to Chester as opposed to the parallel coast route through Connah's Quay and Shotton. In the woods below stood the remains of ancient Basingwerk Abbey, but Holywell was more famous for its Well of St Winifred, a lady who in an era when saints of both sexes were demonstrating startling feats of regeneration, levitation and prestidigitation, had added to the list post-decapitatory liquefaction : her severed head had rolled down the hill, come to rest and given miraculous birth to a spring which has given to Holywell, over the Catholic years, the status of a small Lourdes. As a martyr, Winifred failed to catch my imagination, which evidently required Roman blood and a panther; neither would I have pricked up my ears to be told that twenty years ago Frederick Rolfe ('Baron Corvo') had been lodged in a Holywell schoolroom discontentedly painting banners for the shrine.

The county schools of Wales, at this time, were the recently created equivalent of English grammar schools, Holywell being one of five in Flintshire, with Rhyl, St Asaph, Hawarden and Mold. Normally country children attended the village council school till the leaving age of fourteen, then went to work. If parents were ambitious and had the means, they might remove their offspring, boys or girls, from the council school and transfer them to the County; Holywell charged £2 a term, and when the school had opened in 1896, children brought with them two golden sovereigns. If parents had not the means but were still ambitious, they could enter their child for a scholarship. Pupils were expected to stay till fifteen or sixteen, when there would be an examination for a Central Welsh Board certificate : after that, specializing pupils stayed on till seventeen or eighteen, when they stood a chance of college, usually Bangor or Aberystwyth. Holywell drew its pupils from a circle which included Glanrafon, but my parents would never have considered it as a family possibility. 'Nobody goes from round here,' said Mam, 'except that red-haired Edward Rogers from Sarn, what would it cost?'

Sunday arrived, my father's first since the accident, and a happy one: old books retrieved for me from the ward, toys for the younger two. He was just finishing off the rice pudding – a family ritual – by running his knife round the basin to scrape off the burnt rim, which was my favourite delicacy. He had been telling us about parts for tanks he was helping to make; I sat, elbows on the *News of the World*. 'Well,' he said, popping a scrap into my mouth, 'what news for me?' 'Old Lloyd the deacon has died,' said Mam, cutting bread, 'and they want George to try for Holywell.' My father stopped in the middle of feeding Job and took the news like a legacy. 'Pobol annwyl, great heavens – the *County*?' His eyes were as blue and wide as the day he had kicked from his twelve-year-old feet the dust of Ffynnongroew National School. 'Da iawn, very good my boy' – winking gravely as he gave his preacher imitation – 'Mrs Williams, oes gennym athro yn y teulu, have we a professor in the family?' 'He has got to pass first,' said Mam as he lit his pipe, 'and there's the trip, five miles, how would he get there every day if he *did* pass?' 'In a tank,' said Dad without a flicker, 'I shall have one sent over from the works.'

For three weeks Elfyn and I did extra homework; I concentrated on arithmetic, my weakness. One day I suddenly comprehended, once and for ever, the mystery of Decimals, a name which had frightened me in the same way that, in literature, it would have fascinated. How the decimal-point moves, the practicality of it as a sign, why 1.3 is one-and-three-tenths and 1.125 is one-and-an-eighth, how ten times 1.125 is 11.25 – it all dawned on me with an almost mystic understanding. The neatness of it was so pleasing to my mental eye that I had a glimmer of what higher mathematicians feel when they make a thrilling discovery.

Though I was still not excited, a sense of life was quickening in me. One late Sunday afternoon, I wandered into a disused quarry spangled with gorse, holding a geography primer. I sat in the sun, leafed the pages, Steppes, Tundra, Caucasus, and turned to the coloured map at the end, of the Middle East and of

Asia. On the page, I watched the railway spidering across Russia – Omsk, Astrakhan, past Tibet, Kashmir – and suddenly, parallel with the pleasure of memorizing the names, I was warmed through and through, sitting among gorse in rustic Trelogan, by the feel of the whole world stretching into infinity around me. I saw the familiar afternoon sun (that brushed my hand turning the page, and stroked the sheep as they grazed) shining also on a train as it rumbled along the endless Georgian plains, a Juggernaut bound for Bagdad and thence for the riches of India. It was not a religious feeling, but an intuitive vision of the earth and its marvels, the beautiful and the sordid. Himalayas, Delhi, Samarkand, I loved the look of them on the page. During the sermon that evening, tragwyddoldeb-trugaredd-edifeirwch, I set them all like jewels into my memory.

Each of the three mornings, Elfyn's father was to drive us in, in the greengrocery cart, and fetch us at four each afternoon. 'The cart will bring luck,' said Dad, 'was I not in the same line of business the day of thy birth?' Mr Fidler wished us jocular good fortune in front of the class: 'At it, boys, keep the Home Tires Turning!' On the day, I woke up to a June dawn and for the first time, to the sound of fat sizzling excitedly, as it was to do on the brink of other journeys: for it was the one occasion in my life which Mam felt called for the luxury of bacon (it was only Dad who was served it normally) preceded by potas with the dripping extra-floating with crusts. I stepped into my Sunday boots, extra-oiled, clean celluloid collar. 'Turn the sleeves up,' said Mam, 'so as to wash the wrists as well, and look out for Tŷ Celyn.' She was spreading the margarine less thin than usual, for my sandwiches. 'What is Tŷ Celyn, Mam?' 'I told thee last night, it is the farm just past Whitford where I went to my Aunt Lizzie on my holidays when I was just thy age, from Treuddyn, I had fair hair then, down my back before thy father turned it white, ta ta, be a good boy.' Mrs Morgan the Rest was at her door waving spasmodically.

I knew the scenery for a mile, but after that it was the unknown, Vladivostok, Manchuria; the road flowed away under me as before, but today it unnerved me and I looked only at the

horse and kept my eyes on arithmetic. 1,760 yards one mile –
Tŷ Celyn, I saw a quick vision of a little fair girl standing
serious-faced by a haystack, then gone. Mr Roberts pointed ahead
with his whip, 'Dyna'r Ysgol Sir ichi, bechgyn, there is the
County School!' In front the road dipped sharply into the town;
the other side, as high as us, a hill on which was perched a small
spire and behind, a thick stone windmill-tower. 'Look,' said Mr
Roberts, as if in the Zoo, 'lads from the County!' We saw boys
sauntering to business, men of the world in school caps. The
wide cobbled High Street seemed alive with people; we turned
left at the Victoria Hotel, then dismounted for the steep school
hill where Mr Roberts left us, commiserating as we joined the
satchelled stream. The girls went in one way, the boys down the
road and on to the football field. I was glad of Elfyn.

The school, a warm compact building of brick and slate, was
twenty years old, but to me it could have been medieval. It was
anyway four times the size of Trelogan Council and a maze of
urban bustle, bustling more today with us forty interlopers. We
deposited caps and sandwiches in an overflowing cloakroom,
found the lavatories (mind you go before you go in, so you
won't have to go when you've gone in) and then were shepherded into the Central Hall – lined with bookcases with busts
on the top, classical, dusty plaster – each to a desk with pad,
paper and ink. Names were ticked off by a harassed lady teacher.
Nervous though I was, I could recognize that apart from the
fiddling vision before *The Juggernaut*, Miss Powell was the first
pretty woman I had ever seen, dark waves upspringing into a
hollow tunnel of hair, pink-and-white complexion, rosebud
mouth. 'There's the Headmaster!' whispered somebody, and I
caught a glimpse of a large splendid bull-like figure, in flowing
gown and mortar-board, hands holding lapels, bounding away
into a doorway. I pored over my instructions, trying to blot out
the turmoil of creaking desks and flapping papers. 'Write on one
side, name, age . . .' Silence, but for the scraping pens. '10 years
7 months; educated Council School Trelogan; address –'

A voice, outside a far door. Then the sound of the same door
not so much opening as having its handle firmly wrung like a

neck. 'Look here,' called the voice, nearer. It was a woman's, and from the loudness, in this world of quiet scholastic murmurs she could have been drunk. In a second of panic I thought of the Cap, and waited for a figure to invade us, slap Miss Powell across the face and go home. But this was a mistress, in neat white blouse under a shabby gown and high boots laced militantly and surmounted by a fierce bow. 'Look here, m'dear,' she called, and strode to Miss Powell, 'there's been a mistake, you know, fair play, give me the book of rules ...'

The few English people I had encountered said what they wished to say with limp decorum, moving the lips as if they were egg-shells; this one, while not sounding in the least Welsh, hit every vowel fair and square between the eyes like a boxer smacking a punch-ball, every consonant was wrestled with and left gasping. I realized then, before I knew life, that here was a woman larger than it; I had never seen anybody so unself-conscious. She lunged at a pair of pince-nez fixed to her lapel, pulled them with a superb gesture away from her – there was a terrified zizzing noise from an obedient coil-spring – flung them astride her nose and studied the leaflet on the table. Poised with one boot turned inwards and resting with careless ease on the other, she ate the paper zestfully with her eyes, line by line; then, mouthing the words to herself, she raised both hands in front of forty children, tucked them comfortably under her arms and stood absorbed, awkward and vibrant.

If she had had to fill in the particulars I had just penned with tongue between teeth, she might have dashed off 'Cooke, Sarah Grace (Miss), aged 33 yrs. 6 mths.' – she abbreviated anything – 'Eng., b. Bramley Leeds Yorks, educ. Bramley Nat. Sch. (of the G'd Shepherd) where at th'teen became pupil-t'cher, thereafter self-t't. At 19, Ripon Tr. Coll.; at 22, coll. at Rumilly (Fr.); at 27 took L'n Univ. ext'nal degree, Hons. Eng. Fr., and later acq. M.A.; 1911–1912 asst. t'cher Workington Gr. Sch. C'berland; 1912, H.C.Sch.' Under 'Relevant Remarks' she might have added 'Can't see why the dickens anybody shd thk any of above cld interest any manner of folk, ah well S.G.C.' Atop a vigorous frame, under sensible parted brown hair, the strongly rounded face was pale without being wan, sallow but not unhealthy, 'pallow' might describe it. Helped by the full lips, now pursed fuller in thought, the fairly snub nose widening at the nostrils gave a negroid effect which in 1916 was not appreciated, though a painter ahead of his time would have found in the thirty-three-year-old Sarah Grace a beauty far superior to Miss Powell's winsome looks: high cheek-bones, humorous mouth liberally curved, and a pair of wide, fearless and – even behind glass – strikingly blue eyes.

But, to me, that examination day, she was an English freak. 'See here, m'dear,' she said to Miss Powell, who stood waiting like a pupil herself, 'the Probationers shouldn't be tackling the same papers as the others, it's non sensical,' she made two words of it. The pince-nez zizzed back to her lapel, she paced forward and came right up to me, I was terrified; but she hurricaned past, then tacked suddenly to examine our papers, Elfyn's and mine and two little girls' next to him. 'These are all wrong to start with,' she called, then looked accusingly at the four of us. 'Are you lot Probationers?' I was too scared to answer, and Elfyn spoke up. 'Scholars Miss,' he said. 'Don't say Miss,' she said, 'my name is Cooke – they've got the wrong papers!' she called; then she surveyed us sitting there, four frightened country puppies, scrubbed and open-mouthed, threw back her head and burst into a peal of full-throated laughter. From only one place had I ever heard such uninhibited merriment, the bar at Pen-y-Maes; and once more it flashed through my goggle-eyed head – *could* she be . . . ? 'That would ha' made a fine beginning for the poor nippers,' she gurgled, 'hard lines, dash it all . . .' and strode out, chuckling to herself, eyes on the floor, already thinking of something else. We did not see her again. I was glad.

The right papers were substituted. History: (a) Who was the Kingmaker? (My face fell.) (b) What was the Inquisition? (It rose.) (c) Where was Joan of Arc born, where did she die, and how? (Still up – I could even put the accent on Domrémy.) (d) What was the Rump Parliament? (Down again.) The pens scraped; I stole a look at the clock. It was Mam's morning for turning out the parlour, I tried to see her at the clothes-line beating the rug, but found it impossible – could two such different lives as hers and mine, at this moment in this hall, be going on side by side? The thought was distracting ... Write ten lines on (a) Alexander the Great (a blank). (b) The Catacombs (my pen leapt, I wrote twenty). (c) The Pyramids, I was in luck!

And so it went on, for three days, up and down; my arithmetic was poor but the decimals helped. A week later Mr Fidler stopped me in the corridor, to say that while Elfyn had not quite got through I had just managed it, being thirteenth out of twenty-one passes, creditable considering I was the youngest and entitling me to become a pupil in September, with a scholarship of four pounds a year. Dad was pleased, Mam worried. On Sunday he brought me a Sexton Blake adventure as a token, 'Poll, we must think not of the twelve in front, but of the eight behind!' But Mam spoke of clothes, food ... I assured her that satchel and text-books would be the chief expense, though School Dinner was fourpence. The problem was transport; a bicycle was out of the question. I had just read *From Log Cabin to White House* about President Lincoln, at least I had started at the end with the murder and skimmed backwards, and I fancied the role of poor boy making good, 'Why can't I walk?' 'Five miles each way, at your age?' But I insisted. It was settled. I was to go to Holywell County School.

But I was not impatient for September, and spent the weeks walking about, and tranquilly reading. Though I was capable of seeing myself as the romantic lad with his foot on the first rung, my mind was not yet embracing the reality : that I was a child whose shrouded future was now indicated. For though from the fringe where I stood, the forest looked impenetrable, my path lay dimly defined : a tiny clearing burnt, nettles flat to the ground. Yet I had no thought of any next turn in the trail, but waited, and read. I was still sleep-walking.

Part Two

Holywell, France, Holywell
(1916–1923)

Chapter 10

Sleep-walking to School

'To be sure,' said my mother, 'it will be a stiff collar and not thy ganssi.' But one morning in the Stores she stood next to Rogers's mother : neither, a soft collar and a pin horizontal behind a tie. But you could get most textbooks second-hand; the satchel came through Mr Fidler, third-hand.

September, the new rhythm. The first morning, the satchel, at my back, contained my birth certificate and extra sandwiches in case School Dinner turned out a myth or poisoned, Mam having read in the *News of the World* of a class of infants in Ireland wiped out by mushrooms. Sunday cap on, in my pocket my 'blwch', a shallow tin containing the weekly shilling and eight-pence (five dinners) and six half-crowns towards the books, I set out into the rising sun, my first five-mile marathon. Striding down the road, my shadow longer than me, I turned and saw my mother still at the gate; I waved, she waved, shook her head and went in.

I was so intent on getting there in time and trim, that I again observed nothing of the journey; turning into High Street I was ten minutes early, just right. I called at the Town Hall, timidly proved my legitimacy, continued up to the school field, touched an imaginary finishing tape and sank on to my haunches against the wall among the piping throng, a footsore short-leg Lincoln. 'Tywydd brâf,' said the boy next to me, 'nice day!' I was flattered, he was at least eighteen, could he be the Head B— then I saw he was in rags, with running nose and a straw in his mouth. He loped off, wreathed in smiles, waving to pupils and talking to himself; he was Wil Wirion, Silly Wil, who wandered happily round the fields all day and took a puzzled interest in the school. I observed with relief that I was dressed like everybody else, then spotted a boy in a stiff halter, a poor red-faced outsider from the wilds of Halkyn. He was pointed at; it might have been me. Did the tailor who first dubbed them Eton collars dream that they would one day be taboo in the best rustic circles?

A bell rang and we filed into the Central Hall, each snatching a hymn-book: girls one side, boys the other. The staff stood poker-facing us, two masters (war-time) and four mistresses, Miss Cooke on the end. On the dais, the Headmaster – the handsome farmer-bull – read a short lesson in Welsh, during which I craned to scan the gold-lettered Honours Board: 1909, Edward Williams, County Exhibition of £30 a Year – 1913, E. G. H. C. Williams ditto, what a number of us there are ... Then he stumbled into English, to the effect that the war – er um – could only be won by writing – er um – on every ruled line, but he finished within the minute, announced a hymn, and a pigtailed girl crossed importantly to the piano; two verses, a curt English prayer, scatter. We, the newcomers, trooped into Form One, where there were boxes of caps to try on, with school crest to be taken home and sewn on the front. Girls settled to the teacher's left, boys to the right; a desk of my own, with a lid and a deep interior for my property, beautifully ink-stained and hacked with illicit initials. Eton, Harrow ... and tonight, I thought as I wrote on my exercise-book over the motto 'Goreu Awen Gwirionedd', Truth is Best 'George Wms. Form One, English' – tonight, arriving home in my cap, I shall be not George, but Eric Wms.

For period after period, a different teacher; books were allotted and paid for, time-tables copied. On top of Geography, Arithmetic and all that, there were four intimidating challenges: Geometry, Algebra, Chemistry and Latin. The first lesson was History, at which I felt fairly at ease, then Geometry, when there were distributed ruler, compass, set-square and protractor, all to be paid for. At the sight of these tools the boys round me came to life and gave the protractors a professional twirl. As they warmed, I cooled; I glanced at the girls making tittering attempts to hold set-squares right, and I knew, with a twinge of shame, that in this I was once more a Mary Ann. I understood nothing, felt a bewildered dunce, and longed for the bell to go.

The last period of the morning was hard; it is to the credit of my mother's housekeeping, frugal but fair, that I now found myself, for the first time, really hungry. It made me understand, for good, that people can forget their principles for food. We trooped into the kitchen and sat at trestle-tables, boys one side, girls the other, each presided over by a teacher. Meat and vegetables; I`prayed with my eyes for a second helping, and got one; then rice pudding, I prayed again and it worked. Then I sat in the field watching football practice, my ten miles a day ruled me out; below, the girls were playing a game called hockey. Boys and girls, walking about, did not mix. It was a fine early autumn day and I could see, past flying football and flying gym-slip, a majestic view of the estuary with beyond it the flat waterside towns of Cheshire, Parkgate but no elephants, and beyond that, in the nothing between land and sky – it was transparent weather – the faint line of Liverpool : Holywell County could watch, from one such clear day to the next, the progress upwards of the Cathedral.

Pipettes, bunsen-burners ... Then the last lesson, Latin, pretty Miss Powell. The language, by Jupiter Liberator, of my Romans and my Christians! The blackboard had no sooner told me that 'puella' meant 'girl' than I understood exactly why 'puellae' should mean 'of the girl', did not Welsh words change like that? The other boys looked puzzled and bored. 'Mensa puellae,' I said in my mind, 'the table of the girl,' and saw Stephen saying it as he looked round Ælia's room, the home she was never to see again, 'mensa puellae ...' The Latin for panther – but that could wait.

At 3.45, the bell. I had packed my homework and was out like an arrow, new cap on head, new burden on back. Boys whistled past on bicycles, wagging insolent behinds : I envied the long-trousered ones their clips. Facing, as I walked, the wooded sunset hillside behind Lloc, I saw the flash of Roman legions; but I was ravenous again and the last mile was a treadmill. I dragged myself through our gate so tired that I forgot I was wearing the cap. 'Duwedd annwyl!' exclaimed Mam, 'good gracious, you look terrible, sit down and eat!' I did, wolfishly. She asked how much the books had cost, then I told her one of my subjects was Welsh, 'But you know that one already!' I had thought so too, but filling in a form, we had been told that unless a parent specified French, it was customary to take Welsh instead. I held up my head for an hour's homework, luckily I knew the Latin, and I swooned into bed. Next morning Mam pressed a larger breakfast on me, then something for the morning break, but I demurred in case I might be caught nibbling and given a nickname.

Chaos settled into order. Seven a.m., Mam would shake me, don't wake Job; seven-thirty. by her alarm-clock on the mantelpiece between Gladstone and Disraeli, I would screw my cap down, pull my stockings up and start off, brisk and well-fed, with shining morning face, willingly to school. Gulping the blade-sharp air, my books at my back, I felt so happy that I walked into the early sun to unheard music. Nobody abroad except one old labourer leading a cart-horse – 'bore da, good morning' – who, the first day, had turned curiously (both of them, it seemed) to see what this was, so early. Ten minutes later, a bicycle. I came to expect them at the same spots, 'Bore da!', and they expected me. As I swung along the road that had once been as strange as the Steppes, landmarks approached smiling, and receded: to the right, visible for a minute behind trees, mysteriously alone in a field, twelve-foot-tall Maen Achwyfan, the Stone of Lamentation, a timeless British monument, then my road curved round the high whitewashed wall of Gelli Farm, reputed to house Roman remains, but how would I ever have time to know? ... Then, under trees and down past the parkland of Mostyn Hall, where Henry Tudor once hid on his way to overthrow Richard the Third, and into sleepy Whitford, as cradled in its hollow as Glanrafon had been. Turning the corner, my eyes went to the sun-gilded hands on the church clock, did they show five to eight? Within two minutes either way, they always jubilantly did.

Then came the lanes curling up past Tŷ Celyn – my mother

hovering somewhere – and rising into the Holway Road, a mile long and populated : on its right, moneyed mansions with black Tudor wood and bow windows and steps up rockeried gardens. In the shadows deep to the left, a disused lead-mine, but on these mornings nothing could look sinister. Bicycles go ting-a-ling, carts trundle; the morning bristles, everybody as happy on their way to work as I, mats wag out of doorways and brooms out of windows and I look back on the early labourer and his horse as if they were yesterday. Across the dip of Holywell, my eyes daily seek and find the school spire and the old windmill behind; down into Whitford Street, sharp left past Schwartz Jeweller and into bustling High Street, where the Town Hall should show a quarter to nine, and does. So I have time to dawdle at windows : Scotcher's Stationer, 'Ten Zeppelins Over London Last Night', Morgan Chemist, Madam Eustace Milliner ... I grow to recognize people : Miss Blackwell who walks every morning to the County Herald office, in the same black hat which she has worn for years and will for many more, and – later – the blind man with the boy-led donkey and cart selling summer water at halfpenny a bucket. School caps from all sides, and gym-slips, up from Greenfield down beyond the holy Well, down from Lixwm high up behind Pen-y-Ball Mountain, but none has walked as far as I, for the Flint and Ffynnongroew pupils are 'the train lots' : the 'little train' that puffs up from Holywell Junction. At the gate Silly Wil snuffles me a wistful good morning, as if he envies me. I have done it again.

Before school personalities, I was taken with school dinners; each day had its two courses and was entirely coloured for me by them. Besides Shepherd's Pie there were two dishes I had never tasted and fell droolingly in love with : Soup, and a suet pudding lined with jam and written up on the Daily Menu as 'Rolly Polly'. I talked of Rolly Polly at home, and one evening found that my mother had tried her hand at it, successfully.

But I also looked round my fellow-boys – the girls did not yet exist – and noted that the train lots exemplified a hybrid quality which new teachers from England must have found perplexing;

we were a mixture of Welsh and English. When we from the inland or the west essayed English, we were so foreign in accent and idiom as to be unintelligible; it must have been puzzling to discover that Dick O'Cordin from Tre-yr-Abbott was not so called after an Irish father, but because on being asked if he could play the piano he had answered, 'No, Miss but I got a 'cordeen.' On the other hand, the pupils from Flint – the east, the direction of Chester and England – mostly children of employees of Courtauld's Silkworks, were openly derisive of the savages from the interior who clumped to school mouthing an uncouth tongue. It did not occur to us, or to them, that their own accent was a Welsh one unrecognizably muddied with Lancashire, Irish and Birmingham. The difference was clearest down at Holywell Junction, where the two clans did indeed conjunct, to board the little train, as diverse as a Spanish and Swedish football team. And I soon picked out the opposite captains. Flint had two, Tottenham (Totty), a waggish boy with a frightening flair for nicknames – you never knew the minute – and his lieutenant, Walters (Wally), a jolly footballer whose father kept rabbits, so Totty called him 'Utch; both were bright at science, but cheerfully illiterate and determined to remain so. The opposite ringleader was Septimus Luke Evans, Ffynnongroew, a lank swarthy lantern-jawed boy as pedantic as his name, dedicated from birth to the ministry; his Welsh accent was so strong, said one master, that he would have been chased down Piccadilly as a German.

Then I began to distinguish the staff, mostly English, or they seemed so to me. In theory the men teachers were as responsible for girls as for boys, and vice versa; but in practice, through the segregation in games and one-sex subjects – Woodwork, Needlework, Cookery – it was much more likely that if a boy showed unusual traits, favourable or not, the senior master would take action, just as Miss Cooke held the female reins. Mr Boyer, whose last post had been Sheerness, must have found the hill-tribe peculiar. He was a peppery little man with a drooping moustache, whom Totty obscurely christened Bummer; as he both taught Arithmetic and had a touchline passion for games, our relationship was a simple one, indifference. Miss Cooke I never encountered – she taught only French to Form One – and like everybody else I ducked at the swish of gown and that ringing call, 'See here you . . .'

The Head, John Morgan Edwards (known as J.M., and to the boys as 'the Boss') came of a remarkable peasant family from Llanuwchlyn, the heart of North Wales. He was a younger brother of Sir O. M. Edwards, a revered figure in Welsh education; another brother was to become Vice-Principal of Aberystwyth (Edward Edwards, known in scholastic circles as 'Teddy Eddy'). O.M. had worked his way to Oxford – Balliol – and J.M. had followed, to Jesus; but he was no scholar, and the whisper ran in the playground that he had done it by tearing in at the college gate in chase of a football. Oxford had in no whit chafed at his edges and he remained imperviously Welsh, with the dry common sense of his farmer ancestors; he was as careful with money as my mother, but had my father's twinkle. There can never have been a good headmaster (and he was a good one) so unlearned : to him, English was to stay for ever a foreign tongue ('Rolly Polly' on the menu was in his hand) and it was an open secret that when he had to prepare a speech, he would trot to Miss Cooke with a sheet of foolscap, like a pupil, so that she could 'put the grammar right'. Indeed he deferred to her in everything, while she showed respect and affection for him; for he had authority, and was a father to his school. He taught Welsh; but as my mother said, we knew it already, so he would leave us with our grammars – in the little room to which five or six of us migrated to leave the rest to Miss Cooke for French – and go padding round the school on his watchdog round, mortar-board tilted happily over one eye like a football cap. I found the grammar as dull as chapel, we talked – in English, perversely – and it was a wasted period.

Dad, the first Sunday, wanted to know all about him. While Mam had been interested in the food and the temperature, he would ask, hammering metal protectors under the family boots, was he really the brother of the famous O.M.? And how was Edward Rogers? Rogers cycled the top road so I saw little of him, but he had spoken civilly to me; unofficial head boy, he was brilliant at Science and destined for college. 'A first-class lad,' said Dad. 'And he comes from a home,' said Mam, shaving salt off the great slab which never seemed to shrink, 'even more poor than we are.' Dad tapped his hammer serenely, then told us about Sam Williams, an old Holywell boy on sick leave from France, who was passing the Mostyn Works one evening as a great bell was being lowered into the furnace to be melted down for the war and great flames roared up into the sky and Sam went flat on the road shaking and sobbing, back in the trenches, poor fellow ... it was my one vicarious and vivid war experience.

Dad would then ask about Miss Cooke, with whom he was much taken. He liked to think she stalked the school in bloomers. 'How's the Suffragette?' he asked, rice-pudding bowl in hand; I said, 'She tells the masters what to do,' and he laughed till he cried. He asked about Geometry; he knew about compasses, from the ships, and scrutinized my toy pair. 'O. M. Edwards,' he said, with a sigh of repletion, and joining his fine fingers in thought, 'bettered himself from nothing, but with a careful Welsh mother like your own and his father a God-fearing farmer of the old school, yes indeed, where's my pipe, Poll?' I felt it wise not to look at her as she reached down from behind Mr Gladstone, who looked not an inch higher above reproach than did my father as he lit one of the spills she had made out of the *News of the World*.

As I settled down, the clement September days waned and winter slunk nearer. Then the morning dawned when I was awake before I was woken, awake but sleepy; a sloth in love with the nest which over the chill hours I had made for myself, a haven radiating genially under the nightshirt from the still-baby legs coiled up into puppy-stomach ... Then it came to me with a thud that what had woken me was the howling wind and rain, through which I was to walk five miles. Mam had to light the lamp, and I ate my breakfast like a child-mariner off to a lifeboat. I huddled into my topcoat and as I said ta ta, I saw in Mam's eyes the same unspeaking look she had seen in mine when it was going to be a 'bad time', Richard weather. This was a bad time, real weather.

I started up the scowling road towards a sun that had failed me; I was tugged back by wind and lashed on by rain. Squelching into Whitford, I could not see the clock, half because of the rain and half because I was crying because of the rain. If I had been dry I could have borne it, but only my satchel was waterproof, it was like being a Tommy carrying messages through gunfire knowing the battle was over and lost. The friendly landmarks were looking the other way and puddles lay in treacherous wait : no labourer, no bicycle, the whole world indoors except me and a couple of bedraggled sheep. In High Street I streamingly espied a few pitying umbrellas, until I caught up with the cocky train lot from Flint, bone-dry under mackintoshes. 'Look,' yelled Totty to Wally, 'one o' the drowned Welsh rats!' Was 'Rat' to be my nickname?

I arrived just in time for prayers, before which my course was set by a clarion command from Miss Cooke, who evidently thought that this morning Body should elbow Soul into second place, 'All damp children to the kitchen!' Ribald laughter, as four pair of boots slopped out in front of me, wet and Welsh. We hung up our stockings, then I sat with my knees as near the fire as I could bear, to make the cloth steam. It was delightful and new to be sitting there listening to the familiar hymn, and I realized with a pang of greedy pleasure, as Mrs Lloyd the cook rolled up her sleeves, that this was Tuesday, Soup *and* Rolly Polly. After prayers J.M. ambled in with brown paper which he stuffed up our trouser-legs to absorb moisture, an old remedy of his mother's; from a headmaster it seemed to me a gesture both odd and good. I spent the morning looking forward to two helpings, and the afternoon cheering up as the weather cheered up. But that night, as I snuggled into bed the wind rattled the windows; back came the thoughts of dead Kate and Nel under the ground, then I remembered the ghastly morning light and the road lost in the scuddy dark. I felt the acute Geometrical angles cutting into my sides, and the lab smells and Totty's jokes and the bleakness of drill, eyes right don't woolgather Williams

as you were, rattle and rain, rain and rattle ... teeth clenched,
I sobbed with self-pity, I can't do it, I can't ... On the stair,
Mam's swift intuitive step, 'Wti'n sâl, art thou poorly?' 'No,
doing my lessons' ... I cried more, then thought if I go on like
this I'll be wet before I get to the rain, and fell asleep. It was
another implacable morning, but I thought of the kitchen fire
at the end of it and felt better.

Next day was fine again, and my spirits were fine too; in the
dinner hour I extracted *The Great White Slave* from the school
library – a boy kidnapped in Tibet – and later there was Latin,
puellae pedes nautarum lavant, the girls wash the feet of the
sailors. I saw the yellow Mediterranean sands, the purple-sailed
galley rocking in the bay, the bronzed boys in their togas, sandals
in hand, the white-robed girls kneeling with bowls of sea-water.
Ave Cæsar ... And romantically intricated with the picture, was
the grammar: the nominative girls verbly wash the accusative
feet of the possessive sailors.

I knuckled down to ten miles a day, a routine to toughen
physical and moral fibre, forcing me to dash away tears and grit
teeth against the elements. In school I made friends and no ene-
mies: I laughed at class jokes but made none. Any adventure I
had was imaginary, and all my boldness in my own head. I was
happy to obey authority and a time-table, a timidity encouraged
by the importance of shillings and pence. Only once did paper-
money come to my startled notice: standing at the Central Hall
shelves and turning the pages of a library book, I chanced upon
a pound-note. I was so scared that I ran up to Miss Cooke as she
passed, and handed it to her. It was to be her first recollection
of me.

The last day of term, the annual Prize Distribution, when the
partitions of the Hall were stacked away and the whole Sunday-
bested school squeezed in, opposite an audience of Governors
and Parents. The staff were Sunday-bested too, as much on trial
as their pupils had ever been; Miss Cooke and Mr Boyer wore
shimmering purplish plumage. The Boss, even more bedecked,
rose like an unwilling taurine sacrifice to deliver his Report, and

rising changed from a fine figure of a country Head into an out-size schoolboy at a viva, wrestling – before a Board of parents – with a foreign tongue in which he knew, with every word he uttered, that he was losing marks. Edwards Minor (M.A. Oxon.) was doomed from the start. The pupils who had sat through this before looked sideways with a soundless schoolboy groan, but poor J.M. hated it as much as they did, he was Father Making a Fool of Himself. 'Whereas heretobefore the poss-ition of a cater-ing school – er I mean a school catering for a mixed poppilation, in North W – W . . . (a dead parent-watching pause; 'Winnipeg,' whispers Totty) Wales, in the avenues which we explore, we turn out s – s – s . . . ('Sausages,' whispers Totty) standards ass high ass any . . .' Then part-songs and recitations, then the prizes for the previous year, the athletes winning storms of applause for even Drawing Certificates. Then tea in the long woodwork room, bara brith, coloured cakes, jellies, things I had never seen and now mouth-watered after; then the walk home, suddenly without incentive for I had no hunger. Home, I opened my term's report, I had not thought of such a thing. Not too scold-ing; good for Latin and English, 'pays attention, vocabulary ex-cellent', bad for Arithmetic et cetera, 'must pay attention, lab work weak'.

Three weeks' hibernation, Holywell shut up and put away like a book. Christmas was white, and the snow blurred Trelogan into unreality; I sat reading the *Companion*, a rather dull serial about a money-lender and a Christian home, called *I.O.U.*, a title which mystified me. 'Get out this minute,' Mam called, 'while it is fine.' *Companion* in hand, red scarf, I crunched ankle-deep into snow. The sun sparkled, the snow sparkled back, the air was crisp, I felt healthier than I thought it possible to feel, stopped, and stared down at the familiar rivulet of narrative.

The sentence before me was trivial, 'He looked despondently at the blue sea, as the ship approached the harbour', but in the light poured down by the sun and up again by the snow, with the familiar world around me preternaturally still, the dazzling-black neatness of the letters, the way one followed the other, delicate as fronds, every pin-prick petal perfect, every tip and dot as impeccable as drilled soldiers, hynotized me. In a manifestation oddly born of well-being and sun and snow, I was enmarvelled by the sight of words strung in exquisitely inevitable procession so as to record, for ever, that 'he looked despondently at the blue sea'. My frost-alert mind then moved to another discovery. Why was this story dull, and yet the same words – blue, was, the, approached – had stood in line, in this same journal but in different order, to make for me a world I could not forget, why? Because the procession was not as inevitable as it looked. How wonderful to pick these flower-soldiers of print – flick and curl, curl and flick – and arrange them *in a new order*. For twenty extraordinary seconds, I had a vision of literary creation.

Then the sun went in, the snow began to melt, and I sludged home. But the next week, I told Mrs Hughes I had too much homework for the *Companion*. Not that my 'experience' bore immediate fruit. I wandered and read. The rest of the holidays were marked by *David Copperfield*, much of which I was still not ready for; but in the first part I found enough of myself to hold me enthralled. In Steerforth, I even found my elder brother, glorified and then debased. 'I saw him lying with his head upon his arm . . .'

There were also two grubby magazines (1d.) borrowed from Wally, the *Magnet* and the *Gem*, and a holiday task. The *Magnet* introduced me to Greyfriars School, to Harry Wharton and the Famous Five, Billy Bunter and Bob Cherry, the *Gem* to Tom Merry, indistinguishable from Harry. I thought both childish and preferred bookish Eric, but against my will I was drawn to this monastic world of cells called studies, of clean fisticuffs and quixotic chum-shielding. I had strong hands that looked good when clenched, but it was not easy to identify myself with fairhaired Bob, captain of everything including his soul, Cherry of the long stride and the frank ringing laugh. I essayed both on a walk, and found the laugh as difficult as the stride; I could make it ring, but frankness was beyond me. I shirked the thought that I was better suited for the bespectacled swot, and settled to be the quiet friend clumsy at footer, an accident incurred while rescuing my sister from a runaway pony, good old Williams of the Remove. The holiday task was the most melancholy that could have been conceived for the British Christmas of 1916: to arrange, in a used exercise-book, newspaper photographs 'about the War'. I had only the *News of the World* and a clotted glue-pot lent by Mr Fidler, the glue so strong that it stained the paper right through; but even without that, my photos were of a revolting drabness, messingly exploding shells, smudged nurses, invisible periscopes wavering out of dreary seas forlorn, and a blotched high-hatted Queen Mary shaking hands with a Tommy with high-bandaged head – which was which? It made a sorry volume, came in last, and was burnt.

The spring term, there was harder weather to fight, but I was hardening too. Life in Form One settled down almost into dullness. Latin progressed too slowly for me : through the partition I heard Form Two reciting the third conjugation and longed to be there. English I enjoyed, but my pleasure was marred by my attitude, inside but more and more defined, towards Totty and the Flint lot; a mixture of envy and contempt. Envy for their Philistine insouciance and prowess at games, particularly sunny Wally's; and contempt for their speech.

I did not talk much at school, except Welsh with Welsh boys, partly through shyness but mostly for another reason. Apart from my absorption in the written word, my instinct somehow was to speak English well and with as pure an accent as possible, neither drawled nor falsely refined; I was determined not to talk like Totty and Wally. The morning greeting of the Flint lot as ' 'ow-do', and 'ta-ra' was Flintese for 'good-bye', which would have sounded affected if not effeminate. In between ' 'ow-do' at nine and 'ta-ra' at four, there shuffled a conversational stream choked with banal flotsam which not all the Miss Cookes in Christendom could have sifted away. 'Oh 'eck,' Totty would say, 'you *are* flippin' 'alf-baked ...' The girls talked better, but that could hardly help me. One day, walking out to football after Geography, Wally said, 'What the bloomin' 'eck is the name o' them thingummyjigs on a roof?' I said, 'Isn't the official name weather-vane?' 'Official,' scoffed Totty without malice, ' 'ark at the flippin' walkin' dictionary!' I blushed back into my shell.

On paper though, I showed off. 'Invent three sentences to include inordinate, vehemence, parsimonious.' Wally's approach to this lacked the dash and accuracy of his footwork on the field: 'The teacher inordinates the class to write, if you talk a lot it is vehemence, people that study grammar and that are parsimonious.' I had just read an article in the *News of the World*, and for good measure worked all three words into one sentence. 'Rasputin, eerie werewolf of all the Russias, staggered up to the Czarina, his filthy locks inordinately matted as with the vehemence of the fanatic he flung a mere kopek to the subservient servant for he was a parsimonious monster.' But I confined my gymnastics to the ruled line, and it made me proud of the Ffynnongroew lot, Welsh to the core, that they showed none of my inhibitions. While I splashed knee-deep in the shallows of English, Septimus Luke Evans, without a flicker of his Savonarola mask, the clown-priest, dived headlong into the torrent. 'It iss of our surmissation,' he would boom, holding his lapels and making a square meal of every word in front of Totty and Wally and the world, 'that the effluvia from that part of this edifrice nominated "Shanghai" cannot be assignated to pupils but to Staff and therefore not of human origin, next case pleess ...' He had them foxed; grasping English like a nettle, he uprooted it.

Subject for Composition: 'The East'. I remembered *The Great White Slave* and felt at home. 'Tibet is the roof of the world, and is very enigmatic. It is the cradle of Buddhism. It is more interesting than our religion, and a study of it would not impair us, it would be good to be impartial. Buddha was an exceedingly first-rate man ...' Then followed – from an impartial unimpaired authority, 1000 hours in chapel – a detailed account of Buddhism. ''Ow d'ye spell crocodile?' whispered Wally to Totty. 'Two K's,' said Totty, and tittered uncontrollably. I spelt it to Wally; he looked surprised, and said, 'Oh ta.' I had pushed myself, but it was done now ... 'When I was a marstah in Sheerness,' rasped Totty under his breath, in Bummer's waspish voice; Wally snickered mechanically, caught the teacher's eye, coughed and coloured and smiled. The teacher smiled back and shook her head, I saw him fleeting down the touchline – 'played Walters!' ... 'Coomin' to the pitchers, 'Utch? New serial, exploits o' summat or other.' Elaine! I felt more out of it than ever.

Two days later, after a slab of Algebra, x plus 6 plus y squared, we the Welsh class stumped out, passing Rogers on his purposeful way to the lab, aglow with Science. I was downcast. 'Dysgwch y pedair gradd cymhariaeth, learn the four degrees of comparison.' The Boss was just leaving us to it, when he hesitated and turned. 'George Williams,' he said, 'tyd hefo fi am funud, come with me.' I looked up, surprised: he had never said my name before, and a summons to his study was a serious matter. I looked at the others and followed, was it my Chemistry – by then I was inside. He spoke in English. 'Miss Cooke,' he said, 'hass made a propossal to me. It iss irregular but with your Welsh so good coming from a Welsh home you are to move over to French.'

I stared at him. Miss Cooke had never spoken a direct word to me, had he confused me with another pupil? It was like being told, standing in the Coronation crowd, that royalty has expressed approval of the way you wave and wants you inside the Palace to wave there. 'Go along.' I turned. 'Not back to the Welsh,' he said, 'to Form One.' 'Yes sir,' I remembered Mam. 'Excuse me sir, will I have to get books?' 'Only one.' I sleep-walked to Form One, and heard a trumpet-call, 'Nous avons, Vous avez, Ils ont!' The class repeated it after her. Waiting for the high parrot voices to finish, I knew that my life had begun.

Chapter 11

Down the Alley

I knocked and entered, sensing with a nervous thrill that to the pupils my advent was a surprise. I had never seen Miss Cooke standing before a class; she was rubbing out on the blackboard, great trenchant sweeps. 'Please Miss –' 'I know,' she said without turning her head, 'sit down.' She tossed me a new exercise-book; I caught it and sat. 'Le Roi Georges Cinq,' she wrote in a large flowing hand, 'le drapeau du roi, les drapeaux des rois, le président Monsieur Poincaré.' She chalked the accents like proud combs on cockerels; then she spoke each word and the class intoned after her. In 'drapeau', to make the girls blush, Totty and Co brought out the 'po' sound as weighted as they dared, but it did not distract me; I was alone, for the first time, with the blackboard-face of France.

I thought, this is not past like Latin, I have heard this spoken by the nuns; it is being spoken now by thousands of people, and I am going to speak it too. Miss Cooke said, ' "Le roi" singular and "les rois" plural are pronounced the same, but you can *feel* the s on the end if you listen to the "les".' She could teach. My hand shot up, I did not care if I was showing off – I was – I desperately wanted her to know that she would have no regrets. 'Please Miss –', 'please, Miss Cooke,' she interrupted, 'please Miss Cooke,' I said undeterred, 'why does the plural of "roi" end in s and of "drapeau" in x?' 'S is the usual form but there are exceptions, copy them from Millie Tyrer and don't ask any more questions until you have caught up, it impedes the lesson.' I did not take it as a snub, I had done what I wanted to do.

'Now,' she said, taking the stance I remembered, one booted foot over the other, hands tucked under arms, 'the word "fille", meaning both "girl" and "daughter", is not easy for English people.' I saw Totty look blank, and frown; Wally was baffled. But, I thought, dribbling down a French touchline out of his reach – in Welsh 'merch' means the same two things, what is difficult about it? My promotion was going to my head. Five minutes later I discovered that in French every stick and stone was either masculine or feminine, and that adjectives followed nouns and changed gender, but so did they in Welsh, pen mawr, llwy fawr! After dinner I doubled back into the classroom, wrote 'G. Wms, French,' and spent thirty fleeting minutes copying Millie Tyrer's notes. The recurrent virile thud of the football was no longer a reproach; with its every smack I was smacking back, with a stroke of the pen. 'Le pont, the bridge.' I hardly had to write that, 'pont' is the Welsh for bridge, as 'ffenestr' is for window.

The afternoon walk was the shortest yet, and the least hungry; the day's notes in my hand, in the crisp sun, I bookwormed my way home. I spoke the words aloud, 'René est un garçon, Louise est une petite fille.' People smiled but I did not care. In the twilight of Whitford, a child was crossing the bridge with her mother. 'Louise,' I said to the Welsh air, 'la fille de Madame Pascal, est sur le pont.' 'Any news?' said Mam. 'Oh, this tastes good,' I said, 'as good as school dinner – yes, Miss Cooke is teaching me French.' She looked at me, puzzled. 'The cook teaching you French?' '*Miss* Cooke,' I mumbled between Rolly and Polly, 'the one who talks as if she was a man.' 'Is she going to be like that Mr Hedges? We don't want your father putting her in her place with his soft words, French, well ...' 'It's like Welsh, only different.' 'He went there in that ship of his, do you want some more?' 'Merci, Mam,' I said, 'je suis le fils de Madame Williams.' 'Well,' said Mam, 'you are a quick one, how much was your book?'

Miss Cooke and I were to exchange no personal word, even of small talk, for several years; but the unspoken challenge was taken on, from a dynamo of thirty-four to a tyro of eleven. That night I worked late, I was determined to catch up, and in miraculous time. The next day I rose in the half-dark with more alacrity, and the winter sun seemed to come up minutes earlier, with a cold but gladdening eye. Brain refreshed, I stepped out past Maen Achwyfan of the wise worn face, and found all the words which I had crammed last night higgledy-piggledy into a drawer of memory, now neatly marshalled, 'J'ai un oeil, j'ai deux yeux ...' As I dipped into Whitford, 7.55 to the second, it came upon me that 'cheval' was the same as 'ceffyl' (pronounced keffil) which is Welsh for horse, and that 'cavalier' had to do with both. 'The Keffileers and the Roundheads,' I said to the hedgerows, exhilarated at my discovery: I should have liked Miss Cooke to know of it. Ever after, to me a 'Chevalier de la Légion d'Honneur' was to be an old Welsh farm-hand with a red ribbon in his lapel. Striding past Tŷ Celyn, with a French circumflex, I was aglow with new knowledge, a walking dictionary and proud of it.

I was careful not to exasperate with questions, but by the end of the following week I had caught up. Two weeks later, February weather, with boys running to clamp hands on the hot pipes between lessons, I met Miss Cooke who said, 'See here, Williams, what time d'you leave home?' 'Half-past seven, Miss Cooke.' 'I'm sure your mother would agree that before school you could do with a cup of hot cocoa.' I did not know cocoa. 'You know where my lodgings are?' 'Yes, Miss Cooke.' I didn't but dared not contradict her. 'Right, nip over before school tomorrow.' I did not tell Mam, I thought I would try the cocoa first.

Next morning I put on a spurt, it would not do to take the cocoa and then be late for prayers, and stole up to her lodgings, opposite the school: the Tudor-beamed pebble-splashed villa of a preacher. As I opened the gate a couple of girls looked at me curiously. I blushed, but could be collecting a book, tried to unblush, but they had gone. 'In there,' said a mild Welsh matron, and disappeared. I looked pityingly after her, fancy being Miss Cooke's landlady: 'Mrs Evans, you've dusted my table abominably, four a.m. and not yet light but by jingo I'll have you out of bed before you can say Jack Robinson ...' On the corner of the plush table-cloth, on a spotless napkin, a large steaming cup. I perched on the edge of a chair, sipped, and peered surreptitiously round.

It was a clean drab room overrun by an alien personality, as if the coloured-glass doors facing Holywell Mountain had been opened for sixty seconds to a niney-mile-an-hour hurricane and then calvinistically sealed. There were the remains of a wolfed breakfast: scattered crumbs, an egg-cup on its side and half a cup of tea slopped into the saucer, not by a shaking hand but through an abstracted eye. The preacher's library, as safe behind the glass of the bookcase as the Highland cattle behind theirs, stood marshalled dogma shoulder to dogma, but the hurricane had got at the rest of the room and strewn it with literary débris; yet it was not disorder, but rather order of a tempestuous kind. Stray sheets, splashed with memoranda, spilled over an aspidistra; on the sideboard, a French periodical, its back broken and pages pinned back and scored in red, lay next to a book called Voltaire, both hemmed between a framed Methodist and a cast-iron sheep, while a voluminous newspaper was spread-eagled over the arm-chair: the *Observer*, the name was new to me. On the floor, a pile of exercise-books corrected, slapped-to and flung down like shelled pods, and on the sideboard, next to an umpire's whistle (hockey), another pile open, one on top of the other, meekly awaiting the eviscerant pencil ('rubbish!', 'v. gd.', 'fiddlesticks!', 'well tried'). Blown open on to chair-arm and ledge, every variety of text-book, wedged with book-marks: Latin, French and even Spanish. This last puzzled me, the idea of Miss Cooke being her own pupil was beyond my grasp. Never once at this daily ritual did I see her. Mam approved, 'You said thank you?' 'Mind she doesn't poison you,' said Dad, 'these suffragettes are very absent-minded, she might slip something in out of that Lab, watch out!'

Miss Cooke's next move came on a morning of sleet and hail. 'See here, Williams,' she said, braking amid the traffic of the Central Hall, 'my family are to do with leather, draw your foot on this.' I unfolded a section of brown paper, took it to the lavatories and drew my foot. A week later, next to cocoa, lay an opened parcel; two boots set fair and square for rain and snow, seven-league Yorkshire leather built strip by strip for an infant Hercules. They made what I had on look like a couple of wrinkled old country ladies, but pride insisted that I wear these one more day, to prove that their case was not too parlous. Also, would it not be better tactics to arrive home with the new ones under my arm? I was right. 'What is the parcel?' said Mam. I explained, between mouthfuls. 'Oh,' she said, with a quick glance at my feet, which straight from five miles of muddy highway looked their worst. I knew her unspoken dread of her children going barefoot, to her the mark of destitution, 'Has somebody said anything?' 'Oh no,' I said, chewing, 'Miss Cooke said what good boots mine were, but her family make them, the place is full of boots, they don't know what to do with them.' After my tea I changed into the new ones and stamped around. They caressed my ankles with the gentle touch of the strong; on Sunday I had to change into them for Dad. 'Dear Miss Cooke,' he wrote in his elegant hand, in the ruled book he used for his bets, 'We are very thank-full to you for taking interest' – the pen made a fastidious circle as he pondered the right word – 'in our son's well-fare, and let us hope he will be a credit to us all' – a final hover while formality was decided on, plus abbreviation – 'we remain Yrs. Obediently R. and M. Wms.' 'Poll,' he said, licking the envelope with a flourish, 'Dic goes to the top of the class!'

The iron began to seep out of the weather, and Trelogan grew lighter and younger with every evening that I reached it. Dad was in good shape, we looked forward to Sundays, it was a happy spring.

Leaving the school field, I gave a fleeting look down at the estuary, past the football already thumping; the tide was out, the western light rosy and softer-fingered on the distant sands than I had ever seen it, and Cheshire as mysterious as when it was Africa. A gentler ray picked out a tiny boat. Who was he, down there? A fisherman from Brittany – I knew it was too far, but I liked that – seeking his drowned love? Or from Roma Antica? Would he answer, to a call across the sands, 'Civis Romae sum, amicusque imperatoris ...?' Did he know, as he rested on his sunset oars, that he was watched by a schoolboy? But the field was thickening with ringing bicycles and girls racing down for hockey, I had no time for scenery, it would do when I was old, and I was smartly off. The cyclists whistled by me, mischievous haunches up and down, but though I still envied them, the envy, like everything else with the spring, was not so sharp. As I sped down High Street, my mind lingered with the lonely fisherman. Then I rehearsed my part once more for tomorrow.

There was to be fifteen minutes, before the final bell, when members of each year's French class would recite a page of dialogue from their text-book. Ours was a minute-long discourse between René (Wally) and their English guest John. As John, I had nine uninspired lines – 'en Angleterre on mange des pommes de terre . . .' – but at the end René revealed that I had eaten frogs. 'Des grenouilles?' I answered, 'j'ai mangé des grenouilles? Non . . .' I waited to practise that bit till I got into the deserted lanes, for though all we were to do was stand still and speak at each other, I had a plan. The school crammed into the Central Hall, we appeared first.

I was intensely nervous, but curiously calm. Footballer Wally mumbled and grinned and reddened, but nothing could have stopped me speaking clearly and correctly, or feeling priggish and happy as I did so. When it got to the frogs, I spoke 'Des grenouilles?' as if I had not taken it in, turned to leave, stopped, turned back and exclaimed, 'J'ai mangé des *grenouilles?*' with an incredulous inflexion matched with staring eyes, which earned me the hoped-for burst of laughter. Then the coup de théâtre: I pressed both hands to my stomach, muttered 'Oh non non non . . .', pulled a nauseated face and ran off the platform. In my first part, as a Welsh schoolboy impersonating a London schoolboy talking French, I had brought the house down. If this public test of nerve – to break through the dangerous glass of my own self-consciousness – had been attempted as myself, say in a humorous debate, I would have failed ignominiously; but I had been disguised behind a new language, and that worked the miracle. For ten seconds, I had become another boy.

'Lay *grunnywee?*' mimicked Totty next morning, 'ba goom, 'Utch, e's a downy one, norralf 'e is!' But it was not ridicule, they knew I had meant to be grotesque, and for the rest of the day, girls opened their desks and found frogs in them. I suspected that Miss Cooke had put it down to an attack of showing off; but I had had a squib of success, and I was satisfied.

We broke up for Easter, and I walked home in mellowing sunlight, holding my second report. I was top in French: in firm flowing hand, 'Excellent, phenomenal progress, S.G.C.' The rest was gratifying too, top in Latin and high in English, and even my bad subjects were struggling out of the bog. The world was full of bird-song and long twinkling shadows of trees and promise of good reading, *The Young Fur-Traders, The Swiss Family Robinson, Jane Eyre, The Fifth Form at St Dominic's.* 'This word,' said Mam, bread-knife in hand, pointing to 'phenomenal', 'what does it mean?' 'Good,' I said.

It had been a wonderful walk; it was to be my last. Mr Fidler called, there was a bike going second-hand. Four pounds! Then Mam relented, but I had a feeling that she had no intention of drawing on the box under the bed. Sunday, the report lay next to Dad's dinner. 'Top!' he said, 'what's pheno-meenal, George?' 'Better than anybody else,' said Mam, 'there's a bicycle going.' She looked at me, I went out. When I got back it was settled. Had he suddenly remembered an imminent bonus? ... I learnt to ride with difficulty, having by now a rooted idea that I was physically awkward; try as I might, I was unable to board the machine by vaulting a leg nonchalantly over, and ended by leaning it sideways and bestriding it stationary. It was like sitting on a fence with both feet on the ground, a stance sensible perhaps for a politician, but not dignified in a schoolboy. Then the machine was put away till school, it might wear out; but I did not mind, I was content to walk the fields, read, and do my homework. I was beginning to take to the idea of being top of the class.

It was with a guilty pleasure that on the first morning of the summer term, I rose nearly an hour later than ever before, and set off at twenty past eight. A familiar landscape had thawed into beguilement; my satchel strapped behind the seat, I bowled past Maen Achwyfan and carefully down into Whitford. Near

Tŷ Celyn I passed myself, last term, toiling along satchel on back, and almost waved; a minute later, all down Whitford Street I wiggled my behind, very slightly, a new free-wheel face, and in High Street nodded self-consciously to people I hardly knew, such as Miss Blackwell and the boy leading the blind man's donkey. A small problem, looming large, was the cocoa. I no longer deserved it, but how to tell Miss Cooke? I walked over, reeling after the ride, drank my potion in the still holiday-tidy room, and left a message on a corner of paper. 'Dear Miss Cooke, thank you very much, I have a bicycle, yours obediently, G. Wms.'

Everybody in H.C.S. looked fresh for the summer, including the staff. At noon I was nothing like as hungry as usual, then watched a ritual I knew by name, from Eric and the *Magnet*: cricket. The same boys played it as had shone at football, but with bat and knee-pads their personalities seemed on the way to elegance. The game was so slow that I thought I might have a chance, then I winced at the vicious crack of ball against bat and only ever played as twelfth man. I liked the look of tennis, but that was the girls' game and that was that. As the days grew hotter, during the dinner hour I wandered round the field with John Rees Evans, the boy from Halkyn with the stiff collar. We would roll in the lush grass below the hockey; when it got very hot we wrestled like kittens, one astride the other, laughing, panting, until the prostrate one took the other unawares, heaved him over, pinned him down and started tickling and mock-twisting arms. Sometimes we played leap-frog, and once went piggy-back, jogging along until Totty, fielding near us, shouted out 'Look who's playing dogs!' Loud laughter: we disengaged foolishly and walked away. Bred in the country, I had observed nothing of animal life and had the haziest idea of what the gibe meant; we mooched along past the girl-couples strolling arm-in-arm in soft straw hats, neat and shapeless and heated-looking in their gym-slips and black stockings. I liked the way those with long unplaited hair shook their heads to flick it from their shoulders, then delicately, with two fingers, curved a strand behind the ears. But there were none like Annie.

At a quarter to four, a quick run to the shed and I was one of the Boys. I could hardly be clipped round the ankles, being still in knickerbockers, but at least I could kneel, pump, give my tyre the brisk professional thumb-squeeze, and stand with quickly bandied knees to tweak my trousers away where they had ridden up : they hadn't, but the gesture made me feel like a man. And as I sailed down the hill as independent as any, who was to know from my pursed lips that I could not whistle?

The ride home was a spin through long summer afternoons, which I would lengthen by skimming round through Lloc and the honey-suckled lanes skirting Caerwys. The Holway Road was being refaced; and the tang of hot asphalt was for me a scent to evoke for ever the bland indulgent countryside, the pleasure of pedalling buoyant with thoughts of work done and work to do, and a quiet confidence getting surer every day; I was healthy and relaxed, it was a pleasure to be alive. The two terms of walking had got my body into a training which I would have resisted on the football field, and now I began, without loss of mental zest, to unwind physically. Gliding with gentle pedal along the level roads, where every bird and butterfly, every sheep and cow was a friend to stroke in my mind, I became conscious of an agreeable languor. As over my saddle the smooth loins slid rhythmically up and down between slumbrous hedgerows, without knowing it I was wheeling through my last unawakened summer. I made no friend; still no sign of my elder brother with the honest eyes and the warm hand-clasp, but I was content.

July 1917, enormous news. My father had been transferred to the big Summers' Steelworks across the river from Shotton, a permanent job as fireman, and we were to move to Connah's Quay.

The news was enormous because it signalled a change not only of domicile but of school : Connah's Quay, four miles beyond Flint, lay in the circuit of Hawarden County School. I took a note from my father to J.M., giving the Obedient tidings; in my heart I hoped that steps might be taken. They were, immediately; next morning the Boss sent for me – I was not obliged to transfer, and the school would be responsible for my train-fare, four pounds a year. 'You see,' said J.M., breaking into one of his rare smiles, ' 'rydani ddim eisio dy golli di, we do not want to lose thee.' 'Thank you sir,' I said, and as we shook embarrassed hands, he turned from an enormous mortar-board-and-cane man into a more formal Dad. I was glad, for Holywell was already a part of me.

I could now get excited. Not only was I moving to the English world I had glimpsed that Juggernaut week-end, I would be travelling daily with Wally and Totty and Co! One July morning, the bike sold, I walked from Mainstone Cottages for the last time – we had lived there two years – leaving Mam bustling for the van which was to transfer all the furniture, as well as her and Job and Thomas. There had been talk of my staying to help, but she would not hear of my asking permission 'after them taking that trouble'. There is no doubt that I was at moments a sheltered child. After school I dashed down High Street, turned unfamiliarly off it, settled into the little train for my second railway trip, and watched the girls patter sedately down the steep path followed by Totty and Co charging with satchels flying and pretending to miss the train by a hair's breadth. Girls in the one long compartment, boys in the other. The Ffynnongroew lot kept primly to one end; 'We perceive,' called Septimus, 'a new member of the Order of Flintarian Idiots.'

He was right. 'Coom on Wally, it's my bloomin' turn for the bloomin' corner, yarooh cavey me 'earties – honest guard we wasn't doin' anythin', Good Guard keep yer bloomin' 'air on yah Ah'm poofed!' A prolonged cackle, then silence as the train flowed round through the dappled woods, past the ivy-hallowed ruins of Basingwerk, 'Whorrer flippin' 'ome for 'eroes', past the Paper Mills, 'Poo whorrer flippin' niff', and into Holywell Junction, four sets of lines. The Ffynnongroew lot went one way, we the other, to await a train which loomed mysteriously out of the western nowhere. Bets as to the engine, would it be 'Duchess of Roxburgh' or 'Heart of Midlothian', then the dash for an empty compartment, one of them hanging impudently out of the window to forestall invasion, then a grubby game of whist on an atlas. Besides Totty and Wally there were two second-year boys and third-year Harold Mears, a shifty fourteen-year-old in long trousers who lit a fag-end out of a tin. 'Coom on lads,' he said, 'who's for it today?' I thought he meant a cigarette. 'Give it a rest,' said Wally, 'let's 'ave a sing-song, where do the Flies go in the Wintertime . . .'

They tumbled out at Flint. 'Pick ooz an empty when yer gerrin tomorrer lad, ta-ra!' The compartment was strangely still as I passed behind the little suburban villas, the ruined bulk of Richard the Second's castle, and I now had the fifteen minutes of pleasant solitary confinement which were to be my daily transition from school to home. The villas soared swiftly up to the shooting shadow of a bridge, then swept down into the open, telegraph wires, swoop and cut, swoop and cut, the melancholy Dee sands to the left, then a long tunnel where I stared through the dark window at my other self sitting inscrutably there, more sands, then a shooting bridge, the slow-down, then out of tiny Connah's Quay Station and down the slope into straight endless High Street, I looked up a stubby side-road, was that it, then I saw Job, bright with guidance in strange surroundings; we descended a dark narrow alley between a bread shop and a butcher's. 'Paid a syrthio!' he called gaily, 'don't slip!' My feet clattered down treacherous brick paving, as they were to clatter for the next ten years.

'We live down the alley between Whitworth's and Scott's.' 314a High Street, Siamese twin of 314b, the two known as Bennett's Cottages, was a replica of our Trelogan home, in a very different setting. On three sides we were hemmed in by the backs of dwelling-houses, including Victoria Row, which ranked just beyond that paper-thin barrier dreaded by my mother: it was a slum. I raced past the blistered front door and down the side dirt-path to a tiny brick-paved back yard, separated by a low wall from the yard of 314b. In the wall, knee-high and new to us, a water-tap; in the corner the earth petty, and a banged-together wooden shed, nailed with rough tarred felt but housing a brick boiler and, in a day or two, the coal and a backless chair with tin basin for ablutions. Behind the shed, our ashpit; then a tall fence and the railway embankment, so near that when a goods train clanked to a stop you could call to the fireman.

Indoors was still chaos; but the sun was out, there had been the train and now all new, nothing worried me. Dad was at work. After tea, as I helped my mother scrub the tiled floors, she stopped and said, 'Dost think it will be all right?' 'Oh yes,' I said, touched that she had consulted me, 'anyway it is better than Big Liz's!' 'Yes, it is,' she said and went on scrubbing; I had done no harm saying that. 'The railway is terrible,' she said, 'he never told me, the noise keeping us all awake and smuts all over my washing and children barefoot up in that street, and a pawnbroker, I saw them.'

In the back bedroom, in the deep of the night, I was suddenly woken, terror-stiff, by the thunder of a lion pouncing, hot breath on my face, I shot bolt upright; round the walls raced and roared and rocked a million lights and shadows, taking the shrunken little room by the shuddering throat and shaking it within an inch of its gimcrack life – then, as suddenly, all was over; in one second the sulphurous beast was a hundred miles away, and the room and I huddled back into the silent anonymous dark. The Irish Mail had passed, London-bound.

For the following ten days though, the Flint lot occupied me more than the new house. Next morning I walked up the hill to Connah's Quay Station, again as I was to do for years, and watched the train come serpenting out of the early sun, and halt for me alone; I picked an empty compartment, which rocked me back into my school self. At Flint I hung out and waved eagerly to Totty and Wally, as if I had bribed the guard to keep me an empty. They settled to belated homework. ''Arf a mo',' said Totty to Jimmy Willis, a big awkward boy with spectacles, ''ow many cubic oojahs d'*you* make it, 'Airy Jim?' A loud guffaw and 'Airy Jim blushed, though his hair was short and inconspicuous. Walking out to the field, I said to Wally, 'why is he called 'Airy Jim?' He laughed heartily, 'because he's got 'airs!' ''Airs, what's that?' 'You know,' said Wally breezily, 'between your legs, an' you know what Totty is.' I stared at Willis, bumbling short-sightedly about and teased for his freakish secret. If that happened to me, I thought, I'd keep it to myself.

Yet I was curious. Walking down to the train, two gym-slipped girls in front and two behind, I found myself, half intentionally, in step with Willis. 'Why do they call you 'Airy Jim?' He blushed. 'I could kill that Totty,' he said. 'But you shouldn't have told them,' I said, in a worldly manner. 'But I never did, they pulled me trousers down in the train they did an' all, it's joost a game see, be soombody else next time.'

I settled in my corner, shut my ears to the clamour and opened the homework to which I had given my attention for nearly a year. The same work, but no longer the same boy. I found it difficult to concentrate, for something was looming at my elbow to which I had never given a conscious thought; I had been a candid, even prudish child. As the little train swung me like a giant Gulliver hand not to be gainsaid, round the warm green-wooded curves past Basingwerk, I felt innocence sliding insidiously away from me.

Till now, my secret thoughts had been secret out of fear of ridicule, never from shame. I was ashamed now, this thought was secret-secret. All the people I had ever known – not only family, teachers, Annie, but the intimates of my imagination, Ieuan, Mifanwy, Tom, Jane Eyre, David Copperfield – I was suddenly removed from them. I stared out of the window, with behind me the cackle of the boys, shrill-hoarse, hoarse-shrill, and distantly, through glass, the milder babble of the girls. The sounds came strangely to me. For the first time, I looked down at my own body, Geo. Wms. 11 yrs. 8 mths. I studied the patched corduroy, tight-ribbed over the knees and rubbed smooth inside the thighs; below, the plump black calves and the sturdy boots. Above one knee, I could feel the garter tight round the leg; if I pulled my trousers up and the garter away, the elastic would have stamped a livid pattern on the white skin. Somebody laughed, my face burned.

At the Junction, we climbed into an empty compartment. There seems to be a connection between lubricity and the locomotive; once a train is travelling, with the irremediable isolation of the uncorridored compartment, the powerful shooting of wheels over points, the ruthless drive forward of the great steel body through passive countryside, small wonder that repressed travellers suddenly forget themselves and chase lone frantic women up past foggy photographs of seaside resorts to the communication cord. 'Coom on,' said Totty, 'whist?' 'Boogar whist,' said Harold Mears, 'too 'ot – coom on Totty, 'Ector Baird!'

Poor pimply Baird flushed and shrank – 'I'll bash your ear-'ole in –' but they were all round him, school savages whooping, 'Leggo – get 'is oother leg, Wally ...' I watched, repelled and fascinated. The struggle became so fierce that somebody bumped against the window and there was the crash of the pane breaking. 'Get the flippin' glass out!' I jiggered the pieces off and lowered the window so that only the smooth top showed. 'Can't find 'is bloomin' braces – ooh luke, joost a bloomin' girl – oh no ba goom boot near enoof, aw right lads, fair's fair' and snivelling Hector Baird pulled up under-drawers which only an overworked mother had ever set eyes on, 'Coomin' to the pitchers, 'Utch? Tom Mix, bang, bang, bang! ...' And when they tumbled out, Hector Baird's face was red but dry, and no harm done.

The door was wrenched sternly open by the guard. 'Next door heard glass, know anything about it?' I looked up from my book, 'It was further along.' The train started; Eric, Harry Wharton and I had saved the day. It was cooler now, with the wholesome breeze from the estuary. I began to read, then my child's curiosity climbed on top of me. For the first time, gravely, like a doctor, I examined myself. Smooth as egg-shell. I sat back relieved, pushed the matter into the recesses of my mind, and opened 'G Wms, Form One, Trig'. At the Quay I proffered my season ticket. 'Good trip, son?' 'Nothing to report,' I said and walked modestly home, swinging my satchel. Next week, the holidays.

And with the holidays, seven weeks, my centre shifted to 'the Quay'. In moving, we had travelled fifteen miles, but it was to the doorstep of England, and the fifteen might have been two hundred : we had left a Welsh peasant village for a working-class township where our language was a joke. Our first Saturday, coming out of Bell's Stores, I found two boys baiting five-year-old Thomas, 'Coom on Taffy, say that foony thing again!' He, speaking no English, had asked them something in Welsh, and they were doubled up with mirth. 'Are you 'is broother luke you' – the accent was mixed with Staffordshire, and thicker than the Flint one – 'Taffy wuz a thief ...' My brother burst into tears. I lost control, raised a bag weighted with tinned salmon and swung it like a flail : a yell, a trickle of blood and I walked away, lugging startled Thomas. Shoppers stared after us, muttering; we might have been boys from Alsace in a suburb of Stuttgart.

I knew once and for all that in this tip-end of Wales I was an alien, and would remain one. There was a tiny Welsh community attending the Wesleyan Chapel in High Street, to which Mam sent us our first Sunday and from then on; pitifully sparse, they were simple friendly people, trying hard to fructify a Welsh oasis without the incentive of real exile. The other children in Sunday school were younger and we had nothing in common except goodwill; I was soon giving a series of blank nods while marshalling the new French words I had set aside to ripen during the sermon. Apart from Sundays, the whole time I lived in the Quay I did not make the continuous acquaintance of a single person. There was no animosity on either side, our neighbours were a good-natured clan without pretensions; possibly the class above us had these, the bank managers, the solicitors, the bigwigs in the Steelworks, but I never swam anywhere near their ken. My roots were to the west.

Thomas, alas, was never teased again – alas because insensibly, from now on, our family was to lose its complete Welshness. With my brothers attending the council school and racing home chattering in English, within a year our parents were talking English not only to us but to each other in front of us; within another year, Thomas had lost every word of the language with which he had been taunted. 'Brachdan', bread-and-butter, became 'buttee', but the change was most marked by their names. Thomas became, for life, Tom, 'Mrs Williams, can your Tom coom out to play?' and Biblical Job (Percival he understandably withheld from his mates) was overnight shabbified into Joe; but to their mother, Joe was for ever Job and Tom Thomas, pronounced Tommoss. Her English never became good, she was not a talker and had no leisure for listening; Dad's had limits, but he made a little go almost anywhere.

314a settled into home. Its great drawback, confirmed by the winter, was that it was below sea-level; certain days, through the grid under the tap, water would well remorselessly up and flood the yard. Wall-paper would discolour and curl dismally away from crumbling mortar, and three months after I had stored my *Companions* on the floor in the parlour cupboard, I found them mouldily stuck together for ever. I had to burn them.

But the kitchen was small and not hard to warm, and became the living-room for the five of us. It was dominated by a handsome oak dresser, the only Treuddyn heirloom, containing the family wardrobe and linen. Under the little window which framed back yard and embankment, the hoary horsehair sofa; between sofa and fire – oven and grate, immaculate with blacklead and gleaming irons – my father's chair, hard but with arms; behind him a fretwork rack (Job's work) for his spills, and the cupboard for crockery and groceries. Under the stairs, which occupied a quarter of the room, the 'spench', a dark place of crannies which would have been a huddle of muddle but for my mother's unconquerable sense of order. Besides a sack of potatoes, it stored – on a dozen nails and in rejected boxes on their sides, each in its appointed place – boots, shoe-box complete with rags, brushes and polish, tools, Dad's shaving tackle, old newspapers to be sold to the chip-shop at a penny a bundle, paraffin-can, saucepan, frying-pan, washbasin and an immense earthenware breadpan. On the high mantelpiece over the brass airing-rail, the tea-caddy faces, grimmer every year and by now bursting with laces and string. Hanging from the ceiling, the oil lamp.

Next to the spench, against the stairs, a small round table where Mam stood ministering at a chipped marble bread-slab, or washing up. She had to move for one of us to get to the spench ('Can't you wait till after?') just as Dad had to bend for her to get to the cupboard. Behind the back door, on one nail, the coats of the whole family; in front of the sofa, the main table, neatly table-clothed with yesterday's newspaper. Round the table: Tom and I on the sofa, Job on a kitchen chair nearest the door, Mam in the middle of the room within reach of her bread-slab. 'I am no sooner down than up again, I never saw any boys eat like you.' 'But Mam,' said Job once, 'you've never known any other boys . . .'

Upstairs, the front room was mostly occupied by the matrimonial bed; in the back, I was in a single bed next to the window, the other two in the double. On the walls, 'God is Love' with dim lilies of the valley, 'Jesus Wept' with faded roses, and two rotogravures given away with the *Companion*, one of a putteed private embracing his cloche-hatted fiancée ('Farewell dear heart, I go to fight for thee'), the other of him kissing her, sprained of arm and promoted ('Safe home dear heart, 'tis worth the fight, To see thine eyes with love alight.') Over the tiny empty fireplace, most unexpectedly – again given away with something – a voluptuous female in transparent blood-red draperies, curled up asleep on a Pompeian terrace: Lord Leighton's 'Flaming June', had the 'Lord' made her respectable? On the mantelpiece, a dwarf hand-lamp never lit unless we were ill, when it sat glowing ominously between the beds next to the soda-siphon which seemed essential to any bed-sickness, whether influenza or a broken ankle. Under a bed, the inevitable chamber-pot, never for serious relief; in the small hours of the bitterest night, the improvident one would half-dress and creep shivering out to the yard. In the day-time, for the simpler need, we boys would visit the ashpit behind the shed; often, bemused with reading, I would look up to see the fireman and the driver of a dawdling goods train waving and grinning.

The water schedule was simple; the tap in the yard was a boon, but it meant that in all weathers, one of us had to go out every time the kettle or a bowl had to be filled. In theory we washed in the shed, but the door did not close properly and in cruel weather we would bring in the bowl on to the end of the table, 'Don't splash in the shugger!' Tuesday was the tough day of the week, Washing Day. Breakfast over, Mam put on a no-nonsense expression and an old cap of Dad's, fetched soft water from the rain-butt and retired belligerently to the shed, to wrestle with boiler, mangle, three-legged dolly-peg and a basketful of linen; she would often go in blue with cold, and emerge fug-red and harassed. She hated Washing Day as much as she hated the petty for being attached to next-door's. She intensely disliked being seen going there by her neighbours, even to hang the neat squares of newspaper; wrapped in her shawl, she would open the back door and start back testily, 'That woman's in her yard again ...'

Our routine was governed by Dad's shifts, which had the symmetry of a circle in three parts : eight hours a day, one week six-till-two (mornings), the next two-till-ten (afternoons), and the third ten-till-six (nights), round the clock and start again. Financially my mother could still never relax; every Friday the attenuated pay-packet, three pounds, was handed over by its earner like a drug of which his wife could only be cured by sniffing small portions. Said next-door once to her, 'With me oosband an invalid, Mrs Williams, you *are* looky, a man that clocks in the week round an' fetches 'ome four-quid-ten!' That morning Mam pounded his working shirts with a set face.

She had to concede that the steadiness of his work steadied his leisure. The fact that I was becoming 'a credit' may have helped too; he formed the habit of collecting exam results from the *County Herald* and carrying them in his wallet, next to his seaman's discharge papers, till they blackened and fell to pieces. He was rapidly promoted to foreman, and in his overalls was to tread the mill of his three shifts, except for rare illness, day in day out, Sundays included, for the next fifteen years : a remarkable record for a vulnerable man.

When he fell, he fell. Six-till-two was the tricky week. Round 5 a.m., mostly in the dark, I would half-hear Mam getting his breakfast, both of them silent because of the hour and because of us. There would be the rattle of his tin of 'snap', his dinner, and the purposeful wage-earning footsteps would fade away round the front; winter mornings I would huddle up, remember my own dark Trelogan days, and count myself in luck. But his afternoon return along High Street, where he had rapidly become a figure as welcome as the sun, was not always so purposeful; every hand-wave was a snare. The New Inn was Mam's present enemy. I sensed the situation as I opened the door; either he would be in his chair contentedly preparing his bets, or Mam would be pottering and hovering, 'Look at his dinner . . .'

Summer, we could get safely out of the way; winter, we had to stay in the firing-line. After a couple of false alarms – 'shh . . . no, next door, she's poking her fire' – the heavy boots of that sober-sided Elwy Street policeman would thud carefully down the side of the house, a fumble at the latch, and he was in; a pause, then the door banged shut. He could tell from the way none of us looked at him that we knew, how could we have smiled at this stranger? and at once it irritated him. He would hang up his coat, then sink so heavily into his chair that it scraped the tiles. In the leaden silence, I sat staring at my book, or at the French on the back of the H.P. Sauce bottle, 'cette sauce appétissante . . .' My mother's every muted action was tense with disapproval; she opened the oven, put down his plate, shut the oven, and I knew her mouth was in a straight line. Then, while he ate in the same silence, she would perch upright and stiff at the table, staring blankly past me through the darkening window, hands in lap in bleak dedication. A train would racket by, catching her watery blue eyes into a prolonged unseeing shudder; then, as the sound died, they would settle back into the same stare of hopelessness. He would remember the hullaballoo of which he had just been the jolly centre, sit in stony reverie, shake himself and pad upstairs. The day was destroyed.

Sometimes he weighed anchor even later, when I would squat at our door listening to the silences. One night, waiting for him, Mam had reminded me that Jabez had once given their father a hiding; afterwards, from upstairs, I heard a savage expletive, rushed down and stood between them, bare feet apart under my nightshirt. 'Dad, don't –' but he had me by the ear, up the stairs and back on my bed, legs ignominiously in the air, before you could say Uncle Jab. That was the night I took my mother's part.

But the bad times were not often. Two-till-ten was a safe week, with the New Inn closed by the time he was striding hungrily home with his snap-box crammed with firewood; I would wait up for him, 'And how's the family bookworm?' Ten-till-six was all right too, when Job and Tom's spirits had to be curbed ('How many times – he's sleeping!') but the feeling of Dad safe upstairs made up for it. Just about when I got home from school, he would come down in stockinged feet and easy good spirits, and it was a happy four hours : top of his egg for one, rice-pudding scraps for another. Job and Tom would tell him about last Saturday night, leaning out of the bedroom to catch the usual after-closing rumpus in Victoria Row, the pots flying, the shrewish screams. 'As good as the circus, eh Poll?' Then he would set off with his snap, Tom already asleep in their bed, to keep Mam company. As Richard had dominated each home from 39 Elwy Street on, so he dominated 314a.

Winter evenings, I would set my homework on a corner of the kitchen table, acquiring quickly the habit of concentrating with two to four people active at my elbow; I liked to feel the life around me. But most of my time – that is, every minute of not-too-cold daylight – was spent in the parlour. For ten years, the shrine was to enclose me; once a week Mam would turn me out for cleaning or come in to leave the rent in half-crowns on the dresser, otherwise I was undisturbed.

All the treasures had come again into their own. Facing the empty newspapered grate, the horsehair chairs, one stout and armed (male?) the other low and armless (female?); family photographs, globed glass flowers and birds, clumsy pincushion, grandfather clock, corner-cupboard with sacred tea-set and moustache-cup, waxwork portraits, the two waterfalls. Over the fireplace stood a mirror narrowly framed in faded guilt; on the mantel, candlesticks and gong with on each side, on tiny circles of wool, the rainbow spheres, the shaking-grass. Like the Zoo-dweller, I settled into the far corner of my lair, at the tiny rickety table between the window and the crude cupboard built elbow-high next to the fireplace. Before me a battered old *Nuttall's Dictionary*, donated by Mr H. Price the Chapel, and the books that overflowed my satchel; at my elbow, the sewing-machine and the stuffy scent of the fuchsia brushing the curtains, their lace frayed but stiff with pride.

My ten-year view was not edifying. Ringed by brick and slate, with not a swell of a hill or of a three-syllabled word in sight, I looked out, beyond the unpaved path under my window, on to the few unfenced square yards of tufty weeds and ragged grass which was our garden, its sole adornment a clothes-line and prop. Behind it crouched walled-in ashpits and earth-closets, and behind them, the sullied shoulders and backsides of the High Street houses, with here and there a hopeless window. In the height of summer, with the sun highlighting the dust on the one emaciated thorn-hedge in sight, and coaxing warmth out of every lurking odour, this blighted world showed not one culti-vated thing; not a bud, not a flower, no trace of dignity on the one hand or of indulgence on the other.

Not that I craved indulgence. The outlook from my monk's alcove gradually became a challenge to be defied; I even came to feel that a softening feature would be incongruous, would mar the perfect poverty of the whole face, heartbreaking to any starved imprisoned spirit. For I was not starved, and I had my own freedom. Books forged the key, but for two years they had a rival which brooked little competition. For the holidays, Miss Cooke had heaped into my arms a pile of reading matter – 'nothing on earth like the enjoyment of fine English, mark my words' – which I had stacked next to the sewing-machine, they spilled on to the middle table: most of Scott, *The Mill on the Floss, The Woman in White, Oliver Twist* ... But they were hardly opened. The rival was the Pictures.

Chapter 12

The Silver Screen

It started with a Wednesday-night family outing to the Hip (*The Juggernaut!*), twopence ha'penny each at the very front, a penny for Tom. Suspense beforehand, would Dad have called at – 'oh Mam, not tonight, it's Charlie Chaplin!' – and he hadn't. His spry step down the side of the house – 'hot water, quick march!' – into his best, and we filed up the alley. The film was *One A.M.*; even Mam held her sides and said it was a tonic, then Job and I were given a penny each to call at Ma Williams's Chip Shop and bring them home steaming in greasy newspaper. Then, after entreaty, I was allowed to go every Wednesday, and then, more entreaty, to every Sat Mat for Children One Penny, change of programme.

It was the serials that captured me first. Wednesday, *The Shielding Shadow* (Episode Six, in two reels, 'The Disappearing Prisoner'), with Grace Darmond, fair and entrancingly fragile, and Ralph Kellard, shielding her: when not disguised with wig and moustache, or empowered to be invisible except for a black mask and gloves which wandered eerily on their own, he was a young soldier-lover with teeth as white as his wig had been. The suspense at the end of the episode, death nearer and nearer, then 'To be continued', was a spasm of pleasure. I was so struck with the teeth that I took out the brush Mam had bought me – 'but Mam, I don't need it, I've *got* good teeth!' – for mine must be as white. But toothpaste was unheard of. 'Try soot,' she said. It worked – every morning for years I would scrape my fingertips up the chimney, rub them over my brush, go out to the tap, and scrub: the smoky tastelessness of the recipe became an acquired taste, and my teeth certainly stayed white. Saturday's serial was *The Purple Domino* (Episode Three, 'Plot and Counter-Plot') with Francis Ford and Grace Cunard; when she was not an exotic charmer sitting in a low-cut evening gown in crowded ships' lounges, unscrewing chocolates to fill each with a contraband diamond, she was dressed – for secret missions – in large béret, black tights, high-heeled shoes and a mask.

As the weeks passed, the Pictures dominated my life: the week rose to Wednesday, sank, rose to Saturday, sank for Sunday and rose again. I started an exercise-book marked – insolently, over the school crest – 'G. Wms, Subj.: Pictures Hip. C.Q.' 'Wed. Aug. 22: (1) *Pathé Gazette*; Meal-time in French Munition Factory, America's Splendid Women Army (2) *A Bird's a Bird*, Nestor Comedy featuring Edith Roberts, Eddie Lyons, Lee Moran who find themselves in a harem ... (3) Foxy and Roxy, in person, your own Side-Splitters singing "O'Brien is Learnin' Hawaian", not interesting, (4) *The Web of Desire* in 5 reels; in the Mad City of Destiny, Ethel Clayton ...' Then I would scribble in corners: the wanton doodles of an obsessed mind, skyscrapers with silhouettes wrestling on the edge, or heroes tied to railways. But mostly I drew the heroines; I had neer seen make-up or high heels, and when I was not crudely shaping the perfect profiles of my shadow garden of girls, with names like Blanche Sweet, June Caprice, Jewel Carmen, Louise Lovely, I was engaged on Grace Cunard's exquisite calf, then the curve of her shoe. Then back to work: 'Pathé presents Pearl White as Pearl Walton and Antonio Moreno as Harvey Gresham in *The House of Hate*' – every week I waited for it and was fascinated by the star having given her name to the character and by the whole ritual – 'Episode Seven, "The Hooded Terror". Pearl, trapped in a house haunted by a fiend, is driven along terrible cliffs with death a foot away ...' Scott's *Waverley* ('Chapter One: The title of this book has not been chosen without grave deliberation ...') could hardly compete.

Neither could the 'Variety' sandwiched between the films; I was left cold by the comics in front of a painted Chester street with the local references – 'ee, Ah wuz courtin' t'oother day oop Wepre Drive' – to shrieks of local laughter. But I feasted on the occasional troupes : The Eight Bing Babies, in their dazzling new Song-and-Dance Scena 'Babes in Toyland', were ladies of seventeen dressed as flaxen-haired toddlers in tiny frills over biscuit-coloured tights, holding parasols and tap-dancing in graceful time to the tinny piano. They were radiant beings never to be identified with the furtive hooded creatures who had slipped down the aisle into the little door and must perforce lodge in the Quay. After the final number – high kicks in rhythm with the spinning parasols, 'There's a Girl ... for Every *Sole*-jah!' – I was startled to see two of them pirouette down into the audience and squeak 'Postcards of the Babes, one penny each!' That they should move among us was somehow an offence, and to stop the porcelain visions cracking into painted masks, I shut my eyes. That night, on my haunches in the dark of our bedroom doorway, knowing that my father would be wreathed in smiles and gesticulating, I was able to repeat much of the dialogue. My unbroken voice mimicked the high sharp tones of the Babes, 'Oh deah, I would love to see a reel-live Golliwog, wouldn't you deahs?' and then the chorus, 'Toyland, Joyland, Little-Girl-and-Boyland ...' I meant to sound ridiculous, and when Dad applauded – 'Poll, we've got a houseful o' clever little ladies!' – I did not even feel a Mary Ann. Like the grenouilles, it had been a release.

But such rarities could not oust the Silver Screen. It occupied the foreground of my life, vibrant and near, while fuzzy in the background was the Quay; moreover, while the phantoms were all the more real for being mute, reality was sterile with sound. Avidly, stone-deafly, I watched the quick gay exchanges between Mabel Normand and Wallace Reid, the staccato protests of Anna Q. Nilsson; their vocal inaccessibility, combined with their physical nearness, was perfection. The magic was rendered invincible for me, too, by my indifference to machinery : I heard the whirring and felt the rays play on the screen, but never consciously knew that I was under the spell of photographs off a spool, and when Job told me he had been inside the station and seen a metal box which a porter assured him contained 'the pictures from the Hip', I did not believe him : Norma Talmadge,

Milton Sills, Dorothy Gish, William Farnum all in the Quay lying about in tins?

The music weaved into the glamour of what I watched. Waiting, I would be sitting with twopennyworth of dried dates, a new luxury, reading a borrowed *Magnet* – I never took a book to the Hip – when in mid-sentence the pianist would start. To the music, even my reading matter was transformed, and I could not believe that the two Roman statues could stand so cold while Bob Cherry and Co moved with me into a lyrical world. Shutting my eyes I thought, I am about to watch people *who are going to be there*, in strange rooms, strange clothes, and I pledge myself to watch every ornament on every wall and every earring and necklace, because each will *prove* that this is a reality which will last me till Saturday and then start again. And when I moped along High Street to collect the margarine from the Maypole, all the faces were grey compared to the shadows I had watched; they looked like prisoners of war.

The magic would shed itself on everything to do with it: on the bored girl before the Sat Mat who sauntered up to the back of the balcony to swish window-curtains and blot out the unwanted sun, on the thud of the piano-lid and the lady patting her hair before arranging her pages: on the subtitles, on the inserts of elegant hands briskly finishing notes before my eyes and the serial-synopsis gliding up line by line: on the frantic speckling of the picture round the edges just before the sudden click of 'Reel Two Will Follow Immediately', and above all on the Censor's Certificate, always the first thing to be shown, a palpitating glaring-white document bearing the name of the film and so the proof that it was really here. The title was in punctilious handwriting often at variance with the words: 'THIS IS TO CERTIFY THAT ... *Flames of Passion* ... HAS BEEN PASSED FOR PUBLIC EXHIBITION, T. P. O'CONNOR.' I never wondered what a censor was, it was merely a fatherly message, 'Yes your film is here, enjoy it.'

In between, I half-heartedly explored my surroundings. The High Street which only a year ago had excited me with bustle, I now saw as a grimy prolongation of the same brick and slate that filled my window. The other side of it from our alley, behind the citified Hare and Hounds 'Hotel' and the tiled archway known to Tom and his mates on rainy days as the 'Tel Arch', there was a side street leading past the brickyard and the straggling afterthought-rows of workmen's houses, 'oop the line'. This was a single railway track, disused except for homeless-looking trucks which clanked between the Quay Station and Buckley, three miles up-country, a village by then smutched by pottery works and colonized, from Staffordshire, by Bookley Moogs. To the left, the lone beauty spot of the region – the medieval ruins of Ewloe Castle in a sudden thick and precipitous bluebell wood – but somehow the iron industrial grip was too tight around it for me to penetrate. Inland lay Northop and Welsh Flintshire – Mold, and Treuddyn – but too far.

Were there birds? I never noticed any. From adjacent knolls, in the evening light you could see, over the rammed-flat slate roofs of Shotton and the Quay and the squat arches of Hawarden Bridge, the smoked chimneys of the Steelworks; but even the sun could do little for a prospect which under the loving face of heaven stayed obstinately closed. In the winter, 'oop the line' was a dismal hinterland; between the straggling thornbushes, smeared – it seemed – with rust and wet soot, I would either strut wilfully, stupidly, along one of the rails, one foot jerking in front of the other, or totter between over the maddeningly irregular trestles.

My other excursion was the other way, behind 314a, to the area between our main railway and the estuary. To reach this, I would climb over our ashpit-fence into the cinder wilderness at the foot of the embankment, and follow it for fifty yards past broken barriers and slum backs; here, on my first venture, I saw something peculiarly horrifying which stamped the place for me as a No Man's Gehenna – an alley-cat streaking fiendishly past, its demented head jammed for ever in a salmon tin. At the end, a low wall where I could vault into Fisherman's Row, then under the railway, past a dejected huddle called the Boneyard and exuding a sour smell of boiled leather, into a featureless Rubbishland of slag-heaps, abandoned trucks and sandy scoops up into which the tide sweated from subterranean culverts.

The estuary, which once had meant the amber sands of child-hood, was here a narrow silted channel with rising from its shallows the quay that had once been the pride of Connah, whoever he was. Against the gnawed piles, their stanchions rusty and scrabbled with weeds, a couple of shabby ships; the other side, the flatness of sea-flooded Cheshire merged into the smoke of the Steelworks. I stared glumly down into the ships, but no amount of mind-work could evoke R. L. Stevenson. All was dead.

But in this territory, I had my spellbound errands. Non-picture evenings, I would take a sad pleasure in hanging around the Hip, watching people straggling in, their faces should have been aglow, then looking up at 'the pipe', which ran up the side of the building to emit urgent pants of steam throughout the per-formance. It must have been to do with exhaust (heating?), but to me the endless chug-chug spoke of adventure, and grief, and gaiety. Then I would wander to the back and listen to the faint piano : but that was so frustrating that I only tried it once. Fri-day was set aside for a long walk, through the Quay to Shotton and even as far as Queensferry. It was a dreary excursion, but my quest was not for birds' nests or even shop-windows, but hoardings, so as to drink my fill of the new poster: a graphic scene, in colour, from one of next week's episodes. Some Fridays held more promise than others : once, on the corner of the Central Hotel, Shotton, I found Marie Walcamp staring horror-struck at water from which emerged a giant octopus with one tentacle round her ankle; another time I came upon Ruth Roland, bound and gagged, hanging upside down from a ten-storeyed pagoda next to the Congregational Church, Services 10.30 & 6.0 All Welcome.

Then I would dawdle to the brickyard up beyond High Street, 'Prince's Clay-'ole', a stagnant pool among half-quarried wastes, and tie a pebble to the corners of an old handkerchief, swing it high and watch the parachute miraculously waft a loved and fearless girl over perilous clay cliffs and skeleton-strewn ravines. There, one day in the afternoon sun, I crouched by the lagoon, its shallows ensludged with broken bottles, old boots and dead cats; as other children would have fished for tiddlers, I retrieved from the vile water a wodge of old Hip posters which had been pasted up every week for a year. I scraped off one limp strip after another. *A Daughter of the Gods* Annette Kellerman, *The Beast* George Walsh, *The Birth of a Nation*, The Six Floradora Dancers, *Flame of the Yukon* Dorothy Dalton ... Carefully I toiled, squatting on the slimy stones and clawing after romance with in my nostrils the smell of decay. Love can go no further.

By September, however, I was counting the days till the new term. After seven weeks as a hermit, I looked forward keenly to steaming into Flint, with across my waistcoat Dad's old watch-chain, the watch on one end and my season ticket on the other, and hailing Totty and Co: I would be already an Older Boy. There was a new English teacher, Miss Morris, diffident as a doe, and sympathetic. This was home, a bustle of friendly competition.

But I could not forget. Sitting in class, I saw the first morning as a film through the eyes of the new mistress. Of all these new faces, which is the most interesting? The camera circles down to one boy (the one, surely, who is top in French?) but he is also the Best Liked, a buffoon with great expressive eyes, a mixture of Charles Ray and Charlie Chaplin who will find himself, ere the term is much older, in endearing scrapes. Then a subtitle: 'Young Buster was not called the Holy Terror for nothing. *Buster* ... GEORGE WILLIAMS.' A close-up of Buster, pointing a catapult at two adoring girls. This mood, happily, only lasted a day; GEORGE WILLIAMS subsided into George Williams and got on quietly with his work.

Still, like many children who do not easily make contact, I longed to be popular. I was not unliked, there was nothing to dislike in a solemn-faced polite bookish boy, but I had not the public appeal Dad would have had, and Wally did have. When he was asked the capital of Sweden and said, 'Ee, if it ud been England A'd 'a been aw right,' and grinned engagingly, I knew the girls were thinking he was the nicest. How did he do it?

He did not seem to care whether he was liked or not, a formula as obvious as it was out of my reach. I watched him bounding down to the train, football-boots tied to his satchel – that was it, football! I was strong, my wind was good, the magic leather sphere would be my passport to mass favour.

I spoke to Wally – 'we need a left 'alf, you luke 'efty' – borrowed some boots, and in the dinner-hour joined the others. 'He's the school-captain you know, cool in a crisis and a good mixer', then the whistle blew. The ball came straight at me, I clamped it with both feet as I had seen done, and heard the intoxicating smack of boot against leather as I sent it soaring, the wrong way, narrowly missing a goal for the other side. A squawk of derision, then it seemed some time before the ball ventured my way; then, just as I was wondering what the French was for football ('ballon de pied'?) it came straight for me like a thing possessed. I headed it hard, in the right direction. 'Played Williams,' snapped Mr Boyer, and I forgot French. After that the ball sailed my way more than once, but each time I muffed it; I could head and run and aim, but each time that it meant wresting the ball, the fear of being kicked in the groin was so strong that nothing would have made me plunge headlong. My thoughts wandered again; I saw Wally whisk the ball from Jackson, who appeared to have just missed smashing him with a hip-high kick. I felt cold, what did this remind me of? Glanrafon, Beating Day, only no shilling. Next day Mr Boyer asked me if I would use my dinner-hours to tidy his lab. Le ballon de pied was not for me.

But he let me have a bit of quicksilver to take home to Tom, who sat for hours over the gleam of amorphous beads slithering wickedly over the table and marvellously joining up again. And I helped anybody with their lessons who asked me, and even made quiet jokes. My time-table, for several years, was to be a simple one – in term, up at seven, sometimes six in the summer, the train at ten to eight, home soon after five, tea, then homework and 'general reading' till bedtime; twice weekly, the pictures. In the holidays and on Saturday mornings, I sat and read, or walked and thought. My thoughts were of my reading, the pictures, and the secret world I had glimpsed in the train. Sometimes, without warning, these last thoughts would wash disconcertingly over the others : such as the Saturday, hunched in my parlour-corner over logarithms, when I found myself deep in a daydream of stumbling in a wood upon Captain Ralph Kellard of the U.S. Army, gagged and tied to a tree by Huns, and before cutting my hero free, subjecting him to the indignity of the train. But such lapses were fleeting.

Gradually the marshmallow of the films became judiciously mixed with the more staple diet of school. I was finding homework easier and easier, even Maths, there was no exam for two years, and I began to read – conventionally but steadily – every sort of novel, alternating school library (books which I dutifully covered in brown paper) with swops of current reprints : Dumas, Stewart Edward White, Dickens, Mrs Henry Wood, Lytton, Marie Corelli, George Eliot, Vachell, Mrs Humphry Ward, the Bensons, Fenimore Cooper, Jack London, the Brontës, de Vere Stacpoole, Hichens, Le Queux, Borrow (*Lavengro*, what was the 'sin against the Holy Ghost', just saying bad words about it? The next second, out of panic, I spoke several and worried for a week). English set-books were *As You Like It* and *A Tale of Two Cities*. Neither the jocosities of Touchstone nor the skirmishings of the lovers appealed to me, and I did not once visualize them in a theatre.

The Dickens was a different matter. The Everyman legend on the front caught my imagination every time, 'A Tale Which Holdeth Children from Play ...' School-book though it was, the sweep and grandeur were irresistible, and for the first time I glimpsed that the magic mined out of the *Companion* and the Pictures could also be found in a classic. I once more bestrode the wings of imagination, but this time not my own : I was borne aloft by the pinions of a great writer. 'Six tumbrils carry the day's wine to Sainte Guillotine ... Thou powerful enchanter Time, change these chariots back to what they were, and they shall be seen to be the carriages of absolute monarchs, the equipages of flaming Jezebels!' Sitting in our kitchen, twisting the watch-seal at my navel – as I did ceaselessly when absorbed – I felt my spine tingle; and going out to fill the kettle, I saw the embankment and the peeling shed and the ashpit through a shimmering mist which rendered them powerless to demean me or my family.

There were many such luminous moments. From the trance of Sunday-school I would race home to Sunday tea: tomatoes, cake and a white cloth, 'Don't play with the soft shugger while you're reading, how many times ...' and *The Cloister and the Hearth*. I had until half-past five, when Mam would prepare her own excursion from hearth to cloister by brushing her long blue-black coat, shaking out the tippet with the tiny flat fox-head and taking down the button-hook for her best boots, while Dad brought out his shaving tackle and propped the little cracked mirror against Disraeli. There we would leave him with a cut-throat razor hovering delicately, like a brush between palette and canvas, over a face half foam-flecked workman, half gentleman of leisure, 'Give my love to the preacher, whoever he is!' Mam would advance along High Street at a hymn-book pace, the three of us blankly in her wake, Job and Tom bribed with caramels. I whiled away the walk by taking longer steps than usual and giving quick side-long looks into the shrouded shop-windows to see if I was getting any taller, and once in the pew I sank back into my barefoot journey to Rome with Gerard. Weekdays, returning absorbed in the train, those other thoughts safely at bay, I would hear overhead the warning whoosh of the Quay bridge, stir like a trained sleeper, close my book, descend, show my season, 'good morning I mean night I mean afternoon,' and walk with Romola into High Street Florence.

Miss Cooke taught me French and Latin, in a class of thirty of which I stayed steadily head in these two subjects as well as in English and History; at the foot of exercises, and on my term's report, she accorded me in her bold hand the word 'Excellent', from her there was no higher praise. I hardly ever saw her outside class; I have in my mind only one fleeting picture of her in the Central Hall, I must have been crossing for a book, standing talking flushed and distressed to a weary khaki figure, a former pupil on leave from the front, 'How can one bear the thought of such waste, dreadful dreadful ...'

But though I had no contact with her, her influence on my work was considerable. The possessor of an original and unpredictable mind which in letters could sprawl over eloquent pages, as a teacher she lauded and displayed clarity, simplicity and – a word she used often, pursing her lips lovingly over the difficult vowel – 'la mesu-u-re'. I remembered everything she said and applied it to other subjects. From the blackboard, she taught me to mark cases and tenses clearly, imperatorIBUS, tenEBAM, 'The only thing the examiners want to know, poor overworked beggars – is whether you get the *ends right*.' She taught me how to make memory-notes from prolonged reading matter by boiling down and then starkly classifying, under heads, sub-heads and sub-sub-heads. Underline key words, and don't crush your stuff, it's hard on the eye, jolly well spread yourself', rebellion against J.M.'s war-winning obsession, but she was right:

Influences of the Revolution

I. Domestic.   (1) On the peasants. Their commons to be confiscated.

                (2) On the middle classes. Forbidden to navigate rivers which gave rise to :

                    (a) The Battle of Doncaster.

                    (b) The March to London.

                    (c) The Destruction of two public services :

                        (i) The Tees Bridge.

                        (ii) The Brighton Toll-gate.

II. Foreign.   (1) On France ... etc.

There were also foretastes of Fowler's Usage. *Don't* start a sentence with 'but' or 'and' unless you are bent on it, *don't* say 'disinterested' when you mean 'uninterested', *don't* put 'each other' when you mean more than two people; she would then write, with a splurge of chalk, 'The three sisters loved ONE ANOTHER.' She had a theory, as true as it was astute, which she scolded grammarians for not respecting : when instructing the right thing as opposed to the wrong, *never* write it the wrong way to show what you mean, write 'The French for "marriage" has only one r – "le mariage", *don't* write 'The French for "marriage" is not "le marriage"', for the eye will photograph that and confuse it with the right way. Also jolly well make your *own* vocabularies : get a note-book, divide into sections, Dress, Occupations, Furniture, Nature, Idioms (a) personal (b) general, and ladder it down the side so you can thumb it open. Don't abbreviate Monsieur Madame and Mademoiselle, it's rude, don't put Xmas for Christmas, place the stamp symmetrically in the corner of the envelope, in dates say 'eighteen hundred and thirty', not 'eighteen thirty'. And so on, scores of bits which I retained till they fitted into a mosaic of discipline. Christmas Prize Distribution, I was top of my form and was awarded a gilded, stamped and unreadable *William the Conqueror.*

Dad's pleasure in this was spoilt by his own Christmas present. Like many financially unstable characters, he still thought himself a wily penny-saver; there now arrived a long awaited parcel, in return for a postal order sent to the journal *John Bull*, '20,000 Bran-New Working Men's Footwear, Surplus Stock, Write NOW ! ! !' Dad was unwise enough to open it in front of his family, and lifted up a pair of boots. They were not bran-new, they were not new, they were not second-hand. They were old boots : down at heel, their eyes bleary from old laces, still muddy. It was, out of many, Horatio Bottomley's most cynical gesture. Said Dad incredulously (he never swore in front of us) 'But the bugger has sent them by *post!*' 'But has he?' asked Mam mildly, in Welsh, 'haven't they walked?' I knew better than to look at my father.

But he had got over it by Boxing Day, when he got into his bowler-hatted best and we all went by train to Chester : the matinée of the pantomime at the Royalty, *Dick Whittington.* Dad had assured me the Cat was six feet high. We were the first in the Early-Doors queue for the gallery : no stools, but mufflers and sandwiches. As at the Hip, we boys were to go on ahead and grab the first seats; racing up the endless steps, I heard the blithe clang of the first tallies through the cubby-hole, tumbling out for *us*. We settled in the middle of the front row, on old newspapers Mam had brought; for thirty seconds, as I bit the cold rail and looked down into the glowing emptiness, we possessed a theatre, licensed by the Lord Chamberlain to the Welsh Family Williams. We even owned the great sign behind us, 'Beware of Pickpockets'.

This was more special than the Hip even : the steady clamour as the gallery filled, the smell of dust and soap and gas-jets, the taste of the apple and orange passed along by my mother ... Then, beyond the murmur of the milling auditorium far below – fairy-story children in the boxes, with rows of chocolates before them – a weird miaowing which for a second I took to be the Cat stretching himself; when I realized it was the orchestra tuning up, I leant back. rapt, against a strange pair of knobbly knees. The overture, my first, made the Hip piano sound meagre indeed – 'Give me a Cosy little Corner', 'Let the Great Big World keep Turning', 'Goodbye-ee !' – and then the curtain superbly rose – I remembered la Belle Russe at the Opera House – on the glitter of colour, the sheen of silk tights, the shrill babble of voices; the Williamses had been swallowed up into the great family Gallery, a silent constellation of eyes sharper than Dick's cat's eyes, all glittering watchfully in the dark. For me the magic of the Pictures was to stay supreme, in a pantomime there was nothing for me to identify myself with, but the Royalty had cast a spell which was still over me as we drank tea in the pie-shop under the Rows before catching the train. For several years the Boxing Day Matinée was to be our treat.

The rhythm of the spring term, 1918 tick-tocked staidly on with its two-faced days, the Quay face merging, through the train, into the Holywell one and back again, and punctuated by the long interior week-end. With the summer the train became close again, nudging-hot, and the smells of baking nettles and hair-oil and asphalt grew strong and pervasive; caressing, but without arms which one could have pulled away. Sidney Mills had joined the Flint lot, from another school; a ripe fifteen, he was a handsome long-trousered curly-headed fellow who wore clock-socks and hinted at female conquests: it was decided by Harold Mears that he must be taken down, literally. At the Junction, as we filled the compartment, I recognized with misgiving the beat of my heart: there was once more something conspiratorial about the guard's whistle, the sudden shudder of the train, the isolation. The windows had not been opened for days, it was a luggage-racked five-pound-fine oven, the hot seats padded fat and bouncy like rough dusty thighs.

One minute Casanova was sitting with knees coolly crossed, the next there was the old welter of arms and legs, he had been unbreeched and humiliated, and we were all sitting back, flushed, laughing. For the first time, in this ritual of horseplay, the victim had not been one to arouse pity, and my feeling was unalloyed: one of excitement to see a supercilious sex-god lying back a broken doll, too old to cry but young enough to pant with humiliation, nacreous teeth biting into lower cherry-lip as his arms strained to get free. A couple of days later, I found myself sharing a compartment with him. He had reassumed his air of lofty savoir-aimer, but his ordeal had made him more approachable. I decided to question him about the laws of reproduction; I knew about unmarried mothers, Hetty Sorrel in *Adam Bede* was a marked figure, but love to me was as unreal as in King Arthur's day. Sidney Mills told me, crudely but without prurience, how babies are born.

The shock I had was that no couple, even married, could have a child without all this; there was in me such a cleft between the romantic and the physical that the idea of their mingling was untenable. Must I believe that Lorna Doone and Jane Eyre endured this sniggering schoolboy act? Did this not make them party to the secret thoughts which their company had helped me to evade? I felt the victim of a mass hoax, literary and cinematographical. Then, day by day, I got used to the idea that such a business might be tolerated, en passant and out of pity for an empty cradle, by Mary Miles Minter and Marguerite Clark by arrangement with Jack Mulhall and Jack Pickford. I accustomed myself to the facts of life.

Chapter 13

Pubertas, Pubertatis

With the summer holidays life became flat again. Waking, I would hear the chug of a goods train coming to an uncertain halt; just when you thought it had, one slopping truck would clank its buffers against its neighbour, which would then give the next one a great ignorant shove, 'Coom on, move over!' and so it would go on. In that stuffy bedroom, it was the most hopeless of sounds. How different from the middle of the night, the Irish Mail! By now I was so used to it that in my sleep I waited, and if one night the train had not run I would have opened uneasy eyes. For I had tamed the fiery lion, it was now my own swift-pounding chariot of light, my nightly reminder that while I slumbered, life moved on, Euston-sure; there was a terminus. And at the back of my sleep was a permanent blur of myself seated in the train in a bowler hat, Annie opposite and a picnic-basket between us, a pheasant I had shot outside Gyrn Castle.

These were the days I resumed my barren walks up the line, blackberrying or collecting the dock-leaves with which Mam polished our tiles green, or roaming through Rubbishland where my behaviour – for a week or two – would have looked erratic. I used to spend an hour jumping from the tops of surprisingly steep dumps, back up and down again. This was to get thin; I had the idea, from a random teasing remark in class, that my sturdy growing body was too podgy and my stockinged calves too plump, and even thought of answering the Antipon advertisements in the *Picture Show*, of fat old men miraculously melting into youths.

But this wore off and I would just wander, arranging to arrive at the quayside in time for the only excitement thereabouts : to watch the moribund sands tingle into life at the approach from the west of a sinister stir in the air, nearer, nearer, until it turned into a low foaming marching wall the implacable length of the horizon : the tidal wave. It brought the river to spurious life, frothing and jostling and muttering, and ghostly sailors seemed about to swab the gritty decks. But in time the same tide would seep despondently away, often leaving tragedy in its summer wake. One evening, as across the sun-kissed reeky ashpits Frank Bellis's practising trumpet cried sadness to the long-shadowed world of bricks and momentarily transfigured them, Tom came pelting white-faced down the alley, 'They're dragging for Billy Roberts!' I would surface quickly from the depths of Stevenson or Rider Haggard and run up into High Street, knotted with groups on the same errand, sniffing platitudinously at disaster. 'Ee, boys will be boys, they will that, any road it's the waitin' that's 'ard, it is an' all ...' The sands still gleamed wickedly from waters that had receded, their work done; the figures standing hopelessly by, the silhouette of the boatmen with their grappling poles, gave sudden importance to the little urchin who had been as indistinguishable among his mates as one flagstone from another, now a tragic figure that filled the sky and gave even this landscape stature.

But next day, with the body laid in the Dead House, everything simmered back to normal. We were sworn not to bathe, but I secretly frequented steep stairs leading down to the sand, used prosperous years ago for boarding craft. I would watch the tide creep up step by step till it reached just below a horizontal bar embedded in the sea wall and the pillar opposite; on the top step, sheltered from the wind and any passer-by, I would stoop, stealthily undress, climb down steps breast-high into the swirling water, leap out and swing Tarzan-like from the bar, my body swaying in the sea, well out of my depth. The intention of this was athleto-hygienic, but the sense of danger and of the forbidden, the new feel of my body naked out of doors, the sly slapping of the tide – all meant that however cold the water, I entered the sea in a state of disturbance. Though even the healthiest adolescent could not stay proof against the dour northern current, and I would end struggling into my shirt with dripping knees chastely up to my chin, each time I looked for-

ward to the discomfort of a ritual which consistently failed to
qualify as a healthy dip in the briny.

The winter term, my English essays became more elaborate; I
knew that from behind her thick glasses gentle Miss Morris was
not missing much, and that she might pass on any unusual effort
to Miss Cooke. Then one school morning in November, we were
heaved out of routine and packed home cheering with excitement borrowed from our elders : the war which had touched me
so little was over. We ran down hysterical Holywell High
Street, hastily Union-Jacked, but by the time I had reached the
Quay my champagne was flat. It seemed wrong to arrive home
from H.C.S. before mid-day dinner; was I the one boy in the
country who would sooner have stayed at school on Armistice
Day? But what was I to do with myself? I had sevenpence, saved
out of the sixpence a week Mam gave me, to cover pencils,
sweets or – nearly always – the Hip. An urge which had been
forming for months suddenly crystallized. I wanted to tell a
story, on paper.

I walked down to Fewster's, bought a wad of foolscap, sat at
the kitchen table, and wrote across the top, in flowing scroll,
'HEARTS OF YOUTH, a novel by George Williams, aged 13;
Chapter One, The Eyes of a Viper'. I resisted putting 'Episode
One'. Then, in impeccable copperplate, 'The sun sparkled and
shimmered, one summer's day in 1602, as a boy and girl walked
hand in hand in a beautiful garden outside Paris.' With a facility
derived from writing essays straight off, I altered not one word.
'The boy René was tall and graceful, his blue eyes fathomless :
the girl every whit as fair.' One well-behaved cliché glided after
the other on oiled wheels : 'the scent of delphiniums wafted over
the well-tended paths'. I had never seen a delphinium, but it
sounded exotic. 'He held her to him and gazed into her liquid
eyes.' A line later, the reader was to raise an eyebrow at the news
that this demonstrative pair were brother and sister : I felt as yet
unequipped for a love story, but the romantic convention was
so strong that from the start their devotion overstepped the
mark. ' "My dearest," she breathed, with no idea of the turmoil
to come . . .'

Turmoil it was to be. She was kidnapped by a Turk seeking recruits for the Imperial Harem, whereupon her distracted brother followed via dungeons, bandits, shipwrecks and stolen horses racing for leagues until 'at long last the shimmering Golden Horn'. After bribing his way into the Palace he beheld 'a sight ne'er yet vouchsafed to white eyes: the veiled Harem, lying on their divans in various languid attitudes and wearing agates, emeralds, sapphires, garnets, rubies, onyxes, beryls, topazes, turquoises, pearls and diamonds'. It is hardly to be wondered at that the girls looked languid, considering the weight they were carrying. René was captured, fastened by the waist from the highest minaret and shot at with red-hot arrows, watched by all affrighted Constantinople (Chapter Seven, The Human Pendulum). Miraculously he escaped, rescued his sister from a fate I knew little of (she apparently knew less, for her only comment was 'My jailers were harsh, but from the Sultan I had nothing to fear'), and the last chapter left the pair safe in Paris, with no cloud except presumably what would happen to either if the other married.

I wrote 'The End' on page 68 and after class, hot in the face, casually informed Miss Cooke that I had written a novel. 'Heavens, what next ... well, the handwriting's good – Miss Morris, look at this!' If only I could have handed them a printed book with a picture on the cover, René swinging from the minaret ... But I had started to tell a story, gone on telling, and finished it. The script was returned to me a week later, with a good-humoured compliment, 'You have certainly given your imagination full play.' One wet dinner-hour, in a forbidden class-room, I showed it to Millie Tyrer and Eira Parry, 'An adventure story, you know, just came to me ...' They were impressed, 'Oo George, what lovely writing', and I was enjoyably reading aloud – 'the girl every whit as fair' – when in walked Miss Cooke; after my casualness, it was humiliating. 'Back to your cloak-room girls and Williams, keep to the boys' side, get along.' My parents were impressed by the handwriting and the length, but I did not offer it to them, how could they be interested in the glamour of the East? It did not occur to me that possibly Dic the Mariner knew more about Constantinople than René and the Sultan's harem put together.

Neither Miss Cooke nor Miss Morris had criticized my first work, and it is understandable why. Having in the past fallen under the spell of the second-rate, I had reproduced it perfectly, and it is not possible to pick perfection to pieces. At Christmas the novelist hung his stocking for the last time, orange, apple, pencils and drawing-book, but first there was Prize Distribution. It was gratifying that the applause when I advanced for my prize – a first, *Canute the Great*, again unreadable – was not humiliatingly less than Wally's for his Woodwork. I also won *Kim* in soft red leather, a 'Special Prize for Hygiene'. 'Hygiene,' said my mother, who on Olympus would have been Goddess of Cleanliness, 'what's that?'

After the ceremony, with the unaccustomed fall of school darkness, the spluttering gaslights gave the Central Hall an exotic look; the pupils were special too, in their Sunday best, some boys sporting their first long trousers. Girls took turns at the piano, plucking out languorous waltzes that delighted and disturbed. Dancing was not a school subject, so any attempt at it was holiday fun; couples would link up, mostly girl with girl, but occasionally a blushing boy would venture to be taught by a girl, half in parody. It was a restless hour; one waited, flushed and adrift, teased into an expectation which had to expend itself in laughter, a carefully diffident display of prize-books, clowning, and parlour games. Then the train, unfamiliar too by winter night-light; between Flint and the Quay, with Totty and Co's laughter still in my ears, the blackness flashing past produced a reaction of loneliness.

My standing with my schoolmates continued to be good but I still had no friends. Every advantage has to be paid for : while my obsession with the written word was gradually helping me to pull down one wall – the frontier between me and the cosmopolitan world – it was also building another, the barrier between me and my immediate fellow-creatures. The friends I had made on paper, from my *Welsh Singer* trio to David and the Tullivers on the Floss, were such that nobody could live up to them, and the Chum who accompanied me invisibly over Rubbishland had not materialized. Three weeks' holiday, what now?

Walks up the line, into the working-class weather, past the dead-sea brickyard with the old tins and the cat-corpses; from our ashpit, I would look up at the wise bland moon high in the heavens, free of the Quay. Indoors, the Christmas fire and the holly Job and I had gathered up the line; outside, carol-singers wooed the night air of the grim little town. I tiptoed round to the alley, looked up between the high ravine into High Street, turned and pressed myself against the right wall; it was the side of the bakehouse attached to the bread-shop, and at night it was toast-warm to the touch, a voluptuous private moment. Voices, footsteps – might one of them halt? There would then be the moonlit gleam of eye and smile, strong hand on my shoulder, humorous, stern melting into forgiving, forgiving hardening into stern, 'George!' ... But the steps jaunted by, with raucous laughter nothing to do with me. A last look at the moon, and back into the safe Spartan womb of 314a, back to the book.

These holidays involved an idea of Mr Boyer's, an essay on 'a Visit to a Factory'. One dark evening, Dad six-till-ten, I set out over Hawarden Bridge with a note-book and pass, to the envy of ten-year-old Job who already looked forward to working in Summers'; and like a stray insect I scuttled through a vast street-less city of black sheds, interminable rumbling walls, swivelling cranes, belching chimneys, wagons snarling along rails. I ought to have been excited by the pervasive all-powerful activity, but apart from pleasure that my father was a part of the machine-metropolis, I was conscious only of ruthlessness. I stumbled upon Dad's shed; though we both knew that I was expected, I was as proud and puzzled to see him as he was to see me. He introduced me to his mate Mr Hughes from Flint, whose son Ivor was due at H.C.S. in a year's time. 'Well,' said Dad to him, 'this is the boy!' I realized, with a swelling of the heart, why the cuttings were so grimy : privately and in good taste, he was beginning to boast about me.

They were guarding some sort of machine, and feeding it oil, cinders and – for all I knew – sandwiches. But I evinced interest, and wrote as if I were from the Press. Dad showed me round : a pounding nightmare of glutinous pistons entering serpent-like into hissing abdomens of steel, wheels and rods writhing in an inextricable rhythm to the inaudible music of a witches' sabbath : then the shed where, six feet away – he held me back – I watched a gigantic cube of molten steel throbbing along with red-hot sparks pouring from it. It had a malevolent beauty that held my look like love. Then there was a great pit of white bubbling wickedness that only had to be looked at to burn eyes out of a head. 'Has anybody ever fallen in?' I whispered in a shout. Dad knew me well enough to give the answer. 'Know why they put that rail? Boy slipped, never seen again.' I shivered and asked about carbon monoxide; I was gratified to find that he knew more chemistry than I did. I walked out of the money-making cauldron and was glad of the mute estuary night; if that was life, I wanted no part of it. Mr Boyer found my essay a dull effort.

By the middle of the spring term the film drug was losing its power. I found myself bored by Eddie Polo and Buck Jones and began to anticipate the vistas of scrub and the masked heroes rearing horses against the sky; there was a lull in magic, enlivened by a class-book – the horrifically unsuitable study of madness by Maupassant called *Le Horla* – and by the discovery of *Bleak House*. But *Bleak House*, long as it was, came to its end. Then the Saturday afternoon, a windy day of sun-chasing clouds that felt like the beginning of something, when outside the Hip, yet another W. S. Hart poster was suddenly covered with a slip, 'Special Show Sat Mat'. I was relieved, but not sanguine. A thin audience of children; as we waited for the pianist to enter and the windows to disappear, a weedy boy whom I did not know whispered to me with a leer, ' 'Ere, ever been to bed with yer sister?' It was an unexpected question. 'I have no sister,' I answered politely, and moved to another seat. The pianist attacked what looked like a sheaf of special music, darkness, then 'OWING TO THE NATURE OF THIS PICTURE NO OTHER ITEM WILL BE SHOWN'. This dismayed me – no choice? – and when Mr T. P. O'Connor flashed on I gave a sigh of frustration. He had written one word, and I could only think of sermons. 'Intolerance.'

'A Film by D. W. Griffith.' A preacher? Words faded in, 'Out of the Cradle Endlessly Rocking ...' then a veiled figure, in a shaft of mysterious light, seated at the cradle of the world. I sat forward. A close shot of a book, *Intolerance*; the book slowly opened, on to the words 'Love's Struggle through the Ages ...' I never sat back.

The film was as bold as the title. Four stories forged ahead like horses drawing a chariot; with the cradle the focus moved mesmerically from one to another, to and fro, till the tempo mounted in four crescendos to a triumphant dénouement. The old hypnosis crept up to my head; the Quay, my family, school, my secret thoughts, everything dissolved away and the only reality was my two eyes fixed on the flickering screen.

Story One was modern, made unforgettable by a last-minute rescue from the electric chair, Story Two about Christ, no less, from manger to cross, suggested by a shadow, a hand, a foot, Story Three the Massacre of Saint Bartholomew, Paris 1572, but Story Four was the one marvellously mine. It was set in Babylon, around the corrupt splendours of the Prince and Princess Beloved, with in the market-place the Mountain Girl, a tomboyish creature of sixteen, auctioned as a slave. On the very night of the Great Feast – soaring flights of stairs, barbaric pillars, immense stone elephants, with high above, revellers no larger than bees simmering in silhouette against the city flares – commotion, look, on the great wall, something ... Subtitle 'The moving finger writes, and having writ ...' Then the siege, on a staggering scale, battering-rams, molten catapulted rocks, ladders shooting up from vast engines, the defenders hurtling to their doom, every battle I had ever read of came to thrilling life. The Mountain Girl, struck by an arrow, sank happy and unwept to her death, day dawned on the horror-stained streets of Paris and the sun went down on Calvary. As the light faded from the three crosses, my heart was wrung by a tragedy which had been harangued past my deaf ears every Sunday since I could walk.

Sinking into my parlour-corner I had no recollection of my walk home; gradually my impressions assembled. Babylon was the real wonder, and even more than the Feast and the Siege, the Mountain Girl had ravished me, the sexless adolescent tossing her short hair at the crones around her and aping the boys by wiping her hand across her wide beautiful mouth as she drove her cart breakneck over the plains to warn the Palace. My love for this androgynous creature was twofold: one moment I worshipped her as an enchanting girl, the next I saw her as a wild dedicated lad, my friend across three thousand years.

This last was quick to flower into another vision, of myself as this boy. Home from school in the parlour, I would pull my hair down into my eyes and strain at the reins, face working and eyes flashing when they were not darting to the mirror, a narcissistic Jehu. The family abed, I would take the two dusty red pompons from the mantelpiece and fix one to each ear; then I put a hand up the kitchen chimney, crushed my lips with the soft soot and stared at myself sideways in the little shaving mirror. 'George, how long are you going to be, wasting oil?' The nose was too strong, whether for tomboy or boy, but mark how the teeth flashed joyously below the dusky curve of the mouth, 'Coming, just finishing my geography ...' Then again, many an evening, a wanderer in Rubbishland might have been astonished to see a schoolboy, a book under his arm, leap to the battlement top of a grass-grown dump. The Chaldean air thick with smoke, out of the blood-red sunset advances the locust army, arrows whistle; just as he aims he is mortally struck, in a close-up. The face twitches, empties of expression, the knees give, the Mountain Boy rolls down the slope to oblivion, scrambles up, brushes himself down, picks up his Algebra and walks home to fish and chips.

It was not long before Geo Wms the film star – Roy King, I would call myself – gave place to the novelist, though there was one week-end, in passing, after which Miss Morris had a glimpse of Geo Wms the dramatist; she had set 'a short piece, in dialogue, based on an historical episode'. I still had not seen or read a play, not counting *As You Like It*, but the result was *The Blue Band*, a forty-page 'drama' set in Paris the night of the Massacre, not the easiest piece to stage as it had twenty full-stage scenes lasting half a minute each. But that was a flash in the pan, the Easter holidays were devoted to Book One – a novel must now be planned on the scale of *Bleak House* – of *The Tombs of Terror*, a romance of ancient Thebes. The copperplate flowed as impeccably but the style was richer, stickier : a mixture of the *Sunday Companion*, Dickens, Lord Lytton, and Griffith subtitles. For the plot and setting, I heaped into the stew-pot *Out of Egypt* and the suspense from every serial I had ever seen. 'The Sun Sets! The great molten mass is sinking o'er the rim of the deserts. What is that couchant figure so sinister in its sublime immensity? The Great Sphinx . . .'

The hero, not unexpectedly, was a hermaphroditic streetdancer described as 'the boy Pearla'. 'His face was wonderfully fair for so trying a climate, with an expression almost magnetic. . . . Healthy red lips . . . His whole soul was in his dance, a wonderful feeling which can only be acquired by some people . . .' The Princess Nemesis saw him dance – Chapter Six, The Leap to Fame – but there was a secret society of priests with a green viper whose bite turned the victim to stone. Towards the end the copperplate got out of hand as it sprawled drunkenly on; by Page 107 the novelist had lost all proportion and was working up into a frenzied spiral of suspense which he knew in his heart must taper into nothing, the victim of its own excess. Chapter Twelve, The Death Knell. 'A minute to live! A mumble, a hiss . . . In a few minutes Pearla the Sacred Dancer of Mystery will be a solid statute . . . Death! Death!! Death!!! Two seconds to live!' End of Book One, to be Continued. It never was.

With a present from Miss Cooke of *The Irving Shakespeare*, my clutch of books – penny bargains, prizes, discards – had swollen to fifteen, and at Dad's suggestion we spent an engrossed Saturday sawing at two old orange-boxes, a penny each from Ma Williams the Chip Shop, to make a primitive two-shelf bookcase which just fitted the top of the cupboard next to my parlour-corner. I unearthed an old paint-box and gave the raw whorled wood a coat of maroon along the edges; with the books in place, it seemed to be beautiful. My pleasure from now on was to watch the shelves steadily fill.

In the meantime the disquieting spring flowed towards summer. One early evening, my parents had taken my brothers to some sort of Sports, and for the first time ever I found myself alone in our home, in a silence unique and strange. I felt suddenly hungry; with an impulse as irresistible as any in the calendar of sin, I went into the parlour, sat on the floor and opened the little cupboard in the dresser where my mother kept her sacred store of sugar, butter, jam, and raisins. One by one, I opened the little parcels and scooped out a small helping of each; as I ate, vile and gluttonous, I thought I heard a step, and knew that if my parents entered I would never recover. I put everything carefully back and reopened my book, sick and slightly more conscious of wickedness than ever before or since. Was it a strange by-symptom of growing pains? One Saturday, just as I began to dread my darkening upper lip drawing the street-call 'Beaver!', the end of the kitchen table was cleared and Dad gave me a shaving lesson with his razor. My secret thoughts were pressing forward, and I needed to be talked to. A sensible young master would have been a help, but from my elders and my books there was silence.

Silence too from the Silver Screen; but the pictures moved, and film-makers did not find the Censor difficult to hoodwink. While I liked some of the girls in class and was at ease with them, my visions were of the grown women I saw on the pictures. Between those two impassive Roman matrons in the Hip, Mr T. P. O'Connor tended to introduce a shadow-life unsettling to a schoolboy bursting out of his clothes at knee and elbow. Once the heady upheaval of *Intolerance* had settled into something to be lived with, it was the Babylonian orgy that stayed: flower-strewn bodies writhing on stair after stair, luscious odalisques, glimpsed in slow passing where a halt would have broken the spell, their bare breasts moving shamelessly to unheard cymbals. In 314a back-bedroom, when I was not leaning in a sheet over the bedstead balustrade of the Palace I would be half-lying, biting at a pomegranate under gold tables where besotted carousers sprawled in a dubious twilight, Children's Mat Sat One Penny.

Temptation drew nearer in the person of Theda Bara, as Salome or Cleopatra : a heavy-lidded heavy-mouthed courtesan writhing slowly on vast couches with a bangle round the ankle of one naked foot. It was the foot, somehow – close enough, from the twopenny-ha'pennies, to handle – that told me the rest was mine. Of that rest, I saw the bosom swelling under its jewelled helmets, the veiled curve of the hips – no, the gym-slips in school had nothing to fear. And when the hero, rugged in white breeches and stripped to the virile waist, sank on the edge of the couch, leant at an acute angle and placed his hand on a plump rump – 'the Southern Night, Marvellous One, is made for Love ...' – the lights clicking up, for the variety turn, found me in no mood for terriers staggering through hoops while their mistress played the xylophone in a crinoline. When I got to bed on those nights, there would follow me into it a series of full-bosomed hussies, accompanied on occasion by their menfolk. By the time I got to sleep, it was a big bed.

Though my books kept a general silence, I received food for thought from an unexpected source. 'Ever read Genesis 39 verse 12?' Harold Mears whispered with a leer. Home, I settled into my corner and opened an English Old Testament. 'She caught him by his garment, saying, Lie with me ...' So that was Potiphar's Wife. 'Reading the Bible,' said Mam, 'good life, what's the matter with you?'

My first examination was to be in July – 1919 – the 'Junior Central Welsh Board', and I was determined to shine; to pass was not difficult, the thing to aim at was 'Distinctions'. With Miss Cooke's precepts in mind, I prepared as for an offensive. I wrote out, and kept to, a self-appointed schedule right up to the night before : 5.30–6 Chem. Revision, 6–7 Trig. ... My weak subjects I placed first, when my brain was clearest; French and Latin I kept for last, as a bedtime sweet. I did useful drudgery during the Sunday sermon, off scraps of paper lodged in my hymn-book : 'Reduplicated Perfects, cado cecidi, posco poposci, tango tetigi ...'

In the lustrous evenings, I jogged my brain and legs by strolling up the line, books under my arm, a scholar gipsy with the gipsy side put away; I would settle into a sheltered corner of grassy clay, and study, sift, list, underline. The important thing, next to straightforward swotting, was to examine the examiner's mentality, and I carried Miss Cooke's idea as far as cunning: draw his attention, early on, tactfully display your wares. 'Describe the climate of Madagascar.' I had no idea – temperate season, rainy periods? – but had just read a novel about pirates. 'It is doubtful whether Antananarivo, the capital of the world's third largest island, so rich in cattle and cacti, would be what it is with a different climate ...' I had the right psychology for examinations; I was nervous, but my hand did not tremble, I enjoyed myself, and Sports Day was an anticlimax.

Then the seven soporific holiday weeks, when the gipsy took over. Up the line there was a shimmer of heat to distort the rails, and I sneaked to the estuary and swung naked and ashamed in the arctic flood. Miss Cooke had given me a beautiful *Golden Treasury*, illustrated with reproductions of paintings, which now exercised a gradual and sensuous effect on me, wooing me to poetry. Written under a woodland scene, with one solitary dreamer seated beneath a great tree, the sort to which I had always been strangely drawn, was 'My heart aches, and a drowsy numbness pains'. I had to read Keats after that. Then a Victorian girl seated at a harpsichord: 'music, when soft voices die ...' That stirred me, in an intimately subtle way, and I knew I was with fine things. 'Get out in the air, lad,' Mam would call, 'or you'll go bad.' Then I would climb our fence and wonder, as I sniffed the Bone Yard, exactly what Lillian Gish and Richard Barthelmess were doing at this minute in California. After the heat of the day, with even the Quay landscape softly whispering, I would ramble, restless and yet lulled by poetry, among the abandoned trucks; in search, half knowing, of a stranger wandering like myself who might answer unaskable questions. But there was only an occasional courting couple primly hand in hand, and the face of Rubbishland was too open to permit of tracking them to their lair; I meandered home, books under my arm.

A week before school, a postcard: 'You have passed Junior,

with distinctions in Hist. Eng. Lat. Geog. Welsh and Fr. with Conversational Power. Well done JME.' Dad put it in his wallet, where it was followed by the *County Herald* cutting. These were not joined by a small certificate I brought home from chapel, to the effect that Master G. Williams was for life a member of the Wesleyan League of Total Abstainers.

The winter term was a lull. Rogers had left for Liverpool University, having got his London Matric; I learnt later that privately coached by Miss Cooke, he had passed in French in the unbelievable time of three months, from scratch. Miss Swinnerton joined to teach Geography, pleasant and unpretentious; I was lucky in my school elders, Miss Morris was one of those quiet teachers of literature with the gift of unobtrusively planting – in soil where it could again flower – her deep and loving knowledge, and even the two Inspectors were characters. Mr Robinson was a bluff, wise, brick-faced sergeant-major of a man, with a humorous respect for Miss Cooke. 'I could not do without her,' J.M. said to him once, 'what a blessing for us all she never got married.' 'All?' said Mr Robinson, 'does that include the man?' J.M. told Miss Cooke, 'Ho ho!' she chuckled, 'touchée!'

The other visitant was Miss Sadie Price, a fascinating by-product of Welsh puritanism: the brilliant daughter of a (Calvinist) Head of College in Bangor, she had been born fifty years too soon into a world which forbade a gentlewoman to give proof of intelligence. She had taken her Cambridge degree as a son would have sown wild oats – by stealth: and now showed her independence, a pretty witty spinster in her forties, by rhyming Inspectress with Actress and touring the Welsh county schools wearing paint, powder, over-fair hair massed over the ears and a pair of white fur-topped boots in which she tripped from class to class as unembarrassed as an elegant chamois. Friendly though she was, being inspected by her was something of an ordeal; I stood trapped between fixed seat and desk, talking halting French and assailed by my first waft of feminine make-up and perfume. Everybody, staff and pupils, looked forward to Miss Sadie.

Said Miss Morris innocently one day, questioning us on

Macbeth, 'Looking at that photograph in the Central Hall, it seems a pity it can't happen again.' I studied the picture, a startled group in drapes and Viking helmets, dated years before, and felt the same unexplained urge as when I had imagined presenting Elaine. There was no dramatic society, the Central Hall had only its small foot-high platform, and I still had never seen a play; but that night in bed, I worked out a production of *Macbeth*. I cut difficult crowd scenes and switched others: Septimus could be Duncan and Macduff, scenery a cardboard battlement, the witches voices echoing from behind a curtain, Millie Tyrer Lady Macbeth, a strong voice and would take it seriously. In the train next day I mouthed Macbeth – a drum for effects – and discussed it, engrossed, with Miss Morris, Millie, and Septimus; the bell rang – the Macduff scene suggested by a sign-post 'To Thames ½ mile' – out of the grey, Miss Cooke. 'See here Williams, what's this footling idea of getting up a ... I don't care if it *is* an exam play, you jolly well knuckle under and get ready for your Senior, *Macbeth* indeed, now get along ...' She banged into the Mistresses' Room, left me pale with rage, and stayed in my bad books for the rest of the term.

My mind turned back to writing. Sitting in the gathering shadows just before last bell, looking up from the stone naked-ness of winged Icarus in my Latin Reader and listening to the melancholy twilight choir rehearsing in the Central Hall, I thought of *The Young Visiters*, which had just created a furore, by Daisy Ashford aged nine; though unconscious humour was not quite what I was aiming for, I had my dreams. I dreamt of J.M., one morning at prayers: 'in view of the s-s-sensational news that the enthralling new romance by George Williams, yet to take his Senior, *Woman Thy Name is Serpent*, has passed the half-million mark, I announce a half-holiday.' Tomorrow I would be fourteen, the landmark beyond which I knew that Mam, without saying anything, would look upon me as a tolerated non-earner. I must have mentioned something to Miss Morris, for on Christmas Eve there arrived one of the most sensible presents ever given – *The Lure of the Pen* by Flora Klickmann: a fund of advice, racy and practical, to the would-be writer, analysing the problems of sincerity, readability, cliché, and second-hand emotions. It was everything that I needed in the way of a constructive dressing-down, from a kindly Miss Cooke of Fleet Street, and reaching out for *The Tombs of Terror*, I gave the novelist no quarter. Across whole pages I wrote 'Grossly Overwritten', then in the margin 'why five adjectives when two would do?' and across the last page ('Death! Death!! Death!!!') 'hysterical over-emphasis, ludicrous'. I was growing up.

The Count of Monte Cristo; then I was deflected by the Eisteddfod. This was held, every first of March, the feast of the Welsh patron saint David, in the Central Hall; the three houses into which the school was divided for sports, Gwenffrwd, Alun, Pennant, competed in everything from solos to woodwork. Wally was captain of my house and I became his right-hand man, enlisting every member for every sort of competition; I felt a sport, one of the group. I tried my hand at nearly every item, even spending an untalented evening doggedly copying an old Christmas-card. 'Recitation, two minutes.' I had lately been taken with Mrs Nickleby's hare-brained dissertations, and blended a passage with bits from other ramblings of hers; every night in bed I mouthed till I was letter-perfect, then alone in the train shriekingly practised a high mincing voice, interspersed with my old high-spirited whoops, emerging demurely at the Quay to be stared at by puzzled travellers. To step forward in the packed hall in daylight, with no rehearsal and the heat and excitement of contest after contest, was a valuable exercise of concentration. Having announced 'Mrs Nickleby', I stood and – for a second – thought, shall I lose my nerve and just recite it? I clamped one hand primly over the other, set a poker face, and shot up into falsetto, 'Kate my dear, a warm day always puts me in mind of roast pig ...' There was a gasp and a giggle, and I was off. It was like riding a dangerous motor-bike. I got first prize.

With the holidays, Easter 1920, *Monte Cristo* was devoured to the end, then walks to and from Flint Library, eight miles, good for me, to borrow more. One title caught my eye, *The Ballad of Reading Gaol* – a crime story? Answered the librarian severely, 'You could call it that, the author was disgraced.' 'Oh?' I said, sniffing mystery. 'Brilliant fellow too,' he continued, breathing on his spectacles, 'Irishman, d'you know Ruskin, *Sesame and Lilies?*' What had he done, a German spy? Sinn Fein? I went home with Edgar Allan Poe and emerged drowned in horror and determined to write like that, no more no less.

With my mother to Bradley's, to buy my first long trousers for next term, with low shoes showing the socks. Then, unseated maybe by April softening into May, though I knew as little of the juices of nature as of the sap rising within myself, I became more and more restless; books could not hold me. My dreams were of initiation – into what? – visions of a leafy bower from a Renaissance painting: tumbled rosy limbs chequered with shadow, an overturned wine-glass drenching the grass and beyond the trees the sunlit turrets of an indulgent society . . . One Saturday afternoon I was bound for home along the frequented path from the river to Shotton. An elderly ragged figure lunged towards me in the crowd, put his arms out, said 'Ah me boy!' and drew me paternally aside to a gap in the hedge. I thought he knew Dad and wanted to give a message; then, at the moment when he swayed against barbed wire and I realized he was drunk, he leered between odd teeth, 'How is everything, eh?' and with people passing two feet away, put out his free hand, grubby but expert. He was thwarted by my jumping back a foot, stumbling, and stalking home. What hot water my backstreet Bacchus got into I never heard, all I knew was that my cheeks were still burning when I sat down for my Saturday shave. The episode settled into the back of my mind like an obscene purring cat, and on my meanders my eyes took to roving absently, behind them a rag-bag of shabby thoughts.

Two Saturdays later, eve of term, I found myself near Hawarden Bridge, with the grey Steelworks not even hiccupping with life and the dreggy river with its boats overturned in mud. It began to rain. I was scrambling for home when I saw a figure under the bridge; without thought, yet instantaneously, I deflected. 'Nasty afternoon!' I said heartily, and wished I were wearing my longs. 'It is an' all.' He was a rough fellow in the ageless limbo of the twenties, ginger hair under a cap and a day's growth of ginger beard, shabby khaki overcoat: a pale square amiable face. He lit a Woodbine, with stubby out-of-work fingers, 'Fag? ... 'Sright, keep out o' temptation, from the Quay?' He was from Queensferry, not a neighbour. Silence.

My heart beating, I was as crafty as an old man. 'You must ha' been in the war.' 'Ay,' he said, 'Western Froont, copped it Ah did, God this rain ...' 'You must ha' seen soom terrible things.' I had said 'soom' to sound matey. 'Norralf I did an' all, boot ye get used to everythin', it's clearin' oop, Ah'm off –' 'What sort o' things?' 'Oh, 'ouses on fire an' that, dead chaps an' that –' 'Is it true,' I said, 'the Germans did all that in the papers?' 'Oh,' he said, blowing smoke down his nose, 'ye mean like rapin' an' that? Well, ye can't believe all –' 'What's rape?' I said quick as lightning, my face just below his, eyes wide under the school cap. We were alone in the world. He looked down at me and laughed. 'You know,' he said, 'takin' a woman by force, like.' 'What way?' Then I added, 'I don't know, properly.' A pause. He rubbed his stubbled chin. ''Ow old are ye?' 'Fourteen last November.' 'Garn,' he said, 'ye're older than that.' 'No I'm not,' answered the spider to the fly, 'I'm only just shaving, will you tell me?' Pause. 'Let's walk along,' I continued, 'the rain's stopped.' We reached, in the long strip parallel to path and moribund water, a hollow of thin grass mixed with muddy sand. He spread his khaki and we half sat on elbows, facing – across the river – the square red-brown seedcake of Summers' Offices, and commanding the desolate landscape on each side.

We parted smartly and amiably; he walked away for ever, stolid, lonely, harmless, to merge into the stream of prisoner-of-war faces and thence into the millionfold multitude of the average man. I strode home past the kind stone-faced shoppers, my eyes to the ground, at peace but guilty, guilty but at peace.

Chapter 14

Sleep-walking to Babylon

Sooner than confide in any of them, I would have taken my troubles to the beasts of the field. But even without help, the situation was not serious; the sense of transgression, like mud left on a garment, dried and flaked aseptically into dust. The first day of the summer term, Silly Wil greeted us loudly at the gate, still snivelling; I felt from his vague smile that he knew all about me. The first Saturday, too old now for the Hip Mats, I walked up to St Deiniol's Library – attached to the embattled Gladstone home in Hawarden, I had a pass. As I nosed along scholastic shelves, my eye caught the title *What a Young Boy Ought to Know*. It startled me, and I expected mild pornography; it turned out to be priggish but outspoken advice to a creature like myself.

It did me good, and through the rest of the term I was the first to leap at Mr Boyer's swimming lessons, after school in the indoor pool attached to St Winifred's Well. The heat in afternoon class was enervating, and the essays we were studying echoed the summer mood : Jefferies' 'Meadow Thoughts' – 'the mind wanders deeper into the dreamy mystery of the azure sky . . .', Leigh Hunt's 'Hot Day' – 'now ladies loiter in baths, and people make presents of flowers . . .' The pool was set in mouldering stone, its temperature icy; after the dawdle down through the hot town, came the knife-sharp anaesthesia of the water. Because it was not a team game, I took to the exercise and found I could swim; I was leading a Healthy Life, and could look Eric and Jim Hawkins in the eye. Learning the breast-stroke and curbing the passions formed an operation doubly gratifying.

And the Senior was looming : I marshalled my forces even more thoroughly, and again enjoyed myself. For the holidays,

Miss Cooke again stacked books on to me. French this time, some the set-books for next year, *Athalie*, *Le Bourgeois Gentil-homme*, La Bruyère's *Caractères*, *Atala*. Greedy though I was, I found most of them indigestible. Racine is the most adult of authors, with a classic simplicity bound to deceive the most pre-cocious student by his look of poverty : to the immature eye, the exquisitely right can look like the pedantically trite. But there was Bazin's *Le Blé qui Lève*, and *Tartarin de Tarascon*. It was pleasing to be reading a French novel, written for French people – published in Paris! – with no difficulty for a whole sentence at a time. Miss Cooke sent me a pound to take Job and Tom to Chester to see the Roman remains; coming back I shut my eyes at the railway bookstall, held my breath, and splurged twelve silver shillings on a dozen monthly magazines (*Nash's*, *Cassell's*, *Windsor*) so that I could Study the Fiction Market.

In the meantime, while passions might be curbed, they could not be quite scotched : there were miracles beyond St Winifred's compass. Once or twice the heat of nature, within and without, would meet in combustion, such as when I sat late in the stifling parlour, the August dark gathering around me after two hours' steady reading, and was taken unawares. Leafing through my Shakespeare, I chanced on *Venus and Adonis* : 'Graze on my lips, and if these hills be dry, Stray lower ...' In the stuffy twilight, my eyes ran like chased hares down the pages, plucking out the inflammatory lines. 'With blindfold fury she begins to forage ... Her champion mounted for the hot encounter ...' Thanks to England's national poet, a Young Boy forgot all he Ought to Know.

'Passed Senior, with distinctions in Hist. Eng. Lat. Welsh Arith. Fr. with Conversational Power, congratulations J.M.E.' It meant another item for my father – the Arithmetic surprised him as much as it did me – and with the winter term, 1920, a decisive advance into adulthood : instead of a roll-call of thirty, we in the Honours Form were seven, and free of the sub-jects I liked least, Maths, Chemistry, Drawing, of everything except French, English and History, which we were to prepare for 'Higher', the final examination in two years' time. With only three teachers, women with the rest of the school on their hands, most of our periods were unsupervised; there was no exam in sight, freedom became irksome and lessons unimportant.

In the French class, though, there was no slacking. Miss Cooke no longer intimidated me, but standing in that small room before a staring arm-folded audience, she was a force : her personality demanded a university platform facing a gallery, and why she never bestrode one is a vocational mystery. Her presentation of the première of Hugo's *Hernani* – the booted foot on the other, hands under arms, lower lip jutting and head butting – was memorable. 'Look here, Romantic Movements don't start with pallid poets writing pallid rhymes, they jolly well get off to red blood and red waistcoats. That night in Parry' – it was her one verbal affectation, to pronounce the French capital not as Paris or even Paree, but Parry – 'that night in Parry in 1830, those rebels against Classicism filed into their loges, Gautier flaunting his red waistcoat – and a thousand pities, say I, that in Dublin fourteen years ago at *The Playboy of the Western World* they didn't wear the same instead of chucking stink-bombs' – a characteristic side-volley – 'up goes le rideau, silence, Doña Josefa stands motionless' – the vowels lengthen rhapsodically :

' "Serait-ce déjà lui? . . . C'est bien à l'escalier
     Dérobé . . ."

– ça y est, hisses and cheers, the crime is committed, le jeune Victor has dared to carry a sentence from one line into the next and so perpetrate the barbaric Caesura – uproar, the die cast and by jingo, the Romantic Movement launched.'

Her intensity as she swung from one language into the other sometimes dislocated her h's – ' 'Ugo's 'ateful hattitude to women' – but we never sniggered, any more than at Parry capital of France. Another day it would be the trim sly epigrams of La Bruyère, but the powdered wig did not fit; she was much more at home as de Vigny's *Moïse*, with a ruthless organ-beat French of which the prophet himself might have been proud on Sinai :

' "O Seigneur ! J'ai vécu, puissant et solitaire,
     Laissez-moi m'endormir du sommeil de la terre !" '

The little room bulged, it was like watching Mrs Siddons play Lady Macbeth in pince-nez in a railway-carriage. And if mad Wil was outside, crouched in threadbare overcoat under the dripping evergreens – his nose dripping too, when not sniffing for crumbs of knowledge from the magic casements – he must have been astonished. But she was never grotesque and never showed off; it was a projection of literary treasure by a teacher who was the rarest of anomalies, a full-blooded spinster.

There was no official Head Boy: I shared the position with Wally, football captain and still in the Seniors, and was also train prefect, Intervening in fights and expectoration in front of lady travellers, stern but every inch a man. I was happy; the only thing I consciously missed was money, which cast a shadow faint but unmistakable. On the chapel outing to Rhyl I had no extra pocket-money for ice-creams for me and Tom, and kind Mr Price slipped me a shilling; nobody ever visited 314a except a stray relative once a year, when Dad put on his best and there were small cakes from Hewitt's and the tea-set and we boys sat in a corner while they gossiped in Welsh. But nobody looked right in our house except us. More and more I felt that I ought to be bringing money in; Job, at twelve, was a paper-boy in the evenings for Bennett's, and even Tom helped him on Saturday nights. I once suggested that I too should sell papers. 'No,' said my mother, 'what about that homework?' 'And a good thing too,' added Dad, 'we don't want the *Football Echo* put through old Mrs Coppack's letter-box, do we, and the *Woman's World* landing on Johnny the Bruiser?' I now had a shilling a week, but it did not go far; I looked longingly at the second-hand book box outside Cruickshank's – grubby Nelson's Classics, *Kipps*, H. S. Merriman, Anthony Hope – but I would have had nothing for the Hip. Then, about to succumb to self-pity, I would remind myself that Mam did her best. There were treats: Sunday tea, Christmas mince-pies and plum-pudding, and once a year she made toffee which we would smell boiling before she packed it into a jar, in jagged pieces and tasting wonderful.

Suddenly Miss Cooke, who seemed to do nothing without

suddenness, said to me, 'See here, have you a good doctor in Connah's Quay?' 'Oh yes,' I said, 'we go to him for the 'flu.' 'Give him this and have your chest overhauled.' My mother was alarmed, 'Have you been coughing? ... No? Sending people to the doctor, well ...' 'Chest like a barrel,' said Doctor Owen, 'footballer?' 'A bit,' I said, with a glow which did not disperse. It was some time before I found out why Miss Cooke had sent me.

Meanwhile she enlivened the term with an innovation : she arranged for her pupils to correspond with a school in France, the Welsh side to write in French, the French side in English, each to include friendly corrections. While the others were mildly interested, I was excited; to me any unknown hand-writing had the same removed fascination as the glimpse of a face – anybody's face – first seen in a mirror, and the idea of a live French boy sitting in France, biting his pen and then writing 'Mon cher George', was beyond anything stimulating, would he enclose a laughing snapshot ... ?

Day by day fresh names were given out, 'Eira Parry, yours is Germaine Froissart, start "Chère Germaine" and end with "votre amie" feminine – Eric Jones, Edmond Toussaint ...' Millie wrote pages to Yvonne Avalon, who sounded like a film star. But my turn never came. I was puzzled, baulked, and too proud to ask. Answers began to arrive, and during a chess game one wet dinner-time – an idea of Mr Boyer's – Wally showed me his : 'sounds daft, 'alf of it!' I fingered the meagre graph-paper with envy. 'Dear Friend, I write with much of plaisure, I have fifteen ears ("Fifteen, 'eck, he oughter be in a flippin' circus!") and I habit with my father, my mother is died, I am unique son (of course, fils unique) racount me if it please you your life, I love receve your response ...' 'Ha ha, talks like a bloomin' girl!' I walked away in anger; each mistake had for me the grace of a boy speaking haltingly out of a costume painting.

Then one day Miss Cooke said casually, 'Oh George Williams, you'll be hearing from a French lady, a teacher at the school, who will be kind enough to correspond with you and set you essays and correct them. Here's a sheaf of stamps, and mind you

191

use the thinnest paper – I'll give you a wodge later.' 'Yes, Miss Cooke.' Round the corner I kicked the water-pipes in a fury of frustration. 'What's the matter?' said Ena Mills. 'It's my French, she's arranged for me to have a mistress!' 'Dear me,' murmured Septimus, 'there's French for you, when does it start?'

But I was not to be cajoled, had I not been fooled? I refused to recognize that Miss Cooke wanted my French expertly tuned and that letters in broken English would not serve her purpose; but when my eye caught, next to my tea and tomato on the newspaper-cloth, an envelope with exotic stamps, my pulse had to quicken. 'It came through the post,' said my mother, 'whatever is it?' My first letter ever, come hundreds and hundreds of miles ... Greyish envelope, tinged with blue from the thin thin lining. A clear smallish fastidious hand : 'Monsieur George Williams, 314a High Street, Connah's Quay, near Chester, Angleterre', how odd it looked ... I turned over the envelope, 'J. Tardy, Vincentier-en-Genevois, Haute Savoie, France'. I opened it, Mam watching as if she expected it to explode in my face. 'Cher George Williams, Miss Cooke vous aura certainement prévenu ...' Signed 'Sincèrement, J. Tardy'. I studied it phrase by polished phrase, savouring the flavour of idioms penned by a spinster but composed for me alone. 'Have your tea lad, is it from the French boy?' 'No,' I said absently, 'it's from a woman.' The bread-knife hovered in mid-air. I explained. Next day I wrote back, at length and in fanatically correct French, between the cracks of which I meant the lady to glimpse an amusing correspondent. 'Chère Mademoiselle (never abbreviate titles), Je vous remercie infiniment ... (Shall I tell her it's my first letter ever except to Annie? – no, sounds too childish) J'apprécie votre gentillesse ... J'ai deux frères, mon père travaille à l'usine ...' The amusing correspondent would come later.

For Shorthand-and-Book-keeping students, the school had a gigantic typewriter; Miss Cooke set me to learn and I was soon typing my French essays on to the thin paper, dotting-in the acents afterwards. 'La différence entre Thomas Hardy et Arnold Bennett' ... Back next week would come the sheaf, scored with a rash of tiny red corrections, clear and exact. 'Cette tournure n'est pas française ... Pas clair, qui désignez-vous par "lui", il faut refaire la phrase ...' It was another challenge, and invaluable.

In the meantime the novelist re-emerged. Dipping into criticism – Gosse, Quiller-Couch, R.L.S. – I discovered that Dickens's heart had run away with him in *A Tale of Two Cities* and led him to overwrite, while Geo Eliot's head had stumped off with her in *Romola* and led her to produce a treatise. Geo Wms would rise, an adolescent phoenix between their two stools, with a novel which would sober romance with erudition, and spice erudition with romance. I re-read *The Lure of the Pen* and celebrated my fifteenth birthday, a sombre Saturday, by walking the four miles to Flint Library, poring for a couple of hours over ancient Babylon, and making notes in an exercise-book; this continued for weeks. I was as thorough as any student in the British Museum: 'Deities (a) good spirits (b) bad spirits ...' 'Babylonians a Semitic race, pastoral, nomadic, founded by Queen Semiramis' (exquisite name!) 'Sargon, succeeded in 705 BC by Sanherib or Sennacherib ... Walls made from hot bitumen, alabaster slabs used for pavements 20 by 12 feet, coloured plaster-work common, cuneiform inscriptions, Temp. – January Isotherm 70° July Isotherm 80°, coinage the Maneh equals £9.' ... I made maps of Chaldea and a plan of Babylon ('1 inch to 500 metres') more detailed than any I could have done of Connah's Quay: Khatoniyeh Canal, Outer Walls, Inner Walls, Burying Place, the Road of Spoil, Hanging Gardens ...

Next, a painstaking synopsis, (A) Starting Things (B) Developing Things (C) Accomplishing Things. 'At a village near Shusham live two families ... The beautiful Nonair is in ignorance of her parentage and is known as the Princess Beloved ...' Space was minutely allotted: 'Chap. One, The Veiled Stranger 1¼p, The Falls of Drulatra 1½, The Dying Man ½ ...' 'Analyses of characters: Ban-Apli, sneered at but rather manly – Iqaral (I loved that missing u) vain, rather artificial, gives impression of "maturity" – Nalome (the heroine) A. *Outwardly* (a) to acquaintances, cold, unapproachable ... (b) to intimates, high-spirited, outspoken. B. *Inwardly* (carefully study this while writing) (a) more obviously : sensitive, studies Life and appreciates its vastness, etc. (b) poetic insight into the mysteries of the Beyond, possessed by every person of ordinary "soul-power" . . .'

Then I wrote : ' "The Mists of Babylon", Chapter One "Mul-Ge" : A man stood on Tirpaz Crag, peering into the seething gulf of the valley . . .' The style aimed at economy; determined not to overwrite, the author sometimes lapsed into dullness : 'He had an air of restrained tragedy which obsessed vaguely the observer'. Every Saturday from darkling five till bed-time, I wrote in my icy Montmartre attic : ground floor with fire and warm smell of ironing and shadowy Mam, Dad, Job and Tom. By the time Nalome reached Babylon the copperplate was again beyond control, and I took my first professional step by starting to scribble in pencil, double-spaced for revision. Occasionally research showed through like a bone – 'steps of white gypsum' . . . 'The Ishtar Gate is placed where the Processional Way threads past the Temple of Rinmach' – but once or twice promise glimmered, 'The river fought with the storm, as if goaded by the seven terrors of darkness, a darkness of death's making . . .'

I sank back into a dream-world, happy in the company of my characters. Walking up the line, now prickly with northern winter, I looked down at the swollen ditches for a bird's eye view of my mighty Waterfall of Drulatra; at dusk, when the silhouette of Sandycroft furnaces tinged the sky with red, I saw the lights of Babylon. I was working, steady and absorbed. Then one Friday, February 1921, looking forward to next day's session, continuing from 'What either fate or the gods had in store, Ahteris knew not . . .' I was told by Miss Cooke to call at her lodgings on the way home. I went, clear of conscience, for she often dispatched me on messages, 'Slip down to Miss White's with this note, pick up the book in the hall, read the chapter on Voltaire, and make your comments.' She was stooped over Latin exercises, mouthing between gulps of tea and scoring weals of correction. 'Sit down.' 'Yes Miss Cooke.' I waited on the edge of her sofa. She looked up, dropped the pince-nez and focused sternly on me. 'Do you realize that the fifteen years of your life have been spent within a radius of seven-and-a-half miles?' 'Yes Miss Cooke.' 'Look here,' she said, 'would you like to go to France?'

Chapter 15

En Voyage

'Well?'

'I'm sorry,' I said, 'I thought you said would I like to go to France.'

'I did. Would you?'

'Yes Miss Cooke.'

'The Headmaster agrees that as you are a year ahead, you could stay for the summer term in the care of Mademoiselle Tardy. Now your parents, what'll they say?'

I was still staring. In those days, even to a broadminded parent the project was to sound as bold as it would seem, now, for a pupil to be included in the Everest Expedition; I knew that for my mother, it would be the equivalent of hearing her son proposed as the first schoolboy to reach the moon. 'Well,' I said, 'the cost – ?' 'That's my affair, an investment I happen to think worth making. Tell them there'd be a man from Thomas Cook to see you across London and Parry. I can get you an old trunk. Break the ice tonight, get along now, good luck.' She had already seized the next exercise-book. I mumbled 'Thank you Miss Cooke' and stumbled out.

London, Paris ... I felt the same as when she had put me on to French, poignantly exhilarated. In the train I sat with a book open, thinking of my mother; Dad would be on my side, but I knew that if she said no, he would back her up. Two-till-ten, how to get him alone? – no, together, him sitting back cutting his Warhorse 'baccy, her plaiting her twin horns of white hair and Dad joking about them, she was always in a good humour then ... But her first thought would be, why didn't he tell me when he came home – no, beard her first.

Both boys were out playing. Over my tea, as she lifted down

the lamp to trim the ragged wick, I was more chatty than usual, in a jerky way. 'What's the matter?' I looked up quickly. 'Mam, Miss Cooke wants me to talk to you.' My knuckles were clenched. She frowned, 'Have you done something wrong?'

'Oh no,' I said eagerly, 'they want to send me to France.' She stood, the smoking poker in her hand, '*France*?' Yes, the moon. 'Yes,' I said, 'Miss Cooke will pay for everything, for me to stay with her friend Miss Tardy' – Miss sounded more respectable – 'a nice lady of good family.' 'Pay for everything?' She had stiffened at the magnitude of the obligation. 'Oh, just the fare and the bare room –' 'Who is going to take you there?' I swallowed. 'Thomas Cook, a relation of hers that would take me across London and – anywhere in France' – keep Paris out of it – 'an experienced gentleman that takes children of six across, never mind grown-ups. Mam, do you think Dad might say no?'

Unintentionally, a master stroke. She considered. 'Drink your tea, he might, it is a big step.' I made a fresh move, a sharp one, 'Mam, will he be on our side?' But she was sharper, 'I haven't said whose side I'm on, what if you got took bad?' 'French doctors are the best,' I said, 'there's one called Pasteur who's the top of them all, and didn't Doctor Owen say I had a first-class chest, this is why she wanted to find out.' A pause. 'Yes,' she said, 'you get your chest from my side, Thomas from *his* side.' Leave well alone. I did my homework: History, not French, in case the dream was smashed. Suppose he strayed on the way, France indeed, get up to bed this minute ... No, home on the dot, wreathed in smiles, what's in the oven Poll? After supper, me trying to read and twisting my watch-seal, he got out his pipe. 'Tell your father.'

With each detail his face lit up more. 'Paris! Bless my soul d'you hear that, Poll? ... Thomas Cook? No, George, he won't be a relation, she'd be a rich woman if he was, he'll be working for that big firm, Dover to Cally will you go?' His regard for Miss Cooke was, as ever, blended with the conviction that she was some sort of pedagogic clown. 'Trust her to keep us on the hop with her marching orders, she'll be in the House o' Commons next!' Then he looked serious, 'Poll, dymwa rwbeth rbeth

ini feddwi amdano, be 'di dy farn di?' Welsh, which now they
only spoke in front of us at the most serious of junctures, 'here's
something to ponder, what dost think?' 'Wn i ddim,' said Mam,
'I don't know.' 'Well,' said Dad to me, 'ar y daith, have a good
journey!'

That night I was a long time going to sleep; no sooner had
I done so than the Irish Mail thundered and lightened through
our box of a room, this time whirling me with it, Chester, London, Dover, Calais, Paris, Paris, Paris ... At school, I was half a
day's wonder; *The Mists of Babylon* was put away, cut off for
ever like *Edwin Drood*, but for a happier reason. I wrote to
Mademoiselle, tempering excitement to grammar, 'je trouve
difficile à exprimer mon émotion ...' Forms for Dad to fill, the
passport photograph taken in the shed-like salon on High Street,
my first since Talacre, aged five. As a copy was to go to
Mademoiselle, I must be at my Hollywood best: frank blue-
eyed look at the camera, modest but vital. The man took the
picture a second early, and the result was the loose-lipped ex-
convict to be found in three passports out of four: I was morti-
fied. 'Je ne suis pas beau, mais j'espère que je ne suis pas aussi
laid que ceci ...'

Then preparations. When my mother saw that apart from
extra shirts, socks and pyjamas, all I needed was an alpaca
jacket – the tropical ring of it! – she scaled my trip down to
Everest proportions. It was I who insisted on the pyjamas;
thanks to the pictures, the nightshirt was becoming yearly a
more ignominious garment. To Mam 'pie-jams' represented
English foppery, but I pretended Mademoiselle had mentioned
them. Finally Dad and I lugged the trunk home from the station,
sent from Leeds and an immense scarred affair with a curved lid
and straps like thongs; it squatted in the parlour like a battered
baby elephant, stirring my blood every time I entered. Gradually
it half-filled; no bottom drawer for a bride was so meticulously
plenished. 'How many handkerchiefs, do they blow their noses
like anybody else? ... You can't clean your teeth with soot over
there, they'll think you been brought up by Red Indians ...' I
bought tooth-paste, pour la France. My only book would be Dau-

det's *Lettres de Mon Moulin*, for I was determined, once Dover receded, that not one word of English would come to me or from me. I also packed a tiny black Bible, 'i Mr George Williams o'i ddosbarth ar ei ymadawiad i'r Ffrainc, from his Sunday-school class on his departure for France.' This was included out of sentiment.

When the marching orders came, Mam was glad of them. 'H'd-case for necessities for journey, so that trunk can be registered thru. S'dwiches for train. Don't leave Chester Stn. At Euston, stand quite still on platform waving h'k'chief periodically for Cook's man' – Dad said 'Wouldn't a flag-pole be better?' – 'who will see to trunk and take you to h'tel. Send p.c. of safe arrival to parents and S.G.C. ... ON NO ACCT LEAVE HOTEL DURING EV'G. Arrange called 7.30 a.m. ... Cook's man will see you to b't-tr. Leave 6d. in bedrm for m'd, 6d. in d'n'g rm. Lunch on Fr. tr. ...' Dad admired the document, 'When you do a thing, do it right ...' Said Mam, 'What if this Cook's man doesn't turn up?' 'Worse Poll, what if he *does* turn up, an' sells the lad on to one o' them boats?'

'Good-bye, Miss Cooke, thank you very much –' 'Thank me when you get back, I'm taking a small gamble on this, and it's up to you to see I bring it off, good-bye, my regards to Mademoiselle Tardy ...' The day dawned, sunlit and crackling with travel. Dad was back from work – ten-till-six – the bacon sizzled, the boys off to school, good-byes, with Mam flushed and her eyes darting round to make sure nothing was forgotten. Dad and I dragged the trunk out through the front door, 'Ta ta, don't forget to wave from the train, ta ta ...' On my first home-leaving, the impulse must have arisen in her to kiss me good-bye; but it was too late in our relationship to embark on an embarrassing gesture, and we trundled off. In the alley, I put my end down, turned and waved; Dad waved too, mischievously, and we disappeared. Neighbours stared, Dad met three separate mates, 'Mr Summers let me off for a trip round the world!' In the station, I peered into the tiny ticket-hole, 'London third single.' '*London?*' In exchange for the astronomical fare, a cardboard 'Euston', boldly in print. Over the bridge with the trunk – it looked very shabby in the sun – then we paced the platform, not talking much, but easy together; we had never been alone before. My train drew lovingly upon me, like a jewelled negro out of the spring morning.

It had nothing in common with the one in which I had sat, on this very line, every school-day for nearly four years, this was *my* train, put together bolt by bolt for this day, 7 April, 1921 A.D. We heaved the great trunk into the van and Dad shook hands with me, heartily and with shining eyes, as if he were bidding farewell to an old friend. Then the last admonition, 'Paid a anghofio dy deulu, na dy grefydd, na be' mae Miss Cooke yn ei wneud er dy fwyn, do not forget thy family, or thy religion, or what Miss Cooke is doing for thy sake ...' His sudden solemn dignity brought a lump to my throat, then he disolved into 'Ta ta, don't get seasick and disgrace your Dad, ta ta!' The train was off.

I sat back and closed my eyes – oh, but first! I hurried to the other window, and there was our back yard; for the first time I saw it from above, gliding past as unreal as in a film, and Mam waving in the door. I waved, she circled slowly out of sight, and I sat again. My fellow-traveller was staring at my label, 'Gare du Nord, Gare de Lyon' ... He pointed to 'Haute Savoie', 'Where's that?' 'The other side of France,' I said, as casually as I could.

But I was still seeing my mother, as in the lightning flash of a dream. The house round her had looked startlingly small, its insignificance made total by being seen from this angle and distance, attached to an identically drab other half. As dwelling after mean dwelling wheeled by in my sun, each indistinguishable from the last, I retained on the retina of my mind – superimposed on what I was seeing – the image of ours. It was like looking at a drawing of a thousand shadowy buildings, all alike, but with at their heart one special one, coloured and shaded and an entity in every detail, the only house: and in the doorway, a frail waving figure, guarding with timid integrity the symbols of her family, from the fuchsia to Queen Victoria full of bootlaces. My eyes pricked.

People and bicycles and cats and dogs whirled by, to the intoxicating rhythm of my flight. If the train were to stop now and roll back, my heart, slowly and surely, would run down and I would die. To the left, in the sun, the arches of Hawarden Bridge stared at me like raised eyebrows; I looked away. Did callous murderers feel like this? Would there one day be dug up from Deeside grass, the skeleton of a – oh, Mrs Evans the Chapel, the little Beibl! I sprang to the window, just in time to wave to her and her niece Fannw; excited though I was, I would have felt badly if I had forgotten. 'The other side of France?' said the man, 'all that way by yourself?' 'Yes.' I was going to add 'to school' but sat back, important. It was when the train forged out of Chester, with me in a corner of my first express and Daudet open on my knee, that I felt I was leaving myself behind at last. I fingered my passport for the tenth time, and could not understand the careworn reserve of my fellow-travellers – were they not going to London too? In the tunnels I saw my shadow self, it had a new aura; out of them, I looked up at the spring cumuli fleecing past, my first English clouds. London! I thought of every book, from *A Welsh Singer* on, in which I had visited the capital, and the rhythm of the rails took up names and wove them into mine, Rotten Row George Williams Piccadilly Circus George Williams Tower of London George Williams ... I dozed, then woke hungry. Unpacking my sandwiches, as I undid the finely tied string and the folded grease-paper I had a fresh vision of my mother; my eyes clouded again. Then I began to eat, and was to give no thought to her or anyone else in the British Isles for some weeks.

The afternoon rattled on, I read; then, so as not to waste time when I got there, I wrote on my postcards 'Arrived safely after pleasant journey, George.' An hour before London was due, I stood in the corridor to watch out for it. What did I expect? Babylonian walls wheeling slowly into silhouette ... Hill behind hill – Ludgate, Haverstock, Primrose, Holborn – St Paul's looming out of a cloud ... Bungalows thickened, thinned back into fields, re-thickened, was this it – fields again. I sat down, tried to read, looked up and saw, slithering past, endless sheds and clothes-lines and allotments, like the Quay only denser. I asked my neighbour where we were. 'London,' he said.

But the swelling sooty majesty of Euston restored my spirits. As our rails smacked into the maze of others, the shoals of house-backs – some on wounded cliffs, some hobbling up in storeys from the ground – became Zola-esque rabbit-warrens, a drama in every room: the lone signalman watched us with a tolerant London smile, one more train lumbering home, and wiped his hands on a rag while his wife waited a mile off, strangled on the mat inside the front door. Then into clanging pillars of darkness – halt – out – a hundred haunted hurrying faces – and the novelist turned back into a country boy waving a handkerchief, not an easy thing to do in a crowd with nobody to wave to. I was tapped on the shoulder by a nondescript man in a peaked cap. I said 'Miss Cooke?', and knew it was an absurd gambit. 'Miss? *Thomas* Cook, Williams? Follow me, right?' We passed another Cook's man helping an old lady into a wheelchair, and I realized that I too was itinerant flotsam. The trunk emerged, bigger than ever. 'Yours?' asked my indifferent male governess, 'blimey, goin' to the North Pole?' But by the time he joined me in the taxi I had forgotten him; he did not want to talk either, it was a perfect trip.

Shaftesbury Avenue, a flashing farrago of names, Moscovitch The Great Lover Queen's Nightie Night Evelyn Laye Globe Her Husband's Wife Marie Löhr, limitless noise, movement, buildings, crowds, red bus after red bus streamered with the names of plays, His Majesty's Chu Chin Chow Fifth Year ... I was overwhelmed but not frightened – staggered more, like a toddler swept up by a mammoth of a mother and folded to a gargantuan bosom. In the same way that stepping into the Quay I had known that never was I to take root there, so in this taxi, with at my side the dullest of strangers, I knew that this was where I belonged, Pavilion revue L'n Paris and New York Nelson Keys Violet Loraine Criterion Cyril Maude Grumpy, Eros winging his eternal false promise of erotica, Piccadilly Ritz Green Park Hyde

Park Corner Victoria – 'that's you, in the morning' – and the Wilton Hotel. The revolving door scared me at first, I only knew them from film comedies; I waited till it was stock-still and slid through. In my room, my head throbbing with the magic-lantern jumble, I sank on the bed. There was a gas-fire, the first I had ever seen, with a sign 'Shilling Meter'. A week's pocket-money? No fear ... Electric light! I switched it on and off. Had I really seen Eros, a corner of Buckingham Palace? I unpacked my tooth-paste, laid the pie-jams on the bed, went down to the dining-room and sat for ten minutes while the waiter waited for my elders to join me, then he decided I was a dull orphan and strolled up. Nagged by the thought that cakes might be extra, I decided to risk it and had the tea of a lifetime.

I wandered down, posted my cards, and took up a stray *Evening News*, my eye glancing off the headline – 'Miners and Owners Clash' – and alighting for good on the theatre-list. New Oxford, The Dolly Sisters in *The League of Notions*, Prince's, Madame Sarah Bernhardt in *Daniel* – the greatest actress in the world, within walking distance! – Playhouse, Charles Hawtrey in *Up in Mabel's Room* with Beatrice Lillie ... Beyond the revolving door, the dark, and in the dark the lights of London. ON NO ACCT LEAVE HOTEL. With ahead of me the first unshackled evening of my life, a London evening at that, I faced the fact that a dozen wild horses, each manned by a Mazeppa of a Miss Cooke, could not keep me indoors. I went up to my room, brushed my hair, washed my hands – free soap – got into my raincoat, put on my school cap, took it off again and left the hotel.

I strolled carefully, zigzagging like a crab to avoid the figures closing in on me, past the looming booming Station – demain, en route! A guardsman, black and glowing red, skittered up the steps of the Gentlemen and joined his lady friend; they crossed, I followed them, an inch in the wake of his stick, and found myself staring at the photographs outside the Victoria Palace. Daisy Dormer ... Three minutes later I was in the gallery watching the orchestra tune up. The theatre was much grander than the Royalty Chester; turn followed dazzling turn, then

Daphne Pollard shrieked a lunatic ditty about Cleopatra's Irish ancestry, 'Her mother's name was Cleo, her father's name was Pat ...' And as I sat spluttering to myself or dreamily held by music and spectacle, it kept washing over me like a warm wave that I, George Williams, was in a London theatre, surrounded by dozens of other theatres, each humming with its own dark and spangled life.

I followed the crowd safely across the road, and ate my cold supper in the empty dining-room. The napkin intimidated me, then I watched the only other eater and laid it negligently on my knees; I shied at coffee, which I had never tasted and was extra. Back in the lounge, I watched a woman in deep conference with a man; she showed him letters, then wiped her eyes. Was he a private detective, or were they preparing a blackmail coup? She took two pills, swallowed them and laughed shrilly. A drug fiend? I walked past them, tripped on the carpet, blushed and went to bed.

It was the first night ever that I had spent alone. I wondered why I had a curious feeling of being hemmed in; it was the pyjamas. I read Daudet aloud, demain je serai français ... I switched off the light, and the momentous day swung to a standstill. Mam standing on the stage of the Victoria Palace, waving up to me in the gallery and calling, 'Your father's name is Richard, and what d'ye think of that?' and Miss Cooke standing like a rock in a whirlpool of Euston, a rock in a peaked cap and brass buttons ...

I opened my eyes to sunlight and sprang up convulsively, but I was early. I left the 6d. for the phantom m'd, went down to breakfast, realized nothing was extra, and fed myself for the day: grapefruit (first time, very bitter), honey (first time, very sweet), eggs, toast (first time since Pen-y-Maes, it reminded me of Annie). The waiter came up, 'It is customary, y'know, to leave something for the staff.' 'I have done so,' I answered, lifting my saucer. He looked, I thought, a little like a discomfited schoolboy. The Cook's man arrived on time, glanced at me twice to make sure I was the right one, paid at the desk, and we walked over into the station. 'Do anything last night?' 'Nothing much,' I said, 'dropped into a music-hall, passes the time.' He gave me a look, but said nothing. Suppose he writes to Miss Cooke? He handed me my tickets, checked my passport, and we parted unmoved.

The boat, my first, was calm. On deck I scanned my first Frenchman, I had overheard him speak fascinating broken English to a porter; he wore a bowler, un chapeau melon. I was preparing my first French sentence when a gust of wind lifted his hat into the sea. He clapped hands to head with an imprecation and turned to see if anybody was sniggering. I took the plunge, 'Monsieur, vous avez perdu votre chapeau melon.' He looked at me, I was smiling foolishly. 'Merci monsieur,' he said, 'je n'avais pas remarqué,' and walked away. He was vexed with me but I did not mind, so pleased was I with his answer and with having understood it.

Calais was different : shrieks, curses, fulminations, the blue-smocked porters might be gabbling Arabic. I climbed into the train and was followed by a French couple, the woman discussing their luggage with animation; I caught one word in twenty, 'figure-toi', 'épouvantable', and realized that while the written word – 'ne pas se pencher au dehors' – might be my friend, the spoken idiom was a wild stranger to be patiently tamed. When the collector asked me about changing in Paris, I failed to understand him and the Frenchman interpreted. Where was my Conversational Power? Lunch in the dining-car – 'consommé, monsieur?' – restored morale, but not enough to sample the red wine.

At the Gare du Nord, my waving mouchoir attracted a figure which, for a bewildered moment, I took for the same Cook's man who had seen me off at Victoria, so tediously alike were they. He talked English, I answered in monosyllabic French, and the conversation lapsed. He drove me across Paris, through the Grands Boulevards, name after name on kiosque and theatre front, Raimu, Baur, Francen, Dorziat – hundreds of people at café tables in the sun – Guitry, Printemps, Cocéa, Dearly, Chevalier – 'c'est l'Opéra? ... merci' – la Gare de Lyon; I was deposited in the salle d'attente, to await the night train to Bellegarde, then wandered cautiously over platforms till I wearied of the clang and bustle. The rows of paper-backed books had the glamour of success which a railway terminus never fails to impart, 67ième Mille, 78ième Mille, Prix Fémina, Prix Goncourt ... I fed too on the names on the trains, Wagons-Lits, Orient Express, Simplon, Vienne, Bucharest ...

Darkness came, the dark of my first nocturnal journey. I bought a picnic as ordered, hired neither pillow nor rug, and burrowed into a corner, P.L.M. written at my head, with a French family going as far as Mâcon. They looked curiously at my school cap. The daughter was scanning *Je Sais Tout*, and I followed what she was reading; I ate a hard-boiled egg, my first, my first ham-packed French bread, and a delicious bar of chocolate, then – a seasoned night-bird – collected the rubbish and tossed it under the seat. The light dimmed, and I looked out at the ghostly moonlit landscapes whirling by : two figures immobile at a gate, a spectral horse at a level crossing, a line of shrouded houses, one anxious window, candle-lit – a dying mother? the last rites, a sob in the doorway? – wiped away by a row of poplars pencilled waveringly by the moon. Tunnel, bridge, bridge, tunnel ... A small dark house, does a little étudiant stir at our arrow-lightning and thunder, and dream of Constantinople? By now I was under my raincoat, cap on the rack and knees huddled into chin in the corner, and tallying little with my Irish Mail picture of myself, bolt upright in a bowler with jolly Annie and our picnic-basket. Tunnel bridge, bridge tunnel ... I tried to visualize my family, had I really been with them *yesterday*? – but I saw them less clearly than Annie, at the wrong end of a telescope ... Tunnel bridge, station-lights sweeping over me, I'm in bed at 314a no I'm not, bridge tunnel ... I'll never get to sleep now, je ne dormirai pas ...

I woke in ice-blue daylight, alone in the compartment, and looked out at a jagged cliff shelving up to a tree-clumped sky. The Alps! I stretched, cold and blurred, went and washed carefully, then brushed up, beard not too bad but I wished once more that I were fair, regardez ce blond avec les yeux bleus, cleaned my shoes with lavatory paper and sat again.

Having thought for weeks of the approaching Vincentier – the boys and girls, the classes – I suddenly found myself face to face with the fact that for three months I was to spend most of my waking hours with a woman I had never seen. I was alarmed. I had never been alone with Miss Cooke except for brisk marching orders, and an hour with her, never mind a day, would be an ordeal. And in not many minutes she would be awaiting me, a strapping French Miss Cooke, perhaps cross-eyed and gabbling shrill and unintelligible like the woman at Calais! I shivered queasily, fixed my cap on the back of my head, and practised my look : a strong alert face, albeit warmly shy. We were slowing for Bellegarde. I decided not to be found leaning out, but to hang back and then step down.

The train stopped. I waited for a girl with pigtails to alight and get well out of the way, then descended, alert and warmly shy. A squat woman with glasses and a gap in her teeth waddled towards me, tears rolling down her cheeks and called 'Enfin, mon enfant, enfin ...' I recoiled, she tacked just past me and engulfed the girl with the pigtails. I almost lost my cap, and anyway parted with my strong warm look; I was straightening myself when there was a voice at my shoulder, 'C'est George?' I turned quickly. 'Je suis Mademoiselle Tardy.' I shook a hand and stammered my speech. 'Enchanté de faire votre connaisance Mademoiselle.'

It was Annie.

Chapter 16

Deux Amours

The same merry brown face, faintly flushed under bright brown eyes. Mademoiselle Tardy was thirty-four years of age, to my fifteen and Miss Cooke's thirty-eight. We walked to the van; she was small, with delicate feet and hands. 'Par ici, ce sera vite fait – pas trop fatigué? – vous avez faim, oh si! – par ici ...' I said only 'oui' and 'non', but was immensely relieved to understand her, though I could tell that for my benefit she was slowing down. Then, waiting for the trunk – yes, la malle – I said, 'Ma malle est lourde.' 'Ah,' she said, then as it hove into gigantic view, bubbled into delighted laughter, 'Mais ce n'est pas une malle, c'est une maison! Vous auriez pu voyager dedans!'

The empty restaurant was silver-grey with French dawn; I insisted on café au lait. As she chatted, tentative but easy, I ate delicious brioches and observed more closely. There was no doubt of what she was, her manner to the waiter was correct, even severe, but she seemed to me the gayest school-teacher in the world. Under a plain-ribboned brown straw-hat, I noted lips delicately full over healthy teeth, and a nose unexpectedly strong – 'oh, j'ai le nez de mon père!' she was to exclaim, pressing it into a beak – with at the neck, under the sober spring coat, the soft flick of a lace collar meeting at a brooch. Again correct, even severe. Yet from the wayward lock of hair to the small pointed shoe, she was feminine.

'Et Miss Cooke?' 'Miss Cooke va bien, merci' – like her I pronounced it Mees – 'et j'ai promis à elle –' 'Non, "je lui ai promis", vous permettez que je vous corrige?' with a teasing smile. I continued, corrected, 'Je lui ai promis de vous faire part de son amitié.' She bubbled again, 'Vous avez appris ça par coeur!' I laughed back, I *had* learnt it by heart. 'Miss Cooke,' she said, 'est une brave personne.' It was the first time I had heard Miss Cooke remarked upon by an adult, it made her sound unreal, almost departed. Two young men crossed, wearing bérets; I took off my cap and put it in my pocket. 'Ah, le petit Anglais disparaît! Et à sa place quoi, what is to replace the little foreigner?' I chose my words solemnly, but with a twinkle to answer hers: 'Un petit Français, avec un béret.' She clapped her hands, 'Très bien, bravo!' She shared with my father his gift of approaching the most mundane topic with a non-seriousness to lighten the heaviest heart; I noted the trill of 'trrrès' and 'brrravo', and vowed to acquire it to the manner borrrn. She settled the bill; I was not old enough to resent being paid for out of a female purse, and kindled to the gesture as something intimately protective, marking too the graceful way she lingered breathingly on 'oui' – 'oui-i-i ...'

We got into a compartment with one other traveller; it was stuffy, I must have suddenly looked tired. She opened a book, 'Vous allez fermer les yeux ...' I closed my eyes, then a delicious scent; I opened them. She was dabbing something on a handkerchief, and looking at me. I blushed. The tiny bottle said 'Eau-de-Cologne'. 'Dites-moi George,' she said smiling, 'si nous nous disputons, que ferons-nous, what shall we do if we quarrel?' I answered, 'Nous nous battrons, we will fight.' I had shirked the r. The man looked up from his paper, she laughed and coloured. Then I dozed and did not really come to till we stepped into my tiny bedroom, old-maidish-fussy with doilies and crucifixes; Mademoiselle explained, as she closed the shutters over the early morning, that old Madame Sallicet was letting it as an international gesture. She showed me a blue box by the bed embossed with white marguerites, 'pour vous distraire quand vous avez le mal du pays, for when you are homesick', and tiptoed away. I clambered into my pyjamas and my morning-bed, feeling like a luxurious invalid, opened the box and found it full of chocolates each in a crackly brown bucket. Before I could close it, I was dreamlessly, warmly asleep: warm from a new-found radiation to which I was too tired and too young to put a name. ✱

Stirring in the half-dark, I had no idea where I was; the plash of water and the caressing fingers of dim light through the shutters joined to coax me voluptuously out of sleep. I creaked the shutters open. I was on the third floor and looked down, in the flat afternoon light, across a tiny shrubbery on to the dusty square where the worn fountain was placidly playing. To the right, the Hôtel du Cheval Gris, with a peeling legend 'Savon Cadum'. Not a soul in sight; it looked like a dream, as if all that journey had never existed, and yet here I was. The sun came out and deepened the picture as a horse and cart trundled through, driven by an old Welsh peasant from Trelogan. This is mine, c'est à moi ...

I dressed, crept down and out on the road, into balmy air and the scent of new country – dust, petrol and whiffs of ultra-montane leaf and blossom. Two boys passed, in bérets and black thigh-long overalls, carrying portfolios and munching dry bread and chocolate. Behind them, a hurrying figure with books : it waved. She was hatless, and looked younger, in a brown dress to just above the ankles, with paniers that fluttered as she walked, 'Alors!' The boys looked at me curiously. 'Vous avez bien dormi? – oh, vous étiez mort!' She laughed, and brushed lightly at the wisp on her brow; her hair, curly-brown flecked with grey, was parted down the middle and drawn above the ears to a soft bun at the nape. I followed her into the house opposite, up dark stone steps into a shuttered room; she opened them, 'Voilà, mon humble home!' She pointed across to my gate : every evening she would look to see that I was going straight in to bed and out of mischief. I retorted, wrestling with French, that when she and old Madame were well asleep, I would creep out ...

Her 'home' was shabbily tidy : many dog-eared books, heavy dining-chairs of tooled leather, a wardrobe, a stove out in the room and an alcove with a wash-stand and a single monastic bed. On the chest-of-drawers, a photograph of a striking young woman in mortar-board and tight bodice of another decade. 'Qui est-ce?' She laughed, 'Mais c'est Miss Cooke, elle est si changée?' I was taken aback; the picture looked like a girl, I had never thought of that ... I would keep my shaving kit in the alcove, and shave and wash here during the day, the lavatory was off the stairs, eau courante, and look, electric light! She made coffee, on a spirit-stove, then we crossed to the Cheval Gris to meet François the cook, a flushed motherly peasant, 'Enfin le petit Anglais!'

We walked along the street – 'bonjour Mademoiselle' – everybody staring surreptitiously; le petit Anglais had been talked of, and I enjoyed my situation to the full. We stopped and Mademoiselle bought me a béret, which I put on at once, at an angle – 'mais c'est un Français!' We walked past the Mairie, an imposing little square mansion; opposite, set in dusty playground, the Ecole Primaire Supérieure. Boys and girls shared teachers, but unlike Holywell dwelt in separate wings and never met. I was presented to Monsier le Directeur, polite, correct. I was to attend all classes except Mademoiselle's English one – 'oh ça, non!' from her, and from me. Walking back, I said would she please tell me everything I did wrong, not only French but social behaviour. She said 'bien' : just now I ought to have waited for Monsieur to turn to me before saying 'Au revoir, Monsieur,' and then waited for him to put out his hand before putting out mine, also it was incorrect to point. She bowed to passers-by; I bowed too, admiring the formal grace of her demeanour. 'Je vais devenir élégant,' I said, 'comme vous.' She threw up her hands, 'Comme moi? Oh pensez donc ...'

Dinner was at eight, in the hotel where I was to eat en pension with Mademoiselle Marot, a plain pleasant young woman who taught French, Mademoiselle Roget, dim and kind, and my Mademoiselle, who was obviously, in her delicate chaffing way, the strong personality. I felt strange at table with three women, but made up my mind to enjoy it. It was understood that they should talk away unless I felt like joining in, so there was no strain; though as soon as they forgot I was there I found them impossible to follow, and again realized what a climb I had before me. I sipped red wine; it tasted like medicine, but I would not have admitted it. I learnt that dining at a house one leaves one's napkin crumpled, while en pension one rolls it into a demure ring; I learnt that while at an English table both hands rest in the lap, in France one hand should be negligently on the cloth. I learnt that a high test of a foreigner's French is how he will deal with a positive answer to a negative question, such as 'Il n'est pas ici?'; his instinct must be to say 'oui' (wrong) and if he answers 'si', then he begins to know the language. I watched the way they laid table implements quietly, side by side, and added it to what I had already gleaned at home about dealing with soup noiselessly and peas knifelessly. There were many plaisanteries. One of the few regular pensionnaires was a vapid coquettish lady of forty; Mademoiselle had named her 'la Parisienne' and her toilette was dissected with an airy malice which enchanted me.

After dîner, I walked with them round l'église, then along the Promenade des Tilleuls – lime trees, I added the word to my store; this was to be an evening ritual, 'prendre le frais', while they chattered and joked and even hummed snatches of songs. I confirmed what I already half-knew from Mademoiselle's letters; the school was the equivalent of Holywell, and drawn mostly from the peasant-farmer class. Vincentier was the nearest French village to Switzerland and only four miles from Geneva, a metropolis made doubly impressive, and unpopular, by the bad exchange; the Swiss were derided as dull moneyed outsiders – 'ils n'ont jamais souffert' – and it was hard to imagine that their language was French. We both went back to Mademoiselle's room, I read aloud for fifteen minutes – 'articulez donc, articulez!' – then 'bonne nuit, dormez bien ...' and I rattled downstairs and over the dark still-warm street, by now deserted. I opened my gate, turned, and saw her standing at her window. We waved, I clambered up to my eyrie in the old lady's mausoleum, and I slept, my new and shuttered sleep.

School started at eight instead of nine, but like everything else, I embraced it. I was up at seven and went over to the Cheval Gris for breakfast, which I was given in the kitchen, by Françoise: for the first time, I ate eggs sizzling in a hot metal plate with handles, found they were called 'oeufs sur le plat' and decided to have them every day. Then school; Mademoiselle

Marot introduced me into my class of boys – rather younger than me, to give me a start – and made a speech about 'notre jeune ami anglais' who was to be treated like anybody else. The friendly stares embarrassed and gratified me. First lesson history, French history : I admired the beautiful writing and the furious application, and noticed that all exercise books were meticulously covered in reddish-brown paper, inscribed 'Cahier d'Histoire' in perfect copperplate : tomorrow, mine must be too. I also took shy sly looks at my camarades. Perhaps shabbier than at home; many tabliers – the black aprons I had noticed – but mostly on the smaller boys, and one or two wore separate black sleeves on elastic to protect cuffs. Otherwise they looked much like the Holywell boys – ah, but they were français and the blue sky was français, and I was français too. Every minute I learnt something : Waterloo was pronounced Vatterlô, Marseille and Lyon had no S.

The next lesson was Arithmetic, and I realized immediately that for me this was – and must remain, with all the sciences – a waste of time. As the numbers were spoken, I could not visualize them quickly enough to write them down; the master tested me with a simple sum, and I floundered as if I did not know one word of French, it was galling. But the break was noisy and exhilarating, it was a change to be striving to speak as well as my schoolmates instead of better, I was offered broken chocolate and doggedly tried out phrases. Déjeuner at the hotel, back to school. To the amazement of the class, and my own, I was top in Dictation : I had learnt a language by eye which they had lisped by ear and were only just learning to adorn with silent s's and e's. Dictée would be my favourite subject. And at four, 'Au revoir George, à demain !' and I called back, béret well on back of head, 'A demain Edmond, travaille bien !'; what with the tutoiement and the r fearlessly trilled, you could not tell me from him, and I wished all Holywell could hear me. Two girls were waiting, with their serviettes – portfolios, I was to get one tomorrow – and one spoke to me, a pretty girl. 'Je suis Yvonne Avalon, vous connaissez Millie Tee-rère?' 'Très bien, elle vous aime beaucoup.' 'Est-ce qu'elle est jolie?' 'Assez,' I said, 'mais pas aussi jolie que vous.' Blushes and giggles, her friend asked about Eira Parry. I bowed au revoir, and walked home munching bread and chocolate and feeling homme du monde; no meal till evening, but who wants le thé?

I passed two boys shorter than me: I was happy to observe that while at home I had been of medium height, here I was tall. I never heard anything said, but obviously I was a more strapping protégé than any of the village, or Mademoiselle either, had imagined; le petit Anglais looked seventeen. To me everything French was picturesque, even the conventions, and I could hardly realize yet that Mademoiselle moved in the rigid corridor of French small-town academics, much narrower than either Holywell or Connah's Quay; next day she was to tell me there had 'been a complaint' that in greeting I did not raise my béret with the right hand – I was left-handed – and later I found out that any time she walked along the street after dusk, alone, and passed Monsieur le Directeur, the situation was delicate enough for them to ignore each other. It must, surely, have seemed unusual that the same circumscribed young woman should adopt an adolescent who shared meals and her single room, though it never crossed my mind. What crossed hers, I never knew.

I waited for her in our abandoned walled garden, finishing my bread at the table under the pear-tree. She arrived, with cahiers, prettily out of breath, 'Pouf, il fait chaud! ...' I sprang up, took them from her and told my day. She found me brown paper and I covered my exercise-books, while she talked. Her class had asked questions about me in English: why does he look so French, and what is a Welsh, a Gallois, apart from being a subject of the godlike Prince de Galles? I asked about the girls I had just spoken to: one was 'très bien élevée', the other 'pas du tout comme il faut, très nerveuse, très ...' She gave a neatly censorious sketch, while I observed the precision of phrase and gesture, the whole touched off with a twinkle of mockery. Oh, had I written to Miss Cooke? I hadn't, I had put off switching to English, and it would be my first letter to her – but of course, I would write in *French*! 'Chère Miss Cooke' – Meess, I said to myself – 'Eh bien, je suis déjà français! ... La campagne de

Chester à Londres est très monotone ... j'ai vu à Paris des mer-
veilles qui ressemblent à un rêve. Je porte un béret ...' As I
wrote, on cahier paper, Mademoiselle corrected compositions,
distributing tiny fastidious comments in the margins like a pretty
nun depositing Friday fishbones round the edge of a plate. It was
difficult to visualize Miss Cooke. 'As for Mademoiselle, I would
need a whole letter to describe her, her hat is brown with a
row of small roses, and she wears brown stockings, the colour
of her dress. Our only regrets are that you are not with us,
another letter next week.' How to finish? 'Sincèrement à vous'?
Distance, somehow, made her less forbidding; I dashed off 'affec.
à vous' then, to balance with a playful flourish, signed myself
'Georges'. In her answer, Miss Cooke wrote 'By the way, don't
ever abbreviate letter-endings, i.e., "affec." for affectionately.'
Her own letter ended 'Yours affectionately'. I never shortened
it again.

Mademoiselle talked of her; they had met in college at Rumilly, in the year of my birth, she eighteen and Miss Cooke
twenty-two. Then she had gone to college in Bournemouth, she
pronounced it beautifully, I longed to hear her English yet did
not want to, ever ... 'Oh cette Mees Willoughby' – again perfect
– 'quelle drôle d'Anglaise', then to stay with Mees Cooke's family
in Leeds, where she had become greatly attached to Mees
Cooke's father. I saw it all through her eyes, amused, friendly,
cool. Then – 'au travail!' – a gruelling exercise which was to
happen daily. She handed me a page, twenty lines of Flaubert
chosen for integrated syntax and rich vocabulary; for ten
minutes by her watch I pored over the passage, then she shut
the book and I transcribed from memory, into my cahier.
Fatigued from school and the increasing heat, my brain was
slow to photograph such detail. 'Oh là là, de la concentration,
voyons!' Where my memory failed me, I was made to realize
how poorly my invention tallied with the masterly original. It
was toil, under the poirier, as hard as digging, and she was a
merciless little overseer. But she had planned une petite
excursion.

Sunday morning, she brushed her finger-tips with a fluid to

remove ink-stains – her own recipe – and we set out. Besides her, there would be Mesdemoiselles Marot and Guillemet, a stout red-haired teacher with an ugly jolly face, with me as cavalier. As we joined them at the tramvé, I raised my béret with the right hand. After one mile the frontière, passeports – then we swayed past the fat glossy Swiss villas to Carouge and into Geneva. The immense stone Calvin did his glowering best to stare me out as a reminder of my Llanrwst forbears, who could never have been as Independent as he looked now, monarch of all he sightlessly surveyed; but he did not succeed, the April morning was too warm and the lake too inviting.

It must have been the finest day, anywhere, since the day I was born. To the rhythms of Offenbach, gracefully bantering between piano and violin, the steamer sighed along the glass-clear water, under a sky washed blue; everybody was in summer clothes, relaxed and happy. Vineyards, in serried ranks with every twig accounted for, trooped down to the toy lakeside towns; these were luxuriant with geranium and shrub and a grass that had been laundered blade by blade. People tripped off down the plank, while knots of others tripped on, even more ribboned and white-shod and bright-haired, to the lilt of opérettes; lucent with youth and sun, they were invisibly armoured for ever against all disease including the common cold, immortal. Mademoiselle Guillemet sang, in a low voice as melodious as her face was clumsy. We passed Ferney and talked of acid little Voltaire, but today it was hard to imagine acidity; we passed the woods of Coppet, and they told me of Madame de Staël; we passed Lausanne and I brought up Gibbon.

Déjeuner was under a canopy; I watched my Mademoiselle carefully lift up the back of her skirt, smooth down her white petticoat on to the stool, and drape the skirt behind her round the stool, so as not to crease it. The meal was marred only by a waiter who spilt sauce down Mademoiselle's Guillemet's front and was casual about it; all three turned from holiday-makers into the institutrices they were, as they dabbed water and made outraged well-bred throat noises, 'Ohhh c'est bien suisse, ils n'ont jamais souffert, ohhh ...' People looked round, and wondered at the embarrassed adolescent with the three maiden aunts. But the sole was perfect, my first; the white wine, my first, tasted teasing-cold and less like medicine than the red; and the band played a popular tune, 'La Jolie Jeanne', which Mademoiselle Guillemet trilled as she lifted her glass to my Mademoiselle, who blushed and bubbled as I learnt that her name was Jeanne.

Our goal was the Château de Chillon, mountain-girt at the end of the lake, the grim Byronic fortress which on this lamb-gentle day softened its reflection in the pellucid water. We wandered through vast empty banqueting halls, the lake shimmering on their ceilings, up into sinister turrets, down into dread dungeons. Though I was stirred, I suffered, as I was always to suffer, from the double blight of sightseeing : immediate soreness of foot, and the stultifying presence of other sightseers, even French ones, 'Oh là là ces pauvres prisonniers, quelle horreur ...!' By the end I longed to be sitting down reading about it.

But on the journey back, in the sloping afternoon light with elegiac shadows in its wake, and on all sides a languorous marriage, by the sun, of he-mountain and she-water, the placid tiredly happy people sauntered back aboard, trailing summer music. Sigh of mouth-organ, thrum of guitar, dying fall of concertina, all had become a dream in a gently rocked cradle. Could it last? Oh oui, life must stay like this – on my return I shall go every summer Sunday to my own mountains and valleys ... Back in Geneva, I stared up at a palace; said Mademoiselle, 'It is where stay all the rich and the famous.' I looked at the sign and said, to make them laugh, 'One day I shall stay at the Hôtel des Bergues,' and high in spirits we settled outside a great café with more music, had an extravagant glass of wine each, and ate petits pains very slowly so as to stay longer. After the sun, with the music and the crowds, the wine went to my head and my French improved, 'On dirait un Français!' Back into impoverished France, bonne nuit, the turn at the darkening gate, the wave to the slim figure in the window, and the cradle-dream of the day to be carried into the dream of sleep.

My secret thoughts had settled down; in the hospital for my

weekly hot bath, lying soaking and unused to it I found them awake, but apart from that – yes, there was Françoise la cuisinière, jolly and fat and smelling warm at breakfast. One night I dreamt that old Madame Sallicet opened my door and said 'Quelqu'un pour le petit Anglais'; then she beckoned, and Françoise entered, in her apron. Madame went out, I heard the door lock, Françoise opened the chocolate-box, popped one into my mouth, giggled, and pulled the bed-clothes off.

Mademoiselle was at the other pole from this, smelling fresh of eau-de-Cologne, flat-chested like most of the girls and – d'ailleurs – bandy. It was Tuesday I noticed this, when it was Mathematics and I was leaning out of the window watching for her walking down the street from school : waving to her I thought, what a pity when she has such delicate hands and feet ...

'Chère Miss Cooke, Nous avons fait une si jolie promenade ... I am working very hard ... Mademoiselle has bought for me a new suit ... We eat cherries at the hotel ... Affectueusement à vous ...' In answer, a fresh order : every Friday afternoon a private Italian lesson, from Professor Arzani, of the University of Geneva. Italian! It was not a school subject, and I could tell that Mademoiselle put it down to an eccentric whim; with the exchange, the fees must have seemed exorbitant. To save the tram, I made it a rule to walk the whole of one way, 'Par cette chaleur, pas possible ...!' The Professor was an affable little man; it was a relief to be with a male teacher, and I was flattered by his astonishment at the miraculous ease with which the Welsh accent could soften into the Italian. He was an amateur photographer and took a snapshot of me, in my shirt-sleeves, which I was relieved to find an improvement on my passport. Mademoiselle, unable to forget the Swiss franc, put me in mind of my mother, 'How long did the photo take?'

I enjoyed the dawdle back to the tramvé, along the wide prophylactic Swiss boulevards, swept clear of dust and untidy longings. But I was cluttered with my own longings. During this wonderful summer these were my only public moments alone, and I would linger for five stolen minutes at a cheap bookstall, directing sidelong glances at the cover of *La Vie Parisienne* : plump poules de luxe bursting in saucy colour out of their corsages – no concession to fashion here – legs in the air, tiny aphrodisiac heels a metre apart but dimpled knees maddeningly together. The journal was too unwieldy to smuggle up to my bedroom, and I decided on a fly-blown novelette showing a fiercely moustached man on a bed, bending a horrified beauty backwards over it like a bow : *Passions Bestiales*, Roman Sensationnel! But sitting in the tram with my Passions shielded by my Italian grammar, I found I had been cheated into buying the *Sunday Companion* masquerading as pornography; it was the bow without the arrow. No sooner was the victim horizontal – 'jupe déchirée, seins meurtris' – than the door was burst open by her brother and she safe from a fate which may have been worse than death but was the only one I was interested in. *Venus and Adonis* was streets ahead, and *Bestial Passions* ended up in the ditch at the terminus. Mademoiselle was correcting under the pear-tree. 'Et Genève?' 'J'ai bien travaillé,' I said, 'et j'ai regardé les livres dans les librairies.'

Incited perhaps by Miss Cooke's Italian campaign, Mademoiselle started one of her own : or, befitting her, more a feminine manouevre. It was before déjeuner, we both had a free hour, she at her desk and I shaving in the alcove. 'Ecoutez mon Loupino' – a pet name she adopted for me (whipper-snapper? young hopeful? anyway I cherished it) – 'écoutez – mais George!' To free my brush of drops, I had thoughtlessly shaken it over her bed-cover, which looked waterproof. 'Mais c'est mon lit, quand même! . . . George, la musique, c'est tr-r-ès important, je vais vous faire cadeau de leçons de piano.' The piano! I had gone on envying the girls who sat after Prize Distribution and struck out those waltzes; I jumped at the idea. Madame Sallicet's shrouded salon, crowded with bourgeois bric-à-brac, housed a grand piano; twice a week, for an hour, the room was wheezed open like an over-stacked family vault, and the instrument prised apart like a coffin. I would sit squarely before it with tiny old Mademoiselle Ronce perched beside me, her bird-voice

drowned by the metronome, 'Bémol, si'il vous plaît, bémol ...'
As my scales thumped through the room, ferns shivered their
distaste and the bronze cavaliers on the piano rattled with rage,
while the ticker wagged just in front or just behind, grimly
right where I was always wrong. I had no talent, and so no
application. 'Ne désespérons pas, voici une jolie petite valse ...'
The rheumatic brown-spotted little fingers came to sudden life
and darted up and down the keys like eight drunken old grass-
hoppers. '*La* la la *la*, la *la*, oh que c'est mignon ...' I looked at
my hands, planted between my knees like turnips. It was not
fair.

But my French advanced like a racehorse, my r's trilled into
place, and the stern insistence on logic and clarity was fine
training. I was also careful, in the playground, to learn all the
slang I could; I would say 'chouette mon vieux' if pleased and
'la barbe' if bored, muttered 'merde' to myself on walks and
once said it to startle the ladies : 'George, ce n'est *pas* comme il
faut ...' The days grew hotter, a sensual heat of stone and dust
and fruit and flowers which I had never known. The secret
thoughts on Bath Friday strayed to other times, such as the
twenty-minute siesta after déjeuner, the verre de vin rouge still
rough on the lips, in my stifling shuttered twilight. Then some
morning, with the air unbearably oppressive, every leaf hanging
parched, without warning there would be lightning and thunder,
then rain. Not the half-hearted drizzles I was used to, but a
deluge that lashed the cowering village from end to end, boiled
up the dust into a rage, and streamed off the beaten trees in
dramatic torrents. The world was furiously awash – 'que ça fait
du *bien*!' – and then it was over, the sun would shine and the
village emerge fresh and gleaming from end to end. Next day the
heat again, slowing the brain, quickening the blood, creeping
the flesh.

'My dear Son George, I am very sorry to write this letter with
recieving nothing for three weeks since your first note informing safe arrival and the French Lady etc., every day we expect
the postman but nothing your Mother is worried to death please
write, your affec. Dad Mam, Job, Tom, PS. Llythyr os gweliti'n
dda, a letter from thee, please.' I was overwhelmed with re-

morse; it simply had not occurred to me that I had not written. I was scolded by Mademoiselle, who gave me the money to telegraph, 'All well written love.' In my letter, I calumnied the French posts by implying that at least two had gone astray, 'other people have found the same thing ...' Forming the English with difficulty, I felt crafty as well as heartless.

When I had finished, 'Et le jeu d'échecs?' said Mademoiselle. In the hotel I had noticed a stray set of chess and borrowed it to teach her; it became regular, after the twilight walk under the limes, for us to pore over the board in a pool from the lamp while the evening folded its sun-warmed wings around the spinster and the student. Muffled and occasional, a bicycle bell, a hoof on the cobbles, a whistle, the caress of the fountain : in between, the soft fall of the chess-men into the box. 'Oh que je suis bête, je n'ai pas vu ...' I would see a letter on the table. 'De qui?' 'Quelle curiosité!' It was from her nephew André, aged ten. 'Chère Tante Jeanne ... Je t'embrasse tendrement ...' I felt a twinge, and recognized it as jealousy. I looked at her, she was frowning over a pawn. 'Tante Jeanne,' I blurted. She looked up. 'Je suis aussi un neveu,' I said.

She looked surprised, uncertain. 'You are a nephew only for the moment,' she said gaily, 'tout passe, tout lasse, tout casse!' 'What is that?' An old proverb, that life is all breakages and exhaustions and changes of heart, vous apprendrez un jour!' I ignored this – 'et ce vous-vous,' I went on, 'pourquoi pas "tu" et "toi", why cannot I call you "thee" and "thou", as in Wales?' She smiled, aloof, amusée. Confusée too. 'Tu insistes,' she said, bantering, 'que je te tutoie, thou wilt have it that I call thee "thou"?'

I looked at her; a bicycle bell, a snatch of street song, our lamp-lit intimacy was complete. A frontier had been crossed, the gossamer bridge into the fragile country of calf-love, where innocent-scented grass and leaf shrink from the touch and the half-pleasant pain is as intangible as a breath of fresh eau-de-Cologne. 'Oui,' I said, 's'il te plaît, tante Jeanne.' Then I added, bantering too, 'c'est d'ailleurs bon pour mon français.' We finished the game; I waved at the gate, went to bed, and fell asleep thinking of Tante Jeanne.

I woke up dreaming of Françoise.

'Chère Miss Cooke, Il fait très chaud, we have not waited two weeks before writing this time! . . . We are reading in the garden, I am learning Verlaine by heart. Tante Jeanne is devoted to her nephew André, and has adopted me too . . . The pears are ripening every week. We are both very happy. Yesterday Mademoiselle Marot sent me with a message to Tante Jeanne who was teaching the girls English; when I entered she stopped speaking absolutely and became so red that the class laughed, for they knew how she does not wish me to hear her English, it was very amusing. In Italian, 'ci', 'ce' are pronounced 'tchi', 'tche'. Affectueusement à vous . . .'

More excursions. Ferney, chez Voltaire; Coppet, chez de Staël. The swaggerest home in which I had set foot was my own lodging in Vincentier – a grand piano! – and the idea of opulence in the house, as opposed to the riches of the mind, was completely new to me; I beheld the eighteenth-century splendours of tapestry and brocade, gilt and ormolu, panel and parquet through museum eyes, they were dazzlingly unreal. 'Quelle élégance . . .' My feet ached and a drowsy numbness pained. Then one Saturday, the whole school, boys and girls, climbed to the top of Le Salève, the long cliff-like mountain which dominated the countryside: a spectacular view of Genève and the lake, with mountains on all sides. It was one of the rare occasions when the girls and boys mixed; high-spirited chatter rang through the warm-cool mountain air, there was sun, sky, space, life, they made Edmond Toussaint recite Wordsworth's 'Daffodils' to make me laugh. But I was vaguely dissatisfied. The novelty of them all being French was wearing off; they were as amiable and unarresting as Holywell. Yvonne Avalon was pretty but giggled and had thick ankles, one or two of the boys were comic and had buffooned their way into my affections; but I felt apart from them, not because I felt alien – on the contrary, the more I saw of them the more Welsh they became . . . No. I realized once more that the time I felt lonely was in a group.

A corner began to sing 'Frère Jacques'; the linking of the

childish harmonies on that noble mountain, with all earth and heaven chiming in, was moving. But it was not enough.

'Ce Lambard,' said Mademoiselle Marot one day at déjeuner, 'il porte un maillot blanc, ça fait beau garçon, il est d'ailleurs intelligent.' Who was this, whom a white jersey had transformed into a handsome boy, clever as well? He was in the class above mine, and this afternoon she was bringing him in to ours, to sharpen our wits.

Yes, I had half-seen him; the jersey certainly made a difference, enhancing the black cropped hair and restless green eyes. He was a slim boy of my age, with a fresh complexion, delicate features pure in profile and full firm lips. He looked cool, even in the jersey. His manner was quick without being eager; next to the other Savoyard peasants, heavy of foot and face, he was a tingling little greyhound, with a habit of flicking back his hair with a nervous movement of the head. Mademoiselle Marot asked him to read aloud from *Pêcheur d'Islande*. He rose, with heightened colour and a shy assurance, and read of the two young fishermen, working and singing by the midnight sun. 'Eternel soir, ou éternel matin, impossible à dire ... Yann s'occupait bien peu d'être si beau ...' The Florentine-page felicity of his bearing, the musical countrified French, the tentative awkwardness over the long words, all combined to win me. Then the flawless profile was bent, deep in work; but at a joke, his concentration would dissipate into a wide flash of teeth and childish glee. Once or twice he whispered to his neighbour, and they laughed together; I felt the same twinge as when I had seen the letter to Tante Jeanne. The lesson over, he tossed back a lock of hair and hurried out. For me, the light in the room of twenty gabbling students had visibly lessened.

At dîner, to my three spinsters, I was full of Lambard; I agreed about his looks, and Tante asked me to describe him 'pour exercer votre français'. Engrossed though I was, I noticed that in front of the others she said 'votre' instead of 'ton'. 'Le nez droit, la bouche forte, il est beau ...' 'Ah,' said Tante Jeanne, delicately imprisoning her napkin in its ring, 'on sera romancier

– mais George voyons, pense donc à Françoise!' In my abstraction, I had crumbled my bread into pellets; I tidied the cloth. We strolled sous les tilleuls, and I learnt that 'notre petit héros' was a pensionnaire in the dormitory with a dozen others, only going home for special week-ends. Walking in the midst of three women, the last of the departed day still wreathing the dusty scent of the lime trees around us, I saw the wild-animal boy climbing into his orphaned bed, and it struck to my heart. Their pleasant interest in my interest in him only served to make him inaccessible. I announced that next day I would offer him chocolate, a geste d'amitié franco-britannique – 'bravo George!' I fell asleep thinking of Lambard. I cannot remember if I dreamt of Françoise.

Next morning I went up to him, 'Tu aimes *Pêcheur d'Islande*?' I had thought about the 'tu', all the boys used it but I felt that from a foreigner it might sound forward; smiling with a boldness I did not feel, I was holding out a chocolate melting in a too-warm hand. He looked startled (offended? oh please, non . . .) then smiled and took it. 'Merci – tu connais bien John Godfrey Jones?' Any discomfiture at his interest in pimply other-side-of-the-globe J. G. Jones was wiped out by the 'tu', and we talked, haltingly.

I saw him every day in the break – ten minutes of jolting and ball-bouncing and leap-frogging – but a meeting alone was out of the question; I was tied to Mademoiselle Tardy, and he to the other pensionnaires, who were strictly surveillés. The image of him as something unapproachable grew stronger. I would see him sauntering gracefully round a corner, en promenade at the tail of a dismal crocodile, béret on the back of his fine dark head; I would glimpse him sauntering gracefully back, when his smile and wave had such a transitory quality that I wished I had not seen him. C'était tout. Frustration lent enchantment to the view.

One Saturday evening, strolling with my ladies, the lime trees headier than ever, I heard through the twilight, from the direction of the school, sweet music. We walked up to the knots of people. In the shadow of the playground wall, an itinerant fairman had put up a tiny merry-go-round for tomorrow and the baby-eyed wooden ponies were being put through their battered paces, shyly dipping and rising to the thin waltz. I espied, standing near a car, a large blonde woman in a fur coat, and a man with a reddish moustache; I nudged Tante Jeanne – 'des Anglais!' My reaction was triple – I was a Français marvelling at foreigners, a Welsh boy eyeing the grand English he had read about, and a British subject moved at the sight of compatriots. People stared, 'Des Anglais!' The two looked careless and distinguished, I was proud of them; Tante Jeanne looked from me to them, amused, 'Mais dis-leur bonjour!' I would surprise the tourists with my sudden greeting, also show off to the ladies the English they had never heard me speak; I approached timidly, doffing my béret, and my voice sounded strange as I said 'Excuse me, I am here at school ...' They smiled politely. They were Swedes. I apologized and went back but behind my rueful smile I was childishly disappointed.

But the merry-go-round started up and Mademoiselle Guillemet began to hum the tune, then to sway to it; the sweetness of her voice made her thick waist graceful. Tante Jeanne joined in tentatively, her voice a little sharp; I was glad, if she had sung like the other I could not have borne it. 'Ah, les pauvres pensionnaires!' I looked: above the deserted school-yard, the dormitory windows were crowded with faces that hung towards the music like pale flowers drooping for water. I picked him out at once, his collar loose like a jerkin, how could I ever have thought a nightshirt ridiculous ... One of them began to sing to the music – a tune which was the rage that summer, 'C'est Mon Homme' – and the other boys took it up, guying it happily. 'Oh, mais ils font la Mistinguett! ...' The people round me laughed, somebody clapped, and I felt the old unease at watching a crowd enjoy itself, deepened by the pain of seeing Lambard unapproachably part of the crowd. Then, at a command from behind, the faces melted from the windows, blackness; next to us, the yearning jaunty tune. I turned away to examine the ponies. Walking back with the chattering demoiselles, I was silent.

In the lamplight, the chess came to a standstill. I sat, elbows on the table, staring at the pieces. not seeing them. 'George, tu es triste?' I looked at her. She spoke again. 'Tu as le mal du pays, art thou homesick?' I nodded slowly, my underlip trembled, my head sank on to my arm.

What troubled me? A drift of homesickness, induced by the two false Anglais; the heartache, certainly, of a thwarted friendship; but there was also an emotion regarding the woman opposite me. I saw, as in a picture, the two of us sitting in this teacher's home : not a paper to be seen, everything in its place, the virgin pallet drawn defensively away to the innermost wall of the alcove. The game lay between us, and somehow the stale-mate stood for everything. I had a premonition of sterility.

I heard her put the chess-men softly away. 'On ne va plus jouer aux échecs,' said said, 'no more chess.' In French 'échec' also means defeat, it was hard to tell if that was in her mind. I recovered, 'Pardon, je vais mieux.' 'Tu es un Loupino assez compliqué, tu sais!' Then she told me of when she was an étudiante for three months in Paris, and sat for melancholy hours on a balcon sur la Seine, 'Ah, si jeunesse savait . . . !'

Next morning all was back to normal. Composition française, a private task set under the pear-tree : 'une promenade que vous aves faite', my mentor counselling me to keep within bounds 'ton imagination un peu "weird".' I discarded Le Salève and wrote 'Le Carrousel', a short story about my best friend killed in the war – a poet-poilu, fine head, graceful, shy, we had quar-relled over a jeune fille – the merry-go-round comes to our village, to remind me intolerably of the times we all three spent together – suddenly, to the very waltz we knew, there strides, round the Mairie, an erect slim figure : the returned prisoner. 'La frêle musique nous berçait, je saisis sa main entre les miens . . .' Her little red-inked pen darted punctiliously, 'Non, entre les *miennes*, une faute sérieuse . . .'

For la Pentecôte, Whitsun, she took me home with her to Vallorce, a petit pays near Thonon; in the train I sat opposite her and next to Yvonne Avalon, also en permission. Our three-cornered talk was rendered more constrained by the fact that in the tunnels my hand would dart out, squeeze Yvonne's and dart back just in time, leaving us both flushed and looking out of opposite windows. It seemed to both of us the thing to do.

I was curious to see Mademoiselle in her own home, a farm in a cluster of farms. Her married brother was a drawn unhappy-looking man married to a vague housewife who seemed some-how to have failed the family; the younger brother Fernand, thirty, in overalls, was a fine-looking fellow, 'Oh you should see him dressed up to go to Thonon!' But he did not unbend either. Only the two running children – 'parle-nous en anglais – non, en gallois!' – brightened a household that smelt of constraint. Anxious not to let Mademoiselle down, I was polite and affable and made a point of telling Fernand how good his sister had been to me. I was all the more taken aback next morning, when she took me aside and said sharply, 'Fernand n'est pas content de toi.' Her brother annoyed with me? Her lips were pressed : 'il trouve que tu es trop familier avec moi, que – que tu es insolent ...' Me, insolent? Apparently it was because I had tweaked her affectionately about her refusal to speak English. She seemed angry with me, and yet to be justifying herself; I was lost. Clearly there must have been a strong bond between them; expecting a childishly formal pupil, he had been faced with a shaveling who plainly maintained a closer relationship with his sister than he or any man had ever enjoyed, and he must have said to her 'Qu'est-ce que c'est donc? This boy, when he is not calling himself your nephew, talks to you as if he were your fiancé, it is not comme il faut!' No wonder she was flus-tered. For the rest of the time I had no idea how to behave – sulk, or bow and call her Mademoiselle? The week-end was not a success.

'Bonjour Lambard, ça va?' ... Excursions; the annual school trip through Aix-les Bains, to Haute Combe, hot and tiring; we picnicked on the grass, below the grandiose tombs of the Kings of Savoie, Lambard inaccessible as ever among the pensionnaires, 'Bonjour Lambard, ça va?' ... An evening visit to the Grand Théâtre in Geneva was much more eagerly awaited : Madame

Simon in *Le Passé*. I was fascinated, but not carried away. Considering this was the first play I had ever seen – a strong drama, played by a reputable company surrounding a star of renown – it seemed odd to me that neither this evening nor consequent ones made an impact on me to be compared with that of the Hip or even the Chester pantomime. Later I realized why: whereas at home I had seized on make-believe as an escape from daily life, here I was so under the spell of French, and the French, that I needed no escape ... 'Bonjour Lambard, ça va?' 'Chère Miss Cooke, Do you know the game "corbillons"? After dinner Tante Jeanne and I played, each has to think of a word ending in "on", very good for my vocabulary, at the end we realized nobody had thought of "garçon"! It was very amusing ...'

Then came the afternoon when Lambard called to me and said 'Mon père m'a demandé si tu aimerais passer deux jours chez nous.' Would I like to go home with him – had I heard aright? I walked away on air, and burst into the garden where my task was laid out, to translate from Hardy's *A Pair of Blue Eyes*. 'Tante Jeanne, je vais chez Lambard!' As I spoke his name, she pursed her lips. I scented trouble but blurted on, 'his father has written to ask me, next Saturday and Sunday –' 'Out of the question.' I looked at her, thunderous and white, 'but why?' 'It is not convenable,' she rapped, 'what of his family? You are in my charge, it would not be fair to Miss Cooke – what sort of food, and where would you sleep –' 'But Tante Jeanne, his family is good enough for him to come to school, and farmers just like your family, with the same good food – also he has written to his father that I will come' – not true – 'and if you forbid it his father will be insulted!' Facing me under the tree, across our battleground of translations, she was strong but I was stronger. She knew that nothing, nothing would stop me. I had parried her query about food, but not the one about quarters; I was aware, as she must be, that as Lambard had three or four brothers, I must share his room. But if she had brought that up, I was ready with 'Pourquoi pas? In Wales I share a cupboard, with *two* brothers!'

My vague feeling of guilt made the prospect doubly attractive,

every time I thought of it I felt my heart beat, it was a dream ...
Saturday afternoon came, I packed a knapsack and took it in to
déjeuner; Lambard arrived as I drank coffee with my ladies, and
waited shy and shining at the next table. It was strange to see
him sitting there, where I had first heard and talked of him;
it was like seeing a wild bird suddenly in a cage. Mademoiselle
was affable and the atmosphere easy; I kissed her good-bye,
over-brightly, and the two of us stepped out into the afternoon
heat. 'Alors,' he said, 'on part!' Moi et mon ami Lambard,
ensemble. Béret marching next to béret. I had my wish.

We walked, and he talked; the musical irresistible voice
seemed to set the pace of our march. Dusty straight road after
road, avenues of poplars, valleys, vineyards; more avenues,
more valleys, more vineyards. Walked and he talked. Talked.
Talked. He told me his family, the names of his brothers and
sisters, whom the married ones had married. 'Tiens,' I said,
'tiens ...' In our path, gleaming malevolently, we found a
sloughed snake-skin, and I wrapped it gingerly away, for distant
Tom. The voice, still musical but less irresistible, enumerated
the camarades in his village. Then he told me how flattered he
had been that first morning, when I had offered him my chocolate – I, the first foreigner Vincentier had ever seen! That had
never occurred to me. Then he told me the number of cows on
their farm, their names, the names of the calves. 'Tiens,' I said,
'tiens ...' By the time the shadows of the poplars were lengthen-
ing over the parched roads and the cool of the evening approached, the cool of friendship was on its way too; my
Lambard, the mysterious stranger for ever disappearing round
corners with mute eloquent farewells – Lambard was a bore.

He was an amiable bore and I could not but like him; but his
intelligence was chained to his desk and away from it he had
nothing to offer – neither wit, fantasy nor buffoonery, neither
sulks, violence, nor even maddening reserves of silence. There
was no silence, and the most dedicated house of love will slowly
subside over the corner-stone of prattle. 'Ma tante Alphonsine a
des migraines, elle habite Annemasse!' 'Tiens ...' 'Tu as des
tantes, toi?' 'Oui,' I would counter, marching left, right, left,

right – 'j'ai une tante Sarah et beaucoup de tantes à St Helens dans Lancashire ...' Sacré nom de Dieu, I sound worse than him, la barbe la barbe ... His village swung into view, in a gentle valley. The farm was primitive beyond my imagining: tiny windows, cracked uneven floors, large close rooms sparse with rickety furniture, everywhere the shadow of near-poverty; in comparison, the parlour in 314a became a dwarf-museum of Victorian gentility. It was like one of those inns where travellers are benighted in historical novels. The smell of manure was overwhelming. The family made me welcome (they were a row of grey tombstones, could he be a changeling?) and I was touched that they had asked me, but they were as reticent as mon ami was voluble. Supper was a hot strange mess of pottage so richly seasoned (garlic?) that it made me queasy. Bed-time, and the family monosyllabically retired; we were to share a double bed in an alcove of the living-room.

I lay watching him, as he chattered, pull his Renaissance night-shirt over his head and then his trousers down over his stock-inged feet. The shirt had tousled his hair, and by the flickering light of the one candle, his fine eyes glowed like one of the paint-ings in the Musée de Genève. But the likeness was a speaking one. He had talked himself out of my heart.

He climbed between the sheets, where I was as taciturn as his family; after the long walk in the heat, I was tired too. He blew out the candle and was soon rhythmically, mercifully asleep. I could sense the fresh warmth of him. My blood-brother, my forbidden hero – together for ever, en route for the Crusades, we find ourselves rough-bedded in the sharing dark of hostelry after hostelry ... and it means nothing to me. The impaled butterfly, the bird in the cage, tout passe, tout lasse, tout casse ... In two minutes, I was as unconscious as he.

Sunday was a haze, to be forgotten before next Sunday: family mass in the tiny church, then, for dinner in the broiling farm-house, another immense steaming plate of greasy fare which made me dream of cold brawn and a tomato – 'mangez donc M'sieu George!' – I had to plead slight sunstroke. I missed Tante Jeanne. I spoke sudden effusive good-byes, and at the station felt dull and kind towards dull kind Lambard. As we both said 'Till school Tuesday!' and the train took me away from him for ever, I had a feeling of release.

She stood in la gare de Vincentier, as she had stood in Bellegarde years ago – two months ... I descended; she had her back to me, scanning the front of the train. 'Tante Jeanne!' She was pale, with under her eyes circles of – was it insomnia? But when I kissed her – a kiss that meant 'Nothing to fear, le Loupino is back, allons, un sourire!' – she knew that all was well.

'Chère Miss Cooke, J'ai passé le week-end chez mon ami Lambard avec sa famille. I shall not be going away again because Mademoiselle becomes worried, she fears accidents.' I rejoined my ladies en pension. Lambard's name came up once, twice, then for the third time and down to the ocean-bed.

My Italian improved and my music deteriorated; then, as hot heads began to tighten with approaching examens – the grim French anxiety of jail-birds praying for acquittal – so my sky began to darken with intimations of departure. The evening walks became tinged with melancholy, and the hour afterwards in the lamplight – chess, reading aloud, la conversation – was never free from the feel of something ending, of music slowing into a coda of indefinable sadness. The teasing had lost its sparkle, and now went with an ironical shrug. Mademoiselle appeared sometimes to be as joylessly distrustful of life as my mother, without Mam's humility; while the other went unarmed, this one seemed fortified with a knitting-needle, bright and sharp. The laughter was contaminated with a whiff of cascara. She discussed my future. 'Tu seras sans doute quelque chose, thou hast talent and wilt have force of character as a diplomate pour la perfide Albion, by learning to hide thy feelings.'

'Wilt thou be proud of me?' I said, pitching my note into her bantering key. 'Ah,' she shrugged, 'where will I be?' 'But here,' I said, 'still a teacher.' 'Oui,' she said, 'la vieille fille – mais reviendras-tu, espiègle pigeon? Wilt thou ever return, sly pigeon?' She knew that her mockery was hurting me, but she was determined, and now called me 'vous'. 'Mon pauvre Loupino, ce soir you sit in a room in Vincentier opposite a schoolmistress, as you have sat many nights. But the day will come, George, when you will sit in a London diplomatic mansion with wife and children and success and you will look at a map of France and ask yourself, "Haute Savoie? Now that name reminds me – wait, was it not there that one summer …"' She was laughing, but not happily. 'If you think that,' I said, 'you have wounded me.' 'Ah,' she said, 'jeunesse! Tout casse …' I went to bed depressed.

'Chère Miss Cooke, We are sitting in the fields of wheat, where they are mowing; I have just read aloud Maupassant's *L'Epave* and Mademoiselle has been very amusing about his view of love. Le temps passe si vite …' I had reverted to referring to her as Mademoiselle, I did not know why.

The packing and the adieux – adieu Françoise merci, adieu Mademoiselle Guillemet, a rivederci Signore – it was all softened by the journey to come. The first week of August, we set off together for two weeks in Chamonix and thereabouts, so that I should depart with a vision of the French Alps. We climbed funiculaires into the blazing sun, then down again into the chill evening hollow of the town; I noted the steep precipices, with fir-trees serried shoulder to shoulder, I would describe them, in a story, as an immobile green army ranged in military order from the lowest stream up to the towering sky – 'des phalanges' … 'C'est excessif comme image, mais pas mal.'

We saw everything, dutifully, and like a married couple who know the divorce is to come, made no mention of separation, falling back on polite exchanges – 'savais-tu que la Savoie n'est française que depuis 1860?' – interbarbed with sudden shafts that must have lacerated the archer as much as they punctured the target. 'Tu te souviens, quand tu as dit "nous nous battrons"?' Indeed I remembered. 'If we disagree, we will fight', but though by now I trilled the r of 'battrons', and though we had not fought, except for one moment, in the dark, over Lambard, I did not know her any better than that first day, whether I dubbed her Mademoiselle Tardy or Tante Jeanne.

I loved her, the eau-de-Cologne smelt as fresh, yet she was

doing everything to make me uncomfortable in her presence. Her mockery – of me, herself and much besides – was as subtle as before, but no longer gentle; as we circled from salle à manger to salle à manger, past a frieze of ambulant humanity, shapeless or corsetted, shadowy or raucous, she was a quizzical grande dame sitting with a lorgnette at a circus. 'Regarde cette jeune femme qui ressemble à Yvonne Avalon, qu'elle a l'air bête avec ce collier et ce bleu!' The girl's beads were perhaps too heavy for the too pale blue dress, but she looked lively – 'non George, pas tout de suite, sois comme il faut ...' So I remembered to count ten before looking. *Was* she vulgar? Yes, Tante Jeanne said so; and in imitation of her, I would interlace my filed nails and draw her attention to a young man abstractedly picking a back tooth with an index finger. Even the ones she approved of, she somehow mantled with ridicule, 'Oh qu'elle est comme il faut, elle marche comme votre Queen Mary, elle est *bien* ...' One would suppose that in the higher air, where above giant rock and diluvian snow the mountain-tops communed majestically with the annihilating heavens, the few mortals in the funicular must shrink to the size of ants – no, lift up thine eyes to the hills and lower them to censure thy fellows, 'Oh cette Anglaise, quelle voix, écoute ...' The Englishwoman *was* being rather loud, and pointing. I looked out and up; Mont Blanc itself was not safe, was the snow perhaps a little excessive ... ?

'Miss Cooke m'a écrit, tout est arrangé, c'est une vraie femme de business.' I was to spend four days in Paris with Miss Cooke on her way here. Miss Cooke ... I suddenly heard from the Mistresses' Room a burst of Homeric laughter, which could no sooner have emanated from Tante Jeanne than from the Mona Lisa ... But such apostasy was rare; we were Sainte Politesse and her disciple Young Prig, on a carping holiday. It ended at Annecy, in a packed hotel, nothing available but a two-bedded attic into which was brought a tall screen : our last night, we shared a room. Even then, it struck me as odd that a woman so conventional should accept this as natural; at the desk, I was assumed to be her nephew – I loved to call her 'Tante Jeanne' in front of strangers – but felt a little old to sleep in the same room as an aunt. Yet I was glad, we were en famille and it somehow made the parting easier. What she felt, again I do not know.

Next day – I was to leave by the all-night to Paris – we rounded the lake on a steamer built for families en vacances and lovers holding hands. It was a trip to lull the senses into dreaming, and this last day dreams were best at bay. Dîner was in the hotel garden under a plane-tree, where the special sun of this special summer lingered with me to the last; my picnic for the train was brought in a carrier-bag. We talked, we joked. Had I enough francs until Miss Cooke took over, had I counted my laundry, no holes in my socks, oh mon Dieu, here is one ... She sat darning under the evening leaves, sitting fastidiously on her petticoat with her dress safely tucked up, suddenly more as she had been, insouciante; my spirits were good, for I was incapable of imagining the morrow. We strolled to the bustling station, disposed of my trunk – 'ce n'est pas une malle, c'est une maison!' – had coffee, joked, talked ... Then I clambered up, hurried to my window, lowered it smartly and was about to call down – with an English accent, to make her laugh – 'Nous nous battrons!', when the words crumbled on my lips; she was in tears.

The train moved; she saw me and looked first to the left, then to the right, as if she could not bear for me or for any other traveller to see, 'Ce n'est pas correct' ... The curl of hair was vagrant on her brow, but she was not free to brush it adorably aside : in her effort to control herself, she was pressing her palms together, over and over again. My own eyes blurring, I knew that this was what 'wringing the hands' meant. As she stood there, I had a superimposed vision of her in a few minutes' time, turning and walking away into her future, which was a tunnel – of her own making – narrowing inexorably down the academic distance. 'J'écrirai,' I called, 'j'écrirai, Tante Jeanne!' She smiled, then waved, then laughed as the train, with every gentle ruthless turn of every wheel, snapped thread after fragile thread. She was gone.

Chapter 17

De Retour

Of my four days in Paris I have the memories of a drugged
patient, drugged with love for an enigma – 'enigmatic', at last
I knew what it meant – part spinster, part siren. I was to weld
the two, in absence, into a portrait of perfection.

The Cook's man took me up the boulevard Saint Michel –
the Artist Colony sprawled at open-air cafés, pas du tout comme
il faut – to 212 rue Saint Jacques: under an arch into a dark
cour, troisième étage, a clean shabby student-pension. Miss
Cooke was due later; I slept in my cubicle till an urban August
afternoon prised open my smarting eyelids. I wandered into the
little salon and sat at the peeling desk, the hooting traffic making
me hotter. 'Tu me manques affreusement ...' It did not render
'Paris is meaningless without you' but my heart was too full for
eloquence. 'I would I knew where is thy balcony, I would go
and look up at it ...' I filed my nails.

A babble in the couloir, an unmistakably English voice –
'merci Madame merci' – and Miss Cooke blew into the stale
room, a clean salt wind from choppy Channel and northern
moors. I had never seen her in a hat. I rose, smiling self-consciously. After the other, she towered; I flinched before the ro-
bust gestures, the resonance, the piercing blue eyes, 'You look
jolly well, welcome to Parry!' The first mot d'anglais I had
heard for four months sounded a note at once alien and familiar
which I resisted violently; she was more a stranger to me than
Miss Ivy Jones who followed her, a pretty new teacher from
Flint whose blue dress ... perhaps a little light?

Which do I speak? Shall I parody a French boy and sweep
them into the charade – 'non non, je ne connais plus l'anglais,
seulement Feesh et Cheeps, bonjour Mees Coq ...' I wish I

could have been as accomplished, it would have made for fun and ease. I blushed and mumbled 'Yes thank you.' Miss Cooke turned to go, then pointed ('n'indique pas avec le doigt') – 'what on earth's this?' 'My béret,' I said, rolling the r. 'A berry?' she said and laughed heartily, 'great Scott Ivy isn't that priceless, now les chambres ...' I sat miserably back to my letter. 'Miss Cooke vient d'arriver comme un tourbillon, I had to speak English. All the time at Versailles I shall think of Chillon and Coppet ... I am wearing the tie from thee bought in Thonon yesterday – *was* it yesterday? – and facing me is a calendrier with the Savon Cadum baby from the wall in our dear Vincentier. I can hear Miss Cooke asking about the blanchisserie and the Opéra tonight. Her French is correct, but not like thine, Ton Loupino.'

At dinner I insisted on my own carafe de vin rouge, 'Good gracious Ivy, look!' We were joined by two strange Anglaises, teachers, and they all naturally talked table-shop while I sat in their midst, swallowing silently with one genteel French hand on the table. 'Mind you Miss Proctor – is it? – the status of the married teacher, would you not agree' – the unexpectedly polite warmth with which she could woo a stranger was lost on me – 'to blazes, I say, with the Minister of Education!' Her laugh pealed out, and the others tinkled a delighted echo. Merde merde, je m'en fous, am I always to be surrounded by schoolmistresses? Yet the person I half-long – so intensely – to be with, is more a schoolmistress than any of them ...

Out of the jumble, little was to stay with me : my sleepily losing the Opéra tickets, Miss Cooke scolding me, old Madame Painvin praying to Saint Antoine and finding them in the waste-paper basket: the Opéra – *Faust* – a welter of chandeliers and devilish trapdoors and marble staircases and trumpets out of which I was woken twice by a peremptory dig. Then the evening at dinner when Miss Cooke averred, with sense and sensibility, that the sooner the Germans were accepted as part of peace the better, 'what about the generation growing up in Berlin now, poor beggars ...' Madame was serving soup, and Miss Cooke asked her opinion; till now a frail retainer, she put down a plate and drew herself up, eyes blazing. 'Mademoiselle,' she rasped, 'ne me parlez pas des Boches, je suis de Metz. Twice in my life they have strangled France, twice. Forgive? Jamais...' She retired, trembling too much to pick up the plates : it was the only time I ever saw Miss Cooke silenced.

Then the Comédie Française : *Les Femmes Savantes*, when at some shaft against bluestockings, she jogged Miss Jones, 'Old Molière's got us to a T, m'dear, ho ho ...' and *Ruy Blas* – pageantry and breadth (what did depth matter?) – when the Queen spoke of

> 'Le beau soleil couchant qui remplit les vallons
> La poudre d'or du soir qui monte sur la route ...'

and Miss Cooke whispered to me, 'Ah, les vers d'or de Victor Hugo! ...' I tingled to her enthusiasm, forgetting that Tante Jeanne would have spoken the same words more elegantly – and with sarcasm perhaps? (Miss Cooke could be sarcastic too. 'Je continue ma lettre. She has gone out to buy books. Just now I was at this dreadful piano practising my scales, she put her head round the door and called, in French, 'Ah, la belle musique, le Paderewski gallois!', laughed very strongly and walked out. Imagine-toi, I cannot practise again.')

To my relief, Miss Cooke did not launch into French with me, but I enjoyed tackling officials, to show her how fluent I was; once, in the middle of an animated question to a gendarme, I realized that I had halted my ladies two feet from an open pissoir and my French left me. I dreamt of their finding me deep in sustained idiom with a camarade, but it never happened. And the sightseeing was all wrong. Miss Cooke, who in a Holywell class-room had evoked the excitements of Rome and Parry, was for that reason the last person to accompany me on the spot; dawdling through vast Versailles, footsore behind the two of them – 'there he is, for heaven's *sake* keep up with us!' – I glumly saw the Petit Trianon as something she had conjured up to illustrate Michelet. I ought to have been nostalgically alone.

Then the trudge through the Louvre, scribbling – at her elbow and behest – my hackneyed impressions of the stock masterpieces: the Mona Lisa, discernible a mile off by her knot of hypnotized tourists ('inscrutable') and the winged Victoire ('one would swear she is in flight . . .'). What I did not scribble was the effect, like the brush of fingers across my palm, of the plump sprawling Rubens women, pink-tipped, luscious and biteable as fallen pears. Neither did I include one overheard comment, in front of a gigantic canvas where naked sinners hurtled to Hell with writhing round them every sort of apocalyptic monster: womanish eight-legged wolves and two-headed serpentine women. A lady tourist stood thoughtfully next to her husband, then pointed an umbrella at one of the figures. 'Tiens trésor,' she said in one breath, 'elle a six nichons quel génie, look dear, she's got six tits what a genius . . .' He murmured agreement and they strolled on to pass judgement on the more soberly endowed Vénus de Milo. I was glad my two Anglaises had not heard; had I known it, Miss Cooke would have been delighted.

Then Bonaparte's resting-place ('tons of marble, emphas. insig. mortal remains beneath'). Looking down from the circular balustrade – the ladies had mislaid me en route for the tattered flags – I felt so wearied by the heat, and by the autobuses lurching sickeningly round the mazed streets, the smell of petrol, the metallic gale in the Métro, the sightseers, the sights and now the megalomaniac grandeur of this mausoleum (could he ever have been a dark student of fifteen, inches shorter than me?) that I rested my arms on the cool mottled edge and my oppressed head on my arms. A tug at my elbow, a gendarme, 'Pas permis monsieur.' I went my usual red and dragged on, surely the only visitor who ever, at the height of a tourist afternoon, fell asleep on Napoleon's tomb.

The fifth morning, Miss Cooke bustled off to the Gare de Lyon to join Tante Jeanne (the irony!) while I departed, from the Gare du Nord, into exile. Miss Jones accompanied me, an easy untalkative companion; as we settled in, an Englishman entered, had a misunderstanding with the porter, turned to us others and said, 'Could somebody explain?' Eagerly I half-rose, but his look glanced off on to Miss Jones, who interpreted haltingly.

It was a long day, just time to cross to Euston – too fast to

read the names of the plays bannered across the red buses –
then the late afternoon across England. I absorbed, without
wanting to, the cool sunlight, the size and trim solidity of the
train and the gleaming neatness of the double railway-track, all
more quietly authoritative. Chester was almost dark; we caught
an express, first stop Flint. This meant that we rattled through
Connah's Quay, at Flint Miss Jones alighted and I waited an
hour for the slow train back; the procedure fuddled my mind
and divorced me from reality. How large the pennies felt! . . . In
the train, looking at the faded photographs of straw-hatted
Welsh beaches, I heard the local accent as in a dream, I did not
even mind people staring at the béret which I had worn jea-
lously all day. At the Quay, in a midnight daze – 'c'est moi?' – I
heard my feet echo down the deserted street and down the alley.
314a was dark, I had written that I might miss connections and
not to wait up. A flicker, the turn of the lock, and Dad in his
long drawers holding a candlestick, 'Well, well, well . . .' Bemused as I was, his handshake pleased me. We whispered, he
lifted the plate off my cold supper, Mam called down 'Are you
all right?', he padded up, their door closed. In the silence,
everywhere the smells of home. 'Qui suis-je,' I whispered, 'who
am I?' From the parlour, the tiny familiar clearing of a metal
throat and the grandfather clock, which had announced my
arrival into the world to a parlourful of greengrocery, greeted
me afresh into the stuffy little cave where my brothers lay sleeping. The cave closed gently round me. De retour.

I was stirred to see my family again – I had a tiny boat for
Tom, from Thonon, with two French sailors sitting in it, and the
dried snake-skin – but I was uprooted, dépaysé, a sickness aggra-
vated by having nobody to tell. The first morning Dad, two-till-
ten, accompanied me to the station for the trunk; it struck me
with a pang, as we walked that all through my summer he had
been treading his mill, seven days a week. There had been a bad
strike, a soup-kitchen under St John's Chapel, pianos sold for a
song, but for once his conviviality had done Mum a splendid
turn : through pot-fellows at the Old Quay pub, his knack with

boilers had got him transferred to Crichton's Shipyard next door
and he had worked all through, to the envy of his mates. I was
glad to remember the envelope which had awaited me this morning – I had not yet appreciated it – containing a First Prize from
the National Eisteddfod for an essay I had sent in, before France,
on 'Cynghrair y Cenedloedd', the League of Nations, three
guineas. My first wages.

With the trunk we tramped, in unison, down the hill as once
we had tramped up, only this time there were more curious
eyes. I was still wearing my béret. Dad had the tact not to
mention it. We put down our burden for a breather. 'Off again?'
he said. 'Oui oui,' I answered, and blushed; he laughed de-
lightedly – 'takes time!' – and I knew it would be a story for
his mates. But I could not enjoy it; I seemed to have difficulty
in breathing the very air. I was comforted by the knowledge
that there was no snobbery in my emotion: the milieu for
which I longed was a peasant one, lower socially than the Quay
– indeed, if I had returned to Glanrafon, I would have felt the
change less acutely. And I was unable to show off, which would
have been a comfort; I reflected with a sigh that if I had returned from bel canto in Milan, I would have been rushed on to
every platform in North Wales, breaths bated, pins dropping –
but no, I had come back speaking French, Mammyzelle from
Arm-in-tears, and there was no public for me. In the parlour,
Mam creaked open the trunk as if it was Pandora's Box and continental flummery might buzz out into her hair; she found all in
order, even the socks darned. 'I must say she has looked after
you, where shall I put your French hat?' That settled it: I folded
it regretfully away.

It was Saturday, and I wandered up to the football ground,
as lost as an escaped convict; I heard the meagre crowd – 'ger-
router-vit, sock the bloomin' thing, kick the boogar!' – and it
sounded irremediably foreign. I leant against a tree and longed
– with a physical ache so intense that it should have lifted me
off the ground – to be leaning against a French tree in Vincentier, listening to French voices. Those could be as uncouth –
ah, but they were French. Yes, it was snobbery ... Back in the

parlour I said aloud, 'Un billet de troisième pour Bellegarde, s'il vous plaît ...', then set out the empty chocolate-box with the white marguerites, and arranged my pencils in it.

All this I poured on to long tissue pages to the woman who sat immobile at the core of my affliction. I described my walks, what I was reading, what Tom looked like as he ran in from play, 'Il a presque neuf ans, he reminds me of thy little André, tall for his age and with his joyful green eyes, thou wouldst find him a charming child' et patati et patata ... I was as garrulous as poor Lambard and not helped, in my disorientation, by Tante Jeanne's first letter. It started 'Mon cher Loupino', but while the tone was affectionate it was somehow guarded, and the envelope next to my tea turned her again into the shadowy pen-teacher of last winter. She described her week with Miss Cooke, at our hotel in Chamonix, a pedagogic honeymoon which must have been about as successful as Queen Victoria entertaining, for a long wet Windsor week-end, Sir John Falstaff. 'Elle est devenue eccentrique ... Thou hast written to me of her in Paris, so I feel free to confess that I have passed three difficult days. Imagine thou, in the train after a mountain walk, in front of three strangers, she changed her stockings! We have had discussions about our countries which could only end in bitterness, and when she laughs it is to make the room look round. We have no longer anything in common. Elle est impossible!' I did not notice that she made no mention of the one thing they still had in common. Myself.

My feelings were mixed. In Paris I had indeed rebelled against Miss Cooke, and now found my rebellion confirmed by the opinion which was influencing me most; yet it was distasteful. I remembered Annie turning against Dad, and realized that though I did not think of myself as being fond of Miss Cooke, she was one of the family, halfway between father and mother. Years later, coaxed, she wrote me her side, magnanimous and lucid. 'Mademoiselle Tardy was that French product, a gifted woman so deep in the rut of la vie de province that many things had got beyond her imagination – spent most of the time telling me how badly England had behaved over the war – well, I couldn't stand for that. I was sorry for her, but it was a tough week. I had probably changed, but by Jove *she* had. Heigh ho ...' Clearly a Yorkshire cliff, at odds with an underground Gallic stream as subtle as it was erosive, had majestically crumbled. It was the end of an entente cordiale.

But not for me. 'Comme j'ai aimé ta lettre, it has brought a breath of the great world of affection and beauty ...' I would sit staring at a map of Haute Savoie, my finger tracing the road to Le Salève, speaking the names of places I had heard of but never seen, La Roche-sur-Foron, Cernex ... Then I would settle to read *Trois Contes*, with tucked in as a book-mark the wrapper from one of the slabs of Chocolat Menier just received. As the nights drew in, I walked up the line; with wind rising and rain scudding. I stood on a bushy slope – the stage of the Comédie Française – and spouted from *Ruy Blas*, at the top of my voice, in a parody of the splendid agonized whine of French tragedy :

> 'Eh bien! moi, le laquais, tu m'entends, eh bien! oui
> Cet homme-là! Le roi! je suis jaloux de LUI!'

Then I let myself go mad, and bawled improvisations from bass to falsetto and back: 'je t'implore, mon amour – je m-e-e-urs dans un enfer sans nom, CIEL!!' Behind a hedge I heard titters, scrambled down and away, but felt relief. On my way home I saw, soaring from the sinister gleam of the Clay-'ole, the Comédie Française itself, with against the glimmer of the Steelworks, de Musset's suffering stone silhouette. Superbly alone in the theatre, I enter a box, King Ludwig of Bennett's Cottages, and the curtain rises on *Ruy Blas* with all of us – the actors and I, at the heart of the grievous town – immune. I was a Francophile.

One dies or gets better, and I did not die. By school in September, though the poplars at Holywell Junction were a poignant reminder, Flintshire was more in focus and I was composing sustained sentences in English without feeling disloyal. After my years and years abroad, I found the Honours Form strangely the same; the news was that Septimus, at sixteen, was the youngest local preacher in North Wales, 'verily a theocrastical

wonder'. I was modest about my summer – 'very nice, not unlike here' – but what I longed for and dreaded, was Miss Cooke
asking me to read aloud. It came, a passage from the *Préface de*
'Cromwell'. My voice wavered, but they sat impressed; if only
I could have sung it, merde alors ... 'Excellent,' said Miss Cooke,
'but don't do the rolled r, it's a little affected.' I stood with a
dead look, this was a blow between the eyes. Now or never.
'Next, the effect of Lamartine –' 'I'm sorry, Miss Cooke,' I said,
'but I've got too used to the Parisian r to lose it.' A pause. 'Well,'
she said, 'I still think it's jolly well affected.' Had it been an in-
stinctive back-kick against another French voice? All this was
written to Tante Jeanne, eight close pages soon to settle into
weekly gossips which for two years were to be my regular outlet – 'il est dimanche après la chapelle, I wonder if thou art
having supper ...' – and interspersed with evocations – 'it seems
yesterday we walked back from the Gorges du Fier and disputed
as we went, dost thou remember?' – tumbling sometimes into
the coy – 'dost recall my eating cherries in the tram and a certain old maid forbidding me? ... I would give much to spend
my life with thee, je t'embrasse bien, Ton Loupino.' Her answers
stayed correctly, distantly affectionate.

Before mid-term, just as I was about to drift, marching orders :
London Matriculation, January. And Miss Cooke did not plan
to play the strong cards (French, English, History) but a chance
on the draw – hold your hosses, in the Mistresses' Room – Latin,
Italian and Greek. 'London Matric,' said Mr Robinson the Inspector, to J.M., 'what on earth for?' When told the subjects,
'That's different,' he said, 'that's what I call a Cooke plan.'
'George,' said Dad, pleased, 'she's driving you ahead!' Yet it was
not driving. Outwardly a docile subject, I was the horse that has
to be coaxed, force would have been fatal; and this particular
trainer, with a deportment uncoaxing to the point of gaucherie,
would seem to have exercised, without knowing it, a psycholo-
gical understanding of her charge.

For Greek, I had three and a half months, from scratch.
'Rogers had less for French,' she said. J.M. proudly provided his
old Oxford grammar, I allotted one morning to the alphabet and
that evening, from Cruickshank's grubby book-box, in exchange

for four of my meagre library – I was angry at the parting – I acquired a shabby Liddell and Scott dictionary which had started at Harrow before going down the Hill; its main disfigurement, driven deep in ink sideways into the eight-hundred pages, was the initials of an owner who must have been as suspicious of his schoolmates as if his parents had sent him to Borstal. I spent a nice hour lifting each bruised page like a paw and shaving the edge. Once I had taught myself the rudiments, Miss Cooke instituted a postal course, in Greek and Italian, from London; twice a week I sent off the papers, back would come the corrections. I had neglected Italian for Greek and my first Italian report, in a stern male hand, forced me to sit up : 'weak, doubtful'. I slogged at it; Miss Cooke somehow procured old copies of the *Corriere della Sera* and I compiled vocabularies. Once Mr Boyer was sitting over us and called to me sharply, 'Put that newspaper away and get on with some work.' It was good to answer, 'It's Italian, sir, and it *is* work.' Miss Cooke, evidently as an insurance against overtaxed strength, commanded me every morning into the Mistresses' Room, at a moment when it was empty, to the top shelf of the cupboard where she had placed a family-size bottle of Scott's Emulsion ('World's Finest Cod-Liver Oil, Keeps Colds at Bay') and the tablespoon which I was to fill, empty at one gulp and wash at the tap. This became a morning ritual till I left school.

My father's imagination was caught by the Greek alphabet, he examined it for minutes while I thumbed through Liddell and Scott to discover with wonder the simple words whence came so many I knew. It was enriching to find that $\dot{\alpha}\nu\epsilon\mu o\varsigma$ turned into anemone, Daughter of the Wind, and $\ddot{\upsilon}\pi\nu o\varsigma$ (sleep) into hynosis; I loved the book of $\ddot{\eta}\lambda\iota o\varsigma$ the sun, and $\ddot{\alpha}\nu\theta o\varsigma$, a flower, and if I had known that hydrogen came from $\ddot{\upsilon}\delta\omega\varrho$, water, I might have melted towards Chemistry. For Prize Distribution, a breather, I officiated as a reciter, and chose a mock-pompous rather Dickensian monologue on Mother Hubbard – 'Let us examine Ladies and Gentlemen this touching poem anent an unfortunate widow and her canine friend' – which squeezed reluctant giggles; then 'Daffodils', first straight then in broken English as Toussaint. I had the sense to stand stock-still, let the parrot-accent speak for itself, and the giggles became laughter. Neither was too long, I had learnt something and felt again the exhilaration of turning into somebody else.

Back to Greek that night, after my letter thanking Tante Jeanne for the exquisitely bound *Divina Commedia* she had sent me pour Noël. I sat the exam in Liverpool, where Uncle Jab met me at the ferry as he had met my mother forty years before. Any time I had asked Mam about him she had answered proudly, 'He is still keeping his head up in the Tea,' and whenever he came to my mind I had watched him swimming in a vast steaming brown vat. He had been married many years to a grocer's widow whom he had met at his first wife's funeral, and at 27 Wadham Road – still Bootle – presided over a three-ringed family : his, Auntie Soph's, and their own two sons, a little older than me, Clwyd and Ioan Emlyn. The latter (Ioan is the Welsh for John) had had difficulty with his birth certificate, finding at the indignant age of fourteen that the registrar had put him down as a girl by the name of Joan Emlyn. Auntie Soph was a pretty woman with a taste for coquettish hats; placid and wise, she enjoyed being teased as a fool and kept the straight face of a droll, 'They said I was the best-looking girl in the Vale of Clwyd, George, but you can't expect this lot to believe that – but look at you going to foreign parts, and coming back with not a mark on you, wonderful . . .'

And a lot they were, in-laws and step- and grand-children barging in and out of the communal kitchen; it looked like any kitchen, but for me this one throbbed with the feel of a great grimy seaport pullulating on every side, I heard the midnight foghorns and thought of Conrad. There were Clwyd and Emlyn, apprenticed to a blacksmith, changing in fifteen minutes from oil-faced savages to natty boys-about-Bootle, as Welshless as Job and Tom, a trilby over one ear, 'Mam, got a spare bob for a workin' lad?', young Nellie, married to Auntie Soph's son Bob, a radiant elder sister like Annie, cutting endless bread-and-butter for Soph ('You do it Nell fach it always comes to pieces for me') and on top of the three families young Welsh Tom Jones, as much of a foundling as Fielding's and less a lodger than an extra son : an endless traffic patriarchally regulated by Uncle Jab of

245

the chuckling walrus-moustache. As inflexibly Welsh as J.M., on Sunday he rounded up his sheep, into the pen of the same Trinity Road Chapel where my parents had met. In the evenings I loved sitting in the midst of them all, cramming for next day. 'Hush the lot of you,' said Auntie Soph, 'George is bettering himself.'

The last night, off with Nellie and Bob to the Apollo in Pembroke Road, Priscilla Dean in *Under Two Flags*: But my last morning, a cultural call at the Walker Art Gallery. Besides Müller's 'Tivoli', with its Italian skies over a leaf-clustered landscape where I could imagine sitting for eternity reading all I had ever longed to read, I was inevitably drawn to Poynter's 'Faithful Unto Death' – a centurion on guard at Pompeii with the city perishing around him – and bought a postcard to pin up in my parlour-corner. Unexpectedly, like Shakespeare, the Liverpool City Fathers catered for another side of me with Lord Leighton's 'Andromeda', pinkly naked except for snow-white robes caught perilously by a cord over broad arched hips, and even more successfully with Albert Moore's 'A Summer Night': four Greekish maidens, likewise near-nude, rolling (there is no other word) on a long divan against the night sea, one lazily trying to sleep, one lazily doing her hair, one with hands lazily behind her head, the fourth lazily stretching. I was glad it was January.

Back in 314a, I had the feeling of coming from optimism to a straightened hearth; Mam seemed more harassed. My aunt had kissed me good-bye, my mother did not kiss me welcome, and it irked me. But the news came that I had passed, and I returned to authorship. Selling my books had rankled, and it became my obsession to acquire some of the guineas dangled in the Press – 'Housewife Earns £4 Pin-Money, "My Husband Laughed till he Saw Me in Print!"' I would settle for a pound a week, or even five shillings. I consulted *The Lure of the Pen* for its appendix of periodicals and their requirements: 'MSS should be typed, with stamped addressed envelope.' On Saturdays I toiled up to Holywell and sat at the giant typewriter in the centre of an echoing plague-empty school, with the week's chants and chatters and screeches all dead on the floor like old newspapers; every key struck was like a pistol-shot in a vault. Dispirited, I disobeyed rules and hauled the monster home for the week-end, staggering down High Street feeling like old Bob yr Hendre with his stolen anvil.

I wrote, and I wrote. 'Modern Travel', article for *Daily Mail* (500 wds, shld be racy, topical, 3 gns): 'Every time I holiday abroad, my French porter has grown more emotional and will quarrel over a suitcase as if it were a woman ...' The Editor Regrets ... Short Story for *Pam's Paper* (humorous, sentimental, shld appeal to yg g'ls, preferably middle-class bckgrnd). As I typed my title I winced, then remembered that at first Dickens had had to write down: 'Wendy Comes a Cropper'. ' "Botherosity" ' she whooped as she threw her tennis-racket across the drawing-room, Wendy was a lass given to strange oaths. Then 'Cecil!' and she was back like a boomerang, tugging her protesting fiancé. ' "Steady, Wendy child!" ' The story was a boomerang too. I aimed higher (at *Nash's*, dram. stories for intell. public) with 'Who Knows?', and it was better. It was in the form of a letter ('Let me, Edoardo da Persa, tell ...') describing the writer's revenge, in an Italian community, on the friend who had betrayed his betrothed; he has trapped the seducer into a cliff cave with a ten-foot drop into the sea, and drowned him. Turning to escape, he hears a rumble; an internal landslide, he is cut off, and the tide rises as he pens the confession which he will put to sea in a bottle. 'The water is at my feet. Is this God's judgment – at my knees – where I now go, shall I meet my enemy? Chi sa? Who knows ...' But the Editor again Regretted. I lent it to Miss Cooke, who returned it with a single devastating comment: 'the Mediterranean has no tide.'

These abortive efforts might have become depressing but for the School Eisteddfod, March 1922. In addition to essays ('An Imaginary Visit to Princess Mary's Wedding'), poems, bad drawings and even a setting of Christina Rossetti's 'My heart is like a singing bird' grimly picked out on the school upright, I submitted a short story which, not being aimed at Fleet Street, was an advance. I had been impressed by Katherine Mansfield, and tried to base on personal experience an account of a Welsh boy living on a farm with his undemonstrative mother; he goes to stay with happy-go-lucky relations in Liverpool with whom he finds himself more at home, until a telegram recalls him to his mother's death-bed. It was a shot at truth.

But more important, at the time, was the Trial Scene from *The Merchant of Venice*, myself as Shylock, Connie Wray as Portia, hair up under a mortar-board, and Eric Jones a willing but inaudible Gratiano whose part had to be cut to the bone, just enough left for Shylock to interrupt. Walter Jones Ffynnon-groew, school goalkeeper, made a somewhat stolid Bassanio, who at the same time found it impossible to keep still, as if constantly expecting the ball; and Septimus Luke – the Rev, as he was now known – was a perfervid Welsh Antonio hot from a soul-saving tour of the Lagoons. He looked so scraggy with his chest bared that one had to wonder by what miracle of surgery the Jew proposed to exact his pound of flesh. Owing to the shortage of male recruits (Shakespeare, oh 'eck!) this particular trial had to be presided over by a Duchess of Venice in the person of Mercy Pumphrey, a girl who endured with good humour the nickname of Percy Mumphrey. It was lucky that only the day before, it occurred to me that it might be a risk, in front of the whole school, to have her addressed directly with the line 'The quality of Mercy is not strained'.

My own preparation absorbed me; I studied the photographs of Irving and Tree in my *Shakespeare*; my costume was an old Paisley table-cloth with holes for the arms, Dad's carpet slippers, a skull-cap from an old black blouse ('Don't tell anybody') and at my waist, next to the school carving-knife, the Pen-y-Maes scales with the word 'Bass' obscured by brown paper; for the beard, I found some wire and twined it with cadged horsehair. The family abed, I would hook on the beard, hold out the shaving mirror, and snarl carefully into it. At the performance there was, as always, only the little platform, a near-island in the sea audience; to quieten the school, behind the door from the Boys' Side I struck a gong (Mam's), the door opened, the Duchess and the rest filed solemnly in. At the line 'Call the Jew into the court' I knocked thunderously on the door: the rasp of the handle, Salerino replied 'He comes, my lord!', the door slowly opened, and the star entered.

In spite of daylight and a row of staff two feet away, the scene held thrillingly; then something happened. I had whipped out the knife, at the unexpected moment which evoked the anticipated gasp; sharpening it against my sole as required by the author, and about to turn on Gratiano, I felt – incredibly – a tug at my robe, then a peremptory whisper, 'Don't do that, it'll frighten the younger children.' It was Miss Cooke.

I should afterwards have taken heart from the way I reacted, for it was the behaviour of a professional player, on a first night, in the face of a hooligan audience. I was as angry as I have ever been, but my immediate instinct was to keep my head and direct the anger white-hot at Portia; never can 'Tell me that!' have been spat out with such venom, even Bassanio the goalie was riveted. We won. 'Ma chère Tante Jeanne, Figure-toi que Miss Cooke . . .' It was weeks before I forgave her, and years before I saw the humour of it. Could she, at that moment, have sensed an ambition of which I was not yet aware – 'let's prick the bubble'?

As if to atone, she now began a habit which was to be invaluable to me; every Monday afternoon, she would throw me her ravaged copy of the *Observer*, 'highest standard in the country, study the style'. All the way home in the train, and all Monday evening, I would con it from cover to cover. The leader page – 'The Plight of the German Mark', 'What of the Entente?' – I often found heavily scored ('hear hear!' 'bunkum!' 'Ha ha, L.G. in sheep's clothing again!') but I fear I got to it last, and studied Garvin only for the style. What I went for first, though I still had not seen a play in English, was the theatre page: 'Dramatis Personae' (the news column) and St John Ervine in his heyday. His views seemed to me marshalled with such eloquent clarity, such a compound of the emotional and the astringent, that they rang with truth; I unconsciously noted every tribute and every stricture. 'The essence of drama is struggle', 'no good a good first act if your last is going to let you down', 'every word audible, yet seemed to whisper' . . . 'Next Wednesday evening, Mr A. A. Milne's new play *The Dover Road* . . . Mr Galsworthy's latest drama . . .' For a country cousin who had never been inside one, at sixteen I knew a surprising amount about the West End theatre.

But literature came first. I subscribed to *John O' London's*, a serious twopenny weekly; then, having studied *She Stoops to Conquer* in class, I spent the Easter holidays writing a prose adaptation of *Les Femmes Savantes*, setting the play forward a century and basing the style on Goldsmith's. I even called it *The Diggories*; Clitandre became Mr Joseph Temple, Trissotin Mr Josiah Trimble. I copied it into a note-book and gave it to Miss Cooke. 'Very good practice,' she said, but it was more than that, and she knew it: it was a practical 'merci, de tout mon coeur' for sending me to France.

With the summer, mollifying two hungers, for the flesh and for brother-love, my thoughts returned to poetry. Miss Morris, again at my elbow at the right time, had lent me a primer of prosody; I was never to be a poet, but I felt there must be acres where prose and verse marry and live happily. I became elevated on Swinburne, 'Sister my sister, o fleet sweet swallow . . .' and – a more solid bouquet – on Leconte de Lisle, 'Le sable rouge est comme une mer sans limite . . .' I spoke to myself 'The splendour falls on castle walls' and I wrote: too easily, I knew it, but with love. At Versailles a year ago I had been hot and out of tune, but the muddled kaleidoscope had somehow settled into the clear waters of recollection,

> 'Between the park woods stretching far away
>   Without a breath,
> The palace faces long and low and grey
>   More dead than death.'

then a sonnet, 'Hero for Leander',

> 'Upon the cliffs with tearless eyes she waits
> Through wanton burning noons and timeless nights . . .'

then an English version of the Sonnet d'Arvers,

> 'My soul close guards its secret, and my life
> Its mystery – a deathless love swift-born . . .'

and of de Musset's 'Elégie',

'For the sake of our love,
When I die
Plant a willow above
Where I lie.
I love its silvery leaves, pale bright
And dear to me,
There they'll weep
Their shadows falling so light, so light,
Where I sleep . . .'

'May 11th 1922, Central Hall 3.30, Casket Scene from *The Merchant of Venice*, Portia, MILLIE TYRER; Bassanio, GEORGE WILLIAMS.' The whole school was quickly shepherded in before disbanding. It was glorious weather; as I stood in the masters' lavatory on one leg, pulling on one of my mother's black stockings, I could hear the noise of a crammed cage of birds hoping to get out into the air. Miss Morris was faithfully behind the partition to quieten them first with soft piano music, but it was impossible to capture such an audience; when I said 'I live upon the rack!' and threw my feathered cap to the ground in Italian despair, I harvested a healthy laugh. But it had been worth doing. And Miss Cooke had kept her distance.

The holidays, hot and heavy. I discovered Stephen Phillips, who at the beginning of the century had enjoyed a dazzling London vogue as the playwright who had taken Poetic Drama out of the Closet and put it back on to the Stage. *Paolo and Francesca, Nero, Herod*, such subject-matter could not fail with me (Nero!), and of the language I thought, but it's as melodious as Shakespeare, only simpler, this is *grand*! I spoke aloud

'It is the fault of dreamers to fear fate . . .
For a doom is come upon us, and an ending'

and took a year to realize that the simplicity was false, the grand grandiloquent and that

'The deep delicious poison of a smile'

was not better than Shakespeare, but Shakespeare bled white.

Then E. F. Benson's *Thorley Weir*, Cruickshank's, fourpence, two boys on holiday, surrounded by idyllic woods with pools

251

where they dived into chequered sunlight; I sighed and closed my eyes. It was not quite the same when I took the old train up to Holywell, then up to Pantasaph with plump easy-going John Philip Jones to shiver in icy Llyn Helyg; once we sat for hours on a bank opposite a villa where, according to J.P., there lurked a girl on holiday from the Wirral, 'a typist, wow ...!' She never emerged, and we moped home. Many long sunny afternoons, I would sit marooned in the sun-soaked parlour, wilfully stultified, and when not tormented by the flesh, dreaming awake: in the same sun, I was afloat on a flying carpet, down the Thames, over Tower Bridge, past all the Dickens landmarks, Wapping, Cheapside, Covent Garden, Westminster, and ending up, in the urban evening, inside a theatre out of the *Observer*: Apollo, Phyllis Neilson-Terry in *Trilby*, Kingsway, Mrs Patrick Campbell in *Hedda Gabler*, Drury Lane, *Decameron Nights* (ah!) ... It is all mine. As I thought it, I thought too ... why am I thinking this?

Towards the end of the holidays, I was pitched out of lethargy by 'Subjects for the National Eisteddfod' for next year, at Mold. I had not forgotten my three guineas, and now prospected for a further digging. 'Full-length historical drama, in English, on the Welsh national hero Owain Glyndwr, prize 100 guineas.' My eyes bulged, and once more I spent my Saturdays in Flint Library, gleaning notes for a Poetic Drama, Non-Closet. That winter the spirit of Stephen Phillips was at my elbow as I laboured at my first play. 'Laboured' is hardly the word, for this again poured out with suspicious ease:

> 'Methought the velvet wing o' Cambrian night
> Had folded o'er thy maudlin memories...'

If Sir Herbert Tree had glanced at that with pen poised over the contract for *Herod*, he might have hesitated.

In between methinking and alacking, the winter term bombinated with Recitations. These blossomed through admiring Mr John Duxbury, Elocutionist, a clerical elderly man with a considerable reputation in the north of England. He gave recitals in chapels, and our little Wesleyan colony had had the enterprise to invite him several times, was he not as edifying as a sermon? His rich tones may have had a thin coat of unction, but it did not worry me; even in the setting he was good value. His range was wide, Shakespeare, Dickens, 'A Christmas Carol', the Pickwick Trial, Fagin, Bill Sykes, and a virtuoso rendering of Poe's 'The Bells'. Then, after we had repeated the Trial Scene at a social in Connie Wray's chapel in Flint, it was suggested I should recite at another social; I did – Mother Hubbard and 'The Daffodils' – then sat down to extend my stock. In my *Modern Verse* I found 'Flannan Isle', a fine dramatic narrative by Wilfrid Gibson; then I prepared 'Break break break' done first straight, then again as a French student, then 'The Lady of Shalott', then 'Sergeant Buzfuz', my only Dickens venture, which I presented at a concert in chapel : not helpful to comedy, but it was worth it just to stand under the pulpit, which my mother had thought I might one day grace, and boom out over pew after pew '*Warming*-pan!' Dad asked to read the piece. 'Poll, the boy's in the footsteps of your great-uncle the Reverend, only this one has marched ahead – instead of fire and brimstone, it's chops and tomato-sauce!'

Every week, in return for transport and tea, my field widened; there would be whispers at the front door, could I do the Mancot Church Hall Tuesday week, or the Girl Guides' Tea in Bagillt on the Friday? Said Mam, 'You ought to start charging.' I did, half a crown a time. 'Is there a stage?' I would ask, there hardly ever was, but it sounded good; my approach was unbendingly professional. Though I was deferential to my sponsors, my instinct was to be seen, by them and by my audience, as little as possible before I was announced; on arrival, after the polite how-d'you-do I would disappear and lurk outside. Then, to a running accompaniment of ladies washing-up and children toddling, I aspired to taming one audience after another drunk on tea, pop and seed-cake; aiming at clarity and simplicity, I found that both seemed to work. Then back to our kitchen table and into the Phillips mantle – 'Ho there! What scurvy English knave treads hither?' – then off I would tread myself, sure of my hundred guineas, to the Rechabites' Indoor Gymkhana, where 'the young local elocutionist Mr George Williams will give a selection from his repertwee'.

As this snowball grew, so school receded; my relations with Miss Cooke, since the gesture of *The Diggories*, had deteriorated. The Higher Exam still months away, there was no scholastic bond between us; recalling her scotching of *Macbeth*, I imagined her scofing at my little activities and smarted afresh, though I still dutifully swallowed my Emulsion. Discipline in the Honours Form had so slackened that Septimus and I were banished to desks in the Central Hall, which was like studying in the street. We spent all day staring at passing traffic and making puerile jokes about it. *Macbeth* being a set-book, Miss Cooke was dubbed First Weird Sister, Miss Morris Second, and so on in a welter of inanity and boredom, only relieved one day when Miss Morris and Miss Swinnerton suggested there ought to be an entertainment after Prize Distribution, why not a play, why not *She Stoops to Conquer*?

We would hire the Catholic Hall – a stage, a curtain, footlights! – and I would play Young Marlow. Wigs were made from cotton-wool, and the girls' costumes hired from Liverpool, also make-up, which nobody had ever seen except on Miss Sadie Price. The boys wore red coats, white buckskin breeches and top-boots, our measurements having been posted to Miss Swinnerton's home in a sporting corner of South Wales, where a gig had been sent round with a laundry-basket; so I may claim that once in my life, and early on at that, I have been dressed for a blood sport. The idea was too ambitious, we needed a producer to galvanize the tremulous amateur mechanism; as it was, the responsibility seemed to fall on me. I had no idea of what production entailed, beyond the common-sense precautions of placing furniture, discouraging people from bumping, and insisting on decisive speech and 'keeping it going'. But the challenge of curtain and footlights could not be ignored, and I worked hard, aiming at a standard I knew nothing of. Through three sermons, I thought about the imminent first – and last – night, praying that Ena Mills and Ena Hughes would speak up and that Walter Jones would know his part. The performance was ragged, and to me at moments a shambles; but it was my first play, I stood in bright light, my audience sat in blessed darkness, and I enjoyed it hideously. Speaking clearly the hero's lines, as miscast in my hunting outfit as when I walked the lanes trying out honest Bob Cherry's laugh, I was yet, without knowing it, making a step nearer a goal. We were apparently creditable enough for people to suggest a repeat, but Miss Cooke decreed no, it would interfere with work. Back went the red coats. Tally-ho.

But with the holidays, Christmas 1922, the recitations thickened, one week I earned seven-and-six. At a social in Hawarden, after my encore I stood at the back and watched Miss Eunice Axe of Connah's Quay, another local elocutionist. Miss Axe, drifting into a region of the further twenties which to me at new seventeen lay out of ken, was as unwinning as her name, being bony, black-haired and black-headed, with a harsh voice that had been broken and reset by a local Elocution Teacher, an operation from which the patient had not emerged with complete success. She announced 'Come into the Garden Maud' in carrying tones which somehow turned a tender suggestion into a housekeeper's summons to a skivvy who should have been picking the gooseberries hours ago. No, Tennyson was tonight not in good hands; the black bat Night flew with the clatter of a tin can, and the woodbine spices were wafted abroad like luggage thumping on to a Channel steamer. The deafening applause taught me, not for the last time, that with some audiences violence is its own reward.

Miss Axe and I met over blancmange. Wasn't I the boy always with a book? Through the elocutionary overlay, there now showed gritty traces of Quay: she rhymed 'book' with 'duke'. 'Well,' she said, 'Ay must vamoose now. Going may way?' She did loov rissating, sooch an eskeep, if one didn't tray soomthing one would go pottay, whom did *I* go tew for elocution? 'Nobody,' I said. 'Oh boot if yew don't maind me saying, yew hev got – well to be frenk, a Welsh tweng?' 'I know,' I said, 'but nothing to what it was.' We parted at our alley, 'It's bane ripping foon!' Wait till you meet Miss Cooke, I thought as I raced down, she'll make mincemeat of you.

Next day she was at our front door to lend me *Recitations for Amateurs*, and suggested my accompanying her to her next 'concert', where she could arrange for me to appear too. 'Who was that?' said Mam. 'Nobody,' I said, 'a Miss Axe that recites.' 'One o' them Axes from Cable Street?' 'She's very nice,' I said, but dreaded the next meeting; we had to go by train and I felt trapped. 'Ai've been dradefully oopset, that onnheppy creature.' It was the night before Bywaters and Mrs Thompson were to be hanged – he for murder and she virtually for adultery, he twenty and she twenty-eight – and the newspapers were ringing with her plight; she had been on my mind too. Miss Axe had signed a petition, 'Tew may maind, she did what any yoong woman would do, with Lafe pawssing her bay ...' I told her about Madame Bovary, and liked her for feeling like a woman in H. G. Wells.

But when she suggested walking along the Dee to Queensferry for our next engagement, I felt depressed. 'Well?' said Mam, at the sewing-machine, the same Pen-y-Maes Singer; we were alone. 'I travelled with Miss Axe,' I said absently, 'she's in a state about Mrs Thompson being hanged.' 'For killing her husband with that boy?' I looked up. She continued, whirring the wheel, 'Are you seein' her again?' 'Oh yes, she's asked me to walk with her along the river for the –' The whirring stopped; she was stern and flushed. 'You be careful,' she said. I stared, then flushed myself till my scalp tingled. We looked at each other, mother-and-son turkeys. 'Careful? What d'you mean?' 'Never you mind,' she said, 'count up my divvies, there's a good boy.' I took from her the hook impaling the pile of flimsy Co-op receipts, which every quarter I checked in case she had been duped over her dividends. I found it hard to count, I was working out how to wriggle out of that walk. Next morning at nine, scraping soot for my teeth, I thought of poor Edith Thompson. It was the first and last time my mother interfered in my sex-life.

Chapter 18

Marching Orders (Final)

I finished *Owain Glyndwr* ('Grim-shadowed by twain warring fates, I die . . .') and prepared it for the post, then to be banished from my mind till the summer. Sitting in the kitchen, my eye was caught, on the week-old newspaper-tablecloth, by the photograph, sideways and half under the syrup-tin, of a young man with burningly serious eyes, with over it 'Dual Role'; I moved the pot and bent my neck to read. 'What's that?' said Dad. 'Somebody that's written a play,' I said, packing my script, 'and is going to act in it at the Savoy Theatre, London, *The Young Idea*, Noël Coward it says his name is.' 'Coward?' said Dad, 'the poor fellow won't get far with a name like that, what are you posting, George?' 'A book for my teacher in France,' I lied; my plan was for the hundred guineas in August to be a windfall.

As things settled down after the School Eisteddfod – Malvolio in the cross-gartering scene – I tended, on Saturdays, to walk out with a girl, not so much the spring as a sense of duty. Enid Wainwright was a demure amiable creature whose mother kept a sweet-shop in Shotton; in her I sought, and found, a resemblance to Tante Jeanne at seventeen. We walked up the line after chapel, held hands, even sat in a field and brushed lips; I liked her, but she was nice, unprovocative and local, three deadly attributes, and my heart was not in it.

A question began to be asked. 'Isn't this your last year, what are you going to do when you leave?' 'I don't know yet –' Then, sitting in the train, I thought, well? For the first time, I faced the future: a road without end, with middle age more remote than Julius Cæsar, and old age less conceivable than eternity.

'The brother of Eira Parry,' I wrote to Tante Jeanne, 'is now a teacher of French, which I shall be one day, je suppose.' It was tacitly understood that if I did well enough in Higher, in July, to gain a scholarship and/or exhibition – the sort that glinted down from the Honours Board – I would take the usual path to one of the Welsh colleges. And when one day J.M. said, half-joking, 'Wti'n edrych ymlaen i Fangor neu Aber, art thou looking forward to Bangor or Aberystwyth?', my smile was modest but my thought lay right across the smile. For I did not want to go.

I could not explain my attitude even to myself. I, whose one idea had been to get out of the rut, shying now at a college career? I who in Deeside had felt an exile from rural Wales ... But I still feel an exile, I answered myself, rural Wales is where I belong, but – I don't want to live in it, I want to have it to go back to. From what? London. But what would I be working at, in London? That I could not visualize, all I knew was that whatever it was, if I went to Bangor or Aberystwyth I would not, somehow, be able to get started.

A week later Miss Morris happened to ask me which I thought preferable for a college career, Wales or England. I replied the latter, and I doubt if she minded, but Miss Cooke – over-tired, she had been ill during the term – sent for me and decreed that such a reply to a teacher who had herself gone to college in Wales was 'abominably rude, the action of a cad'. The cad was shaken and furious. 'Non, c'est trop – does she believe, because she has given me money and books, that she can say to me what she likes? Gratitude is one thing, servility another ...'

My nerves rose near the edge, and at home, the last afternoon of term, they flared. My meal ready, Mam was on her knees doing the grate, raking out the cinders and setting them aside to serve their second term on a good fire; to me they had always been the symbol of our poverty, and did not help now. All conspired: she told me that through Dad, Job was later in the year to start at Summers' as foundry apprentice, twelve-and-six a week; last night, moreover, Dad had been waylaid by friends and she was worried about delicate Tom, in bed with a cold. She moved my term's report, to pour out my tea. Something made me say, sharply, 'Aren't you going to open it?' 'Your father will when he gets in, if he does. Get out of the way so

I can get the treacle.' I said suddenly, 'You don't care about me getting on at school, do you?' She brought her head out of the cupboard, holding the tin. 'Eh?' she said flatly. There was no holding back, I was shaking. 'You never say well done,' I said, 'if it wasn't for Dad I wouldn't be at school now, you don't care ...' My voice cracked on a wave of self-pity which had taken years to well up, I choked over my tea, then looked back at her.

She stood, straight and white of hair, with the eyes of a woman who has been insulted out of the blue. I could tell by the tremor in her cheek that I had hurt her, but the sudden outrage to her reserve gave to her frail dignity the daunting divine-right of royalty. She was unassailable, and I quailed. She spoke at last, her voice hoarse, unrecognized : 'if it wasn't for your father indeed ... If it wasn't for me, your father wouldn't be here, nor you, nor any of us. You don't know what I feel, because it's not my way to brag like some people, nobody knows ...' I thought for one appalling second she was going to burst into tears, but she turned away and busied herself with knives and forks. They sounded like musketry. The scene was never repeated.

Going back for my last term, I felt no nearer to Miss Cooke. As if she sensed this, an attitude which could never have been called propitiating seemed to harden. Brisk requests became barrack-yard orders, 'Williams, take this note over to the Cottage Hospital – no, now!' 'Exit First Weird Sister,' cackled Sep, running round my desk, a six-foot witch, 'First Messenger, right about quick sharp!' 'What does she take me for,' I said, tough, 'a bloody footman?' 'Kindly address local preacher in language fitting to his cloth, thou whoreson bastard.' I looked hatefully at the note. 'Perhaps,' said Sep, 'it's to order some more Emulsion.' I threw *Hamlet* at him, he threw *Macbeth* at me; we put our heads into our desks and shrieked, in unison and falsetto, 'Trouble trouble, boil and bubble' as two first-years entered the hall. They stopped, petrified, and we glared at them till they scuttled across and out.

Amidst all this a cri de coeur to Haute Savoie, remarkable

after a separation of eighteen months. 'Thou hast not written for seven weeks, I begin to think thou hast a wish to have nothing more to do with me, tell me it is not true. When thou dost not write, something is missing from my life . . .' The following week, matters came to a tea-cup boil when Miss Cooke called to me, two boys between us, 'See here, Williams, hurry down to Underwood' – the house she now shared with Miss White, a school Governor – 'and leave this, but don't go to the front door as you did last time, use the servants' entrance.' She tossed me a parcel, I caught it mechanically, sat down and took in what she had said. The last time I was errand-boy, I had taken books and Miss White had asked me into the drawing-room to show me a picture. In my mounting anger, I imagined her innocently mentioning this and Miss Cooke saying, 'I'll put a stop to that, who does he think he is?' What she had meant to convey, of course, was 'This is only something for supper, so there's no need to disturb Miss White.' But she had not put it like that. To fan my indignation, I tried to imagine what my parents would say, then shied off as I realized that Dad would laugh and Mam find the dictum perfectly seemly. 'Just because my mother was a kitchen-maid,' I panted to Sep, humour dead and buried, 'doesn't mean I don't know how to behave when they let me come in by the bloody front door.' 'Inform them,' said Sep, 'that the kitchen-maid's great-uncle was the John Dafis that pulverized the Baptists in 1866, and they will let you come in by the chimney.'

I stared at the innocent bomb of a parcel, what was I to do? I knew she was alone in the Mistresses' Room. I seized it, rose, strode across the Hall, knocked at the door, and entered before she could say 'Come in.' 'Miss Cooke,' I said breathlessly, 'I am not a servant and I go to the front door,' put down the parcel, turned on my heel, and was gone before she could turn round. I avoided imagining the picture of her after I left; she must have swivelled round muttering 'Good gracious . . .', seen the parcel, lifted off her pince-nez and drawn them thoughtfully up to her lapel, 'good gracious . . .' If we had been geographically apart and I had put my protest to paper, she would have written back from her clumsy heart – too big even for her vital body – an apology as lucid as it would have been dignified; but it was as much against her nature as against my mother's to express her feelings through the spoken word. Nothing was said.

From Vincentier, a letter at last, as correctly affectionate as ever, no mention of Miss Cooke, and a copy of *Maria Chapdelaine*. I wrote, 'Quel bonheur, I began to think all was finished between us; thou art more dear to me than before ... Miss Cooke is a bluestocking, if she offers me money after this, I shall refuse it.' Angry schoolboy-waves against an admittedly fitful lighthouse. Dumb insolence set in. As she expounded an impassioned view of Hugo's Napoleonic politics, I would be turned away – only half – gazing out of the window. She had lately seen the Irish Players in *The Playboy* and it had so fired her that she read us the first act; even to our ears, her accent as Pegeen was of a marked eccentricity, but normally I would have been very curious. I sat with my arms folded, looking down into them. Once, in the Hall, I was one of a group in idle talk – 'get out into the field you people,' she called, 'wasting this sun, it's a shame!' The others turned to go; I looked at her for a split second, gave the nearest I could get to a sardonic shrug, and sat down. She strode off. This lasted two weeks, till a small boy told me I was wanted in the Mistresses' Room. She was alone, sideways to me, one booted foot on the pipes, fastening the laces. My chest was tightening, ready with 'Just because you sent me to France ...' 'Look here,' she said without looking round, 'it's one hundred per cent nonsensical, hang it all' – a tug at the laces – 'two people at loggerheads' – a brisk knot, foot back on the floor – 'pax, what d'you say?' I smiled, she smiled, I said, 'I'm sorry, Miss Cooke,' she said, 'I'm sorry too.' We shook hands, and I took my leave.

Next day she sent for me again, the most adventurous orders of all: she had read, in a paper called *Careers*, that there was being offered an Open Scholarship in French of £80 a year, by Christ Church, Oxford. She had taken it in to J.M., 'Look here, it's a long shot but for the fun of it – what about it?' Fun rather than hope, for she reminded me that the scholarships and exhibitions based on the Central Welsh Board Higher were confined to Wales, some even to Flintshire. Looking at the Honours Board, I remarked that Goronwy Edwards, in 1909, had gone to Jesus, Oxford, after winning a – 'Yes,' she said, 'but that was confined to Wales too, this is open to any school in the British Isles, which means you'll be up against the best brains in the country but the Headmaster thinks no harm in a try.' (A witness later told me that what J.M. had said was 'You do what you like, you're a wonderful woman.') 'What will it involve –' I was going to say, 'if I win it' 'for whoever wins it?' 'Three years at Christ Church,' said Miss Cooke flatly, as if it were a jail sentence, 'I understand one of the swagger ones.' The details arrived. French was the prime subject, but there would be papers in Latin, Greek, English and any special subject (Italian – of course!), with no set-books which could interfere with my studies for the Higher at home. With luck the dates, in July, just fitted: I would be able to sit a couple of sessions in Holywell for the Higher, go to Oxford for the three days, and return to finish the Higher.

I sat in the train and thought. There was none of the exhilaration of the day she had first put me on to French, or told me I was going to France, this was hypothetical news: if, as was most likely, I did not win, my problem would be back. If I did win – no, don't dwell on that ... I spoke to myself the words with which, in after life, I was to face any vital ordeal, 'This is an adventure in which must co-operate to the maximum every particle of body and brain and heart, but *not* so important as to make you feel faint and paralyse your powers – look up at the moon and the stars and feel your dry throat soften, for nothing is as important as that ...' 'Just an exercise,' I told Mam, 'means going to Oxford for a couple of days.' 'Who will pay the fare?' 'They will,' I lied (Miss Cooke would). 'Oxford,' said Mam, 'I wonder if your father knows it, is it by the sea?' 'No.' 'Oh,' she said, 'then he won't.' He didn't. But he was much interested. 'Just an exercise ...'

But it was important enough, with my Higher, to occupy every waking minute of the next ten weeks; even my letters to

Vincentier had to grow jerky. I made time-tables for each hour: cramming from six a.m. to eight, the brain pellucid as the sun prising into the kitchen over the railway, then train, school all day, train, evening-study till eleven, a drugged review of facts, dreamless sleep, then awake with the jumble in miraculous order. I arranged to alternate tough learning with re-reading one of the set-books, which I would pretend was for pleasure, which indeed it could be; in the afternoon sun I pretended I was playing truant from Trig by sitting against the wall by the tennis-court with Taine against my knee, knowing that with *Shakespeare et son Epoque* I was killing three birds: French, History, Eng. Lit. After tea – ten munching minutes with Mam's *Woman's World*, Will Mavis Beat Tattling Neighbours – half an hour with Anglo-Saxon, which I found unattractive and therefore back-breaking, then up the line to read *Twelfth Night* straight through as if I had never heard of it. Under a tree – beech, birch or ash? I cared not, I only knew them as le hêtre, le bouleau, le frêne and loved the names – I looked up, tired and relaxed, through the high foliage luminous-tremulous against the soothing sky, I opened the book, murmured 'The curtain rises' and read. The leafy light danced on the page as if taking life from the words upon it, mellow met mellow, 'if music be the food of love, play on ...' Two hours later, in my parlour-corner over de Vigny, and hearing Frank Bellis's sad trumpet – 'Dieu que le son du cor est triste au fond du back yard!' – I thought once more, the ash-pits and the privies have no power to level my spirit, for round the corner there awaits the murmur of a rainbowed world, the welling lands and surging seas of the mind. It was a sweet and monkish time.

Then, fairly near the last minute, a hitch. The first Higher paper was to be Monday morning 2 July, 9.30 to 12.30. But to get to Chester in time for the Oxford connection, I must leave Holywell by 10.15 at the latest. Impasse. Miss Cooke decided, through J.M., to beard the Welsh authorities in Cardiff with a suggestion for which, however, she held little hope. For two days I worked, fitfully suspended, then the monk took a breather; the flesh growled like a dozing beast, turned over, and sent the little ants of study scuttling.

Holywell was a pretty moral school; the football team walked down the Strand Woods in the dark with the older girls, but I doubt if much went too far. Questioned, Miss Cooke would have answered 'Fair play, I think our girls are a decent lot, no rotters.' But that year, in the Senior there were two rotters, as unmistakable as a couple of bad apples, and she knew it. Olwen Pulford was one of those adolescents – strictly brought up, father a preacher – who bewilder their elders by suddenly going wild; 'more'n 'ot stuff,' it was muttered, 'it's married men.' She wore make-up in class till Miss Cooke stood her over a sink; she assured us all that school was tommy-rot and her ambition was to go to London and on the steets. But there was no fun in her, looks which should have been provocatively soft were aggressive : she was a man-eater in a gym-slip. Her inseparable foil was Winnie Roberts, a gipsy-like girl with a sly sullen manner; Miss Cooke need not have worried unduly, for their cynicism took the appeal out of sex and scared both girls and boys.

I was an exception; once I knew that Olwen Pulford had crossed into the country of the fallen, I was drawn. As for Septimus, with the impact of summer he assumed the mantle of renegade parson; looking up from his notes for Sunday's sermon; he confessed himself carnally disposed towards Winnie Roberts. When the Senior girls crossed the Hall, we could pick out First and Second Strumpet by their insolently shorter skirts. One day they were idly patrolling the cricket boundary when Sep and I strolled up; the scene was Parisian in its audacity. 'We beg pardon,' said Sep, raising an imaginary straw hat. 'Don't mensh,' said Olwen, 'Winn, take a squint at a brace o' bookworms come up for air.' 'Not for air, ladies,' quipped the unfrocked Savonarola, 'up for a couple of early birds.' 'You're so sharp,' muttered her morose friend, 'you'll cut yourself.' First Strumpet turned to me, 'What's the matter, scared that Ma Cooke might do a swoop, swallowed the old tongue?' 'No, I haven't,' I countered daringly, 'and I could prove it.' 'Saucy,' said Olwen, and clapped the nails of her thumbs together in mock applause. She drew

Second Strumpet's attention to the cricket, 'Train your peepers
on to the playing-fields of Eton, child, of all the japes, lend me
the powder-puff adored one.' Second Strumpet fumbled darkly
in her slip, Olwen patted her fleshy nose, and I got an aphrodisiac whiff of stale patchouli, a word I fancied. 'Well,' she said,
'we must skedaddle, if you can't be good be careful, hapoo
toodle-oo!' 'Fair ones,' continued the Calvinist roué, suddenly
to the point – 'what about Sat night?'

The two ladies of the market town exchanged a look, I looked
at Septimus. 'Eh byang,' said First Strumpet, 'we had an engagement, with two men – oh, no offence! – what about a randy-voo
under the Town Hall clock?' 'Right,' we countered, à six
whores?' 'Right,' and they moved on. 'So long,' called Olwen,
'Mutt and Jeff!' This was a toxic barb out of the funny papers:
lamp-post Sep was inches taller than me, who was thick-set and
not likely to set much thinner ... Saturday night! It would
make a wonderful break from study. 'Now have they got it
clear,' I said, 'which is which?' 'If you mean,' said Sep, 'are they
aware of the differentiation between Adam and Eve, the answer
is yea verily.' 'No, do they twig that you want Second Strumpet
and me First?' 'They twig.' That afternoon it was not easy to
concentrate. 'Sep,' I said, 'will it be your first time?' A pause.
'Second Strumpet,' he answered, 'will be in the right if she
quoteth Columbus – "shipmates, virgin territory!"'

Even suspended study was important enough for First Strumpet not to worry me again till the Saturday afternoon; but
travelling up to Holywell, washed from top to toe and sitting
with my Greek grammar opposite an old lady – a sunny holiday-
day, how could it not be – I thought of me and Olwen Pulford
in a field. I wished once more she were a laugher and a natural
roller in grass, caught the old lady's eye and went back to my
Future Impersonals. Sep was waiting at the Junction.

Holywell looked unfamiliar, a Saturday-evening beehive. The
Prince of Wales Cinema flaunted 'A Sensational Romance,
Adults only, Smouldering Rudolph Valentino in *The Sheik*!!!'
We put away our school caps. The Strumpets were boldly
planted at the Town Hall, both in flowered dresses with winking

265

belts low on the hips, no stockings, high heels and many beads, the one in a white tam-o'-shanter, the other in a bright red cloche. Both were quite heavily painted and looked flapper-vamps of twenty-five, could we ever live up to it? We strolled carefully up the other side, feeling that our lickerish intentions must be clear to.all. High Street was indeed changed; everybody seemed young, full of sidelong holiday looks, as if the Sheik had descended from his poster and were gliding ghost-robed through the staid town, tweaking skirts and exhaling hot goatish breaths to left and right; by midnight the Strand Woods would be bursting. I wished I had a trilby over one eye like my cousins, and hummed 'I'm the Sheik of Ara-bee, your love belongs to me ...' Our two women were attracting attention; we were thrilled, then embarrassed, suppose Bummer came by, then they waved languidly. We crossed – 'into your tent I'll cr-e-e-p ...' – but as we crossed, they started to walk up towards the Victoria. We tried to look as if this was by arrangement, and five minutes later followed at a dignified saunter. Neither cloche nor tam-o'-shanter was anywhere to be seen. We strolled down again.

Then we strolled up again, trying to look like two bored reporters in search of local colour. Our shoes were showing dust, and I felt a slight film forming on me too. We were about to stroll up even again, when the red cloche bobbed along the top of a wall like an exotic thistle. 'Ah,' said Sep, 'I knew they would not dare –' The girls had two men with them, trilby over eye. They all stopped, one of the men distributed cigarettes from a flashing case and lit them all with one of the new lighters; then they all passed within two feet of us, laughing loudly.

'Wasn't he that auctioneer,' I said, my grammar to the winds, 'that she was supposed to be having a baby off?' 'And the other was that bookmaker.' 'And what odds,' I said cruelly, 'local preacher versus bookmaker?' The two reporters strolled down to the train; the queue for *The Sheik* was round the corner, All Seats Gone, and for us, this lost June night, there was not even flickering vicarious lust to an upright piano. In the little train, we reassumed our caps and sat down into the empty twilight. I held my laundered handkerchief across my face; 'I'm the Sheik,'

I suddenly screamed in falsetto, 'of Ara-bee . . .' Sep did the same, then we both swooped into the bass, 'Your La-ah-ve belongs to me-e-e . . .', cut short by the entry of two startled women. I took my Greek out of my pocket and settled down to the Optative Mood. As we descended at the Junction 'Enter Weird Sisters,' said Sep. It was Miss Cooke and Miss Swinnerton, returning from a trip; we did not even look guilty, consciences were clear. Miss Cooke told me the Headmaster had heard from Cardiff; they had agreed to her most unusual request that I should sit the crucial Monday-morning paper not at 9.30 with the others, but alone from 7 to 10 a.m., invigilated by her. All was set.

Sep and I never spoke to the Strumpets again.

With deflorescence unavoidably postponed, work dominated. As the summer spread hotter and second of July crept nearer, the beat of mental machinery grew every day steadier and more urgent; dates, quotations, facts – facts, quotations, dates – marshalled themselves across sunlit pages carried from kitchen to train, to desk, back to train, to parlour, to sun-flecked arbour, back to corner. Monday the second made a stimulating opening to the big week; when Mam rose at five, for Dad, she called me too, and bacon sizzled. As he walked one way to his work, in the clear dawn, so I walked up the hill, with my suitcase, to mine. I saw yet another aspect of Holywell, deserted, morning-washed, the Sheik exorcised, every cobble cool to my studious tread.

I walked up Bagillt Street, as I had walked for seven years, turned the echoing corner and saw my school empty before me, against the old windmill and the early light. It was ten to seven, not a mouse abroad, not a book-leaf stirring, only the silver estuary far down to the left and beyond it the world. No sound but my step and the chirrup of a bird; I thought of the day I had walked up from the Trelogan horse-and-cart and the same little school had towered over me, a teaming metropolis. This morning there was only Miss Cooke, standing at the front door in the sun, her gown wrapped tight across her middle and her arms folded over her gown, eating an apple. She was holding the school key; on a sill, a pile of open exercise-books. Silly Wil loped up, blinked at the strange assignation, and loped on. We entered the hollow school and settled into our little Honours room, still night-cold. I rubbed my knuckles and wrote name and particulars; Miss Cooke looked at her watch, put her index finger to the slim envelope, drew out papers, handed me one, scanned her copy, and sat down to her correcting. I read, the flickering sun across it, 'The date of *Twelfth Night* is placed as 1600 and 1603; give reasons for these variations' and off. Stamina was all. But there could have been no more tranquil overture; for two hours, no sound but the scratch of my pen. 'The owl scene in *Macbeth* is probably the most powerful scene in all drama, an effect due to its economy. As Dover Wilson avers . . .'

Gradually, at the back of my mind, I heard the school filling, then prayers. At 9.29, at a signal from Miss Cooke, I stopped in mid-sentence, picked up my papers, followed her and joined the rest of the examination in the Central Hall where the six other Higher pupils, scattered among the rest of the school taking Senior, were being handed the paper which I was near completing; I sat at my new desk and finished my sentence. At ten sharp I corrected my last essay, placed it below Miss Morris who whispered good luck, I tiptoed out of the forest of bowed heads (a flash of Olwen Pulford doodling on a blotter) and picked up my suitcase. Good-bye to J.M., who was moved that today I was to see his Alma Mater, then a handshake with Miss Cooke, 'I'll do my best.' I enjoyed the unaccustomed morning walk through the market crowd, one or two stared at the suitcase – expelled? In the train I unpacked my revision – last-minute cramming practically in pill form, mostly Greek – rose hastily to wave to Mam as the express tore through the Quay, then back to 'λανθάνω λήσω, λαμβάνω λήψομαι . . .' In Chester Station I settled on a seat and worked; as my train left, I felt my heart beating, shut my eyes and repeated inwardly, 'This is a trip like any other, I'm in a classroom only moving, calm . . .'

My eyes on my book, I ate sandwiches, then unpacked my soap and washed ready for Oxford. I did allow myself time to be disappointed by the station, which I had expected to find ivy-clad with spires dreaming out of the booking-office; it was like the Quay only bigger, certainly as sleepy. I realized, as I walked past the hideous pile of the Castle, that the city was already deep in the Long Vacation; at cross roads called Carfax I asked a tourist for Christ Church, and he pointed to my right, where Tom Tower dominated St Aldate's. I walked down in the heat, entered the echoing gate of Aedes Christi, the House, and gave the porter my name. He had a moustache and looked rather like Dad, he'll bring me luck, scholarship candidate? He directed me to a few doors along, in Tom Quad, 'Stair Two Number Two, next to where it says Mr H. W. Blunt and Mr R. F. Harrod – no, they're dons, all on vacation.' Mr Blunt's was a large high sitting-room : illumined by the afternoon sun through thick-walled arched windows, to me it was Utopia. The endless books, the desks stuffed with papers, the faded chintzes, the deep leather chairs, the table-lamps, the faint photographs of Roman ruins – everything spelt cultured ease, even the fly buzzing on the pane knew Latin and would disdain an Anglo-Saxon midden. I sat slowly in the centre of the room – first on the edge of the sofa, then right into it with my legs crossed – and saw myself living in this room not as an old professor – noli timere, no fear – but as myself, G. E. Williams, dark, romantic, entertaining a breakfast-party all at my feet in tribute to a modesty that refuses to have its head turned . . .

The fly buzzed, and my ghostly entourage rose like angels through the roof. I shook myself and unpacked in the bedroom; before going off to meet the other candidates, I changed my shirt, brushed my hair, then found I had left my soap in the train. Voyons George, tes ongles – wandering out I saw a thoughtful figure entering the next stair. 'I'm exceedingly sorry,' I ventured, 'but I wonder if you'd know where I could borrow some soap?' 'Oh . . . hang on a minute' – he disappeared and brought out a tablet – 'it's used, I'm afraid . . .' 'It's exceedingly kind of you, I'll bring it back –' 'Please don't bother . . .' He smiled, bowed, and disappeared under his name over the door, and for four days my face and neck owed their shine to the Reverend A. E. J. Rawlinson, D.D., the future Bishop of Derby.

We – the candidates – took one another's measure with cautious bonhomie, eased by the fact that there was no way of telling how good anybody's French was. They were startlingly English, with effortless manners to warm the cockles of my histrionic heart, though I was cast down to see only three; they must be the flower of the realm. We were left alone a moment, probably intentionally. Said the shorter fair one, 'Does it make you feel a *little* like a horse being vetted before the show? A neigh, do you think, or a quick canter round the quad with a ring through the nose?' Another asked a question, to which another rejoindered 'I'm so sorry, I didn't hear,' with such negligent charm that I made a note never to say 'beg par'n' again. '*I* feel,' said the tall fair one with an engaging stammer, 'mm-more like a f-fille de joie in a m-maison de t-tolérance being quizzically l-looked over by the Madame, what?' I was enchanted, I had never imagined that young men of my own age could have polish and sophistication, it was like a play. Then I remembered with dismay that I had just heard French perfectly pronounced, and a pretty wieldy English vocabulary as well – 'quizzically', I had never heard the word said before ... And when I gleaned later from Dad-the-porter that Ford was at Dartmouth, that his father was headmaster of Harrow and that Hodgkin was *at* Harrow, my apprehension deepened ... But what thoughts are these? Isn't this an exercise, just for fun?

I returned to the sealed splendour of my don's paradise, did a little Greek, wrote cards to Miss Cooke and 314a, then walked alone in the vast deserted quadrangle, able to take it in for the first time. I was at last seeing a sight without seers, there was no soul in view. The sun was in its decline, and the giant shadow of Tom Tower lay across the fountain named Mercury, leaving Cathedral and Hall basking in a light for ever medieval; behind the mellow stone, I could sense and smell the deep leather of a million books. And I was sightseeing with unsore feet, for was I not treading my own ground – no, I must *not* think that, il faut aller au fur et à mesure – remember that for tomorrow, not a very usual phrase ... A Poor Scholar. In this place the words acquired a classic dignity which I slipped on like a familiar coat.

As I walked, scholar led to scholarship – no, slow down, heart
... I shut my eyes, and in the murmur of Mercury heard the
fountain at Vincentier. La France, ma France. I would wield my
accents – aigu, grave and circonflexe – ay, and the cédille too –
like swords in battle, God bless Miss Cooke.

I dined with the enemy in Hall: at a long cande-lit table,
four nonentities were huddled together, lost beneath the vaulted
shadows of history and on all sides stared out of countenance,
from under brows raised coolly into white wigs, by one re-
sounding name after another: John Locke, Sir Thomas Coke
Earl of Leicester, George Greville Chancellor of the Exchequer,
Trelawney Bishop of Bristol ... Past them, our reedy voices
spiralled impertinently up and away, transient as wood-smoke.
We retired. In bed, I lipped my notes like an anchorite his missal,
to the boom of the great bell in Tom Tower over my head; but
it did not stop my sleeping soundly. I awoke to sit up in the sun
and eye the notes again. A discreet knock, and a can of hot
water was deposited by strange hands. In the great room the
same hands had laid breakfast to which I sat, alone and thoughtful, as if I had lived thus for many an independent year.

We settled at desks in the small Old Lecture Room, crowded
with paintings of bishops, overlooking trees and the atmosphere
helpfully informal. Then the papers were distributed; pigeons
cooed, ivy rustled, fingers drummed, throats were softly cleared.
But the race was on. After three timeless hours, back to aching
stretching life, frugal luncheon under the inscrutable faces, then
back; at five, a brisk walk over to the Post Office to send Miss
Cooke the papers and my rough drafts of answers with after-
scribbles: 'wild guess ...' 'knew this isn't right, but at least
they'll know I know the word I'm pretending it is ...' The evening I devoted to Greek and Latin. Wednesday followed the same
routine; in the afternoon, French Translation included a sonnet
of Hérédia of which I made two versions, one into fairly literal
prose, the other into poetry, unrhyming but keeping the sonnet-
form; I was careful not to be seen tapping out rhythms in case
the others thought my effort pretentious. For all I knew, though,
each might be producing a poem himself, Petrarchian, ottava

rima – I swerved past the thought. Thursday – the last day – would entail general essays, nothing to cram, so after dinner I gave the Bishop of Bristol a stare back and went to the pictures, the Electra in Queen Street. In the empty summer cinema, I reclined in a sudden bed of roses, watched transparent curtains part voluptuously from the Censor's Certificate, and dreamily savoured a smart-set Hollywood comedy, the naughty heroine ogling through fans and American Adonises hovering stiffly in white ties : Gloria Swanson in *Her Husband's Trade-Mark*. It was a perfect antidote, and the piano gave the monastic toil a distant glow. I fell into bed.

Early next morning, before the French Essay, I read French for an hour. The afternoon session, the last, heavy and somnolent with flies, was the English Essay : 'How do you define the word "Romance"?' My flagging steed rallied on to its hind legs for the last sprint, and I willed myself not to tire. The flies buzzed in vain as I poured carefully on to the ruled lines every last drop of clarity and eloquence and tactful display of erudition of which I was capable.

After the session, a brisk cold-water wash and a clean shirt, to appear dapper at the rooms of Mr Dundas the Senior Censor, for Interview cum – I imagined – Viva Voce. With French at my finger-tips, spiced with Latin, I articulated and shrugged my way to the other side of Tom Quad, where I was ushered in to a pleasant older man who asked me to sit down and smilingly held out a glass of sherry. I was modest, but as he presumably knew my background, I felt I must talk a little to prove that the King's English was like mother's milk to me. I tried to look clean-limbed yet intelligent. Not easy. 'Indeed yes sir, my forbears were Nonconformist to the core – but tant pis, de mortuis nil nisi bonum!' I was just about to relax, feeling homespun, a bright hygienic nice boy, when my host asked me, kindly, what experience of sex I had had.

Sprung on an acolyte sipping his first sherry, it was a blow beneath the belt, in veritate. My brain was suddenly shot through with adrenalin, all cells alerted – what was this? I thought quickly, if I imply I have ruined a series of schoolgirls, will that make me the ideal nominee for the House of Christ? On the other hand, if I'm a milksop I'm not right either ... After a sherry-laden pause I said, 'Well sir, attending day-school, there isn't much hope of being alone with a pretty girl ...' I laughed and he laughed and I drank my sherry like a man of the world. Then he said, with the dispassionate interest of a gardener asking about edelweiss, 'Aren't Welsh women supposed to be very passionate?'

I was in a quandary. I had no wish to give the impression that Miss Cooke's decent-lot-of-girls were a pack of wantons, and yet ... 'Potentially so, sir,' I said, 'but malheureusement they are bound by conventions – quite rightly, I suppose, otherwise the social structure would topple.' Not bad, I thought. 'Quite so,' he said, 'but if you don't have girls, what do you do?' The dregs of my sherry went the wrong way, though I did remember not to say 'Beg par'n.' 'I'm so sorry, sir,' I said, 'I didn't hear ...' 'What do you *do*?' Under the kind gimlet gaze, I felt myself go irremediably red, then remembered *What a Young Boy Ought to Know*. 'Well, sir,' I said, 'Mother Nature being what she is – and one has to be glad one has a healthy body – one is often hard put to it' (punch-drunk with examination, I thought, too many 'ones' and anyway 'hard put to it' is *not* the phrase, oh God ...) 'but I find that exercise and cold water help, though there's no doubt sir, it's a problem!' Just as I heard the whip-crack of thin ice, the conversation drifted towards the safer shores of religion and I issued drunk with sherry but dead-sobered by the unknown, for I had not the faintest idea how I had acquitted myself.

Standing in Tom Quad, once more half in the ancient sun, I suddenly realized all was over. Those gaps in my Latin translation, with the pathetic footnotes trying to show off – all was done, tout passe, tout lasse, everything goes into – of course, 'désuétude' the word I wanted yesterday – too late. Trop tard, troppo tardi, serissime, ὕστερος ... By now I was slumped into the Electra, change of programme, looking round at the few blank town faces, and in my mind peopling the cinema with fresh young eyes and rowdy voices – no No, you're going home tomorrow to do your Higher – oh God, to be told I've missed this, and then have to go on bashing at the other ... As the film started, Viola Dana in *A Night of Romance*, I made a mental note to ask Miss Cooke not to tell me the result of this either way until I had quite finished the Higher, and gave myself entirely to the languorous drinking scenes (any sherry?) with the drooping eyelids and the bare backs. But in the night, for the first time, Tom kept me awake, and I gave ear to other bells ... because I was never to hear them again?

My train was not leaving till noon, but I could not bear to sit in the college; I felt it would bring me bad luck and asked the porter if there was anywhere to swim. I walked down to Folly Bridge and along the deserted Isis where the college boats lay supine, got to a pool where young townspeople were enjoying themselves, hired a drooping costume for twopence and lay in the sun. Tomorrow, Saturday, in my parlour-corner, I must stick at Napoleon, for Monday morning's paper ... I suddenly felt utterly lifeless, slept, woke with a headache, dressed and shambled back. I still had plenty of time, but must pack. In Tom Gate, the porter was in his cubby-hole. 'Oh,' he said, 'been looking for you.' He looked more like Dad than ever as he pointed to the notice-board behind me. A small sheet of Christ Church paper – I recognized the cardinal's red-tasselled hat – was fluttering from two drawing-pins. I moved nearer and read, in careful handwriting, 'July 6, 1923, The following election has been made: To an Open Scholarship in French, Mr G. E. Williams, signed H. J. White (Dean).'

Part Three

Oxford
(1923–1927)

Chapter 19

Out of Harbour

'Congratulations sir, see you next term ...' I thanked him, walked drunkenly across St Aldate's, sent a telegram to Miss Cooke, 'Won George', to Mademoiselle, 'Gagné George' and thought, my last bit of translation for today; I hesitated, then added 'hurrah' to both. Miss Cooke's arrived at the dinner-hour and when she took it in to J.M. he decreed a half-holiday, the first since Armistice Day. I did not wire 314a as I imagined I would be home before it could arrive, also I knew that to my mother the brown envelope could only mean disaster.

The details of happiness do not stay in the memory, and the rest of the day is a tapestry of sunlight and summer sounds. The train-whistle was a salute to me; I looked out at the fustian station, peered at the corner of the sign 'Oxford' and thought; mine. A doze, for ten Elysian minutes, then I woke refreshed. The pill of success was already pumping through my veins; I started to read, like a novel, easily and with affection, my notes on the Causes of the Industrial Revolution. Ugly people joined me and I loved them all; as they gazed thoughtfully out at the sun, I felt from their half-smiles that they knew. By Leamington Spa I was reverberating with hunger and had a large meat-pie. Chester was the same idyllic evening as when I returned from France; but as I got into the local train, this time Flintshire did not close around me. Halfway down the Quay hill two people stopped me, the news had travelled. Down the alley, Mam stood at her line unpegging a shirt; had I really been in Tom Quad this morning?

'Well, well,' she said, folding, 'we heard you passed, somebody from Holywell called, are you all right?' 'Fine,' I said, 'does Dad know?' 'Thomas walked to the works,' she said, following me in with her basket, 'your father called at the New Inn but all right thank goodness, people stopping him all along the road, did they give you enough to eat?' But I didn't mind, the tea she had ready for me was a loving one, boiled eggs and Rolly Polly. Dad had had a pint or two, but not three; home had pulled harder, and he elevated himself from his chair like the rising sun. 'Wel ymachgeni,' he said, shaking my arm, then holding my hand in both his own, 'aelod o Rydychain yn awr, now a man of Oxford!' 'He hasn't finished yet,' said Mam amiably, 'there's this other one.' Between questions, I worked; she was right, the test of endurance was the next two weeks, the danger being to treat the Higher as anticlimax, I dare not slacken. After supper, Mum sat plaiting her hair. 'This Holywell exam, Poll,' said Dad, 'will be like water off a duck's back, and the next will be you and me reaching Oxford – how do you fancy her, George, hair up in them horns and a mortarboard on top?' He smoked his pipe, his excitement an antiphon to my subdued smiles. 'Harrow, but they are the cream, Winston was rared there!' Saturday I worked; Sunday, in chapel, a glow from everybody's proprietary pleasure. Dad all but dressed up so he could warm his hands at it.

Monday morning, school: the foretaste of congratulation, mixed with the stern self-warning, don't lose your head, concentrate ... Fortunately it was only a moment before the bell went for Exams. J.M. behaved exactly like Dad, wielding my arm with the same Welsh words; he had said, I heard later, that after the news he had not slept all night. Miss Cooke I saw for a moment, she shook hands and smiled; but she felt, as I did, that things could wait, for within ten minutes I was seeking four reasons for the failure of Napoleon's Russian campaign. More sunlit evenings of steady cramming, then suddenly it was over, and after a thousand hours treading the waters of learning, I found myself washed ashore, prostrate on the level sands of holiday. Sports Day, my last after seven years; facetious unbelieving farewells. The next days, I drifted up the line in indolent trance; I read *The Hill*, and by the end felt I had been at Harrow myself. Then, like a convalescent, I gave all my attention to a weeks-long competition in *Picture Show*, to identify a series of tiny photographed heads of stars: the concentration lately bestowed on the Pluperfect Subjunctive was now devoted to distinguishing Claire Windsor from Corinne Griffith.

But with August, the National Eisteddfod: 'For a drama on Owain Glyndwr, one hundred guineas'. My morning dawned; I set out very early, on foot, 'just to hear the music'. Mold was bursting with people, and the Pavilion stifling; through endless choirs and adjudications and the Crowning of the Bard – I was disgusted to see Druids tucking newspapers under their robes and blowing their noses – I worked out how I would spend the money. During processions of sopranos, I mouthed my best lines: 'The deathless murmur of a thousand harps ...' 'Thou craven cur, in vain I suckled thee ...' Say half and half, fifty guineas to Mam, fifty towards Oxford, a present for Miss Cooke – here it is! 'Drama ar Owain Glyndwr.' A bespectacled gentleman rose and embarked, in fogey-ish inaudible Welsh, on the pitfalls of historical drama, then 'twenty-five entries we have weeded down to four, Eryri, Ossian, Môn and Gwynfab'. I sat up – me last, impossible to mistake the implication ... He criticized each in turn, with faint praise; I swallowed, programme clutched. 'And now Gwynfab' – should I rise – 'has leant the other way, towards old-fashioned melodrama, and a dramatist must move with the times. The one hundred guineas' – I could hear them clinking – 'will be withheld owing to the low standard.' He sat heavily down, the ugly old pudding. Had the tent suddenly become hotter? The face of the out-of-date seventeen-year-old playwright certainly had. The set-back made me rejoice again at my Oxford good fortune, and as I walked home with my weekly shilling jingling in my pocket, I shrieked 'Thou craven cur, in vain I suckled thee!' in falsetto, and decided the old fool was right.

Gentle walks up the line with Enid Wainwright, gentler each time: the only time I came to life was when she produced a Kodak and took two snaps, one smouldering and the other open and boyish. We sat on stiles trying to make out whether a smudge of hair, oval face and teeth was Eva Novak or Marie

Prevost, not a basis for courtship. 'That Enid Wainwright,' said Mam, 'is a nice girl.' That finished it. 'What's Miss Cooke written about now?' It was to suggest my going once a week to Liverpool for an hour's German at the Berlitz School, and enclosing pound-notes. I obeyed readily, taking a cheap day-ticket from Shotton to Seacombe, then my lesson from an impassive lady in a cubicle, 'das ist ein rote Bleistift', lunching off a meatpie in a workman's café, then loitering outside cinemas scrutinizing the photographs like a detective; if I had enough pocket-money I went inside, continuous, for the degenerate thrill of sitting through a film twice.

One week-end, with a pound Miss Cook had sent me 'for extras', I went for my Deutsche Übung on the Friday, and arranged to stay the night at Uncle Jab's so that I could queue up for Martin Harvey in *Oedipus Rex*. As I sat in the front row of the pit watching the theatre fill, an animated man came up to me from the stalls, said he had taken me for his nephew, and would I care for the free seat next to him: I was delighted and talked freely, it was ideal practice for Oxford. I explained that I had only seen plays in Paris, he said he had noticed that Continental accent, and I confessed that I was a local foreign boy.

The play was a revelation to me. When I thanked my benefactor he asked me was I doing anything for supper, I said yes my uncle and aunt were waiting for me in Bootle thank you very much, and we shook honest hands. Next morning I met Enid at the landing stage; on my way, I made a point of passing the back of the Royal Court, where they were moving Oedipus out and Sydney Carton in. In the sun, wings were threadbare and battered; but scenery was made for footlights, and it was right that it should all look like a busy railway station. I gave Enid a tea-shop lunch and treated her to *Dear Brutus* at the Repertory Playhouse; the impression on me of the two plays, my first in English, was to deepen with the months. Enid was amiable but unable to participate – 'It tells a nice story, doesn't it?' – and I would have preferred last night's companion, though looking back there had been something funny about him. I felt guilty being bored, but it was good to think that I had taken a girl out and spent money on her. Miss Cooke's.

A Saturday walk to Chester for the matinée of *Tons of Money* – again I was impressed, by the craftsmanship of farce – then the preparations for Christ Church, on a scale to dwarf those for Vincentier. The trunk was a problem; the old one had been pensioned off, and finally Dad set his heart on one outside Lloyd's the second-hand shop. Mam sat stiffly up, 'Falling to pieces, is it?' But she had to admit that it was hardly that, for what turned up was a square sea-chest, riveted and heart-of-oaked, built for shipwreck, maelstrom and the sea-bed thrust of the sword-fish; it had a green baize shelf, it just winkled in through the front door and it weighed a ton.

In obedience to the leaflet from the Steward of Christ Church, it slowly filled with knife and singlet and fork and glove and napkin and shoe-horn, 'Good life, what's a dressing-gown?' But no hat, that I knew, 'No Mam, *they don't wear them.*' I sent for Cash's Woven Tabs, and Mam spent evenings sewing 'G. E. Williams' in Gothic letters on to shirts, socks, handkerchiefs and even glass-cloths, which for a moment both she and I had imagined to be made of some sort of spun glass; by the end she was sure that the collar-studs should have my name somewhere. As she sewed, Dad read out from a book which Miss Cooke had sent. 'Poll' – clearing his throat and putting on his modulated reading voice – ' "with Mag-daleen, Christ Church is both the largest, most expensive and the most aristo ..." – how d'you say this one, George? – "Former students inclewed Sir Philip Sidney, John Ruskin, John Wesley" – it's a godly place! – "Lord Canning and W. E. Gladstone" ' – a glance up at the tea-caddy – 'well, fancy ... all the top-notchers.' Mam looked up from G. E. Williams, 'What about Lloyd George?' 'No, Poll,' said Dad, 'L.G. never got up to anywhere like this, poor fellow ...' Mam took up yet another glass-cloth, 'What will you want six of these for?' 'To wash up the cups and saucers.' 'A cloth for each cup?' 'The scout has to have some in hand.' 'The scout?' 'The man who looks after you' – Job was sitting there, back from his paper-round, not the moment for all this – 'it's a rule, they wouldn't let you look after yourself even if you wanted to . . .' I engrossed myself in a murder on the table-cloth. 'Poll,' called Dad, turning a page, 'he'll get enough meat there whatever, the place was started by a butcher, a Mr Wolsey . . . and look, they've called one part of it after our Tom!' But Mam was examining the other idea, 'A scout? In his bare knees, with one of them khaki hats and a whistle?'

In the weekly letter I now exchanged with Miss Cooke, a habit to continue through life, she would enclose a sudden S.O.S., 'don't forget vaccination', then a note that hurrah, she was on the track of a discarded dinner-jacket: 'like this, Mam, look', and I would point out, in *Picture Show*, Adolphe Menjou toasting Pola Negri in champagne. With the new Holywell term, I went to Underwood for tea, presided over by Miss White, as fragile as her china, while Miss Cooke sat on a stool, a tamed lioness holding a cucumber sandwich, who with a swish of a tail could have sent the cake-stand flying through the french window and into the hollyhocks. Waiting for 11 October, I felt between three worlds, then, 314a and – what?

'Annwyl Mr Hughes,' wrote J.M. to an educational benefactor in Caernarvon, 'mi ddwedaf yn fyr, I will tell you briefly of George Emlyn Williams, who came to this school going on eleven years of age, fair in face and fair in mind.' Then, after details, 'We gave him a year of freedom, to read here and there as a bee flies from flower to flower to gather honey . . . Besides the County Exhibition of £60 a year – top in all Wales – he has won a scholarship to Oxford, when he defeated the best in the world. The history of this little Welshman is a romance; he is a splendid reciter, fond of dramatics, and successful in portraying life on the platform. His character is spotless.' He ends with a sentence as typical of him as of my father and their Welsh kind. 'It is necessary to find him another £60 a year: I pray you to milk some rich men of your denomination and send the milk-pail to me, yours very truly . . .' The letter is signed by J.M., but the body of it is copied from his illegible scrawl by a modest round hand which I have to claim as my own. In due course the milk-paid arrived, clinking with £40 a Year for Three Years.

I said good-bye to Miss Cooke. The following week, Miss Morris heard Mr Robinson the Inspector say to her 'Miss Cooke, I promise you a place in Heaven, and if God treats you as you have treated George Williams, it will be a good place. Will you be lonely?' 'Lonely?' she said, 'great Scott no.' 'I see,' said the Inspector, 'one black beetle's as good as another, eh?' She did have her beetles too: the following year J. S. Roberts was to proceed to Jesus, Rica Jones later to Somerville, and Alwyn Fidler was to win the Prix de Rome for Architecture and become Master Planner for the new Birmingham.

From Miss Morris shining hair-brushes, from Miss Swinnerton three pound-notes, books from Miss Sadie Price: 11 October. The sizzle of bacon, sandwiches for the journey and Dad to see me off again, with a yo-ho-ho and a vast sea-chest, I bearing in the other hand the handsome inscribed suitcase from my Wesleyans. His pride was so much prouder than when I went to France that it had to be pressed down into a vat of dignity; his nods to the passers-by were imbued with restraint, helped by the weight we were carrying. Mam waved again to the train, so did Mrs Evans next to the chapel; then I was alone, in dark flannel trousers and sports-jacket, cleaving steadily through the grey morning, en avant, avanti. The engine-driver could not have been more confident of his destination than I was of mine. I will be back in between, Connah's Quay, but only a piece of me. Ta-ra . . .

The afternoon stayed as grey, but Oxford Station presented a new picture: it was seething with dark flannel and sports-jacket (good), plus-fours (strange and devilish), long winding scarves, bicycles, tennis-rackets, football-boots, umbrellas, hockey-sticks, skis, cushions, lampshades, I even saw a case of champagne; but no luggage as valiant as mine, I was the only mariner at an inland port. I saw it on to a van and decided to embark on my university career, in exemplary fashion, on foot; it was a long walk with the suitcase. In Tom Gate, now a forest of bicycles, the porter was busy allocating, looked less like Dad and did not recognize me: the rooms which I had asked for, the cheapest in the college, were one of the few undergraduate sets in Tom Quad, the others being mostly the homes of dons, Canon to right of me and Canon to left. I noticed three youths in short tattered gowns, as I approached Number Six Stair a couple of doors along; inside the stone arch, under time-worn 'Mr J. G. Barrington-Ward', a name shone new-white on new-black, 'G. E. Williams'. I stared, hot with identification. Then I lugged the suitcase up two flights of narrow dark stairs, and breathlessly opened my door. The sea-chest was already in the middle of the room.

Not unprepared for a monk's cell, I found a picturesque oak-beamed attic with worn carpet, sofa, dining-table, coal scuttle, reading-lamp next to a small arm-chair, and the friendly flicker of a fire. I turned on the lamp under its frilly green top, and crossed the uneven boards into the little bedroom; its window, low on the floor and obviously the top part of a tall casement also serving Mr Barrington-Ward below me, overlooked the winking lamps of Tom. I walked back and saw, down through the two front windows, also floor level, the humming traffic of St Aldate's. Not grand, not sordid, the den of a student. I sat on my sea-chest, looked round, and said aloud 'G. E. Williams, Christ Church', then felt that somehow I had lived this moment before. Books to go along the shelf, crockery and cutlery in that cupboard, do sit here old chap, are muffins your line of country ... With the October night on either side, the little lighthouse room was impregnably mine. I had never felt so content.

A knock. My first caller! In the shadowy door, an older man, conservatively dressed. 'Good afternoon,' he said. I said, 'Do come in!' 'Thank you, I just thought you might like to talk things over, anything I could help you about ...' O merde, my spiritual or sexual welfare or both, careful ... 'Do sit down,' I said, for the first time in my life, and motioned to the arm-chair: my chair. A flicker crossed his well-bred face. 'No thank you, sir, for instance your provisions, you can utilize the Buttery for jam and such condiments.' He had a couple of brushes in his hand, for utilization: he was my scout. He looked like a Cabinet Minister. For a second I invested his elongated frame with shorts and a whistle. 'Oh I see,' I said, 'how are you?' and extended a frank boyish hand. It was taken, but only just; I knew I was never to get any nearer to him than this. 'Four nights a week, sir, you are expected to dine in Hall and charged for it ...' I thought, if I asked him to sit down when I thought he was the college soul-saver I must go on with it, and interrupted, 'Do please sit down!' 'No reelly, sir,' he said firmly, 'thank yew, rollers – roll-call – is at eight a.m.' I sat myself, on the edge of my chair, having failed-ish in my first viva voce. He produced a worn gown, mortar-board and surplice which could be mine for ten shillings, 'It's quite the thing, sir, for the gown to look a little shabby, some even tear them on purpose ...' 'But couldn't I have a short gown like the one I saw –' His face cracked into a smile. 'Oh no, sir, they're commoners, this is a scholar's long gown, if you'll excuse me I'll see to my other gentlemen.' They will be dons, to him I must be the church-mouse in the rafters of Fat-Cat Castle. 'Mr Lewis Carroll, sir, was on this floor, next stair,' and he was gone; I had never read *Alice* but was impressed. I enjoyed unpacking, and heard Tom boom six; there was over an hour before dinner (dinner!) and I went for a walk.

It was dark and the streets shone with rain: up to Carfax, down the High as far as Univ, everywhere the bustle of taxis, luggage and lusty greetings, then to the right, down King Edward Street and back into Christ Church by Canterbury Quad. I looked at the names on the stairs, painted white on black like mine, Lord Dunglass, Lord Swinfen, then wandered into eighteenth-century Peckwater, its elegant proportions marred by a surface that was blotched and scaling hideously; but it coolly faced the magisterial pillars of the Library like an unperturbed Lord Chesterfield in an advanced stage of acne. I had heard this was the grand quadrangle, with possibly the most expensive rooms in Oxford. The stones rang with interjections, howls of mirth, quick footsteps, and incongruously – I was never to know it different, night or morning – the tinny jazzery of portable gramophones: from one side 'Kitten on the Keys', from the other the long opening wail of what I was to know as 'Rhapsody in Blue'.

A third lord, ground floor, had a little party, I could see the svelte plus-foured figure silhouetted against panelling, others gliding against chintz covers and cushions provided by dutiful mother or sister. On the table, next to a signed photograph of Heather Thatcher, he was arranging two or three family groups, I had none, was it odd? And then ... what was he doing as he chatted, fastidious hands in the air rattling a long silver teapot and dribbling out of it into stemmed glasses? Cocktails! Loud laughter as the door opened, perhaps it was me, greeted with open arms by all – 'ah!' I must have a nickname – Taffy? Good God no – Holly, for Holywell, yes – 'Holly dear boy, I do want these chaps to meet you – our tame Celt, Holly Williams, Lord Castlereagh – you Welsh wizard, I can't keep up with you, did you stay with the Curzons in Rome – Peter a cocktail for Holly!'

From another window, the cheeky twang of a ukulele. I walked slowly away, into the immense shadow of the Library, under the arch, and into the vast desert of Tom Quad. From the Cathedral, a thin caterwaul of choristers. Seven o'clock boomed from Tom, and my eye searched, below it, along the black crenellation where somewhere I was domiciled. I crossed, was swallowed in the dark under the Hall staircase, descended into dim stone passages and skirted a well-like cloister floored with flat stones in the shape of crosses. I pictured them guarding the bones of a giant don killed off in the Great Plague; the wall-inscriptions, in a cold sweat as they piously extolled long-dead college servants, were suddenly melancholy instead of pictur-esque. I came out into the walled area in front of Meadow Build-ings, where a couple of leafless trees gauntly confirmed that summer was past; winter seeped, through Meadow Gate, from the flat river-fields.

Two gowned figures hurried by with books, then one in dressing-gown and slippers carrying a sponge; a bell tolled. I stopped – again the feeling that this has happened before, is it a dream I have had, which makes me feel I am dreaming now? Sudden laughter from somebody's study, I mean rooms, then in a flash, it was pinned down. The whole of this part – long grimly Victorian building, hoary roofs, cloisters, the stray bell – all was to me a public school out of the *Magnet* and even *The*

Hill. In a community of contemporaries who had already spent years divorced from home, I was lodged alone for the first time : the one new boy. It began to drizzle. I hurried back and changed into my dark suit. My room still looked cosy, but empty. On the table a letter, sent by hand. A letter! The new friend with the key to the door which was not quite opening ... 'Dear Williams, On Tuesday we are holding a Wesleyan Prayer-Meeting for Welsh Undergraduates ...' I washed, put on my gown in front of the small swivel mirror, arranged it negligently over one shoulder, and set forth, puzzled by a riddle. Why does Christ Church, full, seem emptier than in July when it was empty?

The great Hall was buzzing with muted voices. At the long top table, under Henry VIII and Wolsey, the dons sat rubicund and candle-lit as if they had not got up from there all through the Long Vac, and there was a Tudor clatter of tureens, hot-plates, pewter and silver. I found the scholars' table, and slid in next to pale clever freshers with nothing to say. I sorted out fish-knife and fork. 'Would you mind passing le sel, I *am* sorry, Classics are you, my name's Williams, name's Rowse, History, anything on at the theatre – Calder-Marshall – *Irene*, jolly good – Greenleaves – Lennox-Boyd – mustard, thank you ...' After dinner, the J.C.R., the Junior Common Room, on the ground floor next to me in Tom, a sort of club for House undergraduates, all the papers. I asked for black coffee and sat in a corner with the *Isis*, a weekly 'Social View of Oxford Life' which offered me – besides Kreisler and Cortot at the Town Hall and *The Cousin from Nowhere* with Maidie Andrews – Sweaters Ties and Scarves from Walters', an Abdulla after the Dip, a Silver Case to put it in, Haig Whisky, Champagne Heidsieck, College Linen and Furnishings from Webber's, Handsewn Boots, a Fiat, a Course in Public Speaking by the Rev. Charles Bradley, a Buick, a Musical Tea at the Moorish Lounge, and (from Ducker's in the Turl) Special Attention to the Hunting Man. An article asked 'Is there an Oxford Manner?' and the Union was to debate whether 'the Government of Signor Mussolini has proved itself a Menace to the Well-being of Europe'.

Then I sampled the *Sporting and Dramatic*, leafing past the Ladies' Kennel Notes and bowler-hatted Marchionesses ('Captain Oswald and Lady Cynthia Mosley have returned from the Lido – that restless person the Duke of Westminster') to rest at the feet of 'Miss Beatrice Lillie, late of the *Nine O'Clock Revue*, wearing one of the new coat-of-mail evening frocks' next to 'Pavlova, still the Incomparable'. People drifted in, each taller than the last, elegant baby-faced steeples mixed with athletic types who all seemed to have the indeterminate good looks of village war-memorials. As I read 'Miss Gladys Cooper and Mr Ivor Novello in their New Success *Enter Kiki* ...' I collected jumbled ends of chatter, as unfamiliar as French had once been, all in a sad ventriloquist monotone, 'Putrid party don'cher know going to a flick terrific womanizer blotto old boy Belgrave Square Lygon birthday pissed to the wide ask your scout for a broadminded Beaujolais ...'

I took a sophisticated sip at my dolly cup of coffee. 'Tell you,' said one languid knowing voice, 'who I met at Oggie's this vac, Dotty Dickson, they say the Pragger-Wagger hangs round the back of the Winter Garden for hours but can't get off the first tee, I understand she's a virgin, beautiful girl.' I was to verify that the Pragger-Wagger was the Prince of Wales but stayed puzzled by Miss Dickson's status, having just seen her in the *Bystander* looking indeed beautiful, but holding by the hand a pretty child of seven.

There was the smell of cigarettes strangely Turkish; as the air thickened, so the voices thinned, 'Have a beer Ramsay Mac my dear sir is eighty per cent saint and twenty unadulterated shit have a beer send 'em down to the barge to be tubbed give my Phyllis Monkman have a beer ...' I said to myself, you've sometimes thought, my God these women – well old boy, you've got away from them now ... I picked up the *Tatler* – 'People, dearest, are flocking back from everywhere, I'm told the new Savoy Orpheans Band is going to knock London flat' – decided to look as if I had read it already and sauntered out, a man-aping boy leaving a gathering of men, who were actually boys considerably more man-aping than I was. I climbed my dark stair and switched on my light; under the naked bulb, the fire was out. I stood overwhelmed with a wave of emotion as un-expected as it was violent. It was a longing, with every atavistic bone in my body, for the kitchen of 314a, for the eternity of the fire and my family at my elbow – what was this? As I undressed I thought, I have always seen myself as a hermit, but I was a surrounded hermit, this is the first time I have ever been alone. I fell glumly asleep. Through my dreams Tom thudded as it had before, but sterner now that I was in, than when I had been on probation. I was a guest in a great monastic hotel.

A discreet knock, shaving-water and breakfast; I felt now like a patient in some academic hospital. Toast, cornflakes, which I had never seen, Cooper's Marmalade, and the Cabinet Minister in green-baize apron pushing a carpet-sweeper. 'Dear Miss Cooke, Life is new and strange, I have just a moment before lunch – "lunch", you see I am slipping into the expressions ..' 'Ma chère Tante Jeanne, La vie est nouvelle, étrange, j'ai juste un moment ...'

Then my first interview with my tutor, serious, conscientious, reserved; I was to find it difficult to describe his appearance to Miss Cooke, being at the stage when all older people looked alike. As we shook hands I knew that like my scout, he was never to get any nearer and that I would be Mr to the end. He had few words and a vast knowledge of Medieval French, which like Anglo-Saxon held no interest for me. 'Well,' he said, rubbing his eyes with a sigh and looking out of the window, 'I suppose the idea would be for you to do your Pass Schools next March, say French and Italian, then we'll decide, mm?' He looked back at me with a kind smile and I thought, you are the salt of the earth, but it is salt which for me will never have any savour and if Miss Cooke had been like you I would now be huddled in an outer office of Summers' Works adding columns up, wrong. 'The Diplomatic Service, ultimately? In the mean-time we'll leave you to follow your bent, mm?' My routine would be a weekly Tutorial (consisting of my reading to him an essay, say on 'The Philosophy of Diderot' or 'The Tristan Legend'), and as many lectures at the Taylorian as I thought fit to attend, and it was his hope – er – that I would attend quite a few. In short, I had no routine; I emerged relieved, yet deflated. It was a wet morning.

I got back to find at my door a ruddy young man in a thick sweater holding a list, who said his name was Gadsden and did I row. I said no but I'd like to try. 'Jolly good, you look useful, two-thirty, House Barge, any old togs.' Excited, I had a light lunch in the J.C.R. – 'Miss Teddie Gerard aboard Miss Carstairs' yacht *Sonia*' – and strode through the clammy Meadows down to the river, thick-scarved and tough-shorted; the swish of the rough overcoat against my bare knees made me feel daring, as if I were naked underneath. Was rowing to be my sport? A miraculous flair? . . . I climbed into the rocking craft to join other frozen freshmen, and as we lurched out into the mist and it began to spot with rain, I knew the cause was lost. 'All together – no no number three Williams is it, don't in God's name grab the blasted thing like a ruddy poker . . .' As I thrust my oar behind me, plunged it like Excalibur into the pock-marked Isis and nearly capsized the boat – 'I told you for Christ's sake' – I thought, with burning face and frozen behind – yes, back in the Glanrafon woods, a water-beater this time. After an hour we lurched back on to dry land, I never to return except horizontal in a punt. I walked disconsolately home with a boy named Drake-Brockman, who was to play Rugger in a couple of days, 'Welsh, you *must* be good, hefty half-back type, Jacob's looking for men . . .' I cheered up again, and felt sporting as I thumped down my stair in my dressing-gown with soap and towel and crossed Tom in the darkening light. After my bath, tea in the J.C.R. with cakes and chocolate biscuits, but I had had an energetic afternoon, if catching several crabs can be called exercise.

Sunday – no chapel, it was a long time before the freedom of that wore off – was like any other day; two sessions in the J.C.R., over coffee. I made friends. The first was a tall diffident youth named Byam Shaw, who noticed I was reading the theatre page and told me he had a young brother Glen who was on tour playing the boy in *At Mrs Beam's*. The second, after dinner, was a great Apollo of a rowing man named Murray-Threipland, to whom I told my afternoon on the river; he spluttered into his coffee, and it became funny to me too. He asked me back to his great panelled rooms in Peck, and I drank my first liqueur. Simple and assured, he answered my questions about his life in Scotland – I gathered a place like Gyrn Castle – and I told him about my life. He had taken me for a Belgian, I was by no means displeased but proud to tell him I was Welsh. Before turning in, I looked up his father in the J.C.R. *Who's Who*: 'Col., J.P., succeeded to estates above-mentioned from his cousin, Sir . . .' I went to bed stimulated by the thought that I had met two strangers with only their English upbringing in common, and had got on well with both.

I bought a long winding scarf. Lectures were dull and not helped by the many tricorned and bespectacled undergraduettes who seemed to write down everything that was said, including 'good morning', and did nothing to belie the legend that they were of the third and neuter gender. 'Dear Miss Cooke, I enclose my personal acct. so far, you'll agree I'm a man of business! "Provision 3/1½d, Sweater 4/6d, Passe-partout picture 1/6d, Stamps 1/4d, Kettle and teapot 3/-, Merry-go-round for Tom 1/- . . ."' The last was not a device for enlivening my quad, but a new boys' paper for my brother. 'I read that Mr J. B. Fagan is this term to present, for the first time, the Oxford Players, he is the famous producer from the Granville Barker seasons at the Court Theatre, London. The Playhouse is a converted big-game museum in the Woodstock Road, they are to do Shaw, Wilde, Goldoni, etc. After Tom Bell tolls its 101 strokes at 9.20 nobody's allowed out, and if we are out already, on our battels – our bills – we're charged gate-money, so much every half-hour, mounting till 12.20, so I cannot yet be sure I can afford the theatre . . .' After lunch I sat guilty and practically alone in the Electra waiting for the programme to start at two (cheap prices till four) and was then almost bored; and it was *Orphans of the Storm*, which a year ago would have been ineradicable.

The Rugger afternoon was even more of a nightmare than

the rowing. Was the notoriously enervating climate already gnawing at my vitals? How else could I explain why I dressed up as a player of Rugby football and strode up the Iffley Road with Drake-Brockman to the House Ground feeling like one, when I had never seen a game? All I knew was that the ball was not round. 'Welsh, jolly good', the game started, and among the weaving steaming scrumming savages I wandered lonely as a cloud. Suddenly, out of the grey afternoon, the ball came staggering towards me; I headed it. There was a howl, I made a sheepish grin, struck my forehead comically, and shrank back into anonymity. When I told Drake-Brockman I had never seen a game he was so amazed he asked me to tea in his rooms, crumpets and muffins under covers from the J.C.R. Sitting on the rug before the fire, when his scout switched on the reading-lamp and closed the curtains over the Meadows I felt suddenly comfortable. Like the other two, he was easy and friendly, neither sporting turnip nor studious owl. We discussed clubs, of which there seemed hundreds, each with a subscription, Yachting, Cosmopolitan, Mountaineering, Wine ... I mentioned the Dramatic Society. 'Oh yes, the Ouds,' he said, pronouncing it Owds, 'rather special, I'm told with that sort it's best to wait till one's second term. But you must join something.'

I decided on the French Club, which had a modest subscription. There were pleasant meetings at the Cadena Café, with a genial smattering of Poles and Belgians and people who had been to French schools; it was gratifying to air my French in front of undergraduettes. One evening the Belgian poet Cammaerts lectured on 'Shakespeare's influence on Maeterlinck'; I was not galvanized, but sitting on a floor against a pillar I felt in the international swim, it was an evening out and worth the gate-money.

In the meantime, in the J.C.R. I had met two other people with whom, separately, I was to be friendly for a couple of terms, both American Rhodes Scholars. The first was Dwight Evvers the Second, a breezy Mid-Westerner, as new to it all as I was. 'Gee, some of these old guys must ha' been drinking their port way back when they saw the Mayflower off!' I had never heard the accent, and loved it. The second was very different, small and as odd as his name, Leo Pascal Gaspary. Nothing of the lion about Leo; he was more like a charming bespectacled cat, and as contained. At nineteen, he was ageless. He had travelled widely, and as he twirled a ring round his little finger and nibbled at his nostrils with a lawn handkerchief, he would range over subject after subject with the widest of vocabularies, and in a quick drawl which was a mellifluous contradiction in terms.

He stimulated and bewildered me, for he was the proof that accomplishment is relative; in my parlour-corner, surveying over my *Observer* the walls of Philistia, I may have been the lone flower of culture, but in fact my knowledge – of art, music, theatre – was nil. I would sit bumpkin-humble at his tiny feet, always neatly side by side, while he answered questions with perfect simplicity. 'Waal no, one could hardly call Bernhardt' – the r blurred, which in his precise speech was beautiful – 'a beauty, though she *was* d'un certain âge, but she possessed her own kind of self-created halo, partly due to back-combing, ça va sans dire ...' When he talked of Kafka, Clive Bell, E. M. Forster, the Kabuki, I felt as ignorant as Wally and Totty; he had an immense admiration for Shaw's plays, to which I hurried immediately, only to find their cleverness so unpalatable that I was angry with myself, then with Shaw, then with both. I realized once and for all that I was not an intellectual; it was a blow.

But Leo fascinated me. Alone by my fire, I tried to imitate his voice, with in between sentences the intakes of breath; then it came to me that this was not my line. Also my picture of myself as a Spartan was, by him, unwittingly shattered. The first day, I had made it a rule not to light my fire; but the grate looked so depressing that I shut my eyes and struck the daily match. I would find American Leo, presumably central-heated from the womb on, straight-backed in his Meadow rooms at a desk overlooking the rain-swept trees, reading *Edward the Second* with behind him, firm in the fireplace, a paper fan with which he himself might have toyed, a Bostonian marquise. 'Why no, a fire kind of stultifies all cerebral movement chez moi, do please sit down – would *you* like it?' I got him once up to my eyrie for chicory coffee after dinner, but though he quite liked me, he had no special interest in the theatre; he was betrothed to his books. He was the most charmingly self-sufficient person I have ever met; beside him, I felt my own Flintshire armour melting away. He was good for me.

To augment income, it was my plan to compete for everything within reach; it was Leo who told me there was a Prize going, for Eng. Lang., to members of Christ Church. Next morning, after solitary breakfast, I hastened to the Library and collected books; on my way back, in Tom, I ran into Byam Shaw, who told me Glen was hoping to join the Oxford Players next year. I bounded up my stair and into my arm-chair. The traffic swishing through the Oxford drizzle emphasized the crackle of the fire; I was in my quiet room, warm enough if you got near the grate, and I opened *The Anglo-Saxon Trend*, with at my elbow an old H.C.S. exercise-book. A morning of leisurely independence, *my* morning. As I turned pages I thought, tonight my first outing – straight from Hall dinner, a dash with Greenleaves to the pit at the New, then I remembered, no that's tomorrow, tonight I have nothing. The word echoed silently round the room. Nothing . . .

Slowly, in one of those ticking moments of self-discovery which come unawares, I looked up and around me. The urge to study was gone. Gone as surely as a watch is broken which dangles before the eyes a broken spring. The Holywell exercise-book mocked me. In the silence the room, the haven into which I had anchored, was empty. Not empty with me sitting in the middle – empty with me not there. But if I was not there, where was I? Where indeed, the room asked, its heavy black beam athwart my head like a scowling brow – fifth-hand sofa, threadbare curtains, reach-me-down lamp like a thousand others – and *what* was I? I looked down at my orthodox ribbed sweater and carefully too-long flannel trousers concertinaed over rough socks already concertinaed over square-toed, crêpe-soled shoes – *what was I?* An undergraduate figure of straw, a shop-window symbol of Poor Scholar. In consternation I pressed my palms over my flannel thighs, as I had done when they were corduroy, and felt warmth – yes it was me all right. But I saw the truth, sharp and two-pronged.

First, having been shot into a world of adult independence without the responsibilities of adulthood, I was homesick. Second, when I had sat in my parlour-corner, in love with study, it had been a means to an end; now that the end was achieved, I was out of love. I had only to look at Leo, the true student, to know that. At 314a I had lived, passionately as an exile does, for escape – and here, escaped and free, I was no longer living. I did not belong : not because of the social insecurity I might have feared – on the contrary, the atmosphere of effortless privilege was stimulating, I felt more at home with it than some of the other scholars did – what was it then? I got up and looked down into St Aldate's, at the townees scurrying against rain, as indifferent to me as I was to them. I crossed into the bedroom. The worn shaving-brush, the limp dressing-gown, who slept here? ... Down in the quad, the long scarves flowed in all directions, pressing unscathed through the harsh morning on some urgent young errand; I saw one figure espy a friend across the grass, hold his arms wide in mock surprise, and hurry off with him arm in arm. Rugger, rowing, music, the flicks, coffee, everybody was off somewhere. I looked sightlessly down at the shifting pattern of bare heads, never a woman, never a child, man after man after man. I was alone.

Alone, and dreading the thought of an evening alone. Staring out at the quad, I searched further. Was lack of funds at the root of my malaise? Not really, for I enjoyed the game of keeping the battels down – and even if I were to be spending freely and cramming my nights with plays, cinema, debate ... that was not the answer. Was I disappointed in Oxford? No, round me I saw all that I had hoped to see, every type of intelligence, every sort of freedom to discuss anything, to any lengths. But I had no desire to discuss. What did I want?

I walked back to my fire, sat again, picked up *The Anglo-Saxon Trend* and spoke down into it, aloud. 'I want to be in the Theatre.'

Chapter 20

Fair Wind

I felt better. The next night, watching my first musical comedy from the pit of the red-plushed old New Theatre – the cast made doubly desirable to the undergraduate audience by the law that on no account must any of us venture back-stage – I saw myself walking-on, with scruffy digs in Walton Street; even the safety curtain, clanking down with 'For Thine Especial Safety' across it, was a glamorous banner. Off next Sunday to Widnes or Westcliff, one suitcase with 'Battling Butler' all over it, does Jack Buchanan really tell the Pragger-Wagger what to wear and what *is* June's surname? ... 'Don't leave your gown,' said Greenleaves after 'God Save the King', 'you might get progged on the way back.'

'Dear Miss Cooke, I have decided it is part of my Oxford education to study plays, so have bought, at Acott's, a book of Playhouse tickets. I am reading widely over the Classic period, though it is accepted at Oxford even by one's tutor that one plays in term and works in the vac. By the way, he assures me that for a Consulship, knowledge of more than one language is advisable ...' It was only fair that at the end of my three years I should get a First; then I would tell her my future. The family? No, I must wait too, it would be like telling my mother I was going to be a bookmaker, only no money in it ...

Two evenings later, with Goldoni's *Mirandolina*, I initiated my three-year Fagan course in Drama, three shillings a time. Every Monday I would sprint from Hall dinner, long scarf flying, Carfax, the Corn, Martyrs' Memorial, just in breathless time to hear the clock on the little church strike eight. The adventurous drill-hall – unraked, no balcony – had an apron-stage, a novelty flanked by grey-white pillars: an imposing frame for tragedy which tended to overlay Mr Pim Passing By. The company had no money to spend, but offered a standard kept consistently high by the taste of a lovable unbusiness-like man of the theatre. At one draughty première after another, the backstage gong would clang out, darkness, and I would be a creaking chair among many; the reason they did not all creak was, alas, that they were not all occupied. The plays were not always word-perfect: loyal first-nighters began to notice that long speeches tended to be directed thoughtfully at the hidden backs of chairs, a habit which seemed to afford mysterious refreshment to the memory. I was to see a maypole named Tyrone Guthrie, as Vedio in *Monna Vanna*, his first serious role, hasten on with a message, trip, fall his improbable length, rise and deliver the line 'But sire, you are hurt – let me sustain you!' On the first night of *The Master Builder*, after Hilda had embarked on a couple of direct questions which seemed to puzzle Solness as much as they did me, I heard the prompter call, in a strangled voice, 'Get her back, she's in the wrong act!'

One the other hand I was to see in his first leading part, in *Love for Love*, a youth whose name in the programme caused a woman behind me to paraphrase my father on another occasion, 'Poor boy, how *does* he pronounce it, John *Jeel*-gud?' When he got going though, all nose and passion and dragging calves and unbridled oboe of a voice – no peering at the back of furniture for this beginner – the creaking stopped. But the *Isis* could not get his name right either, 'a very interesting performance by Mr Gielgerd'. I was to behold a girl lovelier than any on the films, for this one had the exquisite colouring of the theatre, Faith Celli; I would stare at her in disbelief and think, if I saw her walking along High Street Connah's Quay I would kneel and expect the rest to follow suit. And while I was continuously learning as an actor, Fagan was introducing me to Ibsen, Strindberg, Shaw – at whom I jibbed in performance as hard as in print – Barrie, Maugham, Wilde, Synge, Yeats; from each, as beginners must, I unconsciously drew the threads which in time interweave to form the texture of a playwright's work. Dead Sunday afternoons, on my way to a dutiful suburban tea, I would halt opposite the stage-door and wonder about the exasperating, wearing, exciting dress-rehearsal within; for me the drill-hall front, grey as the grey steppes of North Oxford which were its horizon, sheltered a glowing Bohemian shrine. Then I would stuff my hands down my pockets and stride on, a morose and mufflered Love Locked Out.

I sat for the Prize with Leo as the other candidate, knowing that he would win, and he did; I was almost glad, for it proved my point. 'Tomorrow,' said Drake-Brockman airily, 'I thought of going up to town for a spin, like to come?' By licence from the Junior Censor, he had a small open car; in suits, gowns stuffed in the back, we departed on my first motor outing. Provided we kicked the bolted door in Tom Gate by twelve-twenty a.m., it was unlikely we would be detected, but the chance of mishap added spice; he drove very fast, hair and scarves streamed through the yellowing afternoon. He showed me Westminster Abbey and St Paul's; as we came back into the Strand it was still light enough, outside the Savoy Hotel, for him to point out Nelson's Column in ambiguous silhouette, 'It's the cross-guard of his sword, priceless, and the silly sods never spotted it!' Then we crawled into Piccadilly Circus for my first view of Eros by night, poised against the epileptic rainbows of the West End as they schwepped and bovrilled and sandeman's-ported and splashed the heavens from end to end with the frenzied impertinences of some all-powerful commercial imp; I felt the prodigal vulgarity of the Centre of the World fire my blood and cloud my brain with a potion already, for me, a heady mixture of theatre and sex. This delirium of light saxophones blaring, curtains rising, unbelievably lovely women, romantic men, great stage beds, throbbing kisses, sobbing, laughing: His Majesty's *Hassan*, Wyndham's *The Dancers*, Ambassadors *The Lilies of the Field* with Meggie Albanesi ('Look,' I said, 'they say she's going to be *the* actress'), then to the Globe to study the photographs, *Our Betters*.

We must be gone before any play was over, but we had our plans. First up Regent Street, where Drake-Brockman had heard

of a darkly titillant bar called Verrey's where 'they' were supposed to go, 'they' being tarts. Verrey's comprised a sipping
mother with flapper daughter and – to us – two very expensive
gin-and-its; we were apparently too late for 'them', having
missed the magic hour of the thé-dansant. Then, in a 'dance-
place' in Old Compton Street, we sat on a balcony overlooking
an empty floor; we were too early. Two languid girls with pronounced make-up and a cigarette, looked frighteningly promising; I saw them as women of the town and invested their faces
with a depravity which drew and repelled. But my cicerone
explained that they were dance-hostesses whom it would take a
week to bring to terms. We took an aimless walk. At all the
theatres, the show was on; I felt the familiar rub of frustration.
As we drifted past the Apollo stage-door, *What Every Woman
Knows*, I thought, I'm understudying with two lines in the last
act and just slipping out for cigarettes for Mr Tearle ... Our
last try was a side-street cinema, where now stands the Windmill, with back seats where 'things went on'. The film sounded
unlikely to fan surreptitious passions – Little Jackie Coogan in
Daddy – but we settled into the rustling dark, with dank hands
and dry mouths, separated by twenty seats. Next to me, an
entwined man and woman stared as if I had entered a bedroom,
and went back to kissing as to a meal; in front, two bald men
sat absorbed in Little Master Coogan, whose troubles embraced
me too. At the end, the place was nearly empty. Drake-Brockman muttered sourly, 'Slough for us Williams old boy, Maiden-
head in every sense of the word, Henley and Alma bloody
Mater.' He drove like the wind and we were home well before
the Cinderella minute. I saw little of his good company for some
time, then heard that returning from London, alone, he had
overturned the car and been killed. It was such strange news
that it did not occur to me for months that I had had an escape.

'Dear Williams, Would you like to read for the Maître
d'Hôtel in the French Club production of "La Poudre aux
Yeux"? Tuesday 8.30. Yours, H. Wilson Wiley.' Three minutes
later I was one of the purposeful heads hurrying across Tom: in
the Library I leafed through the Labiche comedy – one scene,

but an effective comedy part. I wanted to stride out of Tom Gate, rehearse the rest of the day, no lunch, back for rehearsals after dinner tonight and so every day for the rest of the term. 'Dear Miss Cooke, I am busier than ever, but have now a "petite distraction" – to help them out, the French Club have asked me to play a small part, it seemed mean to refuse. Mademoiselle Gachet is producing the play in the sacred female precincts of Lady Margaret Hall, it will be splendid for my French; she teaches at Rada, the Academy of Dramatic Art. I have acquired a second-hand Spiers Grammar, a long-felt want ...' The cast, men and women students, were sympathique and it was a heady feeling to be directed for the first time, and by a professional with attack and humour.

La Poudre aux Yeux went well; although the others were more amateur than I was, I felt we were a machine in which I made a cog. 'Dear Miss Cooke, I wore my dinner-suit for the first time (as a head-waiter!) borrowing my scout's coat-tails. After the performance, a small party where I had my first glass of champagne, you would not believe how good it has been for my French. With so many delightful people talking French, it was nice to be able to hold one's own. When I think that but for my visit to France I should never have been in the play – never be at Oxford! Yours very affectionately.' The 'very' had crept in with Oxford. Stage-manager Wilson Wiley – Willie, I overheard, to his friends – was a wise young bird, already playing the part, with a conscious and sober humour, of the lawyer he was to become, 'Women smoking I find rather bad form, I'm an old stick I'm afraid ...' Just as I was mustering courage to get round to it, he told me he had been cast as First Sailor in the Ouds *Hamlet*, and would I like to be put up for the Club. I tried to welcome the idea without eagerness. Three days later, clutching at the *Isis*, I was gratified to read 'On the other hand, the Maître d'Hôtel (Mr G. E. Williams, Ch. Ch.) was an astoundingly exact study.' Would the Ouds Committee see it?

End of Term Colleckers: Collections, a routine call on the Dean – a beautiful gentle-mannered old man in an exquisite drawing-room next to the Cathedral – to be wished a happy

Christmas and to be asked if I knew when Next Term Com-
menced (suppose I said no?). Next evening, our kitchen suddenly cosy and the drawing-room a dream; the first bitterly cold
Saturday night, Job at the pictures and Dad working, I sat
opposite Mam at the family fire. After counting her divvies I
sank absorbed into Zola's *Nana* while Tom made a teapot-rest
for me with his fretwork set. If being an alien on one's hearth
meant feeling like this, I didn't mind ... As I cycled up to Holywell, on the brand-new Raleigh Miss Cooke had given me for
my birthday, I was saddened by the thought that I would never
see Meggie Albanesi: on Sunday she had died suddenly at the
age of twenty-four ... Tea at Underwood, where I was careful
to be unspoilt. I made it clear that while I got on with blue
blood, my own corpuscles still glowed a healthy ruby. 'One
can't change!' I heard myself make it a long J.C.R. a, 'ca-a-n't'.

At Prize Distribution, three cheers for a diffident George Williams, hip, hip ... My parents dressed up and came, their first
and last visit, and for a hurried moment shook hands with Miss
Cooke: long enough to prove to Dad that she did not wear
suffragette bloomers. I was happy talking to Millie Tyrer and
Septimus, fresh from their first Bangor term, but though my
picture of myself, in my own mind, was of a muddled hankering
young man, I felt that I had already travelled away from them.
As the piano played – oh why couldn't I sit down and dash off
'Dancing Honeymoon' – and they spoke of their Profs and what
fun Coll was and what a good crit the Coll play had had, I tried
to talk like Leo, 'My what a good movie *The Four Horsemen*
is!' and then like Willie, 'I can't say I was impressed, but then
old dear I *am* old-fashioned ...' I saw them all with affection,
but through glass. Six long winter Quay weeks, broken by bike-
rides to Caerwys to Millie's family, then a week in Liverpool at
27 Wadham. Telling Nellie and Bob and Auntie Soph about im-
passes with scout and fish-knives – 'well George, we've never
been brought up to *those*, have we?' – I knew that whatever
my difficulties, I had few in vaulting the social abyss: the
bridge, both ways, was mine. We went to the Empire to see
Dorothy Ward and Shaun Glenville in *Mother Goose*, a wedding-

cake of a pantomime; once, when Dick's silk legs were taking a radiant call through the curtains, the folds parted behind her and I caught a glimpse of chaos – man-high diamanté Easter eggs swung into limbo by stage-hands in overalls, giant tree-trunks teetering over a jostle of panto tots – and once more I wished ... Home again, I ticked off the days: o Irish Mail, in seventeen days I follow, fifteen days ... I studied, but even in 314a my heart was not in it, it was in the Playhouse, and Faith Celli's face flitted across our backyard like a lamp. I imagined writing a play with the wit of Bernard Shaw (I had to grant him that) the elegance of Wilde and the fantasy of Barrie. All would be better, the black beam in my attic would lighten with the spring. The spring of 1924.

The term started well: with Rowse and Lennox-Boyd, I went to breakfast with the Junior Censor, Mr Masterman, a handsome athlete who was later, unexpectedly, to write thrillers. We were all fairly tongue-tied, but it was a grown-up affair. Returning, I found a large parcel from the Tyrers, who had a grocer's shop, containing every variety of tinned food 'to keep you going'; beside it, even more lightening to the heart, my last term's battel, which included everything – lodging, hire of furniture, tuition; as a result of my skimping, my income was enough in excess of them for the Steward to refund me thirteen pounds. I breathed freely; my instinct was to send it all home, but my mother refused by return, her resolution as firm as her Treuddyn grammar was erratic, 'i of being thinking this over and i think you will need this extra for a rany day wate untill you of got a earning job.' I went out and bought something that was going to make the difference, a retort to austerity; a shade for my top light, till now naked under an enamel cover. After an anxious hour in Elliston and Cavell, I chose pink satin drooping in scallops and edged inch-long with tiny shiny beads. It looked like the evening wear of a lady-dwarf no better than she should be.

All this counteracted Enid Wainwright. 'What have I done? You were home six weeks and not a word, waved once and never crossed the road, if this is what the grand life does to people, just tell me *what I have done* ...' I felt sorry and yet indignant: I had never made the faintest promise, I had been bored long before 'the grand life', and I had not consciously avoided her, I had thought she was as indifferent as I, and if I had suspected she might be hurt ... I wrote tactfully, feeling I had had a glimpse of 'getting involved'. As a companion piece, a letter from Tante Jeanne, whose image was dimming, though I wrote regularly: too regularly, 'Letters come like clockwork, four sides dutifully filled. Mon cher George, friendship must not become a burden ...' I reflected what a difficult wife she would have made. Miss Cooke, on the contrary, was writing more and more freely, not only personal advice but on every topic from politics to Holywell gossip; her letters proceeded like an ungovernable motor-car, in a series of eloquent spurts punctuated by colloquial backfires. 'Words have a life of their own, sez I, and once written they no longer belong to their creator; you know how I love print, yet it downright terrifies me ...' 'Some of the Bible is like a key opening every room ...' 'If the tragedy of the world isn't the evil wrought by the good, I'll eat my hat ...' 'Miss Morris and Miss Swinnerton are people all the rarer for doing their job quietly, I've felt for a long time – fair play – that a flamboyant nature like mine gets away with far too large a proportion of the swag ...' 'I envy your youth, tho' at that age the joys can be as poignant as the sorrows ...'

The first Sunday, a freak spring morning in January, I went spinning to Woodstock, and had half a pint at the old pub in the hollow of the village, every inch the Oxonian. Then Blenheim, I had the pride of discovering its marvels for myself, and after a wide airy day alone returned light with pleasure. But with nightfall the beam was blacker than ever, my lampshade hung pinkly disconsolate, and loneliness lapped like a chill tide. 'Say,' said Evvers the Second next dank morning as we shuffled into Rollers, in slippers and trousers pulled up over pyjamas, 'say, what about a dance, kid?' I smiled politely, but after we had scribbled our names, teeth chattering, he followed me down

the Hall stairs, 'Saturday night, there's a shindig at the Mogador.'
'I can't dance,' I said, hearing myself say it like him, but after
dinner, walking across Tom to the J.C.R., in a fog, he brought
it up again. 'You don't go to dances for dancin', you go to
dances for sex. You go take a lesson in the slow fox-trot from
one of those dames in the ads, and we'll go dancin', out o'
bounds. Know what goes to this joint? Whores, kid, live British
whores –' 'Look,' I whispered, 'there's Harold Acton.'

A tall plumpish young man loomed up, whom it was impossible to contemplate as an undergraduate; his umbrella was
rolled cane-tight but no snugger than he was, into a long tube
of a black overcoat with spilling from under it pleated trousers
as wide as a skirt. As he advanced out of the swirling mist, it
became clear that it was not just the weather, he was doing his
own swirling. His advent was a sequence of hobble steps which
seemed – his legs were of a good length – to be based on the
ritual of some rompish religion; if his walk had not had elegance, it would have been a waddle. He swayed to a standstill;
in case his kind of soft-coloured features might be mistaken for
the face of youth, he had flanked them with a pair of long side-
whiskers and topped them with a skittishly curled grey bowler.
Bowing with the courtesy of another age and clime, he spoke,
an English flawlessly italianated. 'I do most dreadfully beg your
pardons this inclement night – though I have been resident a
year, I find it too idio-tically diffi-cult to find my way about, I
have been round Tom like a tee-toe-tum, too too madd-ening –
where *does* our dear Dean hang out?' He thanked me profusely,
raised the bowler with a dazzling smile, and propelled himself
Deanward, an Oriental diplomat off to leave a jewelled carte de
visite. 'Jesus,' said Evvers, 'what's that?' 'He's *the* Oxford aes-
thete,' I informed him, 'a Victorian, his rooms in Meadow are
in lemon-yellow and he stands on his balcony and reads his
poems through a megaphone to people passing, and he belongs
to the Hypocrites Club with Brian Howard and Robert Byron
and Evelyn Waugh and all that set, they call themselves the
Post-War Generation and wear Hearts on their lapels as opposed
to the pre-war Rupert Brooke lot who called themselves Souls.

They're supposed to eat new-born babies cooked in wine.' 'I don't like wine,' said Evvers, 'but I'm a hot-blooded son of a bitch from the corn-belt an' this fancy monks' paradise is drivin' me crazy, go get yourself a dancin' lesson.'

I did, assuring myself that it was an investment for when I might be required to partner Dorothy Dickson in a tango at the Royal Garden Party. On Sunday morning, I proceeded up the Woodstock Road – a look at the sealed Playhouse – and in a rather Chinese room, tasselled and pouffed and double-divanned, was received, in semi-evening dress, by Madam Wentworth, a semi-lady who worked the handle of a portable gramophone as if it were a pump. The tips of my left fingers touched the tips of her right, my right tips hovered at the back of her corset, and we went for a walk round the wintry room, a foot apart, to the strains of 'A Kiss in the Dark'. She whispered in my ear, murmurs of business-like instruction, and for a second I thought I was escorting Miss Axe the elocutionist, 'Ree-lex two three ree-lex, when you wish to tarn, signify bay tatching your part-nah evah so slately in the smole of the beck, oops, nevah maind so long as my stocking isn't tawn, two-three ree-lex ...'

By Saturday night I was not ree-lexed at all : at dinner Evvers nodded to me across a candle-pool of chattering celibacy, and winked. I winked back, a rogue acolyte, and felt I was in the sort of danger collegiates got into on the pictures to an upright piano. We walked in our gowns out of Tom Gate. 'Gee what a night, I've heard about these hot-stuff joints but never gotten to one. It'll be a late shindig, but I've checked on the window in Canterbury we can climb in by, after twelve-twenny.' Passing Greenleaves on his way to the Union, I pitied him his evening. A furtive scuttle up an alley, and we were swallowed up by the night-life of Oxford.

The Mogador was a parish hall with half a dozen limp streamers and a depressed three-piece band playing 'Ain't We Got Fun'. Three couples were dancing sedately; I recognized one man as an assistant in Boffin's and another as a scout from my tutor's stair. We wandered up to a counter – 'no hard liquor? Maybe better so, what did old Shakespeare say?' – and the waitress, pouring lemon squashes, whispered to Evvers and pointed to our gowns, bundled under one arm. 'She says there's a rumour of a raid and we better check the get-away.' I warmed and cooled at the same time – to be expelled, sent down! A black disgrace, but the danger was delicious, a manly quandary not to be missed. The get-away was the tiny window of the Gents; we hung our gowns behind the door for the dread moment when the Prog's bowler-hatted 'bulldogs' might heave into view. More couples arrived; I waited for a staid enough fox-trot, and invited a girl in cornflower blue with a concave chest to join me in 'Who's Sorry Now?' She looked as if I had asked her to carry a parcel, but rose, shook herself absently, and lent me three bitten fingers for an uneventful stroll. If this one was a whore – one two three ree-lex – she must be the genteelest in harness.

'Surpraisingly chillay, isn't it?' Yet another Miss Axe, God is this what they think the Oxford accent is? I could see my companion wrestling with a plump girl with an immense artificial rose wilting on her hip; he was making her simper, but the shindig was heavy going. 'Isn't this weathah,' I heard her say to him, 'enough to give you the pip?' Evvers the Second looked perplexed. A splatter of applause, more lemon squashes. I said, 'What's she like?' 'Trainin' to be a nurse and engaged to a nice boy in Cowley, not the kinda joint I figured on but you never – watch out!' This was hissed; I saw a bowler-hat, and froze. We walked swiftly to the Gents and snapped the catch. 'You first!' One leg on the sill, a sharp tap at the door, oh God ... 'It's all rate,' said a voice, 'it's may fioncy.'

We emerged. 'Then for Pete's sake,' said Evvers, 'tell him to hang up his hat, it bothers me.' Fired by our sudden importance, we stayed ten minutes; then when two pallid girls joined forces, bead for bead, and began to shuffle haughtily round to 'I'm Tickled to Death I'm Single' – 'aw nuts,' said my mentor, 'let's skip it.' By nine-thirty the shades of our fancy monastery had closed again around us; we were safely Housed, with bell echoing bell all around. But dreaming spires, as Evvers the Second put it, don't do a thing for hot pants. As we parted inside Tom

Gate, 'Ah Williams!' I heard in a fluty Welsh voice, 'I just called on you, the Reverend Idwal Watkyns whateffer!' We shook hands, he was bespectacled and jolly, 'Wrote to you once about a prayer meeting, remember?' 'Too late,' said Evvers sombrely, 'we just came from one.' 'Indeed, quite right quite right! Well another time, good night!' I went to bed early with *Antic Hay*. Once again Sex had beckoned, and once again, giggling, had vamoosed. But I had learnt to press a lady lightly in the small of the back when wishing to turn.

I wrote to Miss Cooke that I intended trying for a Heath Harrison Travelling Scholarship in French (£75 to spend in France during the next two vacations) and a Goldsmith Exhibition of £70 a year, offered by the Company of Goldsmiths of the City of London. My letters were usually painstakingly accurate, but my plans persuaded me to invent. 'Last week we did a little play in college, a society trifle in which I played the heroine, they're having a photo taken.' There had been no play, not even a trifle. At Italian, I had found myself next to a quiet youth with a delicate ivory face; walking away with him one morning, I realized that behind the shy exterior assumed for lectures, lurked one of the most sophisticated undergraduates in the place. He was Rowley Leigh, in the Ouds and last term leading lady in the 'smoker', Oxford for smoking-concert, or rather revue. I pressed him for a photograph, and after the next lecture, on 'The Morality of Dante', he produced a postcard of himself as Adele Astaire, dark shingle, bows and tango shoes, singing 'Oh Gee Oh Gosh'. This was my chance; when I join, I must have just such a photo to produce. A revue, one minute in feathers as Delysia, the next an unrecognizable navvy ... I went secretly to Germer's in King Teddy Street ('Wigs for Hire'), fished out the matted cheapest – 'for a college play' – and took it back, together with a lip-stick, in a paper bag. I sat in front of my fire combing the wig, feeling something of a methodical maniac, then tried it on; I looked like Medusa in need of a shave. But by the time I had trained the tresses round my sports belt worn as a bandeau, there was improvement.

I called at a shabby photographer's over the road, wedding groups a speciality, and arrived there next raw afternoon with a small attaché-case containing belt, wig, lip-stick and scholar's gown; if I had been run over, it would have made a rum inquest. The little man looked bored; when I emerged from behind the draughty curtain, his expression became belligerent. I was wearing my gown back to front to form a black Grecian line across the collar-bone, the rest a sack reaching to my knees: below, bare feet. With lips cherub-red and hair in ringlets round the fillet of belt, I must now have resembled a slovenly Ganymede in mourning for his late Jove; but I only wanted a head-and-shoulders. He rattled lights and banged shutters; with my square toes perishing on lino clammy from twenty years below sea-level, I dazzled into the sneering camera. I did realize, as it gave an angry click, that this was not the Open Sesame into the Consular Service.

The head came out well – the shoulders burly, no doubt about it – and I ordered copies. Tante Jeanne wrote 'C'est quand même une jolie fille'; Miss Cooke ('Go-od gracious . . .') told me later that when she passed the photo on to J.M. he said, 'If he goes on like this the boy will go to the devil', while Dad wrote 'Your Mam is pleased with her bonny new daughter, now on the dresser between Uncle Jab and Auntie Sarah'. Finally Rowley Leigh. 'What a terrible wig,' he said, but did add that it might get me into a smoker.

Meanwhile, I was able to keep up the illusion of study by twice donning sub-fusc and walking down to the Examination Schools in white tie and mortar-board; I sat for the Heath Harrison and won it, then for the Goldsmith and won it. Neither had demanded special preparation, I was still gathering the fruits of Holywell labour. 'I now have £250 a year, I am rich!' 'My dear Son George, Your valuable present to hand, your Mother and I have put our heads together and she is to have a double-lense Glasses one to see *very* far and one *very* near, so when you come home again you will see her with a lot of Eyes on you. Your affec. R. and M. Wms.'

Then, suddenly, Willie's suggestion materialized; I was put

up for the Ouds and would go through in time for *Hamlet*. 'Dear Miss Cooke, I have been offered a most important part! No, no need for alarm – it is to be the prompter at the second matinée, I could hardly refuse . . .' I was in! The producer was Fagan himself, the Hamlet romantically handsome Gyles Isham, and the London Press was giving the project exhilarating space, 'Is Heir to Baronetcy Coming West-End Star?' The women's parts were taken by well-known London actresses, a custom which spread glamour and excitement as well as allowing students to co-operate with first-class professionals. Three years before, the excitement had overflowed banks; when an enterprising Antony had kidnapped his Cleopatra and married her, some dons felt that the co-operation had perhaps gone too far, the club was still complacently tingling with the romance of Cecil Ramage and Cathleen Nesbitt. I mentioned nothing of them to Miss Cooke. 'Mr Barrington-Ward advises me that Classical Mods would not be a practical switch, even if I knew Greek as well as I do French . . .'

Tuesday, a cryptic message from Willie, 'Doggins is out'. Doggins was old Doctor Counsell, a loved Oxford figure in cloak and eye-glass who for years had sat in the prompt-corner of Ouds productions happily holding the book, open at the wrong page, dreamily appreciative of all he watched. Pressure of work had cut him out of the whole week; and I was to report at seven, curtain up at eight. Tonight. The first night.

It was as if I had been offered a leading part which I already knew : there was all the excitement and none of the apprehension. A sandwich in the J.C.R. – 'hello Byam Shaw, odd time to be eating but I'm due at the New stage-door, bit of a crisis!' – and I hurried off, past the lighted front of the theatre, to the little long-forbidden door. I found myself straight on the stage, in the shadow of a great cyclorama and under a glaring working light; workmen hammering, stage-hands sweeping, young men in shirt-sleeves and plus-fours dusting cardboard goblets. I hung my gown on a nail and tiptoed to the stool in the prompt-corner, getting up when Lockhart-Smith the stage-manager hurried down – shirt-sleeves, plus-fours – with a Temple Shakespeare,

'Christ, it hasn't got the cuts ...' He stood with a blue pencil, consulting his own copy – pages gummed on to a foolscap volume with hundreds of notes and diagrams on each – and swiftly excising from mine. When people ran up to him he was 'Ken' to them all, but as sternly composed as a sea-captain of fifty, 'There's an extra gelatine on the O.P. side, but tell Bobbie or Greville to pop over to the club and ask J.B. first.' The Christian names scattered like sparks, 'Reggie, have you tested the warning light under the stage – and Frank, check that the Ophelia mad wig is back and tell Bert I want a word with him about that bloody awful make-up he put on Patrick, J.P. said it turned Osric into something out of the Insect Play.' Then, to me, 'Williams – is that right – the one thing, Williams, you must do as a prompter is – *don't prompt*, unless there's a dead emergency, which you'll soon spot if you've done some acting, Willie says you have.'

He left me with my Temple; by craning I could see into the wings, otherwise my view was of three-quarters of the acting area. Lights were being turned off; the soft tread of many people passing upstage, whispered good-lucks in the shadows. My corner was two feet from the red plush curtain at which I had stared longingly from the pit, and I could hear the audience drifting in; as the activity near me simmered to orderly twilight, so out there the murmur feverishly grew. Suddenly there was the orchestra – playing Byrd, I found later – and our side of the curtain was a lilting pool of confident promise. Applause; then I guessed, from the multiple chatter swiftly fading out into silence, that the house-lights had dimmed. The curtain still down, the lights on stage came up slow and sure on the haunted battlements. Miles away in the Elsinore air, a great bell boomed the ominous twelve of midnight; then, two feet from me, with an imperious sweep, the curtain rose. From the upper darkness, a voice. 'Who's there?'

The first sight of Hamlet seated apart, six feet from me, black of hair and dress and mien, took my prompting breath away, so it was as well that he knew lines which he spoke with a moving simplicity. The scene with the Ghost, green-armoured and thrillingly resonant, ending on the steps in a slow icy dawn over the battlements, grew on me with each performance. Tirelessly I studied the professional Gertrude and Ophelia, and although I was for the whole week under a spell, I never missed one effect they made, one move or one pause, and every time waited for each one so as to mark its apparent spontaneity – as on 'Get thee to a nunnery', when Ophelia turned, unbelieving, and slowly put her hands to her face ... I was learning. The spell worked all-powerfully, because what I experienced was unique : not having attended one rehearsal, and not once – through five nights and three matinées – seeing one actor out of make-up and costume, I stayed under a continuous illusion and yet an integral part of that illusion.

I was at a play, and in it. Fortinbras would stand two feet from me, I could see the pulse beat in his neck, smell the musty scent of the costume, the tang of spirit-gum – then he was on, 'Where is this sight? ... This quarry cries on havoc ...' As for the Ghost – the only character I would have been shocked to find next to me – I was in luck : it appeared and disappeared on the other side, and I never once saw it out of its weird light. Rosencrantz and Guildenstern would creep up behind me for their entrance – by Thursday I was waiting for them, as with dreamlike inevitability they would form out of the darkness, dabbing at a beard, twitching at the crutch of a doublet – but even at these moments (almost more) they eluded me completely – and yet I can touch them! Not once did I wonder which colleges they belonged to, who they were. And in the interval, stretching my numbed neck in the wings – hark to the safety curtain, 'For Thine Especial Safety, *Hamlet*' – I would have rebuffed any know-all of a stage-hand informing me that impassioned snub-nosed Laertes – A. Tandy (Magd.) – is the spit of his little sister Jessie who is going on the stage, or that Osric the butterfly is the Hon. J. P. D. Balfour (Magd.) and the future Lord Kinross, or that the First Gravedigger, J. R. Sutro (Trin.) is going into films, Horatio, G. A. Gardiner (Magd.) into law and the Player King, R. W. Speaight (Linc.) and a Messenger, J. W.

Counsell (Exeter) into the theatre. I wanted nothing of reality to impinge on a timeless time of trance and romance.

Outside the theatre, I lived a shadow among shadows, for the only students I knew were from Wittenberg: my room a chimera, my bed a kip between one Elsinore and the next. It was only when I sank into my corner and heard the orchestra climb and climb to 'House Out', that the people I knew – Bernardo, Francisco – swam into flesh-and-blood focus. Life began, for me, on the stroke of stage midnight. Wednesday, one p.m., sitting in the J.C.R. with coffee, sandwich and *Daily Mail* – 'he was a boyish Hamlet' – I looked round at two blazered men accoutred for the river and thought, if only I could wear something that told the world I have a matinée! A pair of gold-laced Greek buskins? a make-up towel negligently round the neck? I looked at the clock and left for Denmark.

Saturday night I ate in Hall, in my dinner-jacket. The width of the lapel and my Edwardian pumps were off-set by my being able to remark that after my performance I had the Ouds Supper, in the Town Hall; even without my new wealth, I would have paid the astronomical price. The long and merry night – special permission – was doubly entrancing, for not only was Fagan there with his regal wife Mary Grey and the Playhouse company in the flesh, but I was identifying, from *Hamlet*, players whom I had watched for over thirty hours; it was strange to see the raven-haired organ-toned Prince as a blond stripling with high boyish notes. Sipping my champagne and tweaking my black tie, I made friends with a high-spirited youth who turned out, incredibly, to be the Ghost. The banquet was long and hilarious, with speeches and programme-signing (enviously I saw 'With admiration Lila', 'God bless, Tim', 'Love Gyles') folowed by the Ouds custom of 'toys', the cheaper the better, with attached a single punning line from the recipient's part, to be passed up and down with whoops of laughter; opposite me, the Second Gravedigger was brought a mangled celluloid doll, with a label 'The crowner hath sat on her'. It was the custom to stay up all night, the favoured ones finishing up at Doggins' house, 37 the Broad, for story-telling and tipsy turns and even breakfast; but I knew I was too unfledged to tag on to this, and went sighing home. A bewitched and irrevocable week was over.

Toggers, the big end-of-Feb boat-race, was not enough to click me back into life: I stood for two minutes in a chilled crowd barking out 'House – House – House' and stole away. After the House victory, the Bump Supper in Hall, sconce after sconce; after that, a dozen flushed black-tied rowing gods and their pot-valiant followers stood over Mercury – an honoured custom – and fumbled with buttons in order to siphon ill-assorted drinks into the fountain, but all sheepishly cupping an oar-chapped hand over what – tonight of all nights, surely – could have been flaunted as Head of the River.

Hamlet must now be erased, for a four-week battle against lost time before my Pass Schools; my Italian had weakened and I had to buckle down. I realized that the smoker was out of the question, but several evenings after Hall, sick of swotting, I would walk up the Corn past the invisible townees, down George Street, past the toy-shop and up the stairs to the Ouds. In at the swinging door, plonk umbrella, hang gown and scarf, give weary look at notice-board, glance at letters on the green baize to make sure those bores haven't tracked one down, then saunter into smoking-room. The feel of it was enough to give the form, either there were one or two dominant souls presiding plus-foured on the high shabby-leathered fender, knocking out pipes on the mantelpiece and toasting in liqueurs the closed circle of arm-chairs – 'cheers Clive Bobbie Pat Michael' – or it was a dead loss, a couple of dim aspirants like oneself humbly turning the pages of *Variety* to read how many dollars *Abie's Irish Rose* had just played to in Mamaroneck. Nothing in between.

On the good nights one did not attempt even a side-seat, one oozed into the back room to lean over *La Vie Parisienne* as if seeking a telephone-number. For one was eavesdropping, against the faint background, like a perfume, of Dick Addinsell at the rehearsal piano in the dining-room. I could hear Tandy's high clear voice, then the tap of Ken Lockhart-Smith's feet as Jack Buchanan. But eavesdropping was better than nothing. 'Rowley Patsy Monty Chris, benedictine? Peacroft, five, and would you put a call through to the Queen's stage-door, Miss Compton's room?' (*The Little Minister*.)

Then an aimless walk over to the *Hamlet* photographs, newly framed. Voices were being raised. 'Yes, but stage realism quã realism' – 'Ah but what about Freud's "Technique of Wit" ' – I longed for Noël Coward to breeze in and blow us all away. It was ten-thirty and I must get back to Carducci. A last blasé look at the letter-board as I gowned and brollied myself; on the landing, I stopped to catch the music – 'Love is Romantic, Should not be Pedantic, Please Rem-e-mber, da da da *da* . . .' – and hurried down, anonymous, into the night. Walking, I felt the weariness of the demoralized: of my own free will, I had spent an hour overhearing the prattle of the stage-struck. Did I not even belong in the Ouds?

Work proceeded in spasms, and term ended with white tie and mortar-board for Pass Schools. But this time I was rattling uneasily over the thin ice of guesswork, and emerged with a dread of disappointing Miss Cooke with what would be a palpable reverse. I had to hang about for my viva, and even the promise of France was swamped by four days in wet windy Oxford, vacated indeed. I wandered like a ghost in a ghost town, returning ravenous to open one of Mrs Tyrer's tins; too dejected to get out a plate, I would spoon out peaches and let the juice dribble on to the bare table. In the small dead hours I was awakened by the scrabbling of mice trying to allay their own holiday pangs. The third night, after coffee in an empty J.C.R., I climbed my stair like a half-drowned waif, settled by the fire under my beam, opened a note-book and wrote, desperately, 'A PLAY BY GEORGE WILLIAMS'. I looked at my name as if for the first time, thought how dull it looked, put a wavy E after the George, then vaguely started to scribble.

I should here tell how I wrote, at a sitting, the success the world now knows as *Sinner in the Sun*: I completed two pages. The Riviera, heat through shutters, daughter asleep middle of the afternoon, ex-courtesan mother rousing her to receive visitor, both late at the Casino the night before. Cynical dialogue ('My dear Chloe, there are only two ways to treat men, walk past them or over them') and from the daughter a tense outburst ('All I want is peace and a bird singing for *itself* and not to get something out of me – mother *please*, I shall go mad ...') but this wobbling jelly of three plays I had heard of – *Mrs Warren's Profession, Our Betters* and *Rain* – was never to set. Like Coleridge I was interrupted, by the ghost of Hamlet's father, and nobody was ever so ready to be haunted. R. Newlands (Oriel) had a viva too, he had been to variety at the New and walked out – 'putrid, a disgrace to the English theatre' – and was followed by a fair handsome boy whom he introduced as Walter Bendix, a Canadian actor. The world was changed.

I made chicory-coffee over my methylated burner – grounds floating as usual – and opened a tin : they sat before the fire eating preserved pears, off plates. 'Have a biscuit, Newlands,' I said. 'Oh crikey,' he said, 'call me Roy, Walter here does, and it's terribly Ouds.' I felt snug from head to foot. 'What are you writing, a thesis?' 'No,' I said, 'a play.' 'George E. Williams, mmm ...' 'Not a very exciting name,' I said, 'for the stage.' 'Are you going on the stage too?' the Canadian asked politely. 'Yes indeed,' I said, as if I had been answering the question for years. 'I like the way you say "Yes indeed",' said Roy. 'Do I?' I said, surprised. Walter said, 'Is it a Welsh-ism?' 'Yes indeed, it must be,' I said, without thinking. We laughed, I decided to watch it, but to use it when useful. 'What does the E stand for?' 'My father,' I explained, 'having started me off grand with "George", after the King, thought he'd bring me down to Welsh earth with "Emlyn".' 'Emlyn?' said Roy, 'that's not a bad stage name.' The Canadian said, 'May I take a cookie, Emlyn?' 'Sure,' I said, like Evvers, and we laughed. I asked about Toronto, he had played Marchbanks in stock, and Romeo. Here in my room was a real actor, worth more to me than all the Ouds put together, with the magnetic reticence of the true professional. I walked with them; Walter and I left the ghost of Hamlet's father at the gate of Oriel, then I walked Walter to the

Randolph. 'Good night, Emlyn.' I went to bed, christened. The steady Canadian eyes, and the slow smile from teeth as clean as the Rockies, warmed the vacation dark; I forgot the mice. He had once, looking into the fire, laughed quietly, then bent down and leisurely tied a shoelace. I was asleep.

Next morning I was interrupted by a note from Roy. 'Dear Emelyn,' (careless) 'Can you come to tea, Walter has had to go to London and then home and scnt regards.' I never saw Walter again.

At my viva, I parried several blank questions from the blank authorities, queued up to leave one-and-six with the porter to wire the Wilton Hotel either 'Passed' or 'Ploughed', and arrived in London heavy of heart. In the three years since I had last seen the Victoria Palace – 'Harry Tate and the Palace Girls' – it seemed to have crept nearer to the hotel. I unpacked a clean collar, then thought, whether my Oxford career is skidding or not, I'm going to a theatre: the revue at the Duke of York's. After an uneasy dinner, I was diving into the revolving door when I was handed a brown envelope, 'Passed'.

As far as I can remember, I caught the eleven bus by flying down on to the open top from above; I came to earth in Trafalgar Square, walked up St Martin's Lane and got the last side-seat in the upper circle, for my first West End Show. I bought my programme, strolled into the bar, sweet sherry please, and turned the pages. *London Calling*: this is the title for me, I thought as I sipped my first extravagance. Noël Coward, the name seemed somehow to have become less of a liability ... I floated up to my seat, half intoxicated with relief, sherry and anticipation: the other half was quickly achieved by the overture. An ecstasy which in others might be evoked by Wagner was sparked in me by the lilting tunes of a revue; as I leant over and the piano and the violins and the 'cello all melted into 'Parisian Pierrot', the black beam in my attic melted into honey, my life filled with meaningful music, the overture was Dick Addinsell and Rowley Leigh and Willie Wiley and Faith Celli and John Jeel-good and Roy Newlands and the Marchbanks from Toronto who, before my fire, like Mercury had tied his shoelace, and like Mercury had flown. The curtain rose on twelve beautiful girls, my perfect evening was launched. Towards the end I thought tomorrow, expertly and without visible effort, they will go through this complicated thing twice, every laugh falling into place: this is the theatre – the application, to the exotic and seemingly unpredictable, of professional exactitude.

Next afternoon I paid twelve-and-six to sit in the half-empty stalls of the Playhouse to watch my first London play, Maugham's *The Camel's Back*. Then I took a train to Epsom to stay the night with A. S. N. Parker (B.N.C.); we had met sitting for the Travelling Scholarship, he had acquired one too, and in the beery glow of celebration had suggested we spend the vac in Paris. He was a stodgy Saxon with pale blue eyes, a permanent flush of uneasiness and a tooth-brush moustache; he looked as if he knew that if he laughed, the moustache would fall off. He met me at the station, stiffly affable. The visit was enlightening, for Parker was my first indication that not all Dad's top-notchers, even at the House, came from homes in Mayfair or the Shires. It had never occurred to me that even one or two of the high-powered Ouds personalities had been sent to public schools – whether Eton and Harrow or near-grammar – by ambitious lower middle-class parents. Parker, who in the J.C.R. had seemed to sip coffee against a family background of foxhounds and footmen, turned out to be the son of a Leatherhead solicitor; Mater was the daughter of a rich builder who had built for them a large comfortable bungalow named Brick-a-Brack, with a trim garden peopled by female elves whom I could not help grouping round Mercury on Bump Supper Night. When I realized that Mum and Dad, as they called each other, spoke an amended Cockney, I took to them fast. They called Parker Arthur, but to his grandmother, sitting wrapt with machinery clamped over her head, he was Art, 'Come on Art, give yer Gran a peck, mind me crystal-set, dear . . .'

Looking at Parker with new eyes, I recognized the reserve as social embarrassment, and the moustache as a misguided shot at distinction. People came in to tea. 'Christ Church isn't a college, Mater.' 'Sorry dear, pass the little serviettes, aren't they twee?' I, who had imagined myself arriving at a household unobtrusively kind to a visitor from a humbler walk, found I was Art's rather grand friend in the Dramatic Society – '*Hamlet*, we read about that, didn't we, Mum?' – with an unfamiliar background, 'Brought up in *Welsh*, fancy ...' Parker was fond of Gran, and when I told him how many trades Dad had been jack of, and about Auntie Polly Tickle, his moustache almost softened. I must call him by his first name. Art? No ...

It was a rough crossing; we sat inside hugging a brandy and looking greyly sophisticated, but by the train all was well. Heated by wine at lunch, I confided that I was a virgin and so drew out, from under Art's moustache and past the pipe clenched like a lifeline, that he was too; we vowed that on our first night in Paris, whether our benefactor would have approved or not, Mr Heath Harrison's two Travelling Scholars were going to have a woman. We drove to the place des Vosges, to a pension which turned out to be a crazy hostel overflowing with English schoolgirls; just for tonight we would have beds made up in the passage – 'vous êtes jeunes et forts – pour *une* nuit!' – and tomorrow the litle hotel round the corner, meals avec nous. But we had our keys, got into dinner-jackets, and dashed off by Métro to the Folies Bergère. This trip, the Comédie Française could wait.

En Pleine Folie! 'Front seats old boy, essential ...' The two fauteuils au troisième rang ('on voit bien?' 'Monsieur, tout ...') were beyond our means, but the call of the blood had sounded. We crossed to a bar in the rue Richer for an out-for-the-evening cognac. My hand in my pocket after the second one – 'no Arthur this is mine' – I fetched out a sealed letter addressed to 'Mr and Mrs R. Williams, 314a High Street'. It looked so unfamiliar that I stared, then put it back, must post it ... My wrong-end-of-the-telescope picture of our kitchen fuzzed into the melancholy barman reading the *Petit Parisien*. Pauvre vieux, to be at an age where one might as well be paralysed from the waist down, must be a good forty ... Hot pants, old Evvers avait raison; paying, I suddenly wished it was him opposite me, 'Merci monsieur, voici quelque chose pour vous ...' We crossed into a seething foyer, sank like light-headed plutocrats into our fauteuils – 'Williams, where's the ruddy book of the words?' – and the orchestra struck up into a million erotic flash-bulbs of jazz: 'Bluin' the Blues', 'Vamping Rose', 'Russian Rag', 'Whose Baby are You?' ... The Travelling Scholars had arrived. The curtain rose on twelve near-naked negroes locked in jungle ecstasy. Parker lit his pipe and scrutinized them as if we were at Twickenham watching unorthodox Rugger, but I could not be bothered with him. The spectacle was sumptuous, the costumes opulent, the ragtime dancing brilliant, but we were waiting for les Nues.

On they came, proud hands on bare hips, down a flight of crystal stairs as if descending under warm water, long lazy paces to a caressing tango solo which described each as a jewel, the Beryl, the Ruby, the Diamond; each was marked by a head-dress a yard tall, which was all they wore except for high-heeled shoes and an inch-wide gold tassel slung across the middle. One alabaster goddess followed another, as if roused from some shameless alcove: unbelievable white, flushed here and there with pink. I thought, these are not girls, they are inscrutable women who carry their nakedness with a panache of maddening indifference: wide rolling haunches, insolent navel – 'birth? We were never born, and will never die' – and mocking pouter breasts which at each deliberate step shivered firm-soft. Having reached the footlights, they wheeled slowly outward – quick up-thrust in silhouette – and paced one after the other on to the joy-plank circling the orchestra, with a look which said 'I move to the music, mes enfants, but only because tonight I feel like it.' As they passed a foot above us, eyes drowsing down and through us, one could follow, above the gold tassel, Venus's smooth and gentle swell. Parker's pipe had gone out.

Then they went. Half of me knew they were in soiled peignoirs elbowing through stage-hands to rattle upstairs for a change of head-dress; but my other half relegated them to the alcoves, to les vices sans nom. It was the entr'acte. Art, darkly flushed, put away the pipe and we sauntered into the Promenoir, where les petites femmes were buzzing like Spanish flies, all riggish fur and plump shining black, with baby squeals as feather-light as their eyelids were heavy with mascara and sin. 'Look,' said Parker, sipping beer, 'at those two –' But those two were upon us, 'Tu nous offres quelque chose, chéri?' One blonde, one brune, mature without being – even to us – old, and a wave of perfume sweeping us into a shameless public intimacy, 'Oh les beaux jeunes gens!' But the two British boulevardiers had reverted into tongue-tied schoolboys; if this had been a viva we should both have been ploughed on the spot. La Brune was tapping Parker's perspiring cheek as if about to pick off his moustache and eat it as a friandise. We parried suggestions; la Blonde put out a knee and wiggled it roguishly between mine, at the same time pursing her lips into kissing noises, half joking half professional. As we returned to our fauteuils, 'Know what mine did,' said Parker ponderously, straightening his bow-tie, 'got hold of me, a bit swift I thought.' I longed again for Evvers.

At the end, after a scene in Notre Dame Cathedral in which the same negroes, gleaming-nude, masked and jock-strapped, leapt up through belching traps and slowly, to the music of 'Firebird', proceeded to strip twenty convent novices and beat them with red-hot whips, Art and I emerged in no mood to go home. 'Get thee to a nunnery,' I said to him, and felt pleased with myself. There they were, on the trottoir – 'Ah nos amis Angliche!' 'Eh bien,' blurted Parker, down to brass tacks with a rhyming thud, '*com*bien?' But the answer was as direct. 'Deux cent chacun,' they said together, word-perfect. Art and I looked at each other, two pounds ten each, you could buy a portable gramophone ... But the nuns had done their work. 'C'est tout compris?' I asked, then felt like adding 'le service, tout?' 'Oh oui chéri, allons-y ...' 'Come to the rear,' I muttered; we excused ourselves, and as we stood in the Messieurs trying to feel natural two feet from a venerable old lady, chair-ridden and in deep mourning, 'They're stinging us,' I said, Stock Exchange realistic, 'we shouldn't be in dinner-jackets, what d'you say?' 'Let's give it a try,' said my partner, 'will you have the spondulicks ready?' He gave me his two hundred, I put it away, we rejoined them, 'Allons-y!' We followed jauntily down a side-street into a little hôtel particulier with mirrored hall and a chandelier; first floor, a luxurious room with shaded lamps, two evil black-satin divans, mirrors again, a tiger-skin rug – Elinor Glyn – false flowers, sprawling dolls of indeterminate sex – Parisian Pierrot – and a bidet. 'Ah,' they said, both together, and both together casting off their furs and lying back, each on a divan, 'alors?' La Blonde drew me next to her, and la Brune drew Art next to her; Brick-a-Brack seemed far away. They kissed us repectively and thoroughly.

But neither of us was able to concentrate. 'Eh bien,' purred la Blonde, 'on se déshabille?' Le Brune teased Parker's tie undone and embarked mechanically on the next blandishment. He clapped his knees together and looked about to burst. 'I say, Williams,' he muttered, 'this is a bit off, isn't it?' 'Tous ensemble?' I asked them. 'N'y a plus de chambres,' they piped, 'mais vous êtes amis!' 'Oui,' said Parker, 'mais ce n'est pas comme il faut.' I thought of Tante Jeanne and nearly joined in what James Agate would have described as the cacophonous fou-rire of ces dames. 'Ah,' said la Blonde, 'j'ai une idée!' She rose, tottered past the bidet, one professional breast half out of its black satin, and tittupped a screen twice her size into the middle of the room between the two divans. Again I thought of Tante Jeanne, then looked desperately at Parker; a purple Parisian night was degenerating into a sketch at the Coliseum. 'Alors,' twittered la Brune, 'd'abord les affaires, hein?' I thought, my God it's mercenary, but if it was old Hot Pants the Second, I wouldn't mind the sharing at all. I produced the four hundred francs. 'Et pour la chambre, chéri?' I looked at Art, and tightened, 'Mais tout est compris?' 'Mais chéri,' – a new and sickening note of wheedle – 'tout, ça veut dire qu'on *fera* tout, on va s'amuser mes infants – mais la chambre, c'est cent francs ...' Another pound for the room! My mother's spirit, whether it liked doing it or not, suddenly shot me to my feet, and with me Parker. 'Merci, bon soir.'

The effect was instantaneous: before the word 'merci', two simpering sirens had changed into a brace of coal-eyed viragoes screaming abuse. I took out a hundred-franc note and placed it, on the spur of the furious moment, in the bidet. Parker preceded me to the door, turned, said icily, 'Mesdames, je répète, ce n'est pas comme il faut,' bowed with deep dignity from the waist – a rash gesture, for his fly was undone as well as his tie – and stalked out. I followed. Not that ces dames, through this, had stood crushed and silent; a barrage of execration still spattered us in the street. 'Christ,' muttered Parker, adjusting his dress, 'they ought to be ashamed of themselves.' We had a broody drink. I felt something in my pocket: my crumpled letter home. I posted it, we descended into the Métro, and in the train I sat calculating. 'As one roué to another,' I said as we got out at Saint-Paul, 'do you realize that we could have had ninety-eight such journeys for what we just paid for one French kiss?' The dozen British schoolgirls were asleep, and safe as council houses from two dejected libertines.

Chapter 21

Love's Labour's Lost, and Won

'Dear Miss Cooke, Paris is rewarding, much to see and to tie up with study.' Parker and I had both tried, but we were not meant to be friends : next day, we were disconcerted to find that in the hotel round the corner we were to share a double bed. The only thing we had in common, French, only split us. If it had been Evvers, I should have been flattered to act as interpreter, but I was priggishly irritated by Parker's stolid refusal to work on his accent; as he stammered and wuffled, I had to set my teeth to avoid helping him out. I was not old enough to have either the patience to go on breaking ice which kept freezing up, or the decision to move. We only met at meals and in bed, like a ridiculous married couple hardly on speaking terms; Christian names died by the wayside, 'I say Williams puff puff, is this Lucien Guitry actor-chap puff puff, up to scratch?' A pity, for in him I might have made a good friend on whom I could have leaned : he was certainly solid, as good as dull gold. We travelled to Oxford on different trains, I smuggling back a bottle of eau-de-Cologne for Miss Cooke and a box of lace handkerchiefs for his Mum, a conscience gift. I should have gone to Paris alone, rooming in Montmartre and roaming in Montparnesse.

The summer term brought bland weather and fresh hopes. The Ouds play was not yet, but the club was my first call : *Love's Labour's Lost*, auditions 20 May. My love's labour (lost) would be to lose a Welsh accent in three weeks. 'Dear Miss Cooke, My tutor suggests I now aim at Honours in French, end of my third year, then the same in Italian or History end of a fourth (extra) year.' This meant, as I and Miss Cooke knew, that

323

my tacit objective would be the trophy which dangles, glittering and out of most reaches, at the apex of the academic tree: the Double First.

But I had hopes more immediate, which met two rebuffs, both gentle but definite. The first was my call on Harold Acton in his lemon room, after I had submitted my Holywell poems to him as editor of *Oxford Poetry* 1924. No manuscript was ever turned down with more exquisite tact; under the monochromes and Victorian glass and the hanging megaphone, I was wafted on to the antimacassars and sighingly assured that while my work was polished like a jew-el, what he was seeking was the inarticulate soul-gropings of the undergraduate wasn't it horr-id of him and could he press me to a white la-dy? I left glowing with rejection.

The second set-back left more of a mark. I was just beginning to separate the Ouds members who inspired respect and affection by being their own self and sure of that self, from the pathetic souls who ingratiatingly asked a Committee man to lunch and in the same breath implied it was cheek to approach him. I would emulate the former: quiet and strong. I was, I thought, finding my feet.

One morning I was debating, was it to be a lecture on Romance Vowel-Changes or coffee at the Super? (the lounge of the new cinema, just becoming the eleven a.m. black hole of chic Oxford), when Tim Abady walked in, my House sponsor for the Ouds. I knew he liked me; he wore benevolent glasses and smoked a pipe, but not like Parker. His call was a delightful surprise, but the glasses had a gleam of uneasy cheer. 'Sorry to do this, and please for God's sake – may I sit down – don't take it to heart, but a couple of people – sorry, have you a light ...' – God in Heaven, what can it be – 'it's only,' he continued kindly, 'that a couple of people have noticed that you are tending to – er – call people by their Christian names a bit more than is warranted quite so early – see what I mean – I know you don't mean it ...' Poor Tim, it was an awkward errand – lord, had I called him Tim when he came in, I couldn't remember ... I explained, distressed and hot, 'I've been so careful – made a point, for instance, of not calling Isham Gyles to his face, but it isn't easy as isn't everybody Bobbie and Clive and Gerald behind their backs, and even the stage-hands called Ken Ken, and you see I was at a school where Christian names are used, could you explain to whoever complained ...' As he left he reassured me, but it was a club snub, the more unnerving because I could not recall having consciously offended. What positive proof could I give that I had mended my ways, short of distributing surnames like leaflets? 'Lovely day Tennyson d'Eyncourt, how are *you* Downs-Butcher?' – who in hell would note approvingly that I was fighting shy of Christian names? It was my first and last brush with public-school punctilio.

I sat in the J.C.R., crushed over *Punch*. 'I've never found it amusing either,' said a flat voice: I looked up and saw Auntie Soph as an undergraduate, a large white clown-serious face surmounted by a fringe, with a Scots accent which, I was to notice, stayed carefully in trim. 'Do ye not think,' he said earnestly, 'that it would enliven *Punch* if they had a por-r-nographic section?' Through Oxford I was to be leisurely friends with Angus Rae. I went back for coffee in his Meadow rooms, light from tall windows overlooking trees. I told him about my setback. 'It's a pompous wor-r-ld,' he sighed, 'my lover-r's pompous, milk?' 'Your what?' 'Wrigley,' he said, 'he's at Teddy Hall, and verra mudy:' I plied him. 'Sublimated really, we sit and listen to *The Immortal Hour* together. We have dr-readful tiffs, if his poems aren't going right he doesn't utter-r for days. I suggested the New Theatre on Thur-rsday but it did no gude, he never spoke, sugar?' It seemed a joyless troth. And I could not see how he had thought Phyllis Dare in *The Street Singer* was going to help.

I felt better, and went off to a Play-Reading Circle Roy Newlands had started in his college. My part was 'A Tramp', so I was able to listen to the play; though I was puzzled by much of it, it left an echo like a tune imperfectly caught, which might have been more insistent if Roy's supporting cast had not been earnest wooden-voiced Oriel men. It was *The Cherry Orchard*.

*

Awaiting *Love's Labour*, I saw Oxford soften and languish; the Meadows steamed themselves dry, and clouded over with the green of willows. I watched punts, laden with set-books and His Master's Voice, slide dreamily into backwaters of study; muscles were flexed and loins ungirt for the safe cleaving of icy Parson's Pleasure, and for the not-so-safe lolling in the sly-kissing sun. Coming back from an immoral afternoon in the Electra, Carmel Myers in *Cheated Love*, I switched on the light next to my beam : it was darker than ever in the summer, for the sun seldom penetrated. Under the pink beaded shade, melancholy closed ever my head like a pressed eiderdown. Next term, when Angus moves into digs I'll move into his Meadow rooms, I don't care what they cost ...

But rehearsals lifted me, with ease. Like everybody else I had read for Biron the hero – 'a lover's eyes will gaze an eagle blind ...' – and had been cast for Dull, the constable; but I soon recognized it as a rewarding small part. The play was mapped out in the club dining-room, then we moved to the sylvan setting of Wadham College Gardens, from which I felt impelled to send a card to Wadham Road Bootle. Again it was inspiring to work under a professional, H. K. Ayliff, Costard was played by Willie (I mean Wiley, I was to be shy of first names for some time) a natural droll from whom I was able to learn, Isham's sister Virginia was Jacquenetta, and we enjoyed working together as the trio of rustics. I would walk back from afternoon rehearsal hot and dusty, take off all my clothes, run dressing-gowned into Tom for a cold shower, and then put on a fresh toilette for Hall dinner – 'amusing play to be in, though palpably early stuff, poetry on the precious side' – and then back to the fairy-tale evening. One of my rare lunch-times in the J.C.R., among the *Tatler* photographs and gossip ('... after her serious triumphs Miss Hermione Baddeley in the new *Punch-Bowl* revue proves that she has not forgotten how to be gay, Miss Molly O'Shann is one of the Athos Beauties in the Princes' Cabaret, rumours of the Countess of Seafield's engagement to Prince Nicholas are unfounded ...') my eyes lit up at the item 'Miss Veronica Turleigh and Miss Bertha Philips have been released by Mr J. B. Fagan to appear with the O.U.D.S.' They arrived that evening to rehearse, with charm and humour, before one flawlessly setting sun after·another. 'Dear Miss Cooke, Waiting for my cue under a tree I am reading Ronsard, this morning I worked on *Le Contrat Social*, not a free moment! As well as to Robey and Mistinguett, does your antipathy to actors extend to Irving and Duse?' The days went by like water.

Instead of *Le Contrat Social*, I should have been studying the New Testament: two days before the play, I sat for Divvers – Divinity, or 'Holy Scripture' – a routine side-exam based on the yellowing idea that an Oxford graduate must have a solid religious training, the solidity to be proved by sitting for three hours answering such questions about the Gospels and the Acts as 'How do John and Luke differ about the status of Peter?' Treated by all as a chore and a bore, it had to be got through. Remembering that I had traversed the territory in Welsh every Sunday of my early life, and forgetting that I had observed none of it, I gave the matter three irritated mornings; but on the day, my white tie and mortar-board,·and the set faces, reminded me that this was an exam as searching as any other. It searched me in vain : I bluffed, and was ploughed.

'Everybody fails the first time, a matter of pride,' and the dressing-tents were going up behind the trees. 'Bert' arrived from Clarkson's in London, with costumes and wigs, and made us all up; the scent of flowers and trodden grass mingled with the smell of hot canvas and grease-paint and moth-balls. A telegram, my first, 'Good luck Emlyn yes indeed Roy,' and *The Green Hat*, just published, from Virginia. The weather held (how could it not?) and the sun-drenched opening matinée – in the front row Gilbert Murray, Lillah McCarthy and John Masefield – was followed by exquisite evening, the play melting into the bosky sunset and taking on an elegiac colour which may not have belonged but was very beautiful. Monday brought my first newspaper notice, Ivor Brown in the *Manchester Guardian*, 'Mr Williams made a small part large by a rich suggestion of the well-intentioned lackwit hopelessly at odds with a world of scholars'; I knew Miss Cooke would see it, so my cutting went to 314a. I even acquired personality at the scholars' table, 'Williams – top-hole actress the Turleigh woman, what's she like close to?'

Up to the crest of the summer wave; then, avoiding the temptations of Commem Week, such as the Ouds Ball with Hugo Rignold and his Wideawakes, down for three weeks into the trough of 314a, before France for the rest of my Heath Harrison travelling. But the time was as full as it could be in the Quay, for my Italian tutor, euphonious Arundell del Re, had been commissioned to turn into English Solmi's *The Making of Modern Italy*, and had asked me to translate the second half for him, for five guineas. I jumped at it – a hundred and twenty pages of print, a first-rate exercise both for my Italian and my English. Holywell was still in term and tinged with melancholy, for J.M. had died earlier in the year; tea at Underwood, how serious Willie was and how worthy Mr Ayliff, how good the play had been for my English. I tried to amuse about Parker's moustache, but instinctively played down the bungalow and Gran, 'See here George, are you turning into an Oxford swank?' I mentioned – an amused man of the world – the Folies Bergère. Assuming that every youth plays a part in front of his family, Miss Cooke was paying the price for becoming one of my loved ones.

July, I was off; I went up to Oxford by train, taking my bicycle, to leave extra belongings for next term and collect travellers' cheques. I put up at the House, exactly a year – a year! – after my first visit, the same somnolent Long-Vac Oxford. Had it lost its magic? Some of it had flaked off ... Next glorious morning, early, I got astride my bicycle at Tom Gate and set off with a light heart; it was my plan to cycle to Southampton, and then from Le Havre to Haute Savoie. I wore flannel trousers and an open shirt, my luggage a mackintosh strapped on the back and a knapsack on the handle-bars: four pairs of socks, three shirts, shaving kit, and to complete the picture of the Scholar Gipsy on wheels, a pocket *Iliad*. I saw myself – inn after inn – studying a page before falling asleep, when a New Testament would have been more to the point. The lush country was at its best – Abingdon, Newbury, Winchester – and I was independent. I reached Southampton in the late afternoon, a clean-limbed racing cyclist, found a cheap room, washed my socks and ate fish and chips. But by next mid-day, treadmilling leisurely through Normandy villages, the boy scout had relapsed; the French sun was high and bold, I was eighteen, and behind my stolid pedalling face I day-dreamed of arriving at a tiny auberge, only one room to let, run by a buxom russet-cheeked widow of thirty – no, twenty-eight – no, thirty – who presses me to wine for her feast-day. 'Oh que tu as chaud, mon p'tit – on se tutoie?' I am sponging down after the trip when I hear my door, I turn – 'mais regardez où vous allez, nom de Dieu!' I had run into the back of a cow.

Rouen, seen from the afternoon hills with the river and the Cathedral, evoked Madame Bovary; I descended at a cheap hotel in a popular quarter, hid most of my francs under my mattress, put on my béret and strolled out There was a statue of Corneille, I had forgotten he was born here. I ate, then came to a music-hall and settled in the queue, in the setting sun; in front waited two women, respectable, in summer dresses, one like my widow. Chatting, she raised an elbow to arrange her hat, and I observed in the armpit, touched by the soft evening light, a tuft of dark hair; she saw me look, but made no haste. I had never thought of this. The revue was a gay rowdy affair, but several times my mind went back to the woman who had lifted her arm so nonchalantly.

As I got back into my room the lights fused, and I lit a candle. It was stickily hot and still; I sluiced myself. Standing in the basin, I suddenly saw with a start, three yards away, a naked male figure, one leg bent, one thigh turned towards me, eyes fiercely on mine as if to say 'Eh bien?' By the light of the one candle, sunburnt face against the cave-dark background, he looked, except for the whiteness of his body, like one of those sullen strapping shepherds in Italian paintings. I stared back, boldly; in the first long mirror I had ever been alone with, I was studying myself. 'Eh bien,' I said aloud, 'you're going out

329

tonight.' The electric bulb clicked on, and the Renaissance masterpiece was no more.

But I went out. In the café-bar of the hotel, drinking a restless bock, I caught sight of a red pompon; a sailor stood chatting to the patronne. The three of us got into conversation; he was a Breton, his name was Yves, but he had never heard of *Pêcheur d'Islande* or le Pays de Galles, and was amazed when I spoke Welsh and he understood two words out of three. Four or five years older, he was a simple lad with curly peasant hair, strong square body and a plain face with an open look : quiet but not taciturn, slow but not stupid. I told him my father had been a marin too, but he was more impressed by my being an étudiant, 'On va boire un coup?' We issued forth into the hot night, and I told him I would like to 'voir des femmes'.

'Rien de plus facile, allons-y, George!' I set my béret at an angle, and followed his rolling gait round the corner into the rue des Cordeliers, a narrow ancient street running uphill between high gabled houses : there was concertina music, shaded lights in every door and the feel of hushed activity, like pubs out of hours. We were pirates seeking a night's lodging. Old women sat on stools in doorways, fanning themselves and calling to one another and to us; we went in past one of them, through a curtain, and into a garish room with a little bar and a concertina playing 'C'est mon Homme'. I saw two young men approaching, both French, both stocky, sailors, one in uniform and the other in a béret, both with the slow maritime roll. From the way they were coming at us, I thought they must know Yves, then I recognized them in the mirror that ran round the room. They were us. This was my night for reflections ... Two women were dancing together. They wore kimonos under which they were naked but for satin shorts and high heels. We sat and ordered deux fines which were served by a respectable patronne, in black and wearing steel-rimmed glasses.

Several customers sat around drinking, dock-labourers and merchant seamen; one stout jolly older man could have been the father of either of the girls, and as they danced past, one of them leant over and kissed him. It was all so relaxed that it felt like a dream of myself as a matelot français. The rhythms of the absent-minded concertina, genial and yet immensely sad, formed the perfect background. A young workman came down the stairs, combing his hair, and joined his companion, who said 'Alors?' The workman put up his thumb and sagged comically at the knees before sitting down, just as a plump pretty girl bounced humming down the stairs after him, pulling on her kimono, and bounced up to the counter. A second after a customer had put his arm round her, she suddenly bleated 'Orangeade!' and was so like an over-weight doll that it looked as if he had pressed a button in her back to make her squeak. She was coarse, but fresh as a milkmaid; it was impossible to believe that she had just been – the concertina sentimentalized my thought as I thought it – that she had just given herself to him, wantonly, for money. Should she not be crying into a pillow, ashamed and ravaged?

She saw Yves, recognized him like a relative, and pulled up a stool. Her kimono swung wide, but she paid no more attention than a typist with a mack over a coat and skirt. As we chatted to her, she talked like a typist too : oui, a medium day, not hectic, not tedious. 'This morning two clients – oui, some feel more in the mood then – and this afternoon two after the siesta, and just now that one over there, a purser, très gentil, bien élevé –' A man entered in a bowler hat, she ran across, kissed him, put on the bowler and waltzed round the room, the other girls screaming with laughter like children and clapping their hands. Rosine was the clown of the regiment.

The concertina trailed on, 'Je cherche après Titine' ... Yves was the ideal companion for me, without guile, yet wise; to him it was like sitting in a café, in two minds whether to order a bouteille, and for me, after months of watching others and myself being bogus men of the world, it was a breath of sordid fresh air. The lady in glasses brought two more brandies, which I paid for. 'Tu montes?' said Yves, nodding to the stairs. 'Je n'sais pas,' I said, glad of the 'tu', 'et toi?' He shrugged, he had been upstairs yesterday, with Rosine; we sat on. A girl in a mantilla sauntered in and sat haughtily into a corner. 'Oh là là!' said

Rosine as I danced with her in her bowler, 'elle fait la grande señora, she never smiles, she places her feet in the air as if they were two hands which must be kissed, but her clients love that!' She squeaked to the music, and I danced close to her, feeling almost as pleasantly professional as she was. The señora was approached by the older jolly man, put her cigarette out, and rose; he paid at the desk, and she stalked upstairs in front of him like a great hostess about to show a new butler his attic – 'oh celle-la!'

We were bidding bonne nuit to all when the jolly man, stripped to the waist, came downstairs for cigarettes and was quickly shooed up again by the shocked patronne, past the gaping kimonos of her charges : I was glad not to have missed that. When we left, it was well past midnight; Yves asked what the houses in England were like and was amazed to hear there were none. 'Mais c'est pas possible!' On the corner I confessed to him that I had never had a woman. He stopped and stared at me, 'Tu rigoles!' 'Non, je te jure ...' He lifted his cap and scratched his curly head, 'Mais à dix-huit ans c'est inouï, thou art *eighteen*!' I saw myself as an urchin who has just confessed that he has never been allowed a proper meal. 'Mais il faut absolument que tu ...' Two women walked round the corner; he stopped in his tracks and whistled, as if for an ambulance. The women laughed and moved on. 'Il est tard,' he explained, smacking his lips despairingly, 'why didst thou not say before, o-o-h ...' Two other women, another whistle, no luck; I began to feel important. A clock struck two, and we were deciding to postpone till the morrow, when – chut! We listened to running water, as from a tap left on; he drew me quickly on, and in the shadows of a shop-doorway we saw a bent figure. A woman emerged, tugging at her skirt, and walked away from us; stout, thirty, vigorous. Yves nudged me, we started after her. 'Elle fera?' I asked, my French slipping, 'elle est possible?' 'Une femme,' said Yves earnestly, taking my arm as if to deliver a Maxime of La Rochefoucauld, 'une femme qui pisse dans la rue fera n'importe quoi.'

I suddenly felt panic. 'Thou wilt not leave me behind with

her?' 'Non non,' he laughed, 'I will wait for thee, mon petit frère, fear not, attends ...' He hurried on and gave the ambulance-whistle. I saw her stop and turn : I heard his low man's voice, then hers higher, then his, then hers, then a stifled giggle – had he told her we had heard? – then a long 'o-o-o-oh.' ... A dog barked, a barge hooted; that low duet in the secret dark, furtive but matter-of-fact – the rumble of the man, the woman's fluted interruptions – was disturbing; I walked up and down. Yves rolled back down the deck of the street: 'difficile d'y aller à deux, question de la chambre ...' She called him back. I was confused, had he meant we should both – they were walking towards me together. 'George – Françoise, cuisinière au grand hôtel.' Françoise, la cuisinière! We shook hands – yes, not unlike, rose-cheeked, good teeth, a couple gold; ordinary, amiable, she walked between us as if she were shopping with friends.

We crossed a great square, an armoured girl frozen in the moonlight. 'Ah,' I said, 'Jeanne d'Arc!' 'Oui,' said Françoise the cook, as if discussing a spoilt steak, 'on l'a brûlée ici.' I noticed a bandage on her wrist : she told me she had been scalded in the hotel kitchen, 'Moi aussi on m'a brûlée! Ah, c'est pas pour rigoler, tu sais, le travail!' She led the way. It was comfortable, and even exciting, to recall that we had just heard her in the doorway. We turned up a cul-de-sac and stood outside dark shutters with a sign 'Chambre à Louer'. Yves showed me an alley to lurk in; they rang, were admitted, the door shut. I waited; just as I was thinking, he has let down his petit frère – the door opened, six inches, I slipped in and followed him down a passage into a bedroom faintly gas-lit, with a large double bed. 'Oh,' giggled Françoise, 'si elle savait que vous êtes deux ...' She put a comb through her hair; I could see under her arms. 'Alors,' said Yves to me, smiling easily, 'qu'est-ce qu'on va faire? Thou wishest alone?' 'Oh oui,' I said uncertainly. 'Then thou wilt be before me' – my state was evidently a priority concern – 'I explained to her so that she would relent.' He put his finger to his lips, left his cap on a chair and went out, closing the door softly behind him.

I took off my béret, placed it on his cap, and looked at Françoise. She was unfastening her blouse, humming a low tune; then she smiled, I caught the flash of a gold tooth. 'Alors mon petit, c'est la première fois?' 'Oui,' I said, then smiled and pulled my shirt over my head. 'Tant mieux,' she said, 'on se lave, hein?' White and strong and naked, fleshy as all of the unattainable canvas Junoes I had ever known, she poured water into the basin and as practical as a nurse, washed me and herself. Our shadows veered grotesquely round walls and ceiling. 'C'est froid, ça peut décourager ...' The water was indeed cold, but not discouraging, 'Ah tant mieux ...' It was a moment which all but the simplest-minded adolescent must face with doubts, and I felt at home; her action excited and at the same time relaxed, it was like being a sexual child with a nurse-mistress. Did some memory dredge up to the surface, of Annie innocently ministering? 'Que c'est bien, viens mon chou ...' It was as easy as falling off a log into four-leaved clover. And nearly as quick, but I was glad not to keep Yves waiting; I pulled on my trousers and opened the door. In the dark of the couloir, I saw the gleam of his eyes and the white of his teeth as he grinned and jerked up his thumb in inquiry. I jerked up my thumb and grinned back. I stepped out, he stepped in, I closed the door.

I could have tiptoed to the front door, but I stayed on the mat; I think they expected it. Her caresses were so fresh in my mind – shameless yet soft, abandoned yet composed, the cajoleries of a maternal libertine who was keeping her head – that it was odd to listen to her with him : where I, the willing novice, had stirred her heart, he was able, with the gentle brutality of a practised lover, to unleash the animal. For a long moment, from his hoarse muffled imprecations and her half-cries, I thought he meant her harm; but when they both subsided into long sobbing breaths, I knew all was well. There was the splashing of water, then he opened the door; they were both naked. She called out, softly, 'Alors mes enfants, il est tard, on s'endort?' She snuggled into the middle of the bed, Yves settled beside her on her left, I went round the foot, took off my trousers, and settled on her right. We were soon asleep.

I was awakened by the distant rattle of milk-pails and of hooves; swimming up into consciousness through the watery dawn light, I wondered where I was. There was in the air a warm agreeable smell; I turned my head and saw her next to me. I sat up on an elbow and looked at her. His dark head was towards us, hair tangled fiercely over his closed eyes, but lips gently open an inch from her shoulder. She too lay peacefully asleep, hair tumbled on the pillow, bed-clothes pushed away, cheek on hand, hand on other hand; she was snoring faintly. I could see the bandage on her wrist. But though her face was sideways she was on her back, knees even in sleep wantonly crooked; with superb impartiality one ample breast went his way, the other mine. I thought, I could lie here for ever, listening to the sounds of a waking town and watching these two asleep like dissolute children. Before last night, had they not been strangers to each other, as I had been to them? They were mine, for ever.

He stirred, opened his eyes and stretched. Then he sat on his elbow, yawned, winked at me, and saw the breast near to him; he put out his tongue and delicately, teasingly, brushed the tip. She caught her breath in sleep, murmured, and slowly woke. He said softly, without smiling, 'On s'amuse?' 'Hein?' then she realized where she was. 'Oh non,' she said, sitting suddenly up, 'le travail, mes enfants!' It was seven, and she was working at eight. We gave her the money for the room, and while she slipped upstairs to leave it for Madame, we tiptoed into the street and waited for her. 'C'était bien, hein?' She came down, we walked to the corner and stopped. 'Attention,' I said, pointing to her bandage, 'à l'eau chaude.' 'Surtout,' said Yves, 'ne t'asseois pas dans la rue, hein?' 'O-o-h, mal élevé ... Au revoir Yves, au revoir George!' She was gone. We went back for a café au lait outside our hotel, where the patronne, who had just turned out my room, handed me my francs from under the mattress with an amiable warning not to leave money 'in the places where the thief goes first'. Yves's laughter rang down the street. In the evening we returned to the maison of last night, and so as to feel independent of brother-help, while Yves sat

335

with his beer I went upstairs with Rosine; she was polite but markedly absent-minded. 'Je ne suis pas toujours gaie,' she said, 'tonight I am depressed.' Her sister was ill and her friend had left for Algiers for ever. She sat painted and moody, and I left filled with romantic pity for her and her kind. Next morning I set off on my bike, Yves waving me adieu.

At the corner of the rue des Cordeliers I dismounted, for a last look up the crooked sun-marked street; it was deserted except for a couple of tradespeople, but I could hear, faintly, the triste trailing rhythm of the concertina, 'Je cherche après Titine ...' Morning love was for sale. I pedalled on, once more the racing cyclist, bound for the Mont Saint Michel. Before déjeuner at a wayside café, feeling loftily sad and protective, I wrote to Rosine. 'Ma petite Rosine aimée, Thou wilt no doubt laugh and show this to the others, but it may be a comfort to feel that a stranger thinks of thee in that prison which encloses thee like a young bird ... Write me Poste Restante Thonon Haute Savoie, Thy friend of last night.' Then I remembered that this would hardly identify me, and added, 'The British one with the béret'. I never heard.

Chapter 22

Mirage

I cycled through Brittany, where I talked Welsh to the villagers, through Saumur – *Eugénie Grandet* – then Touraine and the Châteaux. Every evening I arrived, dusty and thirsty and filled with fresh air, at some chance café – 'vous avez une chambre?' – drank bottles of limonade gazeuse and fell into bed, dizzy with health. Homer was never opened, all I read was the local paper; continuously alone, I felt none of the Oxford pangs, chatted to many strangers, but no more adventures. By the time I reached Lyon my trousers were worn through and I bought a cheap suit with a belt. One beautiful evening, my bicycle in Thonon Station, I walked up the straight hill-road to Vallorce. Between the sun-flecked poplars, I recognized in the distance the slightly bandy walk as Tante Jeanne advanced to meet me. I was wearing the same béret, but ... as I bent to kiss her, I wondered if she could tell that I had had two women.

'Tu parles un français de diplomate, oh que c'est élégant ...' As we walked up the hill, the teasing was taken up where it had left off – 'mais ton costume est *moins* élégant, par exemple!' – but I had acquired a thin skin of assurance which she could not prick so deftly. We went on a trip; this time I paid for myself and more than once insisted on paying for her, 'de la part de Monsieur Heath Harrison', ending up at Dijon, where I would stay for a month of the University cours de vacances. We did not quarrel, but our relationship had nothing to feed on and starved to death. I saw her off, she looked sad, I looked sad. In an access of guilt I thought, I must give her something, rushed off and brought her a bunch of bananas : one of the most gauche farewell gifts ever proffered. As once before, the train drew me slowly away; but from her no tears, and as I sat back I could have prophesied, if questioned, that during the next year letters would become more and more irregular, and that by another year they would have ceased.

At Dijon, I ate at a students' pension where I met a girl from Anglesey, we showed off in Welsh to puzzled Poles, and I realized once more that however metropolitan my ambitions were, I was proud of my peninsularity. Then, seated one morning before a lecturer who dissected Renan and Huysmans with subjunctives so pin-pointed that we might have been medical students, I felt my thoughts wander; and I was conscious, for the first time, of that warm new bubbling in the under-mind which says, 'Take no notice, body and brain, we are just milling around.' We? The million molecules stealthily aswirl far below the closed face, itself absently intent on a bow tie waggling dead metaphors against a French Adam's apple: after the false alarm of *Sinner in the Sun* (two pages), the apprentice playwright was pregnant.

I wrote my first offspring in my chambre meublée, under a glum window facing a back court; for a subject, my instinct had cast back to my first theatre, pantomime at the Royalty Chester. *Cinderella*, a 'fantastical play' in an indeterminate costume setting, retold the story in simple prose, studiedly so, with a pulse of fanciful sentiment beating through it. There was a tender picture of the heroine and a sentimentally cynical one of the Ugly Sisters; the Prince having been revealed as a roué who has broken the heart of one of them, Cinderella goes back disillusioned to her hearth, Faith Celli, to be specially released by Mr du Maurier. The play embodied all I had learnt so far, at the Fagan knee, from Maeterlinck, Maugham, de Musset, Pirandello, Synge and Yeats; there was even an echo of *The Cherry Orchard*, which had stayed with me more than I had thought. The author of *Mary Rose* contributed most of all, though not a gleam of his humour. As I scribbled I could see the housewife opposite peering as she rattled crockery, 'Qu'est-ce qu'il écrit, celui-là?' The Poles told me there was a street like the rue des Cordeliers, but I was not roué enough to abandon my Barrie heroine.

Winter term, 1924: the first day of windy rain did not dampen my arrival into Angus's old rooms in Meadow, up broad windowed stairs overlooking trees. (The door below me was labelled 'Professor Lindemann', but all the terms I was to be there I never set eyes on him; the future Lord Cherwell was to me a myth.) The feel of space and height again pleased me, also the studious waxy smell of furniture polish and the two long shabby-seated windows overlooking the trees; but overnight Meadow One 6 lost its charm. I had nowhere near enough books to fill the shelves, no photo-frames and no cushions, and my lampshade was getting a little battered to be in pink. Also the narrow bed, as Angus had warned me – even I, not spoilt by mattresses, had to notice it – must have been the most uncomfortable in Oxford, sagging like a badly slung hammock. I missed Roy, already walking on at the Old Vic, and my new scout looked exactly like the old one; gradually, with dismay, it came to me that the high ceilings were too far removed from 314a ever to make me feel at home. But the week was brightened by a postcard from one of the Dijon Poles, who had taken down my address, no commas, as 'G. E. Williams Christ Church Oxford'; his message began 'Cher Monsieur Christ'. Also it was good to learn once more, from my battel, that not only was I not in debt, but the Steward was sending me seven pounds. 'Dear Miss Cooke, I am including a cheque to cover the £4. 3. 11. you lent me last year, and the £5 this vac, thank you again.'

I hired a typewriter, spent an absorbed two weeks typing out *Cinderella*, red for the stage directions, bound it with pins and posted it to Miss Cooke. Her reply was a detailed criticism ('too much a mish-mash of realism and poetry') and a portable typewriter for my birthday. I answered, 'You are endowed with divining the dearest wishes of people ... I am making a cup of cocoa, and then to bed.' Next day *Cinderella* went off to a London agent, who replied with kind evasion. Fagan? No, I decided, but it had been wonderful practice. 'As well as going to play the Lean Person in *Peer Gynt* I am in the throes of Old French,

Morphology and the Yod, and planning as you suggest to sit for a Heath Harrison in Italian, life is worth living.' But in my next letter I was forced into the open. 'I foresee an awkward clash, one of the Italian papers is the Monday of the Dress-Rehearsal. If I cannot persuade Professor Foligno to switch the day, I'm afraid the H.H. will have to go under. The Ouds is the only pleasure I have here and I cannot give it up without my work suffering. This sounds a paradox, but I pray you will understand ...' 'Well my boy,' she wrote back, 'it's a paradox all right, gang your own gait and be it on your own head ...'

In November I took part, again presumably so that my work should not suffer, in an 'Informal Smoker'. These were informal indeed; from a tiny curtained stage rigged up at one end of the dining-room, an upright piano down beside it, sketches of the crudest ribaldry were directed at an audience of cackling under-graduates and daringly tipsy dons. I played all sorts of small parts, but also did a number – lyric by G. E. Williams, music by I. Gundry – which was a parody of the music-hall cocotte, 'Je m'appelle Yvette, Yvette des trottoirs, Tous les soirs, je m'arrête ...' The two viragoes had provided unlikely copy. I wore a purple velvet dress and cloche hat, the discarded ward-robe of Gundry's presumably strapping sister; I was not good, had no production and lacked the complete confidence neces-sary for such a characterization, but my French helped. Yvette was photographed and sent to Miss Cooke : 'mm ... striking, but I prefer Dull.' 'I too prefer Dull,' I wrote back, 'but the soul of art is variation ...'

In the meantime I was slowly making social headway in the Ouds – 'Williams, isn't it about time you called me Leslie, now what *is* your name?' – and on my nineteenth birthday I gave my first dinner-party, in my rooms. I asked Willie, quiet and balanced, he was good for me, Tim, Ken and a couple of others, a group conservative yet unstuffy. In the morning I went out to Woolworth's, bought candles and a bowl of violets for a centre-piece, and consulted my scout frankly about sherry and wines. The room was unrecognizably colourful in the candle-light, they toasted me in wines, and I saw them out through

Tom in a red-white-and-brandy glow of friendship. It had been a wildly expensive evening, plus gate-money for five outside guests, but it had been worth it.

Term over, the boredom of Divvers for the second time; then up to London to wait for my viva, for never again would I face Oxford in winter vacation. I stayed my first night with Angus, in Wimbledon; he was the only son of a bow-windowed-detached doctor and wife, dignified Scots a social cut above the Parkers. Sitting in the dark drawing-room with the bronze Amazons on the mantelpiece, and reading, like everybody else, *The Constant Nymph*, I saw the Common outside, then two children running past. They looked peculiar, like foreign pets, and I realized I had not looked at such a thing for nine weeks ... 'Wrigley's latest poem,' said Angus. 'Funny,' I said, taking it, 'to think of Wrigley in this room, has your father met him?' 'Don't,' said Angus, closing his eyes. The poem was a soul-groping all right, in the inspissated dark,

> 'My cracking croak the colour of mud
> My creaking look a glockenspiel and a dud ...'

It was like handling an ugly piece of wood. 'Last week,' continued Angus with a sigh, 'he tried to throw himself oot of his window in Teddy Hall.' 'Did you pull him back?' 'I was at a concer-r-t, the window was tu small.' 'My Meadows windows would be all right.' 'Yes,' said Angus thoughtfully, 'and higher tu. Our relationship is on the down gr-rade.' 'So are his poems,' I said, then felt mean as I thought of my own, smooth as a balloon, and as empty.

'Aboot tonight,' said Angus, 'we'll never get into the first night of *The Vortex*, is it to be the Old Vic or that thing at the Criterion?' *Fata Morgana* it was, the last seats in the pit; an adaptation of the Hungarian play *Mirage*, by Vajda, it had been running since September, the sensation of the season. The little subterranean theatre was buzzing with success pin-pricked gaily by the tiny orchestra; once more I felt myself fill up with excitement and longing. Françoise la cuisinière, Yves, my family,

Miss Cooke – I must get them on to the stage, and me with them, I must ... The curtains parted. At a table, lit by the rays of an oil lamp – skilfully helped by a spotlight – sat a boy intent on his homework. He frowned over a page, a lock of fair hair over his brow, pencil tapping the tip of a white tooth. Then he looked thoughtfully up.

The London success of Tom Douglas and Tallulah Bankhead (she was playing, that night, at the Vaudeville in *The Creaking Chair*) was a phenomenon of the two-faced Twenties. The American accent was unknown and these had particularly attractive ones, with a timbre steeped as deep in sex as the human voice can go without drowning : both were born fond-lings, beings of such allure that with no seeming effort it over-flowed normal domains, and each ruled with authority a shadowy hinterland. The girl, twenty-two, husky-musky and with a face like an exquisite poisoned flower, was empowered not only to make strong husbands in the stalls moisten their lips behind a programme, but to cause girls hanging from the gallery to writhe and intone her first name in a voodoo incan-tation. She radiated like a lazy Catherine-wheel. The boy, twenty-one, slim as a reed, with a look of a vulnerable school-stripling, made every woman in the audience, the mothers and the childless, want to cradle that perplexed tousle of straw; but with his short nose and a wide soft mouth that seemed not to know its own potency, he cast a spell over his own sex, as often as not in unexpected quarters. On the dance floor at the Kit Kat, you would overhear white-tied Guards officers mutter down their partner's shingle, 'That Yankee feller's a top-hole little actor, lump to the old throat, remarkable, been twice, taking a party Monday, know anybody knows him ?'

A pause. He sighed, then read, laboriously : 'The man who first ... wrote philosophy ... in the Hungarian language ...' His voice was gentle, tentative, notes unexpectedly low. His mother at the door, 'Well George ... ?' His whole family on the lonely Hungarian farm are off to a distant ball, but he has his exams. And his name is George ... They tease him for his timidity with girls, he has a flashing moment of mutiny; they all leave, the dogs bark, and George is alone for the night. Silence. An oafish youth appears at the window (Roger Livesey) and tries to persuade him to stow away on the train and visit a brothel in the nearest town; he hesitates, refuses, and is left alone again. Silence. The audience waits, expectant. He tries to work, feels the heat, unbuttons further his wide Byronic collar, looks slowly round as the loneliness invades him – how well I know – rises, stretches, goes to the window and stands with his back to the audience, leaning over the sill; the loose Hungarian shirt is tucked under a sash into tight breeches, in turn drawn into top boots. Silence.

He returns, sits, and turns pages. I think to myself, rapt, enmeshed – but he is turning them as I would, I too have four fingers and a thumb, we have that in common ... The dogs bark. A pause. They bark again. A knock at the door: it is Mathilde (Jeanne de Casalis), telegrams have gone astray and she is here without her husband, George's smart uncle. In front of this femme du monde from Budapest, the boy stands on one foot, then on the other, stunned with shyness. Slowly it unfolds, the long virtuoso scene which has made the play – she amused, even subtly attracted, he tempted, yet scared. 'My poor George ...' At last she kisses him, lightly. He puts his arms round her, clumsy, passionate; she gives a cry, they clasp each other, and hold the kiss. It was one of those moments of sexual enthralment in the theatre when the fall of a programme from a lap, the hoot of a distant taxi, even the sightless stone smile from the caryatids upholding the boxes, underlines an absorption which only those two people can break. Curtains swished down, lights faded up, and I faded up even more slowly. 'My gudeness,' said Angus, 'he's all they say, do ye not agree?'

But I could not talk. The rest of the play showed him in calf-love with a woman who could take him seriously; at the end, irrevocable parting, he left alone with his studies: 'The man who first ... wrote philosophy in ...' His voice broke, his head sank slowly on to his arms, curtain. He took his call, shy, tentative. Ten minutes later, I was standing in Jermyn Street, shy, tentative, staring at the steps leading down to the stage-door

343

and to the inner world barred to me. 'What are we hanging aboot for?' said Angus. I had just vetoed his half-suggestion we should send in our names – 'strangers du' – no ... A girl appeared up the steps, and walked away – Flora Robson, she had played the small part of the sister – then people in evening dress; they must have just left him, how could they look so calm? Tarts passed, then two blowsy old flower-girls, then a couple of sinister night-birds: could it be that a minute ago a farm-boy, lambently innocent child of the Hungarian plains, had been standing on that stage more real than all these urban walkers-on? And there he was down there, still innocent, sitting before a mirror taking off make-up with the fascinatingly mechanical movements of the professional actor.

A shadow up the steps, oh God, he's in a bowler and smoking a pipe, no, Roger Livesey. 'Let's go,' said Angus. Was that Rolls-Royce ... I did not want to know, for me he could only walk slowly up, looking as he had on the stage, and disappear simply into the darkness. We got to the corner and were swung into the rainbowed Circus, dashing and dotting and coruscating over a thousand people all in febrile search of something. I said a vague good night and wandered off to my lodgings, up Regent Street, and then east into Bloomsbury. As I walked I talked to him, then I was him talking to me, I tried to imitate his accent; for into adulation there intruded ambition. I identified him with myself: I am his understudy, I have to play, I scramble into the clothes, why haven't I a short nose and fair hair, curtain up, no, I'm not like him and what a good thing, I have my own way of achieving the same effects, the audience is hypnotized, actors peer through chinks ... and I was at the door of my dark bed-and-breakfast in Gordon Square. But as I tried to sleep, in my coffin of a room, he was back on the stage, with me watching from the pit.

The next morning was suffocated in the yellowest of London fogs; I sat at breakfast, looking at the crumpled wary travelling faces and thought, as I had of Faith Celli, if he entered now like a light, I would fall on one knee and so must they all. I took the Tube down to Oxford Circus, and felt my way down Regent

Street and to the Criterion; the strangled sounds of traffic were
unreal, I stood alone in the Arctic Circle, peering at a large
photograph. Then by underground to Angus's for lunch; I
opened their telephone book. Incredibly, I read 'Douglas, Tom,
13 Bruton Street, W.1. MAY. 1586.' Angus said, 'Let's ring him
up!' 'You mean,' I said, never having handled a telephone, 'that
he might answer himself?' 'He might, I wonder if that hair is
quite real?' 'What on earth d'you mean?' 'So verra fair-r, no?'
'Don't be absurd,' I said. We saw *Our Betters* and *Saint Joan*,
but though I was respectively impressed and deeply impressed,
I was still at the Criterion. My viva, then home; sitting in icy
Leamington, I worked out my new play. I had the title: 'Criterion 8.30 Mats W.S. 2.30 CHAPEL TIME by Emlyn Williams
with Tom Douglas.' A drama of Welsh village life, the shy boy
rebelling against his deacon father, falling in love, breaking
down, lock of fair hair, Hungarian breeches – no, start again . . .

Home, in my corner, I tucked the Criterion programme under
'Faithful unto Death'. I knew well that the only justification for
my sitting in 314a while my family worked – our Tom was now
selling papers after school – would be study, unremitting study;
my conscience gnawed, but I could not help it. I made myself
cycle to Holywell, I made myself take our Tom to see *Puss in
Boots* in Liverpool, where we called at Lewis' and bought Mam
a Christmas cake of luxury soap. (It smelt so expensive that she
secreted it in the Sunday-best drawer, to scent the clothes; it
was there years later, as innocent of water as when it left the
counter.) But watching even a pantomime, footlights and music
could only remind me.

Romantic mania, like the religious kind, has constantly to
link the worshipped one with the insupportable details of daily
life. He would hate this but he would be patient, so will I . . .
Having my hair cut at Garland's, overhearing the familiar banal-
ities, I opened the *Daily Sketch* at the theatre-list – yes, there
it was, 'Tonight 8.30, W.S. 2.30'. To make myself work, I would
even – on dreary Wednesday afternoons, with the chairs up on
the sofa and Mam doing the floor while I washed up – I would
even say to myself, 'In five minutes, the Criterion curtains will

part and show him impeccably at his studies, so will I be.' Five minutes later I would settle into my corner, 'History of Lat. Indef. Pronouns through French', but in another five I was standing opposite the mirror, the understudy, on. I helped kill one day by walking the four miles to Flint to consult *Who's Who in the Theatre*: 'DOUGLAS, Tom, b. Louisville 4 Sept. '03, s, of William Lee-Douglas and Ellen (Douglas), ed. Louisville and N.Y.' My mother's name had been Ellen – well, Elin; he was two years and eighty-two days older than me. I only just took in that I had failed at Divvers again. There is no doubt that my cure would have been a 40-week season, at four pounds a week, one pound sent home, of twice-nightly Rep at Penge.

The spring term, 1925. For the first time I found my battel, as I put it to Miss Cooke, 'rather alarming' – such items as my birthday party, another sherry everybody? – and I warned her that I might have to borrow £25 from her. She had guessed my ambition; 'I see you still see me,' I wrote, 'as the moth round the flame ... All the actors and actresses I have met have told me it is the most heart-breaking profession in the world, so at least I know what I am in for. I am working hard at the *Chanson de Roland*.' I was fined two pounds by my college for failing Divvers twice, which smarted, but I had my Italian to prepare and was quickly rehearsing for *Peer Gynt*, Professor Foligno having promised that I should sit the Monday paper the day before.

But the image persisted. Sitting in the Ouds one evening after rehearsal, in one of the arm-chairs – it wouldn't be long before I'd be on the fender, I had even bought a pipe and had half my heart in trying to smoke it – I overheard Fruity Orchard holding forth to a couple of freshers: a large harmless tankard-wielding dabbler. 'My dear chaps, he's chased by every dirty old man in the West End, supper at the Gargoyle with Nicky Pullingford, gold links from Billy de Wouk who was in the drug case, Tommy's the toast of them all.' I turned to ice, and put down my journal. 'It's not true,' I said flatly. They looked at me. 'It is, old thing,' said Fruity, 'look at that costume, skin-tight pants all the better to lean out of the window in, is *that* the get-up for a

Hungarian farm-hand in this day and age – I *ask* you! His hair –'
'Do you know him?' I said. 'No, but I know people who do – oh
he's a charmer, but you can't tell me he doesn't know the ropes,
d'*you* know him?' 'Yes,' I said, 'and he's a very fine person –
of course the dirty old men are after him like flies, and if they
like to send him links that's their look-out.' I went back to
Theatre Arts shaking with brotherly anger, while they moved
on to Gwen Farrar and Napper Dean Paul. I told Angus next
morning over coffee in the Candied Friend. 'I'm sure ye're
right,' he said thoughtfully, 'but his troosers *are* a wee bit tight
for a far-rm, do ye no think?' I did realize that I had never seen
a photograph in which that rebellious lock of hair was not
rebelling. 'He was doon at the House last Sunday,' said Angus,
who knew everything, 'with that tall heavenly *Tatler* wench
Daphne Vivian, they went out to the Spreadeagle with Rosse
and Weymouth and Brian Howard.'

I was shot through with jealousy. Walking through Peck to
the wail of Monday morning gramophones, I would wonder, is
he somewhere there? ... 'Somebody,' said Angus, 'saw him
sitting in a window in Magdalen.' That was the picture I seized
upon : behind him, a deafening chattering party – Hypocrites,
Union Debaters, what had Peter Quennell really said, was Harold
Acton actually debagged – and Tom alone in the window-seat,
one knee up and a cheek resting on it, looking thoughtfully
out at the deer. 'What was he wearing?' I asked. 'One o' those
high-necked jumper-rs,' said Angus, 'and the one bit of hair
hanging doon and looking divine, Wrigley and I have par-rted.'
Two days later, when a gossip weekly hinted that Mr T – m
D – – gl – s might have leant over the balcony of the Embassy
Club and poured a gin-and-tonic on to Miss Gl – d – s C – – per,
I dismissed it as spite; I also discarded the story that before the
Boxing Day matinée he had tied thread to the furniture to make
Miss de Casalis giggle – this was slander, for to me he was a
paragon of professionalism as well as of modesty. The one per-
son who knew him at first hand was the producer of *Peer Gynt*,
Reginald Denham, who had produced *Fata Morgana*. Somehow,
I shirked asking.

Rehearsals progressed, heightened by the first night, at the

Playhouse, of the Fagan *Cherry Orchard*, later to move to the Lyric Hammersmith and make history. I became good friends with J. P. R. Maud, a gangling high-spirited boy who walked on; then the ladies arrived, Clare Greet, a giggly asthmatic bundle of Cockney mother, and two spectacularly pretty girls so different that they could not clash: Joan Maude, daughter of Nancy Price, just seventeen with auburn hair, a face made more perfect by freckles, and a heart-stirring lisp: and Lilian Oldland, one of the girls in *Fata Morgana* lent for an Oxford jaunt, a warm brunette. They were nice enough to be anybody's sister and also had sex-appeal, a formidable combination. Joan had a start, being unattached – Lilian was twenty-year-old Mrs Denham – and also lustrous from the Haymarket, *Old English*; John (Maud) and I decided that Lilian was the charmer, while Willie and Boy Malcolm fought openly over Joan, who exercised wide-eyed diplomacy. There were two shy walkers-on named Mary and Ann, the daughters of Sybil Thorndike and Lewis Casson; but they were aged eleven and nine and therefore invisible. I sat my Heath Harrison, then threw myself into the endless wonderful sandwiches-and-coffee dress-rehearsal, with masks and chaotic changes, patiently quickened by Mr Denham – 'Reggie' by now, but I was taking no chances – and great beams of light and the orchestra suddenly, thrillingly, beating out the Grieg music.

The first night, I caroused as a Wedding Guest, gibbered as a Troll, drooled as a Lunatic, then prepared calmly for the Lean Person. This was my real indoor test: a sustained scene late in the play. Standing in the wings, in stockinged feet with cloven hoofs fitted over them, I was suddenly conscious of the packed darkness beyond and of the fire of light into which I must soon walk alone. Suppose I were to ... I felt my heart begin to knock, loud. 'Be still, look up at the moon and the stars ...' I calmed, and stepped forward into the blaze, and was secure. All went a little more than well.

Then something which I had long planned: Miss Cooke, Miss Swinnerton and Miss Morris left school Friday afternoon by train for Oxford. I had booked them rooms in the High, and as I was proudly on the stage of the New when they arrived, I left violets to greet them – the violet seemed to be my flower – with a note to say I had won my second Heath Harrison. Saturday morning I walked them round the House, we lunched at the Randolph; I invited John (Maud), who was amusing and correct, which was perfect. During the matinée they went off on their own and in the evening came to the performance. I could not meet them afterwards, there was the Supper: champagne again and programme-signing and congratulations, but this time I was part of it. Toys arrived for me; at 2 a.m., elevated by bubbly, I was touched by the thought of my three teachers asleep in mid-'Varsity. I went along to Doggins' with the rest, John Sutro told stories, Willie did a piece as a yokel, John and I talked to Lilian about the vac, there was coffee and we saw in a sunny February dawn. I went back to the House, had a bath, and called for my visitors with Angus; we took a taxi to the Trout at Godstow, had breakfast, Joan arrived with Willie and others, everybody was introduced, Joan radiant with the news that she was to rehearse immediately for *Iris* at the Adelphi 'with Gladys, and they told me Ivor may join the cast later!' 'Gladys and Ivor?' said Miss Cooke, on the way back, 'sounds like two old Holywell pupils, who are they?' I could not make out if she knew or not. We walked by the river, I saw them off, wandered sleepily down to Angus's rooms near Folly Bridge and collapsed, by his fireside, into a pile of crumpets and a deep sleep. The *Isis* reported (Claud Cockburn) that 'Mr Williams was a diabolical, if not very lean, Lean Person.'

With John, I was now elected to the Committee, which was satisfying as it was exactly as far as I wanted to go, in Oxford, socially. And on my next visit to the New, in the interval my status gave me that extra ounce of aplomb when I popped across the road to the Club for a quick sherry – a chic custom – and answered the inquiries of after-diners, 'Rubbish, but expertly projected . . .' My Welsh accent seemed to be rubbing off, I said 'Yes indeed' only when I meant to and I had difficulty only with the word 'one', tending to say, 'The war against prejudice will be won worn day . . .'

The next move was another smoker, in which I ran on and off in many guises. The book was japed up from day to day, and by the end even I was rather ashamed of the inanities in the way of double-entendre; there was no direction, and the show was retrieved only by individual turns and the gaiety of the number. The hit was 'Jumper Boy', by Addinsell and Leigh: a skit on a craze which had spread outwards from Harold Acton and his set and had made enough ripples in Mayfair to be currently parodied in Lonsdale's *Spring Cleaning*. When Willie, sitting on a table in a double-breasted maroon jacket over black turtle-neck, mauve Oxford bags flowing below and hair smarmed down and forward, announced, almost wistfully, a craving for high-necked jumpers 'in pinks and reds and yellows, just like Ivor Novello's ...' the number had a bite of professionalism which we badly needed.

Easter. I ought to go straight home to work, but as I was saving all my Italian travel for the Long Vac, I felt entitled to start with a week in London. I went to tea with John, who lived, surprisingly, in a great mansion in Kensington, less surprising when his father turned out to be the Bishop of it. That evening, into the Comedy pit-queue for Lilian Braithwaite and Noël Coward in *The Vortex*: an experience to sow, in my subconscious, more than one dynamic seed. I was struck by a novel note in the programme, a mark of changing custom: 'The audience are requested not to demand the raising of the curtain at the end of Acts One and Two, but should they desire it, it will be raised at the end of the play.' They did desire it.

But next night, still under the Hungarian spell, I queued for *Fata Morgana*, now at the Vaudeville, and next afternoon John and I went to tea with Lilian in her dressing-room; even the tea tasted special, like a potion. I stole out, crept through a door and peered down into the wings, at the Hungarian mother knitting as she awaited her cue. I listened; inside the dark walls of the farm-house, as thin as they were impenetrable, dead silence. Then, a voice ... Next evening I was again at the play, sinking back in my seat as into a quicksand. Two nights later, loitering up the Strand – I must go back to that room and work,

I must – I thought, no, I'll just see the opening, 'The man who first wrote philosophy ...' I paid, dawdled into the back of the pit, stayed five minutes, and like a zombie dawdled out again.

For people in the theatre, to take an evening walk on city pavements during the hour after the curtain is up, is to be suspended in a temporal no-man's land; they hear, in back-streets suddenly strange, a hush of between-times – who can these few creatures be, mooning, mooching, slouching? For an actor such an excursion is unnerving, but for a would-be actor that raw March night was raw indeed. I walked slowly into the dark wilds around Covent Garden Market. By the sparse light of gas-lamps, shrouded carts loomed like biers; the cobbles were scattered with broken crates and flapping paper and rotted fruit. A policeman passed slowly, with a quick appraising look; a man on a corner, feet crossed, hands in pockets, gave me an aggressive stare which said, 'Wonderin' what I'm waiting for? Not sure meself, mind your own business ...' A drunken man advanced on me and lurched into the gutter; crouched in an office doorway, with on either side a sack of rubbish guarded by a twisted root of a hand, sat one of those toothless mindless bundles of brutified humanity to be seen, out of the corner of an eye, lurking just off the nerve-centres of London. I saw it grope down to pull filthy sacking round one troglodyte foot and heard it croak to itself, 'Eh what? What? ...' I walked on, past the drunken man in the gutter.

Stopping, I looked up at the scowl across the sky; behind the high brooding offices, my ear caught the rumble of a Strand bus, purposefully bearing busy people to where they knew they were going, the fires of home, the heat of pub or club, longed-for familiar arms, or even longed-for arms of strangers, Tivoli ladies an' gents nex' stop Trafalgar Square, forging confidently on. What am *I* bound for? What, eh what, what?

What have I done today, leading up to this moment? In my five-and-six bed-and-breakfast, I woke too late for the breakfast; after a culprit look at the Old French piled on my table, I wandered down to Piccadilly Circus and had a coffee and a bun in the Coventry Street Corner House, where I was affably greeted by a military-looking man at the same table, 'Two more ditto, waiter, righty ho!' Then he asked me to lunch, remarking that for a young feller up from the country, the West End was bristling with temptations. 'Yes indeed,' I said, and spoke of an engagement. 'Righty ho, cheery ho.' The pleasure of being wanted lasted into Shaftesbury Avenue; I ran into Rowley Leigh and strolled with him to the stage-door of the Globe, past where they were painting 'Fallen Angels'. 'Tallu's just replaced Bunny Bannerman,' he said. 'I'm just popping in to wish her luck,' and disappeared. I sighed and walked to the Tivoli Cinema, sat in the dark for two hours, proceeded to a suburb for tea with Inglis Gundry, he was working hard at music, I tried not to listen – and back up West by seven for a bite in the Strand Corner House, then a waste of two-and-six at the Vaudeville and here I am. What. . . . what, eh what?

Stagger, and I could be with the drunk, indistinguishable. Beyond the carts and the crates, no soul now in sight; was there nothing, at the hub of a city, but the last cynical resort of the solitary male . . . No, I clenched my fists deep in my overcoat and hurried round a corner. The night street looked for a moment like the one in Rouen. Was that where I belonged, a bed shared with a trollop and a sailor?

Like a leaf blown the way it must go, I drifted down Maiden Lane to the stage-door and sent a note in to Lilian asking if she could meet me and John for supper, my first London invitation. Through a gap I could see her in the passage, in her wrapper, read the note and consult Reggie, who shook his head to confirm that she was not free. At that moment Tom passed them, absently hitching up his trousers under the sash; it must be the end of the first act. I wandered on.

Lilian would have introduced me to him, with pleasure; but I paved no way, beyond praising him in terms which must have sounded inordinate. Back at 314a, where I was able to show Dad *The Making of Modern Italy* in book form – he pronounced it, as always, Eye-tally – I settled down to rehearse in *Y Bobl Fach Ddu*, a version in Welsh of J. O. Francis's *The Dark Little*

People, the performance got up by the enthusiastic Evanses of my chapel. It was a sketchy venture, with the minister's pretty wife as the heroine, no producer, no curtain, no lights, presented in the Wepre Church Hall. As the young shepherd hero, I gave an impersonation, in Welsh, of a Hungarian farm-boy ed. in Louisville and N.Y.

The other Tom, our twelve-year-old one, had transplanted a clump of wild primroses from Castle Hill Woods into the meagre dirt bordering the path alongside 314a, and they were miraculously flourishing; but I had no eyes for them. 'As From Christ Church' – on a sheet I had brought home, cardinal's hat well in the centre – 'Dear Mr Douglas. This is not a "fan letter" though I am a sincere admirer of your work. I am in Wales for the vac, playing the juvenile lead in a play (I hope to emulate you and go on the stage). I have ventured to write because we know several people in common – Lilian Oldland, also Brian Howard, Michael Rosse, Henry Weymouth' – well, I had sat next to them in the J.C.R., so sorry *would* you pass the *Bystander*, thanks awfully – 'Yours sincerely, G. Emlyn Williams.' A week later, 'Dear Miss Cooke, A stream of correspondence – letters from Joan Maude, John Maud, Tom Douglas and Willie Wiley. I am working hard ...' I had not expected it, but I knew it immediately: incredible, alone, beside my breakfast. A large flowing hand, 'G. Emlyn Williams Esq., 314a High Street ...' 'Dear Mr Williams, Thank you very much for your letter, I am very happy that you have enjoyed my work. Next time I am in Oxford do not hesitate to come up and say hello, warm wishes, Yours sincerely, Tom Douglas.'

On our newspaper-cloth, it shone like a missal: exactly what I wanted it to be, simple and dignified. The monogram – T.D. interwoven in two pale colours, raised with a thin gilt border, and the middle of the D perforating the paper – might in anybody else have been a little excessive, but the writer could do no wrong. Yet as I tucked the letter into my wallet, next to my spare pound-note and empty diary, I knew that this image must never be defaced, and that I would never meet him.

And I never did. One afternoon thirty years later, walking

along Piccadilly I ran into Daphne Fielding, the 'tall heavenly Daphne Vivian' who had brought him to Oxford. She was waving to a departing car. 'You've just missed Tommy Douglas,' she said, 'he and I thought before he caught his plane home, we'd go back to the Twenties with a nice Proustian luncheon at the Ritz.' I looked after the car as it veered into St James's Street. Should I run after it, à la recherche du Tom perdu? It disappeared. 'Did you ever know him,' she said, 'in the old days?'

Chapter 23

Becalmed, and Adrift

But all through the summer term, for which once again Oxford slackened from chilly nanny into half-beckoning siren, my romantic thoughts of Tom were good diet, rich but not too rich. And I was busy: we – the Committee – cast the open-air play, Rostand's *The Fantasticks*, preceded by *The Two Pierrots*. 'Dear Miss Cooke, I have been prevailed upon to play a waiter as there is just nobody else to do it .. Divvers? Lord – if you'll excuse the expression – that must wait . . .' For I was rehearsing, in Italian – Professor del Re's idea – Pirandello's one-act play *Lumie di Sicilia*, almost a monologue for me, as a peasant; too young, I craftily did nothing to look older, but was well cast. From the Ouds, John Maud came to see it, in Lady Margaret Hall. I had felt it unwise to press others and trusted him to tell, which he did.

Then I had permission, for a weird twenty-four hours, to travel home for one performance of *Y Bobl Fach Ddu*. I ought to have refused; after weeks without rehearsal, the performance was a shoddy one. But the weirdness was significant. Standing in a packed bus to Flint, I felt like a man from Mars; back to 314a to sleep – o Irish Mail I follow thee today, today – waking to hear children, in the next back yard, again outlandish creatures ... and back in the club by lunch. My Ouds life was so sundered from the other that the sortie had been a jumbled dream, a puzzling wrench leaving a pain, as of dislocation. I could have taken warning.

But there was too much to do. As I competed for the Newdigate Prize for Poetry ('Byron') Stephen Phillips again hovered,

'Slow dreaming through the misty length of years
Across the rosy tenderness of time . . .'

355

I did not win. Then in June, in Peckwater, I walked on at a flying open-air matinée of *Medea* given by Sybil Thorndike and Lewis Casson during their London run of *The Lie* at Wyndham's : 'Old Men, H. S. Barnes, G. E. Williams.' The setting was the Library façade and pillars; the performance must have been impressive, and perhaps more than that when Miss Thorndike flung open the great first-floor window, distractedly picked up her recumbent daughter Ann and seemed about to throw her at a startled front row of dons. Changing afterwards inside, I admired the professional bustle with which the Cassons packed before the dash for the London train; as they streaked across to Canterbury Gate, the youngest middle-aged couple I had ever seen – 'Lewis darling, the thermos!' – and into a waiting taxi, I stood looking after them, a dog that had been left behind. But next morning I had the luck to run into eighty-nine-year-old Doctor Lock, doyen of the House Canons, 'Miss Thornton,' he quavered, 'was word-perfect, I could not fault her and I had Professor Gilbert Murray on my knee all through the performance.'

I supported Robert Speaight and Bertha Philips in *The Bear*, a one-act play by Chekhov, then written Tchehov, at Swalcliffe Park, Banbury; I played the servant, the programme reading 'Lukka ... Miss Evelyn Williams.' At last, Ouds rehearsals. The producer was William Armstrong, who had just begun his long reign over the Liverpool Playhouse; as sensitive as Fagan, what he lacked in authority he made up for with a drollery based on artful exaggeration of what he called his old-maid streak. 'My dear boys, don't *breathe* such limericks down the neck of an old prude from the frozen North – no don't laugh at me, beastly new-born creatures ...' He was like a lively don who spends his vacs playing dame in some witty pantomime. Joyce Carey arrived to play Columbine, Agatha Kentish was Sylvette; as the saffron evenings of rehearsal repeated themselves, it got around that Miss Kentish, a charming ingénue, was pregnant (she was a Mrs McCarthy). Overnight she became – for us all, for ever – respected, uncanny, and as invisible as the Casson children.

I was riding the waves, and plunged into shopping. It had to be faced that my dinner suit was no longer à la mode, and for

Commem, which I was determined to sample, you had to have tails. I told myself, and Miss Cooke, that two new outfits would be an investment, true, and that Oxford tailors were so under-standing that I could pay next term out of scholarship instal-ments. My second buy, the details of which I kept from her, was ill-advised. I·knew I was on the wrong track, but shut my eyes and bought a lounge ensemble, loosely double-breasted (first mistake) in light grey-blue (second) and (third, worst) with Oxford bags, which meant trousers wider at the base than my foot was long. Where was the guardian angel – Ken would have obliged – to whisper 'If you must go in for peculiar togs, don't fall for a craze meant for sissy telegraph-poles, why don't you try the old-fashioned pre-war trousers so narrow they wouldn't pull over shoes but *would* make you look a trim cad instead of a short-arsed deck-hand gone arty-party?' But I did not court advice. First time on, as a coward's compromise I sported my pipe, but my flapping calves made me feel sloppily daring.

I made new Ouds friends, and saw quite a lot, in a desultory way, of Old Percy, the club butt. P. R. Shipping (Merton) was one of those students who claim on their passports to be twenty, but are clearly octogenarians who have hastily swallowed a couple of rejuvenation pills and then regurgitated them, too early for the miracle to have mended their looks but late enough for the brain to have turned callow; twenty-year-old Percy had a walking-stick, a middle-aged spread under a thigh-length cardigan, and a Mama who was preparing to travel eighty miles to see him as an eighty-year-old retainer in *The Fantasticks* ('How nice for you, Percy,' three people had said to him separ-ately, 'a straight part at last'). He asked me to his rooms and dodderingly read me his poetry, which depressed me by sound-ing exactly like mine. Shipping Senior, framed on the mantel-piece, looked ordinary but perplexed, perhaps by having fathered a son thirty years older than himself. Other new friends were less eccentric: Reggie Colby, Campbell Hackforth-Jones, John Aldridge who painted, and Jim Courage and Norman Cameron who both wrote. They came to tea, methylated burner and cucumber sandwiches. All was going swimmingly.

Except for one thing. I had worked a certain amount at Old French and Italian, but I had not worked at Divvers. Once more I got to the Examination Schools, white tie, mortar-board; I looked down at the questions. They were simple but factual, 'Who were the sons of Zebedee and how did they differ?' 'Who was the wife of Aquila?' 'Who were the prophets of Antioch?' Not one could I answer; there was no possibility of bluffing my way across thin ice, there was no ice.

I looked round, at the others scribbling away; slowly, regularly, I inhaled panic. Could this be me? The pride of H.C.S., the half-holiday boy? I saw Miss Cooke staring me out, blazing-blue-eyed, and looked at the clock. Three hours! Not one question ... It was a reasonably hot morning. I heaved a deep sigh, felt the invigilator look up, and put my hand to my brow. Three minutes later I passed him, swaying a little, 'I feel faint, sir ...' Down the deserted stairs, my feet echoed in disgrace. As I walked, I willed myself into a trance, and by the time I called on my tutor, I was suitably dazed. 'Sorry sir, but – could I have a glass of water, thank you – I'd been up most of the last three nights, cramming, everything sort of went black – awfully sorry sir ...' He did not look convinced, 'Would you like a doctor –' 'No thank you, sir, if I may I'll just take it easy for the rest of the day –' 'You wrote *nothing*? ... No, to get an Aegrotat you have to produce a doctor's certificate.'

It had given me a whack, but taking it easy for the rest of the day was to include two run-throughs of *The Two Pierrots* and a costume parade. 'Dear Miss Cooke, I'm afraid I didn't finish the Divvers, I had been overworking and fainted, a kind of brainstorm ...' Commem was fun, a sister of Campbell's came up for the Ouds Ball, cordial and decorative; tails, flower in buttonhole, marquee, claret-cup, dance-cards, 'The Indian Love Call', 'Yearning', 'Down on the Farm', 'Marcheta' and the inevitable 'Tea for Two'. Then a strenuous job – business manager for the two-week charity tour, a different village or town hall every night, of *Twenty-One*, a come-of-age revue concocted by Willie and Tim. It was work I was unfitted for, I was determined to do it right, and it was back-breaking; but we finished well, with a big party the first half-hour of which I ruined for myself by opening a letter from Miss Cooke. A broadside. 'If this makes you sit up, good. Your letter makes v.v. sorry reading ... One-eyed nonsense, I've no use for slackers who can't stick it ...' My face riddled schoolboy-tomato with grape-shot, I took a glass of champagne without looking up to say thank-you. 'Fooling about with amateur theatricals, esprit de corps be hanged ... You'll come a cropper or my name isn't S. G. C. ...' Slacker? But I was exhausted! Gulp gulp ... I felt better.

I took a room at the Wilton and had a solitary evening out, *On With The Dance* at the Centre of the World. After a stifling swaying Riviera night I reached Florence, took a carrozza to the Pensione Balestri, Piazza Mentana, and fell into bed. All my activity piled itself on top of me in a last delicious avalanche of tiredness and I slept all day, my ear vaguely conscious of light showers of pure Italian freshening the heat like water. As in Vincentier, I smelt dust, and coffee, and flowers; I slept all that night too, my sleep rosy-clouded with the strumming of serenatas on the Arno bank. Andante andante, Beatrice e Dante ...

For three months I went through what most impressionable Inglesi had been experiencing for two hundred years: a prolonged love affair – no tensions, take-me-or-leave-me-mi-amore – with a country, sun-kissed and wine-warm. I wandered alone among broken columns, around hot still cloisters, through the long calm corridors of galleries, through medieval alleys bursting with humanity and smelling of heaven and hell. As a recess from the tireless symphony outside, of caerulean sky and grapes and white teeth and laughter, I would circumambulate the cool of the churches; but by the end, to my Wesleyan eyes and nose and ears, the holy places were as pagan as the summer day I had left. The echoing dark winked with gold and silver and porphyry : then came the sensuous throb of incense, and round a pillar the sudden stifling caress of a hundred starry candles; beyond them, the shrouded visitant sunk at the mysterious cubby-hole, the agonized murmur of self-abasement ... And even in the canvases glowing on every side around the one un-sexed and grief-stained face to sear the conscience – was there not always, in some corner of the reverent landscape, the odd pouting putto flying as bare as the day he was born, milky-creased and overweight, his baby mind not entirely on the cloud in hand? And what of the Sistine Chapel, with more carnality sprawling giant-limbed on its apocalyptic walls, proud and hungry of lip and nostril, than is to be found in the Decameron?

Hovering between the crumbled cliffs of the Caracalla Baths, I looked up and chose the weed-tufted niche where Shelley had sat to write *Prometheus Unbound*; in Sorrento, I saw an open-air Madama Butterfly scan Vesuvius for her Pinkerton, and the next afternoon, in *Aida*, a crowd of hastily recruited Ancient Egypt-ians raise their long-sleeved arms aloft in adoration of their gods, to reveal a dozen wrist-watches glittering in the sun; an atten-dant whispered to a man near me, 'In the back where they disguise themselves, there is no trust between them.' Under a full Roman moon, I stood in the Colosseum and heard, soaring out of the ruined darkness opposite, a disembodied tenor singing *Tosca*; the impassioned voice winged across the centuries, taking me with it across my own centuries to Glanrafon and to Nero's Rule, and deep in the caverns at my feet I caught, in the moon-light, the glitter of a padding panther. In the evening sun, I sat in a peasant train meandering across the Campagna, thought of Cicero and Ovid and Virgil, then mixed them with Miss Cooke who had first made them real to me; then I mixed the landscape with the great print of Rome on the wall of a Holywell class-room. On a street-corner in Pompeii, in another cross-century trance, I sat street-map in hand on a bed of cindered weeds and watched the setting sun redden the doorway of what had once been a brothel, ave Felix Maximus, ave Clodia Minima, ave Yves, ave Rosine . . .

My personal life was as solitary and as tranquil : it was evi-dently Mr Heath Harrison who had for me the gift of happiness. I did little he might have frowned on, apart from the stray encounters any human must make in an Italian summer, travelling alone and under seventy. I doubt if he would even have minded my determination to spend, of his seventy-five pounds, as few as possible : I had made a bet with myself that I would take thirty home. I settled to a page of Greek every morning, having hit on the solution to Divvers : this time to choose the alternative offered to the four Gospels in English – St John in Greek, which would mean tackling the thing afresh as a Greek exam. I should have thought of it before, χριστός looked quite different written like that. I also started Spanish : Miss Cooke was anxious, I too, for me to try for a Spanish Heath Harrison next year.

A week in Assisi, my window overlooking the Piazza Santa Chiara and down in the distance, rising from the vast Umbrian plain, the dome of San Pietro in Perugia. I worked and walked, and talked to nobody except my landlady and her family in the kitchen. I walked in the early morning and after dark, past mountain farms where I would hear the dogs bark and imagine Tom at his Hungarian studies : walked peacefully, his letter in my wallet, my mind soothed by work and by rest. There was one encounter, an English couple outside Santa Maria degli Angeli. I was wearing my béret and a workman's shirt, and heard a whisper – 'ask *him* . . .' The husband turned to me, 'Scusi – er –' – 'Parlo un po' d'inglese,' I said, 'I spick l'il Englees.' 'Hasn't he a pretty accent?' said the wife, 'where did you learn it?' 'In Roma,' I said, 'then in my collegio in Oxforde.' They were fascinated by me – so was I – particularly when it came out that I was a Count. We strolled back to the Piazza; I was too busy acting to feel mean. 'Archie, why shouldn't the Count join us for lunch, and then come tomorrow as a sort of guide?' I only giusta maneggioed to wriggle out of it. 'Too bad, they've promised us a real British meal, have you by any chance heard of Yorkshire Pudding?' I bowed them a courtly shy addio and walked away feeling quietly attractive. It is the nearest I ever got to the confidence trick.

In Rome, through my Italian tutor I had been offered a bed in a vast mansion, the noble owner in villeggiatura. I had my own key, and felt like a burglar. Up to six, I worked at Greek for two hours, then gingerly crossed the shrouded drawing-room. Moneyed citizens in Europe seem often to turn their backs on the beauties for which their city is loved : it was as if this Roman had said, 'When you are sated with the Seven Hills, I have a nice change for you.' The vast *salone* was like my mother's parlour with every timid item grotesquely magnified into megalomania : it was loaded with fat furniture inlaid with coloured stones like petrified Neapolitan ices, acres of family paint defiantly bemedalled and befeathered, tons of life-size cemetery statuary, brown velvet poufs like giant toads, and enormous beady birds and beasts snarling down from the walls or rampant on angry mosaic. Back at night, zigzagging through the dark with finger-tips spread, I wished I had been given the choice of a night's rest in the Chamber of Horrors.

Then Sorrento, in a *pensione*, I inhabited a cupboard of a room for the smallest sum I paid for a room anywhere, with thrown in the scent of jasmine. But I was out all day. Some mornings I went bathing, sneaking through one of the big hotels to its private beach, which made the stolen sea all the more enjoyable; but most days I would buy fruit and bread and climb with my books to a vantage-point on the cliffs from which I could see Vesuvius and from the summit behind me, wicked sea-girt Capri. There I would study till I lost the sun : there one day I took *Antony and Cleopatra*, looking forward to opening a masterpiece which I had neither seen nor read and immersing myself in it throughout an unforgettable Mediterranean day. The magic did not work; the whirlpools of middle age were not for me, and I sat baffled and disappointed. In the evening, in my dim cupboard, I held up my candle to the London theatre-list, cut out of a discarded *Times* and hung by my bed. In Venice, I found a back room near the station, a tiny house in the Campo San Geremia where I was the only lodger; my window overlooked the trees of a tranquil nunnery, and it was pleasing to find that my landlady was a Signora Gobbo.

I worked and I walked. In my stark room, after my early-morning gospelling, the Sermon on the Mount, in Greek, taking on a new-minted lustre, la signora would bring me up a caffé latte. Then I would work till noon at Italian – I had done enough picture-galleries for this trip – go out and eat spaghetti at a workmen's trattoria, then decipher the mazy walk to the Piazza and take the big vapore to the Lido, where I would lie in the cheap part, half in and half out of the sex-strewn sand; then the vapore again and the walk home to work. Once, looking down from the steamer at the quayside crowd, I noticed among a cluster of golden boys and girls one striking bare-breasted Venetian, a youth even more bronzed and white of teeth than his companions, all carrying bathing shorts and waving addios to friends next to me : remembering him in the distance in Tom Quad, I saw it was Oliver Messel and nearly waved back. Some evenings I would put on my best, that damned light blue, and zigzag back to the Piazza. Once I was standing in the crowd round the band, when it broke into a jolly tune : I was prodded by a fierce youth who pointed to my béret, snatched it off, handed it to me and marched away; the tune was 'Giovinezza', and it was my only brush, the whole trip, with Fascism. I would sit outside Florian's, order one cappuccino and watch the world stroll by; then a frugal dinner and the walk back to my near-nunnery, where – in the house of Gobbo – I would count my travellers' cheques as if I were Shylock.

The last day, I relented and bought lace and brooches, and a necklace of coloured Venetian stones for my mother; just as the dream-like weather of my perfect holiday was about to break, I left for two days on the Lakes, took the train from Lugano, and arrived in London serene and super-solvent. I stayed the night with Angus, we went to see Henry Ainley in *The Moon and Sixpence* and the theatre enfolded me again. Oxford next day : I sat the paper, and left sure that I had passed. I had, the Greek had done the trick, and I went home for the week before the autumn term, of 1925.

Mam had never seen beads like these before, and wore them for best, on the Sunday and for the rest of her life. 'This Venice now,' said Dad, cutting up his tobacco, 'she'll be in Eye-tally, on the Adriatic,' and added, puzzled, 'this Divinity exam, I thought you got through that before?' 'No,' I said, looking up from my Spanish grammar, 'that was a first step to this.' I mentioned the thirty pounds to Mam, in front of Job, but she would have none of it. 'Don't you go robbing yourself, we're all right here, you're not owing any money down there?' 'Oh no,' I said, 'nothing to speak of.' The tie-shop, the tailor, the ... nothing to speak of. 'And now, George,' said Dad, 'when is your *big* exam?' 'Next June, finals in French and Italian.' 'And will that,' said Mam, who was never to lose her flair for hitting the nail on the head with the wrong hammer, 'will that be the end of you?' 'Well,' I hedged, 'it depends how I do –' 'Ah yes,' Dad nodded eagerly, 'you mean if you get one o' them Firsts!' 'Well, a First is very hard –' 'I know it,' said Dad, 'you remember, Poll, when Mr Ferguson from head office stopped me and asked to see the cutting? Well, his sister's boy went to Oxford, a clever lad an' all, and he got a second. "You can't get a First," says Mr Ferguson, "without you work like a black *and* got the top-notch brains," and I said, "Well, Mr Ferguson, we'll do our best, the boy's work goes without saying, and what with his head *and* the benefit of his Dad's free tuition in the holidays, we can lay odds on a First!"' I smiled feebly, he would not leave it alone, 'Poll, when we get to Oxford it will be like that Holywell Do only bigger, mortar-boards and all talking Latin – what a champion day!' O God, I must work, I must ... I did not unpack my Oxford bags.

Back in Meadow One 6, I not only unpacked the bags, I went to Walters' in the Turl and bought a high-necked jumper. I had hesitated, but there was no doubt that they were being worn, impervious to ridicule, by the best-looking undergraduates, if not the heartiest: a garment which with plus-fours and a pipe could have added up to a sturdy effect, did not look quite the same in pink or heliotrope married to yards of lemon trouser. My ensemble was only blue, but I was still miscast, and the first time I sported the jumper in the club I was glad that Willie was safe in the Temple. A better buy, more individual, was a loose slate-blue shirt-cum-sweater, collar attached, worn outside the trousers with or without maroon tie. And in manner, I had the sense not to emulate the nonpareils of languid elegance, but to strike out as a sort of proletarian enfant terrible, hair in eyes, tie awry, tongue eager to shock and woo alternately.

I made a plan. I would work, within reason, but until the February play was over, *Henry IV Part II*, I would enjoy myself in the Ouds. I was loth to face it, but the winter aspect of Meadow Buildings, its gaunt wych-elms dripping in the mist, was more oppressive than Tom : the black beam was invisibly still with me, and daily I dreaded the walk back through the dank past, Plague Corner, the cloister-well with the giant grave ... No, I would do what other gifted and versatile men had done – though I would not have framed those words even to myself – who stow away rowing caps or violins, assume overnight the colour of book-leather and for four months disappear into the landscape of study : the Monday after the Ouds Supper, the butterfly would become a dedicated moth at the flame of learning. As at Holywell and in my dear Venetian cell, from dawn to midnight the factory in my head would hum as the alchemy of imagination transmuted the swot-dross into gold; with the March sun warming the chilblained Meadows, I would sprawl in my window-seat over the *Lais de Marie de France*, then lie in a May punt imbibing Montaigne as I had once read *Twelfth Night* –

But that was to come. 'Informal committee meeting Fri. 6.30. Yrs. Bobbie.' The idea was that the Ouds should explore the territory between Shakespeare and a smutty smoker, and it was decided to invite members to submit original one-act plays, the best three to be presented in the dining-room. As I voted I thought, I'm going to write one, and act in it; and going down to the smoking-room, I was not deflated when I found people reading the current *Isis* in which I was deputizing for Boy Malcolm, the New Theatre dramatic critic. My notice of Madame Lydia Kyasht and Company in *A la Russe* had the distinction of achieving a misprint in the first line : 'A curious entertainment, as bent on variety as a Colosseum programme.' But I made up for it with 'The pointe-work of the ballerine was deft'; I had altered it to 'ballerinas', then in the name of Heath

Harrison altered it back. I was severe, but with pained impartiality. 'The whimsical Chauve Souris drummer grew a trifle tiresome ... Miss Colleen Clifford worked hard giving 'impressions'; her technique is clever, but she lacks personality ... The dresses were tawdry, and the scenery deserves all the vituperation it can earn. Altogether a cheap affair. G. E. W.' I had not studied St John Ervine for nothing. As I avoided noticing the others bent over my verdict, the image twinged my mind of Madame Kyasht sitting in digs in Walton Street reading me too, and I saw Miss Clifford, any minute now, dragging her way past us to her evening's work secure in the knowledge that she had no personality. Craven thoughts. I was challenged about the Colosseum, tried to make out I really had meant a variety show in ancient Rome – gladiators, Christians – but my bluff was called.

By this time I was on the fender, ordering a round of drinks. Suddenly, this year, the club seemed less inhibited, more whimsical, and hadn't people got less tall, more my size? I scanned them. They all looked more like promoted school-fellows than Ouds members: a bouncing fresh-faced head boy biting a pipe named J. B. Fernald, a gentle fag of a Pat Moynihan, a languid cherub in plus-fours (Martin Rellender), a fair quiet school captain with a diffident repose (Charles Garvenal), a hesitant mooncalf (Douglas Cleverdon), and a zany wiseacre with a protruding tooth: a fourth-former by the difficult name of Betjeman. 'My tutor,' Martin was saying, balancing a Manhattan Cocktail, 'is deeply in love, with a deer in Magdalen Park ... Yes, a she, I'm surprised at him ...' 'As long,' said Charles, 'as it doesn't go any further. My house-master had a thing about the Matron's hedgehog, used to disappear for hours and turn up to read the lesson scratched to bits.' They looked even younger, of course, next to Old Percy, who was foolish enough to disclose that Mama had given him a long mirror so that he could practise gestures in front of it. 'How thoughtful of her, Percy dear,' said John B., 'obscene ones?'

I wrote my One-Act Play, revising next day, then typing by my fire. It had come so easily that it was hard to believe, as I wrote 'Vigil' across the top, that it was any good. It was set in a lonely Welsh manor into which stumbles an English traveller, lost in the small hours, to find a young rustic, simple and inarticulate, on guard outside his master's bedroom. Another Englishman bursts in, in a dressing-gown, and the two talk across the immobile boy: the sleeping man has hypnotic power over any who enter his house. The newcomer tries to walk out but cannot, and the scene mounts in hysteria until the boy raises his head: his master has died in his sleep. The two prisoners stagger out, free, while the bewildered sentinel takes up the candle and goes in to the corpse. I had an idea who might be well cast for Issaiah Farmer's Boy.

Vigil was chosen to be included in the Evening of One-Act Plays, preceded by *Professional Soldier* by Patrick Monkhouse, whose father had written *The Conquering Hero*. Robert Speaight and Leslie Nye were cast as the Englishmen, and I asked if John Fernald might produce it; I knew he would do it well. I also roped in Charles as assistant stage-manager, strolled out of the committee-meeting and raced down to tell them that what we had planned was to happen. They were sitting with Martin the cherub. 'Marvellous,' said John, 'your first play, my first production!' 'Let's celebrate,' said Martin the seraph, 'I'll take you all to Fluffy Dent-Godalming's.' 'Fluffy Dent-Godalming?' said John, knocking out his pipe, 'sounds like a deb turned chorus girl.' 'He practically is,' said Martin, 'and the poor thing's in Balliol. He's got a binge tonight, but hates the word and says he's giving a small dance. It's to celebrate the *Cherwell* number.' 'Oh my God,' said John. That week the magazine, handed blithely over for one issue to Harold Acton and Brian Howard, had set North Oxford by the ears: ' "GIRL-MEN AT CAMBRIDGE" – this sort of slogan in the daily papers must cease; Oxford cannot afford to lose her one claim on public attention. Girl-men are hers, and hers ALONE; for the last six months they have provided three dozen London reporters with their daily bread. Shall Cambridge take this away from us? NEVER!' Over the page, a sober Acton review of *The Picture of Dorian Gray*: 'a charming boy's book, we would suggest a cheap edition to fit comfortably into the pocket of a school blazer.'

*

I said, 'Shall we meet here first for a sherry?' 'Sherry?' said Martin. 'You mean a gin-and-French at the George!' 'Right,' said John, 'but damn, I can't come on to the binge, it's Monday,' he was the *Cherwell* critic for the Playhouse. The George Restaurant! Let it advertise itself soberly in the *Isis* as 'Oxford's Premier Rendezvous, Music and Punkahs', was it not the sizzling hub and hob of the Aesthetes? Martin seemed to have a foot in several worlds, having mentioned casually in the Ouds that he had had carnal knowledge of Muriel, a waitress at the same rendezvous.

I had never tasted a gin-and-French, I had never been to a party, I had never been to the George, and I had had my first play accepted. I walked back to the J.C.R., lunched off coffee, a biscuit and the *Sporting and Dramatic*, and for the first time hurried past the Hall stairs and down to Meadow with a light heart. But I could not stay still: before an unpredictable evening, I would lead an exemplary afternoon. I struck out on a long wet walk up to Boar's Hill, and looked down through the mist at Tom Tower, a stolid winter sultan amid an elegant harem of shivering spires. Back, I found the weekly letter from home, in Dad's fine script. 'My Dear Son George, Yrs to hand, hoping this finds you as it leaves us. We are delighted to hear that your Tutor is pleased with your Progress, also that in your little spare time you have managed to write a Play, you must trust to Providence and the good taste of the Committee in general. Mrs Evans Chapel was asking after you in the Co-op, Yr loving F. M. and Bros Job & Thomas.' Then the other laboriously rounded hand, 'i of gott the parlour to do so no more now, are you getting enough nourishment, M. Wms.'

It was the night for the slate-blue sweater with the maroon tie, and I flapped smartly past the poor devils dawdling in to Hall dinner, then once more through the invisible townees thronging the Corn, and up the George steps. As I entered the glittering twittering flower-scented pleasure-dome, beyond the palms the orchestra was playing 'I Want to be Happy'. The other three already shone at the table, John conservative in bow-tie, Charles brushed and quiet and amused, Martin in green shirt and flowing poet's tie, his hair trained down into one eye. The punkah started to whir. 'Martin,' I said, 'you look like a sinister choir-boy of fourteen.' 'So glad, I was aiming at fifteen. When I'm sent down I shall apply for a job as punkah-coolie at the George.' I sipped my gin-and-French; it tasted more like medicine than medicine did. 'Martin,' said John, lighting a Balkan Sobranie, 'which is Muriel?' 'Standing behind Mark Ogilvie-Grant and Ketton-Cremer and serving Harold Acton if you know what I mean – cigarette? Miranda's Dream, rather good.' I took my first puff, and savoured my medicine; the lights and the music and the talk were closing deliciously round me like a great buzzing bubble. 'I asked her to marry me,' drawled Martin, 'but she was engaged to either Plunket Greene or Robert Byron she couldn't remember which.'

Then he told us how last vac, waiting for a bus in Piccadilly, he had been drawn into conversation by a Nonconformist parson – 'one of his *big* non-conforming days ...' 'Martin,' said John, as we pooled for the gin-and-Frenches and ordered more, 'now we're boozing tell us all – are you or aren't you?' 'Well,' said Martin, pursing his lips to make a smoke-ring while he weighed the question, 'yes and no – I'm bi, I suppose.' 'Bi?' I said, at sea. 'Sexual,' said Martin, blowing a kiss to Muriel. 'They do say,' said John, winking at me and Charles, 'that at school you were no better than you should be.' 'Do they?' said Martin, beaming, 'tell them I can't take *too* much credit, if there'd been any girls about I might have got through clean as a whistle. It was really faute de Muriel.' We all laughed so much that even Brian Howard's table turned round. My Miranda's Dream had split; I chewed some crisps and said, 'D'you remember, that's what Noël called *Hay Fever* in his first-night speech?' 'What,' said Charles, ' "Faute de Muriel"?' It was so unexpected, from him, that we nearly fell off our chairs. 'No,' I said, ' "clean as a whistle" – you know, after they'd all said how dirty *Fallen Angels* was. He rushed on from *The Vortex* just in time to say "This play at least, ladies and gentlemen, has been as clean as a whistle".' I had used the Coward voice, a passable imitation considering the background of gin, French and Welsh.

We went out. They were playing a tango, 'La Paloma', and Martin glided downstairs to the music; we followed solemn suit, more clumsily. The night air was bracing; I shouted suddenly, the war-whoop I used to do by myself in the train, and at last – oh joy of friendship, joy of Oxford – I was answered, for my companions took up the cry and all four arm in arm, we whooped across into the Turl. On the corner, the great Playhouse hoarding stared down at us, black on dark red: *Ghosts*, with Alan Napier and Byam Shaw. I stopped importantly and pointed up: 'I prophesy that I shall have a play on at said Playhouse.' 'Why not,' said John, 'if it turns out as good as *Vigil*?' I felt sharply happy, then, seeing cakes in a window, sharply hungry; I had eaten nothing since my J.C.R. biscuit. ' "Clean as a whistle",' said John, 'good old Noël, he's still marvellous value, remember *The Young Idea*?' Old Noël was two months off his twenty-sixth birthday.

We were at the portals of Balliol, where the porter directed us with a sniff; John bade us farewell and hurried on to Trinity for his gown. Once in the dark of the Quad, where every whisker of lawn was Jowett-hallowed and any stone that did not ooze learning at our tread was exuding virility, we tangoed across to 'La Paloma' sung by Martin, and raced up to the first floor. 'M. J. T. Dent-Godalming.'

But there was no need to look for the name. The noise was like a hundred fledgling parakeets, splayed with shill laughter and the tinny rhythm of 'Rose Marie I Love You'. Martin pointed to above the opposite door and grimaced, 'Know who that is? The big Rugger blue, Fluffy said he and a couple of hearties are watching the form and might easily cut up rough.' Two hulking figures in plus-fours and gowns came clumping up the stair just as a maniacal cackle echoed from M. J. T. Dent-Godalming; they glared at us and banged into their sanctuary. 'They can't read or write,' said Charles, solemn and again unexpected, 'but my God they're men!' We could hear Rose Marie running down with a despairing wail and then being whizzed frantically back to life. 'Here goes,' said Martin, holding the knob, 'bye bye Muriel,' and opened the door on to a tidal wave of cigarette-smoke.

Fluffy was winding up the machine: pale face over shiny black high-necked shirt over gold trousers tucked into Russian boots. 'My dears,' he called, 'do you like my Charvet pyjama-jacket? Martin you look divine, what I can see of you without my glasses but I look so heavenly without them it's worth it. I've got something on called Helena Rubinstein Jelly and Whitener, drinkies?' A graceful Sapphic ghost, he now bent under a lamp in order to scrutinize, between wrists which seemed hardly able to bear the weight, a plum-coloured H.M.V. label. I subsided into a corner to scan the murky landscape: scarves had been twined over lights, shadows swayed between me and the fog. The centre had been cleared and six or seven couples were fox-trotting, chattering as they jigged decorously to 'Does the Spearmint Lose its Flavour?', some holding glasses from which they sipped while jigging, it looked hard work. Brian Howard stood at my elbow, his back to me. 'My dear,' he was saying, 'I've only ever seen one passable undergraduette and *she* looked like a vain boy scout.'

Fluffy peered at me hospitably, 'Here's a spare drinkie my dear, do gobble.' I gobbled, then saw Charles leaning against the wall, his eyes moving slowly over the scene as if absorbed in a play. He was the sole relaxed figure in a smoke-laden bird-cage; who did he remind me of, suddenly? Before I could think, he was working his way over to me. 'I say,' he said, the school captain, 'you're not drinking whisky, are you, after gin?' then a couple tripped between us. I wondered about his question, for my glass tasted as much like medicine as the other hand. As I sipped absently, fragments of talk scurried past, a syncopated whirlpool of my-dears. 'T. S. Eliot my dear is a bloody fraud my dear it's the Firbank in me my dear who does he think he is my dear Zuleika Dobson?' Fluffy was doing an intricate Black Bottom, 'I'll Jazz my Way, To Mandalay', but not a word spilled: 'my dear, Bébé was sent down and now in France, Université de Nancy, I wrote him how sweet of them to name a town after me, Oscar never had that ...'

The noise rent my ears, and the room began slowly to swim. I rose, collided and sat again, heavily, on a stool next to the fire.

On a bookshelf six inches from my eye, *The Water Babies*; I
lifted a full glass from the shelf, lugged out the book, and the
print curled into focus, 'One upon a time there was a little
chimney-sweep ...' With the vision of the about-to-be-drunk, I
was in 314a by the fire, the same coal as glowed here in Balliol,
my mother and Fluffy, the coal they used was the same, what
a marvellous marvellous thought to put in a book, *that is life* ...
I took something from my lips, the glass I had lifted. I had
drunk half. I drained it. Then I gave my railway-carriage whoop,
drowned in the whirlpool from which splashed single words:
Dadaism Tutankhamen Mr W. H. sublimation Rimbaud em-
pathy Aldous Julian tone-poem Ufa Rima Diaghileff post-war
neurosis my dear ... 'If you knew Susie,' shrieked His Master's
Voice, 'as I know Susie, oh Boy what a Girl!'

I lurched across – 'my dear my ankle' – and into the bedder.
Four people were perched on the single bed, three drinking and
listening to the fourth, Harold Acton, his trousers draped to
look like a lilac-coloured hobble-skirt. On a low dressing-table
lay a box of Papier Poudré Phul-Nana and a lip-stick. I watched
Fluffy sit before the mirror, take up the lip-stick, peer, put on
his spectacles, apply it with care, put it down, whip off the
spectacles and scamper back to the dance. I took his place,
drained a tiny glass, green stuff tasting like sweets, and cocked
an ear to the voice from the bed, 'But if one finds the words, my
dears, there is beau-ty in a black-pudding!' I shuddered, then
caught the eyes of the owl in the mirror; we exchanged a long
stare. 'Are you me,' I said aloud, as he formed the same question,
'or am I you?' Wait till I get on stage, the mystery will be
revealed, the quarter has been called, my make-up ... I took up
the lip-stick, daubed, and suddenly had a crimson moustache.
Then the ship gave a vertiginous heave – good God, on deck ...
A doorway – help, where am I – a door – and I knew no more.

Ruthless giant arms dragged me to the depths of a whirlpool
smelling of a cesspool, then up through booming corridors of
darkness to a white-hot lighthouse bursting with frantic voices
that blinded and deafened me. Then a tang of soap, I am sluicing
myself next to the mangle before going out to the tap with a

sooty toothbrush, no no there's the school train slowing down for the Quay, run for it you'll miss the exam come along old boy three more steps ... Then the monster wave of smoke and water engulfed the lighthouse, a thunderous crash of glass, I flailed out piteously to defend myself; and I died, mercifully, in action.

Unmercifully I awoke, from a groaning retching stupor haunted by chimes, ding dong what's wrong very wrong ding dong ... daylight; I sat up, and slumped back. My head had been cleft neatly in two, by a tomahawk soaked in gin-and-French, whisky, white wine, rum-punch and green chartreuse; my stomach was a nest of vipers, and my tongue had been neatly skinned and then baked. I was in my own bed, I was naked, but in that flash I had seen my clothes folded on a chair and Charles's scarf crumpled on the boards. He had put me to bed. Mingled with my nausea I thought, had I had a bath yes I had ... I felt so ill that I made myself get up – my scout, thank God, had left me to sleep – then I scoured the red streak from my face and shaved in a trance. My slate-blue hung pitifully drying – washed? – I groaned aloud. The only object on my table was the letter from home. 'Are you getting enough nourishment ...'

My feet dragged to the Ouds, where I found Charles and Martin, who was sipping black coffee as fresh as a bisexual daisy. I drew them greenly to the window-seat, 'Was it awful?' 'First time I've ever seen Fluffy angry,' said Martin, 'he's had three Cachet-Faivres already.' 'I was sick, wasn't I?' 'Sickissimo, on the Rugger blue's bed, they raided the party, Fluffy was debagged, they smashed his spectacles –' 'Don't tell me,' I moaned, shutting my eyes, 'and you took me ...' 'Some gaudy night,' said Charles, 'have a beer.' I felt better, then sat down to write to Fluffy, 'Dear ...' 'Dear what, do I call him?' 'Well,' said Martin, 'I know he's feeling pretty haughty, why not try "Dear Madam"?'

Meanwhile, in 314a, religion was rearing an unexpected head. 'Now for the Latest, your dear Brother Tom has celebrated his thirteenth birthday with buying a uniform for the Sally Army; the first we knew was your Mam catching him testifying in the middle of them all with a cornet on that waste patch between the New Inn and the War Memorial that smells of them goats. It was a shock to her. Your dear Mother has been always one for the Chapels but she feels that this is too much of the Good Thing. But we must let young lads sow their wild Oats in their own way, Yr loving R. and M. Williams.' I wondered if Mam had been reminded of the Praying Stoker.

Vigil went into rehearsal, my first birth-pangs and my easiest. It emerged as I had written it, the other actors were perfectly cast and John Fernald knew what he was doing; Charles said to me, washing hands after rehearsal, 'You know, this is going to be all right.' I was asked to a party in New College, a friend of Fluffy's; a weight lifted, I was not ostracized after all. There was dancing and cup, but I partook of neither, being unsuited to the first and cured of the second. Afternoons, I fell into the excellent habit of long winter walks with Charles, who talked little but well, and – it seemed to me – with importance. 'Dear Miss Cooke, I am concentrating on *Le Mystère d'Adam* and now must rush my essay through to read to my tutor, whose comment will be the usual "Any difficulties?" The idea is for me to stay on a fourth year unless something untoward happens ...'

Vigil went better than any of us had dared hope; I savoured the satisfaction of holding an audience, and heard in the air the faint unmistakable crackle of success. On the 26th I gave a rowdy birthday luncheon, my twentieth – Reggie Colby, Charles, John Fernald, John Aldridge, Jim Courage – with dancing on the table to the borrowed gramophone, after emptying a bottle of kümmel brought by Norman Cameron; I had taken him aback before the meal by suggesting we open it then, and he had explained to me about liqueurs. I then prepared a party for that night, after the last performance, by setting out bottles, glasses from the J.C.R., records, and solemnly arranging the room for dancing. Then, to clear the head, a particularly long walk with Charles; as we returned, the November dark was already drizzling over Oxford, but I was, for today, invulnerable. Then Ouds dinner with John and Charles, I never seemed to dine in Hall these days, though I was steadily charged for my four nights a week. That night Mr Fagan came to the plays, and told John that he would have liked people in London to see *Vigil*.

At the party I drank two whiskies, enough – tonight – to go perfectly to my head. People brought other people, and it was more hilarious than the others. I never found out if Professor Lindemann heard any of it. At a quarter to twelve they all trooped out: I winced at the gate-money I would be charged, and though my head was spinning, turned into my mother by opening wide door and windows, pulling out coals, shovelling cigarette-ends on to the embers, coaxing drinks back into bottles, scouring glasses in the scout's pantry and slipping records back into their brown covers: 'What'll I Do', 'Tie a String around your Finger', 'I Wonder where my Baby is To-night', 'You Forgot to Remember' ... My life in order, I went happily to bed.

Next morning, the shadow of anticlimax: as I walked to the Ouds, the six-weeks vac hovered over me. Only Old Percy sat before the fire, and the waiters were dismantling the pigmy stage. On my way into the office cum dressing-room, I heard a voice on the telephone inside, 'Sorry father, but there it is ...' He came out, harassed; it was Charles, 'What a start to the day ...' Then he saw that his shoelace was undone, bent down and slowly fastened it, who did he look – of course, the Canadian actor who had called ... 'My college has sent me down for next term, for not working.' I continued to stare, 'You won't be the Page in "Henry Four", or in the smoker?' He counted out pennies. 'No, I'm depressed. Come over to my rooms, I have a couple of notes to write first, isn't it bloody?' He hurried out, and I collected my belongings from the play which last night had been all-important, I looked at the tele-phone, then at the coins. I touched them, they were still warm from his pocket.

He was at a desk, writing. I called 'I'll walk on'; catching up with Martin outside the toy-shop, I said, 'Weren't you at school with Charles?' Yes, and Charles had been a dark horse my dear, quite a heart-throb in his quiet way but his own heart wasn't in it, last term he asked a chorus-girl from *Poppy* to tea in his rooms, got her into his bedder and then into his bed, bye bye my dear. I did not stop till I was down Beaumont Street and inside Worcester. I had never visited him, and decided to walk about; something told me that the one way to endow a personality with mystery and a double allure is to enter a room which has been trodden by those feet for months, and wait. I wandered through and stared at the lake. A couple of notes ... I had never seen his writing. I saw his hand, blunt and strong, with at the wrist a blur of faint gold. Back into Beaumont Street. Many undergraduates advanced towards me, lanky, stubby, long-chinned, no-chinned; but I knew him a mile off.

He saw me, and his face broke into a smile. His rooms were like him, warmly unaffected, the desk untidy, with lecture notes in a firm hand; I saw them as a long letter, to me. He made coffee; the door of the bedder was open, and I thought of *Poppy*. Letters lying about, but already I would not think of that but looked rather at the dog-eared script of *Vigil*, 'return to C. R. Garvenal A.S.M.' It looked like a degree. Assistant Stage Manager, he had been employed by me; the thought vibrated.

We took the coffee to the window-seat: one foot up on the cushion, trouser tight over the under-leg, sock concertinaed down over brogued shoe. 'Charles,' I said suddenly, 'I've never thanked you for that night, for looking after me.' He laughed, 'You were in a bad way – stay to lunch? I don't know enough about you, you're going to be a real playwright my old friend, d'you know that?'

I answered all his steady questions, then asked him about his public school. 'I was rather hearty, footer and all that ... Well, there were a couple of what Martin would call romances, nothing very ... Yes, one boy did get a bit difficult, scenes, then tried suicide and went to India.' I said, 'He sounds rather dreary.' 'He was – cigar, no?' We sat on the floor and he put on a record of 'Rhapsody in Blue', which I had heard often enough, since that first Peckwater evening, to know every note.

The long threnodies, even the melting slow movement, combined with the failing winter day to make me somehow apprehensive, and I was glad when he put on 'I Miss My Swiss', 'Thanks for the Buggy Ride' and a marvellous new tune called 'Valencia' to which we snapped thoughtful fingers, he played it twice. Then a piano record, Chopin. As we listened, he fell into an even deeper repose. The morbid chords lingered dangerously in mid-air, before dying into the shadows. He stretched, ruffled an eyebrow and jutted his lower lip in lazy thought.

I jumped up, lifted the needle and said 'I'd better be off.' Beaumont Street was already flickering into gaslight. I felt elated, yet there was constriction in my breast. 'At that age the joys can be as poignant as the sorrows ...'

Racing across Tom, I forced the elation to the boil. I would work, with before me this new and permanent image; I would start this very evening, dinner in Hall, then Fr. Philology by the fire, hammer and tongs, for that First. Then, for the first two weeks of the image-less spring term, I would concentrate on the Heath Harrison, perhaps he would come to Spain for the summer vac, cycling, marvellous – but first 'Henry Four', I was to play two good parts, then work like hell for the rest of term, then we ... I opened my door. No fire and a window open to the twilit Meadows, their chill firmly on the room like a dead hand; I laid out my books, hesitated, changed into my blue, went to the Ouds and dined with Campbell and Pat Moynihan.

I did work in the vac, with the image before me, but it was a time-killing time. If I had been able to take an interest, however superficial, in the people around me – but I lived in a sealed world, communicating by signs and phrases, 'Yes Oxford going nicely thank you no we missed the flu down there remember me to Mrs Roberts merde merde merde ...' Tea at Underwood, though, could not fail to jerk me out for a bumpy hour. 'See here George, they blether about progress but I'll bet my bottom dollar there was more democracy then than now, how's the Spanish?' For Prize Distribution, I steeled myself and donned my Oxford bags; it was my best suit, I had to. 'Good life,' said

Mam, 'there's a waste of stuff for you!' I had intended to sport the high-necked jumper as well but my courage failed me; as it was I walked up Holywell High Street creating a sensation spiced with ridicule, but willed myself not to care. Miss Cooke made no comment.

I counted the days, but I worked. Sometimes, after dark, I would restlessly put on overcoat and scarf – knotted, a vac concession – and hurry up the alley to dim High Street; the few cloth-capped figures of my own age, propped like dead bodies against a brick corner and waiting for something to happen to the barren greasy night – something more than just rain and dirty stories and betting slips – made me think of Covent Garden and I pelted home with the old zest, to a long evening in the ancient womb of family. Mam supplied diversion from Morphology. 'That Mrs Bellis is got shut of that Mr Bellis, he's gone dead, not that he had that much life in him when he was with us, poor fellow ...' Over the New Year, a card, 'What about Easter in Paris? Good luck for 1926, Ch.' I turned it over, my name and address looked as unreal as on the Tom Douglas envelope in my wallet, which I now took out and replaced with the card. I hesitated, then put the old letter in the fire. 'What was that?' said Mam, 'never burn a paper lad, in case you've made a mistake.'

Chapter 24

Towards the Rocks

The new term started badly with a disconcertingly high battel, I was living beyond my means. But nothing could keep me out of the Ouds, I would even settle in corners of it with my Spanish vocabulary. *Vigil* was published in *The Oxford Outlook*, which Graham Greene had edited last year, printing work by Isherwood and Rowse. I sent a copy to Miss Cooke and to my father, who wrote back 'Your play is well mixed together, more power to you.'

We, the Committee, gave a luncheon for Lucille La Verne, a distinguished American actress at the New in *Sun-Up*, and after coffee, when she said she wanted to see Christ Church, I escorted her. She was a four-square body of fifty, and I felt unchivalrous wishing it were Isabel Jeans. Passing Mercury, with ninety-year-old Doctor Lock in front enjoying an uncertain constitutional, my guest came out with the strangest statement ever made in Tom Quad; I had just admitted to having acted at school in *The Merchant of Venice*. 'Ah,' she said, stopping, 'Shylock!' The Doctor peered round, obviously not sure that he had not heard his own name. 'Now Shylock,' said Miss La Verne, 'is a role I am determined to play.' The Doctor wavered, turned again, gave her a bemused look, and went on. She did play it, in London, at the Little Theatre, on 23 September 1929. It seems a pity that the night could not have turned into a memorable one with Ralph Richardson as Nerissa, Jack Hawkins as Jessica, and Portia in the safe hands of Donald Wolfit.

I sat the Heath Harrison in Spanish, but though I made a tremendous effort with a last week of hard labour, I had not a strong enough grounding and was third time unlucky. It did not depress me unduly, for there was 'Henry Four', produced by

379

Bridges Adams, with Harman Grisewood, Olga Lindo and Speaight as Falstaff. During rehearsals, somebody suggested that mine being a big room, why not a bottle party, and charge everybody their gate-money? This was so successful that it became a weekly event; each time after the last guest was gone, I donned the scout's apron and put the room to rights. Daily I expected a polite note from Professor' Lindemann, and it is typical of the impersonality of Oxford life, certainly at Christ Church then, that it never occurred to me that somebody might notice my weekly battel dropsically swollen with gate-money, and so get wind of the fact that I was running a night-club. And nobody ever did.

There were no incidents, and though spirits were high the dancing stayed as stately as ever. The only chequered night was after I met Brian Howard in Peck and he said, 'We're dining first, shall we bring Cara?' 'Do,' I said, thinking he meant some Italian undergraduate; I was halfway to Meadow when I remembered that Cara was Oxford's own siren – but they couldn't bring a girl, they'd be stopped at the gate ... They weren't, for in mid-party Brian slipped in with Fluffy and a white wisp of a boy in Oxford bags, long scarf and green pork-pie hat; she passed among the crowd and danced from here to there, so Eton-cropped that her hair was often shorter than her partner's. Setting out for Tom Gate, Brian was unperturbed, 'I'll put her between Fluffy and Sandy and the porter won't bat an eyelid.' It was next morning before I contemplated the consequences for me if the porter had.

'Dear Miss Cooke, I am working on Pascal and the *Chanson de Roland*, which tails off at the end. For the Easter vac I have decided on Paris; this time, alas, not on scholarship money but it will be worth it for my French and the Bibliothèque Nationale at hand.' 'Henry Four' was exciting for me; as Morton the soldier I didn't look bad in a plain sort of way, and later as old Silence, I had the luck, in answer to Shallow's 'He is at Oxford still, is he not?', to speak the line 'Indeed, sir, to my cost', and get the laugh of the play. A Supper of friendship and fun, Doggins' till dawn, and at five we did *Vigil* impromptu, the only time I have ever played a performance while under the influence of drink. Six sleepy hours later I was shown Agate in the *Sunday Times*: 'I think I spy an actor in Mr G. E. Williams, who gave the small part of Morton very well indeed.' Tomorrow, I start work.

As we dozed over tea and the Ouds fire, Denys Buckley said, 'Who's going to run the smoker now Patsy and Co have gone?' Five minutes later, somehow, it was me, and for five weeks it was a full-time job: getting numbers composed, producing and writing most of the dialogue, work not only gruelling but worthless in view of the low level, in every sense, expected of the book. To only one réplique did I become attached, in the Turkish scene,

SLAVE: The Chief Eunuch, sir, wishes to escort you round the Palace, he is particularly proud of his ballroom.
SULTAN: What was that again?

After the last night, the inevitable bottle-party in my rooms; next morning, before I had time to feel any let-down, John Fernald bounced into the Ouds with a letter, Mr Fagan had arranged for us to play *Vigil* in front of a couple of people in London, at the Fortune Theatre. 'Will be v. happy to A.S.M. again, also to put you up. Meet me Alexis Monday lunch one, Ch.'

'I trust,' said the Dean, framed through his french windows by a perfect garden already sprinkled with a discreet wealth of spring buds, 'that you have enjoyed a profitable term?' I thought of Clara. 'I take it, Mr Williams, that you know next term's date and a happy Easter to you ...' Off with the white tie, kick the mortar-board into the wardrobe; next day, Sunday, was spent time-killing, a stroll through Addison's Walk, where I halted suddenly to realize how importance absence had made this reunion, an evening in the empty club, lounging with one leg over a chair-arm, then on Monday morning I was off. I took the Tube to Leicester Square, stood on the moving staircase elbow to elbow with a slim bearded traveller whom I alone seemed to recognize as Bernard Shaw, deposited my case and at five to one entered the Alexis, a little restaurant in Lisle Street to which Angus had once brought me. I settled at a table for two facing the door, and told the little French waiter that my companion would be here any second.

Five past. I wished I had brought a book. I ordered a sherry, and with it the waiter brought me an early *Evening News*. I glanced at the headline, 'Measles Attacks Cambridge Crew', I had not even known there was a Boat Race, then among the Oxford faces I recognized Murray-Threipland from my first term, a hundred years ago ... On the theatre page, a photograph of Tom; I returned his look, thoughtfully. Twenty past. The door opened, and in my disappointment I was compensated by recognizing John Gielgud, playing at Barnes in *The Three Sisters*. But by twenty to two, I was staring at the stock market. The waiter looked at me uncertainly, for the fifth time; I mumbled 'Coquille'. The restaurant had filled, and the chatter suddenly mocked me, ha ha let you down ha ha ... The waiter was gazing curiously at my hands; they were clutched round the newspaper, the knuckles white. I started on the coquille and burnt my tongue.

'Emlyn, you're looking very unapproachable!' Alan Michelsen of the Ouds, leaving with a pretty actress. 'Sorry,' I smiled, 'I thought after the racket of term I'd have a quiet lunch on my own.' The waiter gave me a cool look. I paid, wandered out and down into Piccadilly Circus and stood on the corner of Eros waiting to cross. Cross to where? I looked at the blank concealing faces; except that they were scurrying, they were the same as in Connah's Quay. Hatless, scarf over shoulder, did I not belong here either? Remorse stabbed me. I should be in my parlour-corner studying, what was I doing at the Centre of the World, a leaf spinning on a muddied stream of dangerous currents?

I eddied down to the Plaza Cinema where for five minutes the music soothed me, then it turned into Chopin; I looked round at the daytime dark, got up and left. Sinking into the foyer carpet, I halted. I had walked out of a film! The Hip, the starveling who had rolled crumbs of excitement round his tongue, the lost paradise ... I went back to Leicester Square Tube and telephoned; I had only handled the instrument a couple of times as business manager, I was still scared of it, and his voice answered me from the bottom of the sea, 'I'm terribly sorry, had to meet my father before they left for the country – left a message for you at the Alexis and had a feeling the waiter wasn't taking it in – come straight here, *please* ...'

At the flat in Fitzjohn's Avenue, he opened the door; the telephone was ringing. 'That was Martin,' he said when he joined me in the spare room, 'Bunny Abraham's father's giving a twenty-firster tonight at the Kit Kat, a cousin's got flu and can you take his place, right?' The Kit Kat! As he went back to Martin, I settled into a blanket of well-being. Oh tails, I'd left them at Oxford, ring John Fernald, not far off for size, fixed ...

I walked down to Marlborough Road with a key in my pocket and back again with the tails in brown paper under my arm, an adventurous undergraduate in the wilds of St John's Wood. But as I walked I thought ... as long as I can remember I've called myself self-sufficient, so how can I have changed in half an hour from a moron to a bright-light lad out for the evening? The Kit Kat's done it ... Letting myself in, I heard 'Rhapsody in Blue' from the drawing-room. I made four attempts at my white tie. 'Let me do it,' he said, 'sorry to breathe down your neck, stand still!' As he manipulated the tie from behind my shoulders, hands hovering warm against my face, I smelt soap and cigarette smoke, and felt the fine red-gold hairs tickling my chin.

Dinner, Rules, a flick, then ... my first night-club, or rather Palace of the Night : shrouded lamps, slaves dressed as waiters, exquisite shingled women, defiant Eton-crops behind long cigarette-holders and above all, a deep-throbbing jazz band. We joined a great flowered table ablaze with a cake; Mr Abraham, a benevolent Old Lad of Threadneedle Street whose Isaac had not only not gone up in flames but was here, Oxford-blessed and come of age, sat waiting to pour out the milk of human kindness, or gin, or champagne, or anything else we fancied. I saw the Charleston danced for the first time; I was flanked by two charming chatty Jewish girls who had come out last year and looked and sounded exactly alike: after coffee, in a Gents which seemed to me lined with precious stones, Martin asked me how I was faring with Miss Rosencrantz and Miss Guildenstern. They and I discussed plays and books without visible strain: 'I've *tried* to learn the Charleston but find it too shy-making, Mummy says it's too indecent but just jogging up and down isn't indecent or is it said she naïvely?'

I was again careful with my wines but felt myself soaring, a sybarite on a central-heated cloud. Then the cabaret: under smoking spotlights, acrobatic dancers flung themselves about and peered politely at us from between their own legs. I danced dutifully – unacrobatically – and enjoyed making myself agreeable; Bunny was toasted, and the evening ended in a glow of thanks and goodwill. Charles and I got home at four; he opened champagne – 'they're away' – and put on a record, his Worcester gramophone. 'Rhapsody in Blue', slow movement. 'Charles,' I said, wine-happy and wrapped in music, 'in Paris I have *got* to work, will you help me?' 'But of course,' he said, 'I'll have to work too, we'll work *and* paint the town, great fun ...' He was swaying slightly with a broad smile that was unlike him, and I realized that he too was wine-happy. He leant forwards suddenly, mischievously, and flicked loose my white tie. 'Easier to undo than to do,' he said, 'but that's life!'

We all met at John's in the afternoon to rehearse, then again at the Fortune stage-door as the curtain fell on the matinée of *Juno and the Paycock*. At five-fifteen we played the play; the handful of audience only enhanced the uncanniness of the setting. After the curtain fell we went down into the stalls to join the Fagans, Sybil Thorndike and Lewis Casson, before they went on to *Saint Joan* at the Lyceum and several of the O'Casey cast. But while Speaight, Nye, Fernald and Williams were being kindly treated by their elders, to me the important figure in the dim auditorium was the respectful A.S.M. standing at attention four empty rows away, with warm under his arm the prompt-script of my play. Sitting beside him in the 13 bus as he read a newspaper, and looking at his face in profile, relaxed but withdrawn, I knew that he was unattainable.

Love is one thing, obsession another. Paris began badly and ended worse, and abruptly. As with all writers in embryo, one narrow-eyed corner of me was watching, just as the sick doctor, locally anaesthetized under the knife, cannot help following – even as he winces – the details of his own ordeal. I found myself able to see another human being, one moment as the magical loved one, and the next – with the cynicism of the observer – as a creature as ordinary as his neighbour, with the mundane defects, and the mundane qualities too, which will reassert themselves when the fever has abated; sometimes, indeed, it is possible, with a devilish double vision, to see the two figures at once, superimposed. And it is not true that a capacity to analyse one's own disease halves the pain. Possessive, though not to be possessed – covetous of that which could not be mine, but which I would reject if it were pressed upon me – I knew what it is to be tormented with thirst when the water is salt and must not be touched. 'My Dear Son George, I am on nights, so writing before going off, your Mother baking. Glad that you are working hard for your last fling at the Studies before the big Adventure, that was a good move to put down the Keel (nautical) in France, reminds me of when you went in 1921 and got the whole thing ship-shape . . .'

Chapter 25

Shipwreck

Walking into Christ Church in the warmth of early evening, I saw the Oxford summer as my enemy. It was a bad time of day psychologically and a bad day, for the term would not get going till tomorrow and the college was ringingly empty. The late April sun lay across Tom Quad, brushing the Cathedral spire like a blessing; and from all sides windows winked on to the spacious grass, calm tolerant eyes mellow with the gathered wisdom of centuries. The sight should have smoothed my spirit, but I zigzagged across with no more sense of where I was than a fly making its way over a framed Canaletto. My rooms were sour with the accumulated emptiness of weeks, and the bookish smell of polish was a reproach; looking out once more over the melancholy Meadows, and hearing the door shut behind me, I knew that from now on I was a prisoner, in a personal jail to which I had lost the key.

I opened letters. 'The view of the Dee from the school field is at its best. I'm reading reading reading, a day crammed with wealth ... I envy you every minute of Oxford, you are promised life itself ...' I put it hastily away. Advertisement, bills, then last term's battel, so high that I sank into the window-seat with a gasp. The gate-money accounted for some, but I had not saved my night-club revenue, and the lunches, teas, wines ... My Ouds bill was proportionately high, and I calculated on a bit of paper that I would end the academic year securely in debt. My mother's gorge rose within me, and I was seized with panic. Then, sorting papers, I came across Enid Wainwright's old letter, 'just tell me what I have done ...' A least I could never write like that ... Couldn't I? Shadows lengthened in the room; it grew more than uninviting, it looked sinister. I walked out without even unpacking and hurried to the Ouds, where I found Campbell and Reggie. I told them about Paris, but touched on nothing which would make me the friend in need. A pity, they would have been sensible and I would have benefited.

My tutor asked if I had worked well, 'Any difficulties?' Suppose I told him? ... The days passed. I cut myself off from the theatre – a frenzied too-late economy campaign – and the Playhouse saw me no more. 'The early history of the French Partitive Article is a debated question, cf. Sneyders de Vogel ...' I went one evening to the Ouds when I knew it would be safe, there was a dinner-party at the George. The club was buzzing with *A Midsummer Night's Dream*; 'I'm in purdah this term, Schools, such a bore ...' Leaving, I saw from the list that he was to play an Attendant to Theseus. 'The tendency to denasalize nasal vowels began in the sixteenth century, while the flectional system ...' By evening, I could not have dreaded my rooms more if there had been a dead body festering in the wardrobe. Reggie had his schools too, in French, and I welcomed his suggestion that I should join him in his rooms in Wadham every morning and work alongside. After every hour we docked ten minutes, wound up the gramophone and talked, to 'Chinese Moon', 'Jealousy', 'California here I come', 'Barcelona' ... I avoided the tunes that jolted the memory, but occasionally Reggie would set me back with an innocent remark, 'Saw Charles Garvenal on the river – no, couldn't see who he was with ...' For five unseeing minutes I stared at a list of Survivals in Medieval French of the Subjunctive of Modesty, then pulled myself together and slogged.

I dined nightly in Hall; Greenleaves, Lennox-Boyd, Auden, Rowse and Driberg all seemed to be working at fever pitch. I avoided the eyes piercing through me from the panelling; the Earl of Leicester, the Bishop of Bath and above all Mr Gladstone were now downright contemptuous. I would then go back to my rooms, and put off the moment of settling under the dusty frayed lampshade by sitting immobile in the shadowed window-seat for half an hour. The silence of the Meadow was absolute, and I longed for Tom Quad, where footsteps had been hurrying by, even if they had made me restless. I sat listening for the real world, for the train-whistle far over the frontiers of my sealed kingdom. 'The equivalent of "quam ut" is "que que", sometimes found in old French; on the other hand . . .' The empty twilight echoed mockingly with old chatter, the parties that should never have been . . . Then tormenting reminders would bare their fangs, with a regularity which my slowly hallucinated mind begin to think was ordained. 'The questionable influence of Charles (turn over the page) the Fifth on European politics . . .' One day, deep in *Tristan et Iseut*, the name Gorvenal leapt at me, one letter off, and my head fell on to my arms; I was as possessed as the man in *Vigil*, and as frantically resentful of my servitude, a bird caught in lime, had that been a premonition? . . . O God, I breathed into the sepulchral air, send an earthquake to swallow up the High, a two-month paralysis of all my fingers, let a miracle happen . . .

It did. The morning of 5 May, I was on my way to Reggie's in Wadham when I saw unwonted activity, many people hurrying, a notice outside Hall. I doubt if any young man being sued for maintenance, or wriggling in the cleft stick of bigamy, could have been more relieved at the news of war than I was to read of the General Strike of 1926. Such was my indifference to the headlines that I had had no idea of its imminence, much less what it was about; I only now took in that we were allowed, even expected, to abandon our studies and help. At five that afternoon, unable to believe my luck, I found myself at Paddington in a squad herding into a lorry, thirty undergraduates who included Angus, placid as ever and good company. I was going to ask about Wrigley but was not in the mood.

We poured out at Hay's Wharf, in the shadow of London Bridge and facing the Monument: there we filed into a tiny ship, settled four to a cabin, ate workmen's high tea in the canteen, then milled around aimlessly in the gangways, holding mugs of beer while a piano played and the hearties gathered round and swung their jorums to the inevitable Gilbert and Sullivan choruses. Everybody was excited to be playing truant in such a new way; I was so conscious of a weight off me that I was floating. Up at seven, we were marched to the quay and given dungarees and our jobs; Angus and I reported alongside a large Swedish vessel out of which swung great crates of cheese, forty at a time. We would heave one up on a truck, wheel it through, down, up, across to a corner, pitch it down a chute into hurtling darkness, and wheel back. The rhythm was utterly mechanical and soothing, so much so – and the crates were so alike – that when Angus said, 'Ye know, I think they go doon the chute, back under the Thames, up into the ship and oot again,' I believed him.

The cheery come-and-go was stimulating, and at the same time I was a workman doing a foolproof job; I thought how my father and Miss Cooke would be amused and yet approve. And we all enjoyed turning a casual eye up to the permanent crowd gaping from the bridge; we were news. Next day it was crates of pig, next cheese again. The food was rough, but we were hungry; in the evening the choruses and early to bunk, it was a healthy life. Saturday night, most of the enlisted were given leave to get lifts and go Up West for a night out. I stayed behind; seated on the deserted deck, our anchored billet spick and span with the silent city above and around, Wordsworth-shining in the evening sun, I closed my eyes and was content. It was like a toothache suddenly stopping; I was a potato at peace. An old salt wandered up to smoke his pipe and we discussed life on and off the ocean; I confided that it was two and a half years since my last woman. 'Blimey,' he said, spitting overboard, 'what'd they feed ye on up there, quinine?' Which seemed the last word on my Alma Mater. I wandered round, captain of the ship and sailing tomorrow for Atlantis : finding a tattered Edgar Wallace, I started to read and fell asleep. I was a potato.

Angus had news of Fluffy; he had been shipped to the Tyne as a navvy, and Gateshead would never be the same again. The usual morning of to and from, fetch and carry; I was thinking how sound I would sleep again tonight, when somebody shouted that the strike was over. Schools 10 June, four weeks to the day.

I did not sleep sound. That morning when in the Ouds I heard him on the telephone, was he in the brown jacket – no, that wasn't till Paris, we had bought it together and he had it on when we had the apéritifs at the – Rotonde? The Coupole? No, that was the other time, when he ... At twelve noon I opened my door in Meadow, and the empty room hit me like a blow. I heard the door close behind me. The prisoner was back, for keeps.

'Dear Miss Cooke, I am concentrating this week on the Pléiade ...' I could not work. For weather, the next twelve English days were the most beautiful I can remember. Youth flowered with the college gardens, and only for me was the sunlight envenomed; I longed for rain. But Oxford hummed quietly with the deep green of watered grass; the lighter green of willows dipped dishevelled and loving into the Cherwell; punt-poles slipped lazily into willing water. 'How is Holywell, Oxford is looking wonderful ... The economy of Pascal's style is certainly to be admired ...' There was the confident zing of tennis-rackets in the Parks; swans reared strong necks, flashed them like swords in the sun and veered downstream in casual quest of Leda. Even the stone heads outside the Sheldonian lifted satyr faces, diseased and crumbling, to the unwonted heat. 'The letter v early became a bilateral fricative, while ...' Even Plague Corner seemed to trail a scent of summer, while from my window-seat the Meadows, thorny resentments forgotten, billowed feathery and kind. For the first time, birds rested on my sill. In Peck faces passed me bright with purpose, with chatter as unheeding of me, the sick shadow that drifted by, as the twitter of the birds. But it was the purpose that frightened me, another reminder that I had none; at a time when every hour counted for getting into port, I was lost, aberrant on a private sea. From every corner, the tintinnabulation of the gramophones, 'Dardanella', 'Alabama Moon', 'Say it with a Ukelele', 'Thanks for the Buggy Ride', thin ghostly echoes. 'The role of the relative pronoun' – I could not work. These days gave me, for ever, an understanding of the lonely.

I could not sleep either, for only the bells were deaf to the summer, and refused to sweeten their clamour with any note of mercy: every quarter of a night-hour, as I creaked over in the sag of my bed, they repeated a reminder ending in an insidious question-mark, 'What's wrong ding dong twenty-four days, twenty-four? Twenty-three days, twenty-three?' And there was not one of those quarters when one face did not loom up into the darkness, give a mocking look, half-vanish and half-reappear; I was finding out what it means to be haunted. I would suddenly adumbrate plans which showed how much I was daily losing touch with reality. Feverishly, as if I had red-letter news, I would rise at eight and run breathless over to Reggie, already tranquilly at work – I would adopt a new routine, I would work all day, desperately, like those geniuses who pour life-blood on to paper while the sun is up and at nightfall sally forth to carouse: the day behind me, I would be a pub-crawler, on beer, in a haze of faces – if among them one face swam in and out, what matter – end up in jollity and sleep, and up at dawn again. Another moment my plan would be, after campaigning all day like a brilliant general in a crisis, to embrace in the evening a task to be disguised as relaxation even during Schools – I would Write a Play, to be next year a staggering novelty at the Playhouse – 'Garvenal, you haven't *seen* it? But your friend is stupendous!' – three people cut off by water, love, frustration, jealousy, *The Singing Pool* ...

Then I would glimpse my madness and sit back, my brain limp again, and wandering. Ten minutes later I would rouse myself, focus on the open page, rise and pace the floor with fists clenched, even beating my head; once I said aloud 'I'm trapped, trapped ...' then stopped and continued, still aloud, 'God, the plays I write will have to have better dialogue than that ...' Once, crossing Peck on my way to Reggie's determined to pitch into Petrarch for a whole morning, I heard from a window the opening chords of 'Rhapsody in Blue', stopped dead, turned back, and found myself in my window-seat trying to remember the etching over the fireplace that first lunch in Worcester when he had called me old friend and we had talked of school, 'One boy tried suicide, a bore ...' He had been pulling at his eyebrow, lower lip pouting thoughtfully. Glancing through a newspaper, I saw the headline 'Aimée McPherson, Evangelist, Disappears into Pacific' and thought, humourless and lifeless, yes what a way out ... I was fortunate that there were no stimulating pills or sleeping-drugs on the market. One balmy evening, when the High smelt of the day's warm dust – Italy, Elysium! – I walked with Campbell over Magdalen Bridge; suddenly hungry, we stopped at a coffee-stall and bought meat-pies. Mine had a sort of claw in it, I was sick. That seemed the key incident of a bad time.

'My Dear Son George, Yrs to hand, I am getting this off as I have an extra shift this week-end. Tom reports nine souls at the Mercy Seat last Sat so watch out, he will be coming to convert all you Scholastic Lot next ... Glad to hear you are putting on a last spurt but don't over-tax your brain, you have a lot on your plate, now for yr. Mother ... i of gott quite used to saying D.V. through Thomas so will see you after the exams D.V. Yr. loving M. Wms ...'

The days began to fuzz into one another, each an abortive neverness that need not have dawned or dusked. One moment I was my own drifting ship, the next a climber slowly leaving behind the happy valleys, up past the grinning Trolls on to the bare equivocal uplands, the eternally twilit solitudes of the half-mind. I must have been eating irregularly, I certainly slept little. I dreamt of exam-papers which were blank, I dreamt of being cornered against a wall and pressed to it like an insect till I was a smear; I dreamt of descending into the blackness of corkscrew-stairs, each downward step exactly a quarter of an inch narrower than the last, down, down ... 'Eighteen days,' said the bells, 'ding dong very wrong, eighteen ...'

What afternoon is it I find myself walking down George Street, on a bad errand – Tuesday, or still Monday? The long sun-rays had swept the road clean and transformed it into a Claude Lorrain avenue – the New Theatre a Greek temple and the overhanging Ouds-window a bower – a highway to enchanted embarcation; the sun looked magically suspended, as if tonight it was to stay and not set. I walked past the stage-door, no longings, and through into Beaumont Street with a springy walk that felt unlike me, into Worcester, and through to his rooms. His oak was sported (Oxford for front-door-locked), the most desolate, or indicative, sight in the world, people were either away or ... ? Just as I knew I was about to beat frantically on the wood I realized I was on the wrong stair. Wildly and unreasonably relieved, I found the right rooms, opened the door, and in the soft evening light, closed it.

I stood immobile, breathing the intimate emptiness like sweet chloroform. I must have looked like a composed burglar: 'Who are you,' said everything, 'who are you?' I went into the bedroom: a jacket lay crumpled on the floor, the brown one. On the chest-of-drawers lay a jar of Anzora hair-oil and a brush, which I picked up as if to put to my nostrils; but I dropped it and walked out again. There was a letter in a jagged envelope; I picked it up, stopped to savour the full tang of degradation, took out the letter and unfolded it. 'My dear Charles'; it could just as well be from a maiden aunt, but the phrase, in its true meaning, swept over me and I sank in the window-seat. I looked back into the darkening room; the silence was as hostile as in my own quarters, and I closed my eyes. Do people ever die by just sitting, and ceasing to breathe? I waited. No, I was alive and – I could feel it – clouding over. The lost vessel had glided, at last, on to the razor-edge of a reef, and was sundering from stem to stern. I got up and returned to Christ Church, to be greeted in Tom by the serene amber mockery of the same unsetting sun. I crossed jauntily, then at the Hall corner I stopped and turned. I looked back across the lordly expanse, to the Gate where I had first entered to lodge for the scholarship and thought, but that was an indestructable child ... Where has he gone?

I pulled myself together, started a letter – 'Dear Dad and Mam, Nothing much to report, only work ...' – remembered overhearing that Garvenal had gone to London, broke off, and walked to the Ouds. As I entered he was sitting on the fender,

lit by a shaft of the same faithful sun, listening, smiling, to the
arm-chairs. He saw me, and the smile flickered into embàrrass-
ment; I turned round as if I had forgotten to study the notice-
board, did so – 'Attendant to Theseus . . .' – and walked straight
out again. Halfway downstairs, I heard a loud laugh; it could
have been anybody, on any subject, but that day it could only
mean that he was making fun of me. I walked mechanically
back through the town ghosts, passed Parker at Carfax, carrying books, just managed to recognize him – that first Paris, the
Folies Bergère, les deux cocottes – and gave him the bright smile
of unhappiness; I sat in my window till it was dark, went to
bed, and listened to the bells till 'dawn. 'Sixteen days! Sixteen? . . .' I subsided into a doze, woke, dressed carefully,
emerged into another perfect morning, walked across Peck –
'Bye bye Baby', 'Am I Wasting my Time' – and along King
Teddy Street. The people looked so unreal that as they advanced
I expected them to walk through me. I stopped, and looked at
the walls of Univ; in the lyrical sun the stones looked the stuff
of dreams – and yet, if I beat my head hard enough against
them, in one minute they would turn a shell that should be
crammed with knowledge, bash bash bash, into a scrambled
egg, shall I try? I lost my way, got into Holywell (why should
a street in Oxford be so called, and why should I see it written
up as if for the first time, this morning?) and passed the Sheldonian, where the satyrs had a special leer ready for me.

Crossing the Turl and passing Blackwell's – books, books, I
shrank as if the rivers of print had wafted me a bad smell – I
rang a bell where it said 'Dr Counsell'. His eyesight was already
failing, and he was not sure who I was at first. I sat down, told
him I wanted to die, and could he give me something. The dear
old man – he had his own problems – blinked, sat next to me,
put his arm round my shoulders and said, 'Now tell old Doggins
all about it.' I did not tell him all about it; I told him I couldn't
work. It is true that I was half-watching the scene, and looking
and feeling as ill as I possibly could; but I must have been in a
bad way, for I took nothing in of being got into my bed, or of
being given sedatives to drink. I woke to find a strange lean man

sitting bolt upright in the afternoon sun, reading a paper. Photographs on the back of it, laughing holiday-makers, children, there had been Whit Monday; I studied them, curiously, across thousands of miles. He looked like my old Cook's men, then I realized he was a keeper. He gave me a cold look, 'Better?' 'No.' I said. 'Ye're swingin' the lead,' he said, 'aren't ye?' I guessed what it meant, that I was shamming illness, stared at him as coldly, and stared away.

I must have been given more draughts, for I slept through the evening and the night, to wake to dim daylight. I stirred, opened my eyes, and saw a figure curled on the floor like a watch-dog, fully clothed and asleep with head on pillow. He was too bulky to be the keeper, I looked again. It was my father. Richard had reached Oxford. I turned my face abruptly to the wall.

Chapter 26

Salvage

Tom told me afterwards that the telegram had arrived as Dad was setting out for work, two-till-ten, Mam black-leading the grate : a nervous break-down, would he come at once. He looked at it a long time, she watching apprehensively; then he read it out, and burst into tears. She put the brush in its box, rose and said, 'Now don't you start worrying where the fare is to come from, Thomas will run about the train, look sharp Thomas.' Then she went upstairs to her tin box under the bed, came down with three pound-notes, lifted out his Sunday blue serge and brushed it.

When he woke on my floor, he was so relieved not to find me being forced into a strait-jacket that he was quite merry. But I must have been fairly odd, for I was quite unstruck by the strangeness of him in these surroundings. 'Mr Warren the scout,' he said over his breakfast, with next to him my un-finished letter home, and me dressed and half-dead in the arm-chair, 'seems a nice well-spoken gentleman, we had quite a chat, for a good while I took him for your tutor till he mentioned his housework, he was three years at sea as a young 'un.' I thought, he knows more about him than I do after six terms . . . After that I only recall, as an isolated flash, our crossing Tom Quad, me with my suitcase and him completely at home as he bowed kindly to tremulous Doctor Lock and the two octogenarian juniors flanking him, 'They breed 'em very old up here, George?'

I remember nothing of the journey or even arriving at 314a. Mama also seemed relieved to find me sane, if dazed and more silent than usual. The trains in the night lulled my sleep. The first moment fully to strike me was when I woke up, in a room smaller even than last time, saw Job and Tom asleep in the other bed, looked across at 'Flaming June' over the tiny fireplace, and knew that I had exchanged one prison for another.

But any prison was better than the first. Dad was not working till two – he had missed two shifts, I realized abjectly – and he suggested a stroll: evidently fresh air had been advised. We went slowly up the line, the first walk we had ever taken. Except for friendly nothings, 'Dad, will Tom be leaving St Mark's when he's fourteen?', 'The harvest will be early, George, by the looks of it', we did not talk. The family barriers were up, and impregnable; this was a man I loved, as he loved me, yet that morning I could no more have discussed my situation with him than with anybody else. But the strange excursion did me good, and when I returned I got out Pascal's *Pensées*, my parents watching me and then busying themselves. But thoughts crept across the page like shadows, and I shut the book abruptly. I had a long way to go.

I must have been more dislocated than I imagined, for I had let slide the question of Miss Cooke. Apparently my father asked his workmate and old friend Edward Hughes from Flint to ask his son Elfyn, a pupil at H.C.S., to go up to her and say I had come home; poor Dad must have thought of writing, but was at a loss how to put it. My letters having given her no inkling, she was stunned; nor was she helped by having heard that day that a gifted young Yorkshire colleague had committed suicide. She wrote to my father that she would come down on Saturday afternoon.

China emerged from the corner-cupboard, including the moustache-cup. Still in a semi-voluntary trance, I was to retain little of her visit, though it was their first meeting except for the handshake at Prize Distribution when cheers had been ringing in all their ears. Crowded with me into the parlour, it was a difficult moment for the three of them, but Miss Cooke cleared the air. Having first greeted my parents – Dad in the blue serge, stiff shirt-front and Lord Mostyn manners – she looked squarely at me where I stood by my books trying to look incapable of sitting an exam. 'You'd feel better, you know,' she said, 'if you got your hair cut.' She then turned to my father, whose face broke appreciatively. The conversation was general, then 'This morning,' Miss Cooke said, 'I got a note from your tutor asking me to persuade you to go back and do your Schools.' 'I can't,' I said flatly, then, agitated, 'I can't, I can't . . .' The subject was changed. There was no suggestion of my going with her to the station: I did not feel up to an inquisitorial walk, and neither probably did she. Dad accompanied her up the alley – 'I will see you, if I may, to the end of the estate' – then she walked past the station and a mile towards Flint until she was given a lift by Doctor Jones of Holywell. She was upset. 'Well, Poll,' said Dad, closing the front door and unfastening his stud, 'we have met her at last. She's got the bark, George, but God bless her, no bite.'

It was understood that I had 'brain fever' and would get better so long as I did not see people; I was let off chapel. Being cooped up with a family whom I loved but with whom I had no communication, in a town of reminders ('They say 'e's coom a cropper poor lad, too good to last') was not easy. But I felt lucky to recuperate at all: my parents behaved with tact and sensibility, and I was indifferent to anything outside. My pre-occupation was the shackles under which I still chafed, of which I could neither speak nor write, not from fear of censure, to which I did not give a thought, but from a dread of others knowing how weak I had been, and still was. I would be sitting in the parlour when a shadow would cross the window; before the knocker knocked I was upstairs, and Mam would be wiping her apron, putting on her chapel face and opening the front door to Wesleyans come to ask how poor George was, peth bach, poor thing. Though I was fond of them, I could not face the gentilities. But it was hard on my mother.

With Schools sloughed off, I sank into a routine of torpor which was the slow way to recovery. I slept late, came down to the kitchen empty but for Mam, and over my breakfast, while she pottered, I read the serial in the *Daily Dispatch*, drinking it in like an opiate. I had a strong dark beard which thrived at the razor's touch, and I would now sit slumped in the parlour for an idle half-hour with tweezer and mirror, solemnly plucking bristles from my chin in the experimental hope that the next crop would sprout less fiercely: one of the more individual forms of occupational therapy.

These were days without false pride. It was the summer our landlord Mr Bennett had decided, like Sir Philip Sidney (Ch. Ch.) on the battlefield, that our need for water was as great as his: under my mother's suspicious eyes, our earth-closet in the back yard was in the pangs of conversion. And after my late breakfast, you could have espied the late Maugham-Coward of Oxford, late handler of three hundred and twenty-five scholarship pounds a year, twenty-one next birthday with father and young brothers all working – you could have espied him sauntering up the alley and across to the Hare and Hounds Outside-Gents with a penny from his Mam. If I had felt embarrassment at my errand, I would have lost it seeing my mother on the same journey, Indoors-Ladies. She, who demurred at next-door seeing her enter her own petty, now crossed High Street, in black shopping shawl and straw hat, with the realistic unconcern of playgoing Majesties of the past proceeding openly to the niche behind the Royal Box.

Buses were by now common, and Miss Cooke wrote and suggested a jaunt. On several perfect June Saturdays we drove all over Flintshire and further, through landscapes to lift up the heart, which I had never dreamt existed. And as we rolled past rows of villas, past housewives hanging washing and children playing, my mind began slowly to dwell on something to which I had hardly given a thought since I began to grow up, and never at Oxford: the existence of outwardly ordinary people. And to observe the rhythm of their days became one unobtrusive factor in my rehabilitation; I sat and let natural life flow round me and into me. These trips must have been the few occasions when Miss Cooke curbed her tongue. She kept to generalities: at Pantasaph, passing the monastery, 'Know who lived for five years just outside it? – the poet Francis Thompson': at Denbigh, 'That's the work-house, and know the Denbigh boy who was dumped there as a waif? John Rowlands who turned into H. M. Stanley the explorer, how many even of you Welsh know he was Welsh?'

We went by bus to Liverpool, where she took me to a doctor in Rodney Street, I imagine a psychiatrist, though I did not hear the word. Apart from the need for evidence that was unfit to take my Schools, she wanted to be sure that I had nothing amiss with me, though – as she told me later – she was jolly well one-hundred-per-cent sure I hadn't. The doctor interviewed me alone; pompous, unsympathetic, after a string of intimate questions he was able to tell me nothing I did not already know. But he did sign a paper, then shook cold hands, a politesse which, as I was to realize when the bill plopped into 314a, had cost me eight guineas: an account to be stored, away from Mam, as the first I would in time annihilate. As we came away, Miss Cooke had made her only pronouncement on my break-down. 'At twenty my boy,' she said, 'such an occurrence is forgiven by society; if you were twenty-five, it would be disallowed.'

Then, a doctor herself, no fee, Miss Cooke prescribed solitary golf, 'You've never had a hobby, that's half your trouble.' In the still-perfect weather I would set forth on my bicycle, up to Northop and along the top road overlooking Flint and the Dee, then higher through Halkyn to the golf course on 'the Mountain', a gorse-clad expanse open to the sky, with in the distance the Denbigh Moors and behind them, Snowdonia. There I would arrive at eleven, take Miss Cooke's clubs from the locker-room and toil over the deserted links. I felt, as usual, inherently clumsy, but enjoyed the drudgery of going round and round, my head as empty as the course and as stupefied in the sun as the sheep I encountered; after my sandwiches, I went con-scientiously round again.

Other days I would sit in my corner, slowly reading novels borrowed from Miss Cooke: *The Forsyte Saga*, Masefield's *Odtaa*, Stephen McKenna, *An American Tragedy*. Like an invalid with a limb in plaster, I was training myself not to lean on that part of my consciousness which was splintered. But sometimes, without warning, I would lurch and give it a jolt. Running up to

a green, for no reason I would see a face, hear a voice, the glow
would fade from the day and my breast would burst with pain,
and with despair that it should be such pain. Once, alone in the
parlour, I found in my wallet an old postcard. 'Good luck
for 1926' ... I sat with my new flimsy defences razed before a
rancid wind of longing, my hands clasped to my head, calling
a name, in a loud whisper, over and over. I recovered, rose to
go out and saw my brother Tom looking at me, crying himself;
I felt bitterly contrite. 'I'm better now Tom, it's only the brain
fever.' And the attacks grew rarer; even a letter which arrived
did not disturb me for long. It was warm and solicitous, hoping I
would be up next term; but I felt subconsciously that I would
hasten my own recovery by thinking ill, so found patronage
between the lines. Notes from Angus, Campbell and Reggie –
Campbell even asking me to come and stay – nobody else. 'Dear
Ch., Thank you for writing, I am quite recovered. In haste ...'
I went into the kitchen to thread a needle for my mother. Oxford
was wiped out.

A bad day was the arrival of my sea-chest, which that October
morning three years ago had swaggered up the hill. When Dad
and I now carried it down again, I felt we were bringing home
some sort of coffin, particularly when I was left in the parlour
to creak it open. I had written to my scout to pile everything in
willy-nilly, and he had. The first thing among the jumble-sale
junk on the baize shelf was the bedraggled pink lampshade,
then a chipped record, 'Chili Bom Bom', then my red Auntie-
Sarah scarf, then a crumpled birthday menu. In my mock-
flourish writing I read 'Consommé Chaud à la Reggie Colby,
Poulet Garvenal ...' I shut the coffin with a thud and went out
through the back – past the ashpit under the railway – to
Rubbishland, where the odour from the Boneyard so assailed
me that I lay face down on the cindery grass and breathed in the
stale smell of burnt leather and failure. This was no good; I
scrambled up, brushed myself and strode on past the hillocks
where I had once feigned mortal wounding by Persian arrow and
had rolled to my lonely death. At the steps where I had bathed
naked, the tide was turning. I walked smartly home, unpacked,

burnt the menu and much other rubbish, sorted my clothes, settled books into my orange-box shelves, and felt better.

After golf, my second and permanent therapeutic was a contraption which Dad had purchased in a high-flown moment on his way from the New Inn, a small box between my corner and the sewing-machine, with half a dozen wires sprouting from it and scuttling under the table into the wall: in the same month when water had come to the back of 314a, wireless had invaded the front. A crystal set, with two ear-phones. It had been another of his sudden buys, for he had not heard of aerials and had to spend a strenuous morning in the back yard with Job and me, rigging up an immense pole acquired from Coppack's timber-yard. It worked: one evening I walked in to find Dad wearing the ear-phones and gaily waving his long fingers in time to unheard music. From then on the crystal was my friend; while the old wives of yore prescribed the tail of mouse and the tongue of newt, I was coaxed back to health by the cat's whisker. I would sit for an hour while the faint dream-sounds of 2LO echoed in my head, with behind, imagined, the fainter surge of London: after the Whispering Baritone, the tinkle of a piano turned the parlour into a cool spacious country-house, then Gwen Ffrangcon-Davies spoke poetry – listening, I would look unbelievingly out at weed and brick – then a great orchestra before which the parlour faded into air and left not a rack behind. The new marvel, oddly, did not bring England nearer to me; on the contrary, the unearthly sounds were wafted from another planet, making me feel more cut off and happily so.

I enjoyed best the night sessions, when I would sit in the dark, one tiny light glowing and ear-phones tight, like a spiritualistic operator in weird touch with Debroy Somers and the Savoy Orpheans; after 'Fascinatin' Rhythm', the applause and the murmur of the crowd. My new play opened tonight, next door at the Savoy Theatre, I have brought the cast here for supper and am kind to all, though pale and withdrawn, for I have conquered weakness and am immune to emotion; the smart crowd dart surreptitious looks at me, for the play is a great success, ah, they are playing 'I'm Sittin' on Top of the World', shall we dance, Fay? Edna? Tallu? ...

The third week in June over – Schools – I relaxed as if a danger was past, and with July tottered one more step forward with the knowledge that Oxford was a desert. Some afternoons after golf, I cycled down to H.C.S. – my first visit, did I imagine it or *did* Silly Wil, at the gate, give me a sorrowful look? – and Miss Cooke, again the doctor, would enjoin me to read to the Juniors in English or to the Higher in French. Once, with the Higher, I conducted a reading of *Caesar and Cleopatra*, taking both parts and showing off to Rica Jones and Alwyn Fidler. I went to tea at Underwood where I met Rogers, now a Liverpool graduate full of honours and off in a week to teach in Rhodesia. Miss Cooke felt, rightly, that it would do me good to see him. By the time she went home to Leeds, I was fit enough for her to broach the future. I was determined to start earning; I would take my Schools next June, but while preparing for them, I would teach in a preparatory school. I wrote to London, to an agency with the utterly Dickensian name of Gabbitas and Thring, and waited; fore-dreaming, I saw myself in a prep school, 'set amid rolling parklands', I would be withdrawn again but popular, a pipe perhaps, and maybe a discreet affair with the Headmaster's wife, or even the Matron, a play about it? ... But nobody wanted me (I had no degree), I relaxed into convalescence, and by August, while I was still golfing and reading and cycling and going for picnics with the school friends I still frequented – J. S. Roberts, on vacation from Jesus, the Edward Hugheses, Ena Hughes and the Wrays in Flint, Alwyn and Ena Mills in Holywell, Millie Tyrer in Caerwys – the under-mind was once more in travail.

The play was the one I had feverishly conjured up last term. I decided that *The Singing Pool* was too conventionally Celtic a title and called it *Full Moon*; after making a synopsis I started the first act in long-hand, then on an impulse opened my typewriter, tapped out what I had done and forged ahead, inventing straight on to the machine, double-spacing for corrections. I found it so much more satisfactory – as I composed the sentences, they assumed authority, even if they were to be rewritten – that I was to continue the practice permanently.

Within a week I was thinking of nothing else. The story was a simple one, six people on a one-house island, in an Italian lake which I endowed with the Welsh legend of a drowned city whose bells can sometimes be heard, in this case (at full-moon time) by people as they fall in love, then the clash between an exiled Englishman and a half-Italian girl over his adolescent son; all through, I saw it at the Oxford Playhouse with Alan Napier and Byam Shaw. As well as my conscious mind, my subconscious was at work; while *Vigil* had dealt with the hypnotic hold of one human being on another, here it was again, as the obsession of a father about his son which had to appear, to a wise onlooker, an unnatural emotion. If I had been told, typing away in the parlour, that there was something of me not only in the father but in the girl, I should have been taken aback.

'What's that you're doing on the machine?' said Mam, as if I were running something up on her Singer. I mumbled 'studies', but did not fool her. She was openly contemptuous – in my break-down, had not the fatal ingredient been theatricals? When it came to revision and final copies, it was hard to ask her for the shillings for paper, carbons and stamps, but I had to. I typed single-spacing throughout, a foolish economy, made six copies, under-ruled the stage-directions in them all, posted one to Fagan, one to Willie Armstrong in Liverpool, one to Denham, one to Dorothea Fassett, a play-agent to whom John Fernald had recommended me, and retained the dimmest carbons. Then the inevitable reaction, a week-long eclipse from which I escaped on my bicycle to play the Bohemian undergraduate with J.S. or the Wrays. I was silly, but it helped me and amused them.

A letter from Miss Sadie Price the Inspectress. She was an old friend of the Lloyd George family; Mr William George, the great man's brother, would like his son coached in French, for Friar's School, Bangor. Also two young neighbours, the Misses Drage, wished to embark on Italian, would I like to go to stay with the Georges for a couple of weeks, coach and look round for more pupils? I seized on it. Now that I was better I was on the point of getting on my family's nerves, and they on mine. Mam was tartly relieved that the severe bout of typing had subsided – never, she hoped, to recur – and my father, who worshipped L.G., was transported: 'Poll, the lad will end up as his secretary!' It would have been churlish to remind him that to have hopes of serving an ex-Premier, one should start with some idea of the difference between the Liberal and Conservative Parties.

But I had my start, up the steep hill of self-respect. My first move was to ask my mother to turn the high neck of my jumper into a respectable plunging V; what she cut off, she was to use for years, though with no conscious sense of the fitness of things, as a dish-cloth. For this home-leaving, in early September, a modest suitcase and no sizzle of bacon; but I heard in myself the simmer of life. I took a train to adventure a new way: not through Chester, through Rhyl. From my seat, one reminder after the other of the past, Flint, Bagillt, Holywell Junction, Mostyn, Ffynnongroew, Talacre; by Colwyn Bay I was an old man who has lived, suffered and forgiven. In a late light as beautiful as over the Campagna, I discovered North Wales: Conway Castle by the sea, the lordly sweep of mountains – 'Every other Welsh peasant,' Sadie had once said to Miss Cooke, 'is descended from princes' – and at every tiny station, as farmers and their families got in and out, the Welsh language came ringing clear and full on the lips. For the first time I was travelling deep into my own country – to my left Llanrwst, home of my father's grandfather; looking out at the threadbare dignity of the farms, through the floor of the train I felt the soil from which I had sprung. I felt it seep through shoe-leather and mix once more with my blood.

Criccieth was a small rambling stone village on the Caernarvonshire sea, and the Georges' house, Garth Celyn, an imposing Victorian mansion on the hillside. In my turreted room, with a glorious view of the sun setting in Cardigan Bay, I became a romantic tutor arriving in the first chapter of a Brontë novel, or even Henry James. It was an unpretentious household: Mrs George a kind mild chatelaine, bearded Mr George the picture of a right-living Welsh deacon, little William and Fraser the

Sealyham. A couple of lessons every morning, and in the afternoon I took Fraser for long blackberrying walks, Auntie Sarah's red scarf over my shoulder ('Newydd ddôd o Rydychain, medda 'nhw, they say he's from Oxford') or I would sprawl in the sun of the ruined castle with Maurois's *Ariel* and dream of Italy. In the evening we would sit round a table and play card-games till bed-time. I wrote to thank Sadie Price.

One evening I accompanied Mrs George up to Bryn Awelon, the hill-top house in which the Lloyd Georges had lived for years; 'he' was in London, but his wife was there. A rosy-cheeked Welsh farmer's-wife with the same country manners which had always been hers, Dame Margaret must have grazed shoulders with the great ladies of London, and if urbanity had not rubbed off on to her, neither had artificiality; she had stayed an apple among the peaches. We talked Welsh, then entered the most attractive girl I had ever seen.

Megan was twenty-four, small, with a tilted nose, fearless grey eyes, a wide blithe mouth and high spirits alternating with flashing seriousness. She had, beside the parental glamour, an aura of her feminine own; I was also peculiarly fascinated by the two-foldness of her personality. One moment she was the sophisticated London miss-about-town, blessed not only with brains and a humour that bubbled, but with the most attractive of English voices; the next, she would break into a Welsh as peasant-flavoured as that of any of my four grandparents. The juxtaposition bowled me over and made me double-proud of her, proud of a London dazzler at home with cottagers under Snowdon, proud of a Welsh girl holding her own in Claridge's with Margot Asquith. So recurrent are the patterns of childhood that the attraction may have been a variant of *A Welsh Singer*: the shepherdess metamorphosed into the urban charmer, and yet both at once.

I questioned her about the London scene, about which she would make sudden incongruous comments in Welsh. It was stimulating to hear of Winston, Ramsay, Father (sometimes 'Tadda') and H.R.H., but even more welcome to know that she had met Barrie, Galsworthy, Maugham, Noël and Gertie. I told her diffidently of my play, but learning that it ended unhappily, she said gaily, 'Oh dear, there's enough heartbreak in the House of Commons without going into the West End for it!' I laughed, but was dashed; there was as little of her heart in the theatre as of mine in politics. 'Dear Dad and Mam, I was invited to Bryn Awelon, Megan is a very nice girl. I have moved into Ty Newydd in the village, very cheap, a nice old lady Mrs Jones, I have the front room and bedroom and buy my food in the shop and she cooks it, they invite me into the kitchen to talk to them, I feel at home. Megan is always up and down between here and London, so three times a week I am giving her tuition in Italian. I will be paid 7/- a lesson, and continue to teach William, his mother wants to brush up her French too, also still the Drages and I am on the look-out for more pupils. Next week I am going to play tennis with Gentilissima Miss Megan, as I call her in the lessons. I feel strange writing this in English, with speaking such a lot of Welsh here . . .'

I knew as I licked the stamp what this would do for Dad, who had not had anything to produce from his wallet for a long time now; I knew also that as he read it aloud he would be promoting me from private secretary to public son-in-law. Half playing up to him, as I walked the hills past the loose-stone walls, hands buried in overcoat, I would day-dream, knowing in my heart that I was much too immature, and too afraid, to move a finger. 'Politics?' I say to her, 'dim fath beth yngenethi, no such thing my girl – whether you like the theatre or not, you are going to marry an actor-playwright and live in an attic in Bloomsbury, your old man may be a genius but I'm a genius too, get your hat and coat and stop crying.' I saw myself meeting her old man; he is obdurate, but as we shake strong Welsh hands he is won over by the strength of my personality.

'Lovely girl Megan,' said her Uncle William at breakfast, out of the blue, 'but she'll never marry. Whoever gets her down the aisle has got to be as tip-top as her Tadda, and where is *he* to come from?' I stirred my Quaker Oats thoughtfully.

On my walks, I made it a daily habit to call at the village

library and scan the theatre page of *The Times*; during these bracing dips into print, I read that *And So To Bed*, a new comedy by J. B. Fagan, about Pepys, had opened at the Queen's with great success. He had not acknowledged *Full Moon*; Armstrong had written nicely about it, Liverpool wasn't doing new plays and don't type single spacing next time, think of my old Scotch eyes Emlyn! Denham had shown interest but thought the play uncommercial; Dorothea Fassett the agent the same, but wanted to 'handle' it – but all that was weeks ago, and *Full Moon* was in eclipse. The Oxford term was near, the Ouds would again be planning one-act plays, should I send one in, go up and act in it and startle everybody I knew? *The Window Seat*, set in Venice; below, the unbearably sad five-note refrain of a street fiddler, I even picked out a phrase on the Georges' piano, a mysterious urchin named Giustinianino; they (who?) call down to him, and he is invited up to explain why he plays those notes over and over again, I enter, cap in hand ... But I knew I was best where I was, paying my debts and the Atlantic wind in my face.

While the lessons with Gentilissima Miss Megan were fun – she was inclined not to take them seriously, but as quick as a bird, with an accent perfect from the start – it was the other way round with Major and Mrs Seckerby and their twin daughters, who inhabited a distressed gentleman's Grange on the way to Portmadoc. All four were loose-covered, from head to foot, in the same tweed; it was a surprise that the motif was not echoed in the table-cloth, and that the snippets had not come in for the tea-cosy and a winter coat for the peke. Once it was bruited in Criccieth that the Drage girls were learning Italian, it became de rigueur, as Mrs Seckerby put it, that I should get to work on the twins' French, 'so useful when they come out'. A power in the Women's Institute, she was one of those frail English matrons whose delicate stems, like those of artificial flowers, are internally wired. Her dreamy eyes watched every penny; both the twins and their father were at her tremulous beck and call. The latter was heavy in body and dull in mind, and Megan and I were never to refer to him except as the Gallumphing Major, il Maggiore Galumfante.

Mrs Seckerby was a woman of crazes, and once her girls were to polish their French, why not their father? The Major looked alarmed, as if she had suggested a course in sword-swallowing; he mumbled that he was starting a cold. The twins were chimney-tall albino girls of seventeen, with invisible hair looped over invisible eyebrows, who looked like two bean-stalks put in the sun to bleach till they have become brittle enough to snap in half at the touch, and then left in the cold; they appeared irretrievably nipped. The Major had apparently questioned the propriety of their being left alone with me, but he could safely have risked Casanova à l'ombre des jeunes filles sans fleur. They spoke only in monosyllables, even to each other – 'thanks', 'I see', 'quite'; being identical, they may have indulged in mutual thought-reading, and a duller pastime it would be hard to imagine. It was unclear to me how I was to make the French language become, in their chilblained hands, a social weapon; but Mrs Seckerby was happy to pay seven shillings for their daily hour. As they were two it had crossed my money-making mind to give a genteel turn to the screw and mention half a guinea; then I had to reflect that as the Major had been so generous with them in the first place in the matter of splitting, the least I could do in the matter of my fee was to emulate him.

Next day the manager of one of the two Criccieth banks stopped me and said that now that the nights were drawing in, if I formed a French night-class he would be the first to join. I went home fired; where would I – but of course, here in my room! A rearrangement of furniture, a derelict blackboard from the council school, donated by a master who was to be in the class, and the setting was complete for many winter evenings. Miss Cooke posted me my old H.C.S. text-books, the master dug up copy-books and I charged a shilling each; nine turned up, so it meant nine shillings an evening three times a week, two bank managers, two bank clerks, the doctor, three school-masters and the chemist, from eight to nine-thirty, the hour spilling over into fun and jokes built on the fascination of there being three such languages as Welsh, English and French. All intensely Welsh, they took to speaking anything strange like babes to breathing, and for me to come from my two albino mutes to their blithe mouthing of 'Je suis gallois, mais cela ne veut pas dire que je suis voleur comme Taffy' was like changing from cold tea to champagne.

For the Seckerby girls were not taking to French. They pronounced the syllables after me with such a heightened colour that each word might have been more risqué than the last; their lips shrank from 'Mes gants sont dans le salon' as they would have from 'My drawers are coming down'. They were named Jane and Amy, and to bring a little splash to the bleached landscape, I addressed them as Mademoiselle Jeanne and Mademoiselle Aimée. This was recieved with a twitch of the lips which was the shadow of a giggle; they even made *me* feel silly when I talked French. But Maman made up for them by speaking it fluently and atrociously, like an athletic cripple. As the girls sat blushing scarlet over the imperfect tense, her head would bob brightly round the door, 'Excusez à moi Monsieur Williams – Jane dear, déjeuner, est-ce que vous avez souvenir à ordonner-vous le whiting?' Then she would join in the lesson, each time a longer sit; by the end of the week she was wreaking harm right and left, for the girls heard much more of her French than of their tutor's.

Then came the morning when I found the Gallumphing Major in the window, behind *The Times*; when next day I spotted him drawing up a chair and making half-hearted notes, I felt I had to make a delicate suggestion in case next time the parlour-maid and the peke might have enrolled in the seven-shillings-for-all. I hinted at a tutors' trade union, which frowned on overcrowding. After that, Papa had seven shillings' worth on his own; knowing he dreaded it, I suggested reading to him and he concurred eagerly. In dramatizing the narrative, I would go to extravagant lengths to see how far I could exaggerate without drawing any reaction at all. All through *La Chèvre de Monsieur Seguin*, with me moaning, groaning, sighing, dying, he watched me glazed of eye. It was like reading to a drugged dog.

The September of tennis and even bathing hardened suddenly into a spiky northern autumn, a toughening which I welcomed

as part of my cure. And as the days darkened, so I felt the subterranean excitement of new London plays preparing for the
winter. Once, walking past a farm off the Pwllheli road, on an
overcast afternoon when I was calculating how many seven-
shillings would pay off the bills pinned in my severe folder, I
stopped short at the sight of a figure seated on a gate : the
resemblance was so strong that I was back in Worcester College,
back in the streets of Paris. It was a farm-hand in leggings and
muffler; he passed the time of day, in Welsh. I did not walk that
way again.

There were motor excursions with the Georges, up the valleys
of Snowdonia, to stand on mountain-tops and see whole pri-
meval gorges boil like cauldrons with sunset light. One evening
– there must have been an election brewing – I sat on the floor
of the Lloyd George car, a happy appendage, with Megan, Dame
Margaret and the William Georges, to drive to Caernarvon and
settle with young William at the back of an immense packed
marquee while the others faced us on the platform grouped
round a stocky fiery figure with white hair flowing and the
voice of a prophet. He spoke in Welsh, which had to remind me
of chapel, but I felt his hypnotic power like a breath; he made
everybody round him disappear, including Megan. William and
I waited in the car for the others, but except for Dad, I had no
regrets : to have been presented to a legend, for a meaningless
second amidst seething humanity, would have been a frustration. Anyhow, writing to my father, I pretended I had met him.

One morning, I bounded out of my attic bed as usual, raced
into my clothes in the patch of autumn sun – too cold to bath
in the morning, that was for bed-time – and went down. Next
to my cornflakes and tinned prunes, an envelope forwarded bv
Dad, with printed in the corner, 'Savoy Theatre, London'.
'Dear Emlyn Williams, It is my plan, if you agree, to produce
your play *Full Moon*, which I like very much, at the Oxford
Playhouse the week beginning January 31st. Let me know if you
agree. Ever, J. B. Fagan.'

I knew then what it is not to believe one's eyes : also to find
that a plan which one has conceived with practical sense, and

411

so presumably thought possible, can come to pass and still appear fantastic. I touched the sheet of paper to see if it was real, mechanically poured out the cornflakes, then sprang up, banged about the room, came back to the letter, then walked again : it was so joyously unsettling that it felt almost like bad news. I folded it into my wallet and walked to my tweedy-reedy twins; this morning I could not have told their parents apart either. The Mam side of me was sensible; it was a wonderful chance, I would watch every rehearsal and miss not one point, and even if nothing more was heard of the play I would have made a propitious start ... But walking those two rustic miles and back, in a daze of salty winter sunlight, through a countryside as alien to the theatre as the mid-Atlantic wastes, my Dad side soared into surmise, with every sort of whimsical elaboration.

'On Friday, *Full Moon*,' I announced to the Welsh sheep, 'will celebrate its hundredth performance, and the young author's former teacher, staying at the Savoy Hotel as his guest, informs us that she always jolly well wanted him to go into the scholastic profession. His parents, it will be remembered, were presented to the King and Queen when the latter visited the play last month. This phenomenal success opens next month in Copenhagen, Oslo, Madrid and Berlin (Elisabeth Bergner as the girl) while in Paris Sacha Guitry is already in rehearsal. The film has been sold to Hollywood for a record sum and will star Emil Jannings and Janet Gaynor; Mr Williams has forbidden the title to be changed to *The Girl from Anywhere*, and when asked if his supping alone at Ciro's with Miss Megan Lloyd George means an impending announcement, he laughed wittily and changed the subject ...' The sheep looked sceptical, and Mam's side took over; I decided I would work here till Christmas, pay off my debts with a bit over, go home till I went up for the play and from then on work at home for Schools in June.

Writing the news to Miss Cooke and to the family, I made little of it; so did they, my father not distinguishing between the Ouds and a professional début. 'My dear Son George, we are pleased to note that you are to have yet another play done at Oxford, I hope it will not keep any actors from their work.

We see by the photo of Megan in the *Echo* that she is back in the Smoke ...' Miss Cooke, 'Hmmm ... As I told you, it's an interesting play, and as to respect for the Unities, Racine would have approved. But don't build castles on sand, find yourself a goodly piece of rock in the shape of an M.A. Oxon, that'll outwear a week at any old Playhouse. . .'

The weather turned stern. Great breakers thundered at my doorstep, the wind flattened the nettles against the castle ruins and whistled through the holes in the hill walls; the street was deserted, past my window stray bodies pressed at an angle against the gale, holding on to hats. But I was beside my fire, warmed too by the nearness of Mrs Jones's kitchen and reading *Tess of the D'Urbervilles* or, eyes wide, *The Loom of Youth* (thinking, thank God, for my peace of mind, that I never went to a public school ...). Then I would knot my red scarf, myself make a Spartan sally and undertake the walk to Portmadoc for a private lesson to the daughter of a lawyer, and dinner afterwards with her parents; then, by a cloud-ridden racing moon, the weird walk back over Craig Ddu – Black Rock – with far below me the ocean thundering and boiling like a thousand dragons moon-maddened and lashing giant tails. The whole Celtic world felt haunted, from the sea-bed with its drowned city of legend to the clouds pulled and dragged and tortured, as they tore along, into the monstrous shapes of portents : I hurried stumbling past the long-forsaken ruins of cliff sheep-pens, thinking of the haunted barn of my childhood and shuddering as I wondered if there were quarry-shafts lurking in my path. But when I reached the safe main road and saw the scattered lights of Criccieth, the full moon reminded me of the play and the new letter in my wallet, and whooping against the wind, I held idiotic conversations at the top of my voice. Once, dipping into a sheltered hollow I let out a yell of contentment, terrified a courting couple, and ran; the girl screamed, and possibly owed to me her good name.

For my twenty-first birthday, Miss Cooke sent a box stuffed with tissue-paper in which nestled, like so many ticking eggs, ten wrist-watches to choose from. 'Well my boy, this is the parting of the ways – the child becometh the man.' 'My dear Son George, Congratulations on your Coming-of-Age, when you gett home for Christmas you will see we have once more gone Up in the World, first water and now the Electoric Light. Your Mam is all the time waiting for it to explode ...' In the middle of the day, after a couple of lessons, I sat for minutes on a bench in the middle of Criccieth and thought, I'm celebrating my twenty-first birthday by sitting on a bench in the middle of Criccieth just looking from sea to village to sky and back, and it is so meaningless I shall always remember it. And I have ... But the evening quickened into celebration mixed with farewell. After my night-class we all resorted to the Lion, to a private room where they had organized a first-rate dinner, with place-cards, flowers, vin blanc, vin rouge, et liqueurs; then speeches, in French helped out only with Welsh, then they drank to 'Pleine Lune'. It was a happy and touching evening and on the way home, winter Criccieth by night was softened by the pagan fumes of wine.

I said good-bye to my pupils and all the people who had been kind to me, packed my case into the back of the Lloyd George car and travelled with Megan and her mother to Bangor, where Megan boarded the Euston express, first-class, reserved, stared at. Oh, the fun of being famous ... I stayed in the car and accompanied Dame Margaret across North Wales. She was to open a school in Chester, and dropped me where the country road dived under the Buckley line above Connah's Quay: I longed to ask her if the car could not be deflected a couple of miles so that she could come down the alley, sit for three minutes in our parlour and so glorify Dad's life. She would have done it too.

This was a strange homecoming, down the line with a suitcase. But I felt hardened, settled back into the rhythm of 314a and studied, slowly, consistently, though somehow, in my heart, not sure that I would ever do Schools. Once I had worn off the self-respect of earned income and the glamour of contact with the great, life over Christmas was not easy; when I saw Dad's and Job's grimy hands, in retrospect teaching bank managers

French in the evenings had a frivolous ring. And my imminent play not only did nothing to enhance my status, it was damaging; my mother just could not see why I had to go up to see it, 'Good life, they'll say the things the right way round without *you* there!' Clearly she felt that one return ticket in a year from 314a to Oxford had been one too many; she could not forget Dad's journey, and neither could I. There was, moreover, a courteous note from Fagan to explain that the play was postponed a month, but he did enclose one of the familiar dark-red throw-away cards for the Playhouse:

Jan. 24	UNCLE VANYA	Tchehov
„ 31	THE PHILANDERER	Shaw
Feb. 7	QUALITY STREET	Barrie
„ 14	THE RUMOUR	Munro
„ 21	ANDROCLES AND THE LION	Shaw
„ 28	FULL MOON	Emlyn Williams
Mar. 7	INTOXICATION	Strindberg

I handed it to Mam. 'Very nice,' she said, adding ' "Intoxication", fancy writing a play about strong drink ... That Shaw with two plays going to your one, is he another lad in your college?' But Dad, realizing for the first time that this was the professional theatre, was very struck. 'I notice here, George, that while they only give the surnames of the other buffers, they give your Christian name as well, now that's a honour, isn't it?' 'Fancy,' said Mam, 'you taking up the Emlyn and dropping the George, is that for good?' 'Yes,' I said. My father took the card to work. Labouring at my studies, I looked forward with quickened pulse to the Savoy Orpheans now that the Fagan play had moved to the Savoy Theatre: hearing the murmur of the dancers in the hotel, I felt that if I were to lean forward I would hear the stage-door keeper, 'Good night Miss Arnaud, Miss Grey, we 'ear Mr Fagan's got a tip-top programme at Oxford!' The band played 'Who' from *Sunny*; sitting in the dark, I moved hands and feet to the beat, ear-bound to magic, rich, famous and more than ever, kind to all.

•

415

But it meant another month. I did not help, over Christmas, in search of music to remind me, by taking a fancy to local dances. Last minute, I would shave at the table, dress in my best, swathe the bell-bottoms into clips and pedal to Flint to accompany the Wrays or Ena Hughes to some sedate hop pepped up with one saxophone, 'When You and I were Seventeen', 'Whispering' ... At the Holywell Palais, I longed to startle the fox-trotting mice by shouting, to the tune of 'Charleston, Charleston!', that inside the prim façade perambulating with Ena Mills to 'Felix Kept on Walking', was caged a metropolitan menace. Was escape imminent? ... One Sunday, biking back in the dark from supper with the Hugheses, I caught up with a cyclist who asked did I come from round here. I said no, London, I was in the theatre – 'no! dear me ...' – opening on tour at the Royal Court tomorrow, juvenile in *No No Nanette*, yes a hard life but it's one's profession, by the time we parted I was ready to turn off for Liverpool.

January 1927, dragged on; then a note from the Oxford Playhouse and a self-conscious saunter to the photographer across the road for a 'publicity picture'; I tried to look unassuming and was glad my blue could not photograph. This was followed by an interview, in the parlour, with a Chester journalist: a harmless-looking creature not much older than me, who asked me simple questions which I answered truthfully. Yes, I had given Miss Lloyd George lessons; yes, she had evinced interest in my play; yes, she had told me that Basil Dean, looking for a Constant Nymph, had suggested her reading for it; yes, if she were an actress she would be right for my heroine, thank you for calling ... Two days later I was brought a picture-paper in which I was appalled to read, under my unassuming photograph, that it was 'not unlikely that Miss Megan may make her stage début in her friend's play: it is stated she is eager to act in it'. I felt myself tingle from head to foot with shame, had a bad night, and next day was brought the same paper, 'Miss Megan effectually disposed of the story that she is to appear on the stage by saying "It must have grown out of a joking remark I made to Mr Williams."' I wrote to her, and it seemed a long time till her answer, by return, 'I knew you had been misquoted – the penalty of success Emlyn bach!'

Then a note from Fagan suggesting that the week before *Full Moon*, I should join the company to play Androcles. I was excited and confused. With my own play immediate, it could not but be an unsettling début; moreover I knew in my heart that to start off in a leading part might mean making a fool of myself, and I did not want to do that twice in a year. I may also have been influenced, without admitting it, by Shaw's description of his hero, 'a small thin ridiculous little man, any age from 35 to 55, sandy hair, watery eyes, arms and legs shrivelled' ... Having answered that I had to study, I felt I could face Miss Cooke more squarely. She was in top form, with a tirade ending up, 'I'm agin' him since the Peace Conference in Parry but he's a great man is L.G. and this bumbler Baldwin is to him what a minnow is to a whale – see here George, you've heard of the Marconi Shares rumpus?' I hadn't, but said I had and she was off. Megan she evinced no interest in – how I hoped she had not seen the paper – and hardly mentioned *Full Moon*; like my mother, she frowned on impending Oxford and talked of Rogers and his splendid start in Rhodesia, for which he was to become Chief Inspector of Schools.

With February came bitter Quay weather; the Dee seeped up into the yard, and washing-day was once more a nightmare. The usual complaints of 'the flu' became more insistent. 'That Joe Crowther's gone dead with it,' said Mam, ironing; she complained of a headache herself and next morning I found her sitting with her hands to her chest. 'You're poorly Mam,' I said. 'I am not,' she snapped indignantly, 'how can I be bad with this house to run?' I went off for some panacea she fancied, but when I got back Doctor Neville was there; she looked very odd sitting flushed and mute in her own kitchen with a thermometer in her mouth. He took it from her and looked at me gravely. I helped her up, she demurred but was too ill, I tried to help her up the stairs but they were too narrow. For the first time in her married life except in childbirth, she took to her bed, or rather to Job's and Tom's, for I had quickly to decide with the doctor that Tom must share the front room with Dad. She had pneumonia, which in those pre-penicillin days was very serious; a nurse would come in later to see to necessities and then call when she could.

I went up and told Mam I was in charge; but even in her daze of sickness, she remembered that while I could apply myself with industry to simple tasks like scouring or washing up, my knowledge of cookery was moronic; I could make a cup of tea, boil an egg and peel an untidy potato, there I ended. I seized on the quick relief of washing up and putting the kitchen to rights exactly as she would have done, even doubling her apron and wearing it; then I was stumped. It was a frantic and humiliating moment. I should have loved, from that second, to take everything over – I had the stamina and the moral drive to do it – the ordering, cooking, nursing; I would have toiled all day and nodded all night, feeling that at last, in this burrow which for years had sheltered me, I had come into my cool efficient own. Mam's voice quavered down, 'George ...' I ran up; it was her shopping morning, and her fevered mind was on Dad's dinner. She muttered 'Taters, meat ...' and lay back exhausted. The sick captain knew that the idiot cabin-boy was at the helm. I could have wept.

Mrs Leadbitter next door ... One of her children was ill too, she had her hands full. I hurried up to Ma Williams' and asked how many pounds of potatoes would be needed to feed four people – one, one and a half, two? It was to become a legend in the Quay that a young man who had spent three years at Oxford should put such a question. Then I had an inspiration – cornflakes! Nutritious, and foolproof. I bought them at the Co-op, went back, lay the potatoes in a saucepan and on to the fire – adding water as a hasty afterthought – hoped for the best, and made tea. Tom, still delicate and tall for fourteen, came home from school with a headache; at half past two, Dad arrived briskly as usual. When I told him Mam was in bed, he looked stunned, went upstairs, came down again, and sat heavily in his chair. His plate was piled with cornflakes. He stared at them dully, 'What's this?' 'Cornflakes, Dad,' I said, 'they're champion with sugar. I had them all the time at Oxford.' He looked from them to me, as if to say 'Yes and look how you ended'; I sprinkled the sugar, more generously than Mam would have liked. Mechanically he took up a spoon, dug it into the concoction and put it in his mouth. He rolled the flakes round his tongue, looked at the stairs, bewildered – he had never once, in ten years, eaten a meal in this room without her – and burst into tears; I was not to know it was the second time in a year for him, who had never done such a thing before. I removed the plate and he pulled himself quickly together; I boiled two eggs, and cut some bread and butter. It was a poor meal for a working man.

By evening Tom was in my bed, as ill as our mother; soda siphons, and the glow of the tiny watch-lamp. The nurse arrived, weary but firmly efficient; Mam, her mind wandering and nagged by worry, was still able to take an instant dislike to her and never called her anything but 'that woman'. I arranged to sleep in the front room, and Job went to neighbours. By next day Tom was worse; as he worsened, so she, through her delirium, sensed with some deep animal instinct that he was losing ground, and herself deteriorated with him. But even a nightmare, if it lasts, has to settle into routine, and somehow we managed between the three: I responsible for the mechanical chores – coal and water, dusting, washing floors, errands and keeping the house so clean that only she could have told the difference – Job helping me out with practical instructions, and Dad falling back on his seafaring days and doing a little rough cooking. There was one near-disaster when I was out shopping; he had propped a newspaper against the fire to make a draught, gone out to the shed to wash, and came back to hear Mam calling weakly down, she could smell smoke – the newspaper had caught alight and then set fire to clothes I had hung to dry on the brass rail. All was well, but it set her back, confirming her obsession that downstairs all was chaos without her.

Though never off my feet, I never ceased to be conscious of my incapability. But I was at least on hand for sick-bed chores at which I became thoroughly efficient; one of these was the continuous preparing, applying and discarding of linseed poultices. In all weathers I was out to the tap fetching water for the boilings, then out again to scrape the cloths clean and throw the rubbish into a corner of the shed, to be cleared later when the outlook cleared. Then there were the other necessities : with this woman who had always been so shy of the physical with her children, it was strange for me to feel completely natural and protective as I supervised the dreary ritual of the bed-pan. When she lay moaning with unease and distaste, white hair fanned unfamiliarly over the pillow, a human being of fifty-eight became a sick and fractious child, little fair-haired Mary of Tŷ Celyn; and at these moments – 'come on now Mam, you'll feel better' – I was nearer to her than I had ever been.

'That woman' brought me news of the alarming number of deaths in surrounding houses, 'Somebody else last night', and I begged her to keep it from my father. Then came the day – he was working nights – when the doctor told me that for Tom the next twelve hours were decisive : he would either turn back to life, or go on his way. All that night I sat between them and looked down at his unconscious face, quite different from Job's or mine, long and high of cheek-bone; now, drained of colour and merriment they were the features of an ascetic, and by the glimmer of the toy lamp, his waxen head looked on the pillow like the effigy of a child-saint. I heard, in half-dreams, the tide of death bubble slowly up through the back-yard tiles and into the house, lapping at the stairs ... Should I pray? ... Then I dozed, then woke, then dozed. Next day he was no worse; I had not prayed, but the tide was swirling and muttering against itself. By evening he seemed – could he be? – easier. It had turned.

But for us all, it was a long and chafing recovery; the poultices mounted into the most unsavoury of slag-heaps. As Mam became less ill she worried more, 'No, George, leave that till I get up, you wait till I see the mess you and that woman have made of my kitchen ...' I had set *Full Moon* aside since a hasty note to Fagan; then it was suddenly here, Monday, 28 February, when the evening clock would chime from the little Playhouse church, as it had so often done for me racing past. Early on, the doctor had advised a half-bottle of Haig in case of emergency; I poured a little out, sat between the sleeping patients, put on the ear-phones (Job had managed to rig the crystal set up here) and on the stroke of eight p.m., drank to my first night. It was my first drink in 314a, and with Oxford-scented whisky going in at the lips and faint orchestral music pouring in at the ears, I was straightaway blissfully intoxicated. Stifled for weeks, the promise of the world came flooding over me : I saw everybody I knew in Oxford thronging in, would the actors know their parts – yes! – would the prompter hiss 'Get her back, she's in the wrong act' – never! I closed my eyes, and the curtain rose on *'the living-room of a house built on a rock ... motionless save for the lazy reflection of water; for an instant, the illusion of complete suspense'*. Then the first line.

SANDING: *Are we to be kept from the world for a night and a day? ...*

Reggie was to wire me. All Tuesday morning, emptying ashes and fetching coal, I made dashes into the house, thinking I heard the rat-tat. At two o'clock it came. 'Audience very favourable, writing.' Well, that was all right ... No, I had to face it, inside me I had hoped for 'Wild enthusiasm, Fagan plans immediate West End' but it was all right ... Then another telegram, 'Your charming piece played beautifully do come see it J.B. and Mary Fagan'. Next day I showed it to Dad – 'you mean she is Mrs Fagan *and* Miss Grey?' – and we talked to the doctor; Mam was getting up in two days, next-door was coming in to help when she could, I'd better go.

Late Friday afternoon, waiting for the connection in the twilight of Chester Station, my Oxford scarf trailing a whiff of moth-ball, I felt as if I were going away, an end and a beginning – and yet (I had to remind myself) I shall be back on Monday, back to the prison ... Reggie met me; I was glad, for stepping into Oxford I felt much more of a stranger than the first time, and apprehensive. We took a taxi to the room he had taken for me in Wellington Square, ironer than the Duke – I could not have gone to my college, not yet – then walked to his digs in

Walton Street, where he had the press notices for me. They were highly encouraging: 'writes powerfully, almost lyrically, though at times his facility betrays him ...', 'except for *Uncle Vanya*, richer than any offering this term ...' Even *The Times* commented 'something of Tchehov and Strindberg ... mystical, with touches of whimsical humour ...' and one paper had 'Unique Event in Oxford – two world premières in one night, by authors with identical initials: at the Playhouse *Full Moon* by Mr Emlyn Williams, and at the New *The Terror* by Mr Edgar Wallace. Both had an enthusiastic reception.'

In bed I heard the chimes, and shivered; but my nursing had left me a good sleeper. Next day, Saturday, I read, and lunched with Reggie in his digs, with Campbell; I had no desire to walk streets which could only remind me of bad times. But Reggie did insist that I saunter to the corner of George Street and the Corn, to look up at the great Playhouse poster five minutes before Strindberg was to oust me. Black on dark red, my name boldly faced three thoroughfares, then a stab as I remembered the night I had made a tipsy vow. Well before the clock struck, I was sitting alone in the midst of a filling house. The house-lights clicked off one by one, as they had so many times, the old gong sounded, the curtains parted and disappeared behind the same pillars. A pause. '*Are we to be kept from the world for a night and a day? ...*' I then underwent an experience rare for a dramatist, I saw a play of mine without having been present at any rehearsal; moreover, while I had once met Byam Shaw with his brother, the other four actors I had never seen. Playwrights react very differently to their own plays; for me the experience was the opposite of what it should have been. Instead of something come true of which I had dreamed, it looked like an orderly two-hour dream, with two intervals, repeating in measured unreality the reality which I had long ago lived through when I wrote it. My feeling was enhanced by the fact that I had visualized Napier and Byam Shaw in the parts, but even the others were as I had imagined them.

During the first scene, I detected in myself a vague embarrassment at hearing my lines spoken, one after the other, in public. Then I felt detached, and stayed so. It was impossible for me to

judge the emotional climaxes, I knew they were coming and
there they were : detached, flat, flat ... I only came to myself
in the intervals, when I hopped outside to avoid overhearing
comments : I looked at my programme : *The Scene is laid in the
Italian Alps, in the Living-room of a House built on a rock in the
middle of a Pool.* I winced at the pretentious capitals – if only
I had seen a proof, and anyway once you're Capitalizing, why
not 'Rock' and 'Middle'? – then, straight from such practicali-
ties, back to the dream. The play was well produced and well
acted, but it was an experience which I did not enjoy and which
I would willingly have exchanged for a revival, for one performance, of the Ouds *Hamlet* with me crouched in the prompt
corner for the ninth time.

As far as I could judge, the audience listened to the play with
interest; I myself by the end was able to discern in the writing a
vagueness – a lack of purpose, was it? ... I went round and met
the cast. 'Glen dear boy,' Alan Webb called, in flannel trousers
and singlet, wiping off his make-up, 'you've misled me, our
author is nothing but one of those 'Varsity boys, Oxford bags
and that great nonchalant scarf, I expected the Welsh Pinero!'
I walked back with them and Alan Napier to their digs, and had
a theatrical supper which fitted me like a glove, kippers and
chips and tea and beer and 'shop'. Names flew, J.B., Granville
Barker, Cocky, Willie Maugham, Leo Quartermaine, Komisar-
jevski, Gerald, Jack Barrymore, Harry Ainley, Stanislavski, and
arguments. 'Nonsense Alan, I agree with the other Alan, I saw
it at the Apollo and it wasn't *lack* of production that killed it, it
was too much' – 'No dear boy, the idea that some actors are
better when they've had a couple of drinks is absolute bilge,
what about timing laughs?' – 'Don't talk to me about first-class
acting in the West End, all you need is to look good in tails and
you're there' – 'Glen, you're talking through your hat, apron-
stage my arse' – 'If *he's* wonderful, then get Fred Barnes, thank
you Mrs Mac dear the kippers were gorgeous, and are the stiff
shirts back? No not a dressy one next week, thank God it isn't
The Circle every Monday ...' I may have looked like one of the
Oxford boys, but this was where I belonged.

Glen and Alan (Webb) walked me to Wellington Square –

'must see old Pinero home, might get another part if we play our cards' – and I arranged to meet them the next night after the Strindberg dress-rehearsal, before my inevitable Monday. Before the curtain rose, the Fagans greeted me warmly; afterwards Fagan was delayed, Miss Grey went back to the Mitre by taxi, and he suggested I walk back with him. Down the Turl, down Holywell; it was a moonlit Oxford, ghostly and Sunday-deserted, as we traced, in reverse, my last summer walk. He talked of *Full Moon*, which had obviously appealed to his Irish temperament; I told him I had felt last night that it was fuzzy and that I hoped to write something with more bite. As we turned into the High, its curve the silver bosom of a stone river, he said, 'I don't often advise this, but have you thought of going on the stage?' Then, as if to appease the stones we were treading, he added, 'When you've done your Schools, of course. Come to me if you need help.' 'I will, sir,' I said. The words had been spoken : and it was right that it should happen here, where I had crossed that morning. Arrived at the Mitre, on a warm impulse he suggested that I should come to London for four or five days as his guest and see some plays : there was no room at their flat at 100 Great Russell Street, but he would book me in at the Kenilworth Hotel next door, would I meet him at the Savoy Tuesday at one to lunch with Ned Lathom, and before I could answer he was inside and I was walking back.

314a? A telegram – no, after last May that would be unkind; I wrote, to reach them Monday morning, asking them to wire me if needed, 'Mr Fagan is paying for everything, and he is *very* anxious for me to go.' No reply, and on Tuesday, after the first night of *Intoxication*, where I enjoyed being introduced by John Fernald to several people as the author of last week's play – and, even more, being handed at the stage-door an envelope containing five pound-notes, my first royalties – I arrived at Paddington. Leaving my case, with in it the enormous *Full Moon* poster, the strips pasted together, I took the Tube to the Strand and walked to the Savoy Hotel, its great entrance reverberating between metropolitan cliffs. Outside the theatre, I studied the photographs of *And So to Bed*, then walked down side-steps, past a bar called The Coal Hole, to the stage-door, where sat a rosy old man. I wandered down Savoy Hill to gape curiously at the wireless doors of 2LO, then back and into the Babylonian foyer, the first West End hotel I had ever entered.

Ned Lathom was Lord Lathom, a stage-struck social figure who had written talented plays in the Coward vein; Ned the playwright was more important to me than Ned the lord, but the riches were an attraction, for I had heard that as well as writing plays, he financed them. I waited. I studied the people endlessly crossing the thick carpets, trying to pick out faces: the air was velvet with success. I waited. But somehow – a compliment to us both, certainly to Fagan – sitting there with the scenery of *And So to Bed* not fifty yards away, I did not feel depressed; I knew that his Irish heart had got him into a muddle. At two o'clock I began to feel hungry, went and had two buns at an A.B.C., fetched my case and proceeded to the Kenilworth. I could not help contrasting today with the Alexis, and being glad. I never met my Maecenas; Lord Lathom died in 1930.

When I called at the flat, Fagan was like an apologetic school-boy, but he had been meticulous in arranging theatre tickets, 'Only one? Don't you know *anybody* in London?' I saw *And So to Bed* first, a graceful comedy pervaded with an aromatic zephyr of literature; the second day I sat in the hotel waiting for a telephone call as to whether, in view of the failure of the play at the Royalty, *The Dybbuk* or *Full Moon* should follow it there at once. This was too good to be true, and I was not downcast when that evening Fagan told me it was *The Dybbuk*. The news was anyway softened by my hearing it between Mr and Mrs Fagan at the Ivy Restaurant and by the thought of – in half an hour – the Hippodrome: Fagan was amused that next to *Juno and the Paycock*, I should want to see *Sunny*, 'An intellectual Oxford playwright at a musical comedy?'

Four days of it, then I broke into my five pounds to buy flowers for Mrs Fagan and went home. In the train, I again had the feeling of suspension, as if I must make no decisions. At Chester, getting into the local train I waited for the claustrophobia, it did not come. I felt as if I were on a visit. I would be seeing the Fagans again, and Glen and Alan Webb – would I?

Our Tom was slowly building up, while Mam testily refused to be a convalescent at all. I need have had no qualms, she refused any help, 'No no, I'd only have to do it again after ...' Dad was subdued, like a child which has been violently reminded that its parent is mortal. My arrival made no ring in the opaque pond of 314a, though there was a slight stir when I unfurled the *Full Moon* poster for Tom and hung it against the stairs, where it reached from floor to ceiling; the great black letters boomed like a fanfare in a cellar. Even Mam blinked, and as I folded it away I could tell that if Dad could have got it into his wallet, he would have taken it to work.

Alone with Mam, I showed her the four pounds something – 'no, you will need it'; then I went up to Underwood, but kept off the London visit except to stress how cultured the Fagans were. Again I had the suspended feeling, as if my whole personality was lying loosely about like a jig-saw puzzle which at a touch would shuffle into place. The March weather relented; I went for long slow walks and worked every day, a clerk at his desk. Sleep-walking, sleep-working.

Only two spikes shot up out of the pond, to show that underneath it was seething with irritations born of illness, worry, propinquity and a congenital inability to communicate. The first was at the monosyllabic evening meal, Mam hovering. Out of nothing, between me and Job, now eighteen and a half, an argument arose about the crystal set; he wanted to bring in his mate to sample its wonders, while I wanted to hear a quartet. With two ear-phones, there was a deadlock. 'Anyway,' said Job, 'why should you get the first claim?' 'Because I'm older,' I snapped, to which he snapped back, 'You may be older, but I'm the one that's earnin' his living.'

Silence, while the clock ticked and a coal subsided. I think Job, a gentle boy, was sorry it had come out quite like that, but it was true. 'Get on with your food, the two of you,' snapped Dad, it was a snappy time in 314a. But I did not smart over the incident, I seemed to be waiting. For the next? That was a week later, one of those meaningless happenings which change the course of life, as a balancing stone can be sent, by a casual jolt, hurtling for ever into the valley. There was not even tension, it was tea-time, I was in my usual place on the sofa, reading, head in a book, never get anywhere ... The parlour arm-chair had been gradually disembowelling itself, and I had lugged it in earlier for Dad to try and patch up, which he had done. 'George,' said Mam sharply, 'do I have to ask you again to carry that chair back?' 'When I've finished the chapter.' Then, so suddenly that I started – he was tired, or his horse may have betrayed him – Dad thundered, 'You get up and do as your mother tells you, *now*!'

Not one word more was said, I stared at him, then at her; family affection was unrecognizably blackened with family hate. I got up, stamped past the crucial chair into the parlour, and sat down. I had four pounds twelve. I opened my folder, and saw Campbell's old letter, 'Why not come and stay?' I rose, put on my overcoat, went out by the front door, gave it a healthy bang, strode up to the station, looked up a train, went to the post office and wired 'Meet me Euston 1.20 urgent.' I went back and packed my suitcase, leaving my books in a neat pile. None of us spoke, pride was raging. Tom sat uneasily polishing his Sally-Army trumpet. I went to bed knowing that Dad would have gone to work when I got up; after breakfast – no bacon, and no conversation either – I slipped out by the front door (no bang), bought my ticket to Euston, my first since France 1921, and settled into the corner furthest away from 314a. No waving, anyway the back door would be shut. If he had not thought of mending that chair ... yet it had been meant to happen and had. I sat supine throughout the journey but nearing Euston, I had a moment of panic, suppose Campbell isn't there? I'll wash dishes, I'm a dab hand at it, get a First any day – Campbell *was* there. I explained to him in the Refreshments, he telephoned his mother in Barnet and I was invited to stay for a week, with a family who were unreservedly kind to me at a moment when kindness meant everything.

'Dear Mr Fagan, You kindly said to me at Oxford that I was

to come to you if in trouble. I will call at the Savoy tomorrow at eleven on the chance of a word with you.' 'Dear Miss Cooke, My plans are changed completely. Or rather I have none, I am looking for a job, anything, anywhere. Will write. Yours very affectionately.' Next morning I walked from King's Cross to the Savoy. The booming front looked suddenly impregnable. But Fagan was in his back-stage office; I told him the facts, and mentioned the dish-washing. His eyes twinkled, then turned serious. 'Well,' he said, 'I really haven't anything, come back this afternoon.' I went and had a bun at the same A.B.C., and when I returned at three, the façade looked less forbidding. He said, 'I could switch one of the boys walking on downstairs back to *Professor Tim* across the road, he's Irish and you're not, and you could take over his bit here at the same money, three pounds a week, you can just live on it, any good to you?' As I stared at him, relief poured into me, and I realized how apprehensive, under my front, the Mam side of me had been. 'On one condition,' he added, 'as an old Trinity man, I insist that you take your Schools and get a respectable Second, a degree never did anybody in the theatre any harm.' 'Yes sir.' 'Then,' he said, 'when the play goes to New York in the autumn, we might discuss your playing the slightly bigger part of Pepys's Boy and understudying Glen Byam Shaw who's going as Pelham Humphrey. You start on Monday, all right?' I had heard that he could exasperate his friends by his Irish vagueness, but that morning of mine was not one of his vague days.

I returned to Barnet buoyant, with daffodils for Campbell's mother and insisting on coming back into town in the evening and taking him out to dinner in Soho, in my city of London. But before that, my parents, though I was still too proud to communicate direct. 'My dear Brother Tom, I start work on Monday, in Mr Fagan's play. Will you post me the following books, postage enclosed, I shall be getting three pounds a week, not much in London so won't be able to save on it. Will keep in touch, your loving brother.' I wrote to Miss Cooke, and settled to enjoy the rest of my last free week. Campbell's eldest brother Oliver, on the Stock Exchange, was having a wonderful year and he and his wife wanted their friends to share it : they adopted me with a generous zest. Oliver took one look at my wilting Oxford bags and sent me to his tailor for a good new suit; I' was starved for entertainment, so with Campbell I was included in a 'cheery' evening at the Gargoyle which included bubbly and staring at a strangely beautiful woman, in black velvet eccentrically to her feet while every other lady was showing her knees, who was rumoured to be Augustus John's model. A letter from a Mr Kyrle Fletcher offering two guineas for a reading of *Full Moon* in Newport, and he would like to talk about it on the wireless (into our parlour!). It was a fine week.

Saturday morning, walking through Bloomsbury to my newly acquired furnished room, I held a committee meeting with myself. Though I had written that I would be unable to save, I was determined to. Plate and spoon from Woolworth's so I can keep cornflakes in a cupboard for breakfast, all other meals in A.B.C.s or Lyons or at coffee-stalls, no fares, walk to the theatre and back – if I stick to this, I can put by a pound a week, by Schools I'll have saved eight pounds ... The room was in Mecklenburg Street, a dingy top-floor back single with three clothes-hooks and one chair with a burst seat, but it was ten-and-six a week and within walking distance of the Strand. I cut the theatre-list out of a newspaper I had picked up in the train and stuck it on a nail beside my bed; an hour later the slatternly landlady entered to find me washing the window and the woodwork, and looked so taken aback I thought she was going to fetch a policeman. I walked to Leicester Square, to Frizell's the chemist to buy my make-up, 'a stick of five and a stick of nine', then down to the Savoy to rehearse with Mr Storie the stage-manager, ready for Monday. In the rack, a letter, Miss Cooke's writing, 'Emlyn Williams Esq., Stage Door, Savoy Theatre, London, W.C.2.' Had she written that with sorrow in her heart? 'Hmmm, I was afraid of this. But I have faith, and three cheers for Mr Fagan of Trinity.'

I was happy to find that I had six lines in my part, now dictated to me by Mr Storie; under the dim working light, I stood scribbling them on the back of Miss Cooke's envelope. My bit opened the play: curtain up on street scene, enter Pelling's Prentice carrying hare, knock at Pepys's front door, opened by Blackamoor, 'Is Mistress Pepys within ...'

Sunday I spent at Campbell's. Walking I wondered – for the first time, realistically – what sort of an actor I would have to be, to make the success which I assumed I would achieve say by ten years' time ... Ten, I would be thirty-one – no, say nine ... I reminded myself that the stars of today, Nares, du Maurier, Ainley, as well as the actors on the brink of success, Ion Swinley, Francis Lister, Ian Hunter, Frank Vosper, were all cast in the heroic gentlemanly mould; my face clouded. To appeal to an audience, was it not enough to be interesting? A wild creature like Heathcliff? Keats? A criminal like that pantry-boy Jacoby who murdered his old benefactress? Do they *all* have to be six foot six, and can't young character actors be romantic or tragic, instead of just comic relief? There must be plays ... But I felt my first part burning a hole in my pocket, on the back of an envelope, and the cloud was gone.

Easter Monday, 18 April 1927, I was to join the cast at the matinée. On my way I called at the British Museum, a gesture of propitiation to my academic gods, and arranged a card to the Reading Room. Then I walked, in the spring sun, down Southampton Row; walking I fore-dreamed, but this time practical. I would work in the Museum daily, even matinée afternoons, for after my bit I could be out by ten to three, and after my Schools in June before America (America!) I would get down to writing a play, a thriller which had been hovering over my mind for weeks. Miss Cooke had decreed that a play respecting the Unities of Time and Place was the most difficult: well, this one, a ghost story, would carry the Unities to the utmost lengths, for the Time would be the time of the performance, and the Place the stage of the theatre in which the piece would be played. I had the title, *A Murder Has Been Arranged*. Once I had made enough money to be out of work for a year, I would get my parents out of 314a and build a bungalow for them, say on the genteel slopes around Hawarden, a bathroom ...

By this time I was in the Strand, thronged with holiday-makers celebrating my début in the spring sun. A red bus flashed round from Waterloo Bridge, with across it 'AND SO TO BED'; the next said 'EMLYN WILLIAMS' twice the size. I looked again, 'EVAN WILLIAMS Shampoo', near enough; I walked along the pavement from which Drake-Brockman had pointed out Nelson's Column. For *George, His Story*, what would be today's illustration? 'A deathly hush as he stood in the wings, then ... the curtain was up ...' Outside the Savoy, a new poster, 250th Performance SPECIAL MATINEE TODAY. At the stage-door Bill Bragg the rosy old man handed me four envelopes. Not bad, nearly one for every line in my part.

I raced up to the stifling hot chorus-room where I was to dress with six other people, and there found the amiable boy who was being moved to the Irish play, George More O'Ferrall, come to wish me luck. He introduced the new boy to the rest of the form, and sitting down I hoped it would not be too clear from the way I handled my five-and-nine that I was not used to them. I got into ballet shirt, brown knee-breeches and short jacket – must buy a cheap dressing-gown – and examined my mail: a telegram from Campbell and his family, another from the Fagans and two notes, from Miss Cooke and our Tom, 'All send love, I was clearing the shed yesterday and found your poultices in hundreds, we had a good laugh ...' Then I got nervous and went down to the stage, holding Mort O'Ferrall's late matted wig. I muttered my part, heard the audience coming in, my audience, and felt suddenly cold. Mr Storie took me in to Yvonne Arnaud in the star dressing-room, a radiant bubble in a wrapper, gurgling – in between brushing her teeth – her own brand of English. We spoke French, she asked me had I done Rostand at Oxford; I made a note to mention to Miss Cooke that actresses know about Rostand, went down to the stage again, stood in front of the long mirror in the half-dark wings, and felt my hands tremble as I pulled on the wig.

A click, and the dark was stabbed by great fingers of light from the street scene within: the fire into which I must walk ... At the same moment there struck up the gay music of Lully, harpsichord and viola da gamba, wrapping us round in our

Restoration world. They may have played it two hundred and forty-nine times before, but this Easter afternoon they were playing it for me. The Blackamoor was already at her post inside the Pepys house, a coloured lady named Emma Williams. 'You two,' whispered Mr Storie, 'ought to go on the halls together.'

Beyond the theatre walls, the faint rumble of the sunlit Strand; in the sacred daylight-dark at the pulsating core of the great city, here I stood at last, admitted. All over London the curtains were rising, on *The Letter, The Constant Nymph, The Gold Diggers, On Approval, The Marquise, The Dybbuk, Interference, The Fanatics, The Ringer, Marigold, The Transit of Venus, The Constant Wife, Yellow Sands, The Greater Love, The Beaux' Stratagem*, and I was a part of it, together with all the people on my bedside list; and now, as I stood waiting, they streamed in breathless procession across my excited mind, Marie Tempest Ronald Squire Gladys Cooper Ernest Milton Ellis Jeffreys Gerald du Maurier Valerie Taylor Herbert Marshall Angela Baddeley John Gielgud Jean Forbes-Robertson Nicholas Hannen Cathleen Nesbitt Cedric Hardwicke Dorothy Dickson Robert Harris Ursula Jeans Leslie Faber Alison Leggatt Keneth Kent Mary Clare Leslie Banks Athlene Seyler Lewis Casson Edna Best Raymond Massey Tallulah Bankhead Allan Aynesworth Fay Compton Frank Vosper Sybil Thorndike Ralph Richardson Edith Evans ...

The music came to a spirited close, applause, silence; above me a voice muttered 'House out'. Under a distant light I could see Miss Grey, drinking water and whispering to a footpad and a fop; she blew me a kiss. I was suddenly gripped with fright, gulped, pulled up my stockings under my breeches as I had when a child, and clutched the property hare. Heart, stop beating – speak up and be natural – remember the moon and the stars –

A rustle and a sweep, like a strong calm wind. The curtain was up.

Index

Index